Student Solutions Manual

to accompany

Beginning Algebra

Third Edition

Julie Miller
Daytona State College

Molly O'Neill
Daytona State College

Nancy Hyde

Prepared by

Brandie Faulkner
Tallahassee Community College

The McGraw-Hill Companies

Student Solutions Manual to accompany
BEGINNING ALGEBRA, THIRD EDITION
JULIE MILLER, MOLLY O'NEILL, AND NANCY HYDE

Published by McGraw-Hill Higher Education, an imprint of The McGraw-Hill Companies, Inc., 1221 Avenue of the Americas, New York, NY 10020. Copyright © 2011, 2008, and 2004 by The McGraw-Hill Companies, Inc. All rights reserved.

1 2 3 4 5 6 7 8 9 0 WDQ/WDQ 1 0 9 8 7 6 5 4 3 2 1 0

ISBN: 978–0–07–730068–5
MHID: 0–07–730068–8

www.mhhe.com

Contents

Chapter 4   Systems of Linear Equations and Inequalities in Two Variables

Chapter 5   Polynomials and Properties of Exponents

Chapter 6   Factoring Polynomials

Chapter 7   Rational Expressions

Chapter 8   Radicals

Chapter 9   Quadratic Equations, Complex Numbers, and Functions

Appendix

Chapter 1

Chapter 1 Opener

18	+	2	+	10	=	30
÷		+		−		÷
3	×	4	−	7	=	5
−		+		+		÷
2	×	0	+	6	=	6
=		=		=		=
4	+	6	−	9	=	1

Section 1.1 Practice Exercises

1. Answers will vary

3. Numerator 7; denominator 8; proper

5. Numerator 9; denominator 5; improper

7. Numerator 6; denominator 6; improper

9. Numerator 12; denominator 1; improper

11. $\dfrac{3}{4}$

13. $\dfrac{4}{3}$

15. $\dfrac{1}{6}$

17. $\dfrac{2}{2}$

19. $\dfrac{5}{2}$ or $2\dfrac{1}{2}$

21. $\dfrac{6}{2}$ or 3

23. The set of whole numbers includes the number 0 and the set of natural numbers does not.

25. Answers may vary. One example would be $\dfrac{2}{4}$.

27. Prime

29. Composite

31. Composite

33. Prime

35. $2 \times 2 \times 3 \times 3$

37. $2 \times 3 \times 7$

39. $2 \times 5 \times 11$

41. $3 \times 3 \times 3 \times 5$

43. $\dfrac{3}{15} = \dfrac{\cancel{3}}{\cancel{3} \times 5} = \dfrac{1}{5}$

45. $\dfrac{6}{16} = \dfrac{\cancel{2} \times 3}{\cancel{2} \times 2 \times 2 \times 2} = \dfrac{3}{8}$

47. $\dfrac{42}{48} = \dfrac{\cancel{2} \times \cancel{3} \times 7}{\cancel{2} \times 2 \times 2 \times 2 \times \cancel{3}} = \dfrac{7}{8}$

49. $\dfrac{48}{64} = \dfrac{\cancel{2} \times \cancel{2} \times \cancel{2} \times \cancel{2} \times 3}{\cancel{2} \times \cancel{2} \times \cancel{2} \times \cancel{2} \times 2 \times 2} = \dfrac{3}{4}$

51. $\dfrac{110}{176} = \dfrac{\cancel{2} \times 5 \times \cancel{11}}{\cancel{2} \times 2 \times 2 \times 2 \times \cancel{11}} = \dfrac{5}{8}$

53. $\dfrac{150}{200} = \dfrac{\cancel{2} \times 3 \times \cancel{5} \times \cancel{5}}{\cancel{2} \times 2 \times 2 \times \cancel{5} \times \cancel{5}} = \dfrac{3}{4}$

55. False: When adding/subtracting fractions, it is necessary to have a common denominator.

57. $\dfrac{10}{13} \times \dfrac{26}{15} = \dfrac{2 \times 2 \times \cancel{5} \times \cancel{13}}{3 \times \cancel{5} \times \cancel{13}} = \dfrac{4}{3}$

59. $\dfrac{3}{7} \div \dfrac{9}{14} = \dfrac{3}{7} \times \dfrac{14}{9} = \dfrac{2 \times \cancel{3} \times \cancel{7}}{3 \times \cancel{3} \times \cancel{7}} = \dfrac{2}{3}$

61. $\dfrac{9}{10} \times 5 = \dfrac{9}{10} \times \dfrac{5}{1} = \dfrac{3 \times 3 \times \cancel{5}}{2 \times \cancel{5}} = \dfrac{9}{2}$

63. $\dfrac{12}{5} \div 4 = \dfrac{12}{5} \div \dfrac{4}{1} = \dfrac{12}{5} \times \dfrac{1}{4} = \dfrac{\overset{3}{\cancel{12}} \times 1}{5 \times \underset{1}{\cancel{4}}} = \dfrac{3}{5}$

65. $\dfrac{5}{2} \times \dfrac{10}{21} \times \dfrac{7}{5} = \dfrac{\overset{1}{\cancel{5}} \times \overset{5}{\cancel{10}} \times \overset{1}{\cancel{7}}}{\underset{1}{\cancel{2}} \times \underset{3}{\cancel{21}} \times \underset{1}{\cancel{5}}} = \dfrac{5}{3}$

67. $\dfrac{9}{100} \div \dfrac{13}{1000} = \dfrac{9}{100} \times \dfrac{1000}{13} = \dfrac{9 \times \overset{10}{\cancel{1000}}}{\underset{1}{\cancel{100}} \times 13} = \dfrac{90}{13}$

69. $\dfrac{1}{3}$ of $\$2112 = \dfrac{1}{3} \times \dfrac{2112}{1} = \dfrac{2112}{3} = \$704$

71. The statement "one-third of the team graduated with honors" translates to

"honors $= \dfrac{1}{3} \times 12$"

$\dfrac{1}{3} \times 12 = \dfrac{1}{3} \times \dfrac{12}{1}$

$= \dfrac{1 \times \overset{4}{\cancel{12}}}{\underset{1}{\cancel{3}} \times 1}$

$= \dfrac{4}{1}$

$= 4$ graduated with honors

73. $4 \text{ yd} \div \dfrac{1}{2} \text{ yd} = \dfrac{4}{1} \times \dfrac{2}{1} = \dfrac{8}{1} = 8$, 8 aprons

75. $6 \text{ lb} \div \dfrac{3}{4} \text{ lb} = \dfrac{6}{1} \times \dfrac{4}{3} = \dfrac{24}{3} = 8$, 8 jars

77. $\dfrac{5}{14} + \dfrac{1}{14} = \dfrac{6}{14} = \dfrac{\cancel{2} \times 3}{\cancel{2} \times 7} = \dfrac{3}{7}$

79. $\dfrac{17}{24} - \dfrac{5}{24} = \dfrac{12}{24} = \dfrac{1}{2}$

81. $\qquad 6 = 2 \times 3$
$\qquad 15 = 3 \times 5$
$2 \times 3 \times 5 = 30$

83. $\qquad 20 = 2^2 \times 5$
$\qquad 8 = 2^3$
$\qquad 4 = 2^2$
$2^3 \times 5 = 40$

85. $\dfrac{1}{8} + \dfrac{3}{4} = \dfrac{1}{8} + \dfrac{6}{8} = \dfrac{7}{8}$

87. $\dfrac{3}{8} - \dfrac{3}{10} = \dfrac{15}{40} - \dfrac{12}{40} = \dfrac{3}{40}$

89. $\dfrac{7}{26} - \dfrac{2}{13} = \dfrac{7}{26} - \dfrac{4}{26} = \dfrac{3}{26}$

91. $\dfrac{7}{18} + \dfrac{5}{12} = \dfrac{14}{36} + \dfrac{15}{36} = \dfrac{29}{36}$

93. $\dfrac{3}{4} - \dfrac{1}{20} = \dfrac{15}{20} - \dfrac{1}{20} = \dfrac{14}{20} = \dfrac{7}{10}$

95. $\dfrac{5}{12} + \dfrac{5}{16} = \dfrac{20}{48} + \dfrac{15}{48} = \dfrac{35}{48}$

97. $\dfrac{1}{6} + \dfrac{3}{4} - \dfrac{5}{8} = \dfrac{4}{24} + \dfrac{18}{24} - \dfrac{15}{24} = \dfrac{7}{24}$

99. $\dfrac{4}{7} + \dfrac{1}{2} + \dfrac{3}{4} = \dfrac{16}{28} + \dfrac{14}{28} + \dfrac{21}{28} = \dfrac{51}{28}$ or $1\dfrac{23}{28}$

101. $3\dfrac{1}{5} \times \dfrac{7}{8} = \dfrac{16}{5} \times \dfrac{7}{8}$

$\qquad = \dfrac{\cancel{2} \times \cancel{2} \times \cancel{2} \times 2 \times 7}{\cancel{2} \times \cancel{2} \times \cancel{2} \times 5}$

$\qquad = \dfrac{14}{5}$

$\qquad = 2\dfrac{4}{5}$

103. $4\dfrac{3}{5} \div \dfrac{1}{10} = \dfrac{23}{5} \times \dfrac{10}{1} = \dfrac{2 \times \cancel{5} \times 23}{\cancel{5}} = \dfrac{46}{1} = 46$

105. $3\dfrac{1}{5} \times 2\dfrac{7}{8} = \dfrac{16}{5} \times \dfrac{23}{8} = \dfrac{\cancel{16}^{2} \times 23}{5 \times \cancel{8}} = \dfrac{46}{5}$ or $9\dfrac{1}{5}$

107. $1\dfrac{2}{9} \div 7\dfrac{1}{3} = \dfrac{11}{9} \div \dfrac{22}{3} = \dfrac{\cancel{11}}{\cancel{9}_3} \times \dfrac{\cancel{3}}{\cancel{22}_2} = \dfrac{1}{6}$

109. $1\dfrac{2}{9} \div 6 = \dfrac{11}{9} \times \dfrac{1}{6} = \dfrac{11}{9 \times 6} = \dfrac{11}{54}$

111. $2\dfrac{1}{8} + 1\dfrac{3}{8} = \dfrac{17}{8} + \dfrac{11}{8}$

$\qquad = \dfrac{28}{8}$

$\qquad = \dfrac{\cancel{2} \times \cancel{2} \times 7}{\cancel{2} \times \cancel{2} \times 2}$

$\qquad = \dfrac{7}{2}$ or $3\dfrac{1}{2}$

112. $1\dfrac{3}{14} + 1\dfrac{1}{14} = \dfrac{17}{14} + \dfrac{15}{14} = \dfrac{32}{14} = \dfrac{16}{7}$ or $2\dfrac{2}{7}$

114. $5\dfrac{1}{3} - 2\dfrac{3}{4} = \dfrac{16}{3} - \dfrac{11}{4} = \dfrac{64}{12} - \dfrac{33}{12} = \dfrac{31}{12}$ or $2\dfrac{7}{12}$

116. $4\dfrac{1}{2} + 2\dfrac{2}{3} = \dfrac{9}{2} + \dfrac{8}{3}$

$\qquad = \dfrac{27}{6} + \dfrac{16}{6}$

$\qquad = \dfrac{43}{6}$ or $7\dfrac{1}{6}$

117. $1 - \dfrac{7}{8} = \dfrac{8}{8} - \dfrac{7}{8} = \dfrac{1}{8}$

119. $26\dfrac{3}{8} \div 3 = \dfrac{211}{8} \div \dfrac{3}{1}$

$\qquad = \dfrac{211}{8} \times \dfrac{1}{3}$

$\qquad = \dfrac{211}{24}$

$\qquad = 8\dfrac{19}{24}$ in.

121. $2\dfrac{3}{4} - 1\dfrac{1}{6} = \dfrac{11}{4} - \dfrac{7}{6} = \dfrac{33}{12} - \dfrac{14}{12}$

$\qquad = \dfrac{19}{12}$

$\qquad = 1\dfrac{7}{12}$ hr

123. $1\dfrac{1}{2} + \dfrac{3}{4} = \dfrac{3}{2} + \dfrac{3}{4} = \dfrac{6}{4} + \dfrac{3}{4} = \dfrac{9}{4} = 2\dfrac{1}{4}$ lb

125. $6\dfrac{1}{4} \times 4 = \dfrac{25}{4} \times \dfrac{4}{1} = \dfrac{25}{\cancel{4}} \times \dfrac{\cancel{4}}{1} = 25$ in.

Section 1.2 Practice Exercises

1. Answers will vary.

3. $4\dfrac{1}{2} - 1\dfrac{5}{6} = \dfrac{9}{2} - \dfrac{11}{6} = \dfrac{27}{6} - \dfrac{11}{6} = \dfrac{16}{6} = \dfrac{8}{3} = 2\dfrac{2}{3}$

5. $4\dfrac{1}{2} \div 1\dfrac{5}{6} = \dfrac{9}{2} \div \dfrac{11}{6} = \dfrac{9}{\cancel{2}_1} \times \dfrac{\cancel{6}^{3}}{11} = \dfrac{27}{11} = 2\dfrac{5}{11}$

7.

9. a. a terminating decimal; rational number

11. b. repeating decimal; rational number

13. a. a terminating decimal; rational number

15. c. a nonterminating, nonrepeating decimal; irrational number

17. a. a terminating decimal; rational number

19. a. a terminating decimal; rational number

21. b. a repeating decimal; rational number

23. c. a nonterminating, nonrepeating decimal; irrational number

25. Answers vary; for example: π, $-\sqrt{2}$, $\sqrt{3}$

27. Answers vary; for example: $-4, -1, 0$

29. Answers vary; for example: $-\dfrac{3}{4}, \dfrac{1}{2}, 0.206$

31. $-\dfrac{3}{2}, -4, 0.\overline{6}, 0, 1$

33. 1

35. $-4, 0, 1$

37. (a) Since Kane's score is 0 and Pak's score is -8, $0 > -8$.

(b) Since Scorenstam's score is 7 and Davies' score is -4, $7 > -4$.

(c) Since Pak's score is -8 and McCurdy's score is 3, $-8 < 3$.

(d) Since Kane's score is 0 and Davies's score is -4, $0 > -4$.

39. -18

41. 6.1

43. $\dfrac{5}{8}$

45. $-\dfrac{7}{3}$

47. 3

49. $-\dfrac{7}{3}$

51. 8

53. -72.1

55. 2

57. 1.5

59. -1.5

61. $\dfrac{3}{2}$

63. -10

65. $-\dfrac{1}{2}$

67. False; $|n|$ is never negative.

69. True; 5 is to the right of 2.

71. False; 6 is equal to 6.

73. True; -7 is equal to -7.

75. False; $\dfrac{3}{2}$ is to the right of $\dfrac{1}{6}$.

77. False; -5 is to the left of -2.

79. False; 8 is equal to 8.

81. True; 2 is to the right of 1.

83. True; $\dfrac{1}{9}$ is equal to $\dfrac{1}{9}$.

85. False; 7 is equal to 7.

87. True; -1 is to the left of 1.

89. True; 8 is equal to 8.

91. True; 2 is equal to 2.

93. For all $a < 0$ since $-a$ is the opposite of a.

Calculator Exercises

1.

```
(4+6)/(8-3)
                    2
```

3.

```
100-2(5-3)^3
                    84
```

5.

```
(12-6+1)²
                    49
```

7.

```
√(18-2)
                    4
```

9.

```
(20-3²)/(26-2²)
                    .5
```

Section 1.3 Practice Exercises

1. Answers will vary.

3. -4, $5.\overline{6}$, 0, 4.02, $\dfrac{7}{9}$

5. 9.2

7. -19

9. $c - 3 = 6 - 3 = 3$

11. $cd = \overset{2}{\cancel{6}}\left(\dfrac{2}{\cancel{3}_1}\right) = 4$

13. $5 + 6d = 5 + 6 \cdot \dfrac{2}{3} = 5 + \dfrac{\overset{2}{\cancel{6}}}{1} \cdot \dfrac{2}{\cancel{3}_1} = 5 + 4 = 9$

15. $\dfrac{1}{c} + d = \dfrac{1}{6} + \left(\dfrac{2}{3}\right) = \dfrac{1}{6} + \dfrac{4}{6} = \dfrac{5}{6}$

17. $\dfrac{1}{6} \cdot \dfrac{1}{6} \cdot \dfrac{1}{6} \cdot \dfrac{1}{6} = \left(\dfrac{1}{6}\right)^4$

19. $a \cdot a \cdot a \cdot b \cdot b = a^3 b^2$

21. $(5c)^5$

23. **(a)** x

   (b) Yes, 1

25. $x^3 = x \cdot x \cdot x$

27. $(2b)^3 = 2b \cdot 2b \cdot 2b$

29. $10y^5 = 10 \cdot y \cdot y \cdot y \cdot y \cdot y$

31. $2wz^2 = 2 \cdot w \cdot z \cdot z$

33. $6^2 = 6 \cdot 6 = 36$

35. $\left(\dfrac{1}{7}\right)^2 = \dfrac{1}{7} \cdot \dfrac{1}{7} = \dfrac{1}{49}$

37. $(0.2)^3 = 0.2 \cdot 0.2 \cdot 0.2 = 0.008$

39. $2^6 = 2 \cdot 2 \cdot 2 \cdot 2 \cdot 2 \cdot 2 = 64$

41. $\sqrt{81} = 9$

43. $\sqrt{4} = 2$

45. $\sqrt{144} = 12$

47. $\sqrt{16} = 4$

49. $\sqrt{\dfrac{1}{9}} = \sqrt{\left(\dfrac{1}{3}\right)^2} = \dfrac{1}{3}$

51. $\sqrt{\dfrac{25}{81}} = \sqrt{\left(\dfrac{5}{9}\right)^2} = \dfrac{5}{9}$

53. $8 + 2 \cdot 6 = 8 + 12 = 20$

54. $7 + 3 \cdot 4 = 7 + 12 = 19$

55. $(8+2)6 = 10 \cdot 6 = 60$

57. $4 + 2 \div 2 \cdot 3 + 1 = 4 + 3 + 1 = 8$

59. $81 - 4 \cdot 3 + 3^2 = 81 - 12 + 9 = 78$

61. $\dfrac{1}{4} \cdot \dfrac{2}{3} - \dfrac{1}{6} = \dfrac{1}{{}_2 4} \cdot \dfrac{2^1}{3} - \dfrac{1}{6} = \dfrac{1}{6} - \dfrac{1}{6} = 0$

63. $\left(\dfrac{11}{6} - \dfrac{3}{8}\right) \cdot \dfrac{4}{5} = \left(\dfrac{44}{24} - \dfrac{9}{24}\right) \cdot \dfrac{4}{5}$

$= \dfrac{35^7}{24_6} \cdot \dfrac{4}{5}$

$= \dfrac{7}{6}$

65. $3[5 + 2(8 - 3)] = 3[5 + 2(5)] = 3[15] = 45$

67. $10 + |-6| = 10 + 6 = 16$

69. $21 - |8 - 2| = 21 - 6 = 15$

71. $2^2 + \sqrt{9} \cdot 5 = 4 + 15 = 19$

73. $\sqrt{9 + 16} - 2 = \sqrt{25} - 2 = 5 - 2 = 3$

75. $[4^2 \cdot (6 - 4) \div 8] + [7 \cdot (8 - 3)]$

$= [16 \cdot 2 \div 8] + [7 \cdot 5]$

$= 4 + 35$

$= 39$

77. $48 - 13 \cdot 3 + [(50 - 7 \cdot 5) + 2]$

$= 48 - 39 + [15 + 2]$

$= 26$

79. $\dfrac{7 + 3(8 - 2)}{(7 + 3)(8 - 2)} = \dfrac{7 + 18}{(10)(6)} = \dfrac{25}{60} = \dfrac{5}{12}$

81. $\dfrac{15 - 5(3 \cdot 2 - 4)}{10 - 2(4 \cdot 5 - 16)} = \dfrac{15 - 5(2)}{10 - 2(4)} = \dfrac{5}{2}$

83. $A = lw = 360 \cdot 160 = 57{,}600 \text{ ft}^2$

85. $A = \frac{1}{2}(b_1 + b_2)h = \frac{1}{2}(6 + 8)3 = 21 \text{ ft}^2$

87. $3x$

89. $\dfrac{x}{7}$ or $x \div 7$

91. $2 - a$

93. $2y + x$

95 $4(x + 12)$

97. $3 - Q$

99. $2y^3 = 2(\quad)^3 = 2(2)^3 = 2(8) = 16$

101. $|z - 8| = |(\quad) - 8| = |(10) - 8| = |2| = 2$

103. $5\sqrt{x} = 5\sqrt{(\quad)} = 5\sqrt{(4)} = 5(2) = 10$

105. $yz - x = (\quad)(\quad) - (\quad)$

$= (2)(10) - (4)$

$= 20 - 4$

$= 16$

107. $\dfrac{\sqrt{\frac{1}{9}} + \frac{2}{3}}{\sqrt{\frac{4}{25}} + \frac{3}{5}} = \dfrac{\frac{1}{3} + \frac{2}{3}}{\frac{2}{5} + \frac{3}{5}} = \dfrac{\frac{3}{3}}{\frac{5}{5}} = \dfrac{1}{1} = 1$

109. $\dfrac{|-2|}{|-10| - |2|} = \dfrac{2}{10 - 2} = \dfrac{2}{8} = \dfrac{1}{4}$

111. (a) $36 \div 4 \cdot 3 = 9 \cdot 3 = 27$
Division must be performed before multiplication.

(b) $36 - 4 + 3 = 32 + 3 = 35$
Subtraction must be performed before addition.

113. This is acceptable, provided division and multiplication are performed in order from left to right, and subtraction and addition are performed in order from left to right.

Section 1.4 Practice Exercises

1. Answers will vary.

3. $\dfrac{9}{2} > \dfrac{3}{4}$

5. $0 > -\dfrac{5}{2}$

7. $\dfrac{3}{4} > -\dfrac{5}{2}$

9. $-2 + (-4) = -6$

11. $-7 + 10 = 3$

13. $6 + (-3) = 3$

15. $2 + (-5) = -3$

17. $-19 + 2 = -17$

19. $-4 + 11 = 7$

21. $-16 + (-3) = -19$

23. $-2 + (-21) = -23$

25. $0 + (-5) = -5$

27. $-3 + 0 = -3$

29. $-16 + 16 = 0$

31. $41 + (-41) = 0$

33. $4 + (-9) = -5$

35. $7 + (-2) + (-8) = -3$

37. $-17 + (-3) + 20 = -20 + 20 = 0$

39. $-3 + (-8) + (-12) = -11 + (-12) = -23$

41. $-42 + (3) + 45 + (-6) = -45 + 45 + (-6)$
$\qquad\qquad = -6$

43. $-5 + (-3) + (-7) + 4 + 8 = -8 + (-7) + 4 + 8$
$\qquad\qquad\qquad = -3$

45. $23.81 + (-2.51) = 21.3$

47. $-\dfrac{2}{7} + \dfrac{1}{14} = -\dfrac{4}{14} + \dfrac{1}{14} = -\dfrac{3}{14}$

49. $\dfrac{2}{3} + \left(-\dfrac{5}{6}\right) = \dfrac{4}{6} + \left(-\dfrac{5}{6}\right) = -\dfrac{1}{6}$

51. $-\dfrac{7}{8} + \left(-\dfrac{1}{16}\right) = -\dfrac{14}{16} + \left(-\dfrac{1}{16}\right) = -\dfrac{15}{16}$

53. $-\dfrac{1}{4} + \dfrac{3}{10} = -\dfrac{5}{20} + \dfrac{6}{20} = \dfrac{1}{20}$

55. $-2.1 + \left(-\dfrac{3}{10}\right) = -2.1 + -0.3 = -2.4$ or $-\dfrac{12}{5}$

57. $\dfrac{3}{4} + (-0.5) = 0.75 + (-0.5) = 0.25$ or $\dfrac{1}{4}$

59. $8.23 + (-8.23) = 0$

61. $-\dfrac{7}{8} + 0 = -\dfrac{7}{8}$

63. $-\dfrac{3}{2} + \left(-\dfrac{1}{3}\right) + \dfrac{5}{6} = -\dfrac{9}{6} + \left(-\dfrac{2}{6}\right) + \dfrac{5}{6} = -\dfrac{6}{6} = -1$

65. $-\dfrac{2}{3} + \left(-\dfrac{1}{9}\right) + 2 = -\dfrac{6}{9} + \left(-\dfrac{1}{9}\right) + \dfrac{18}{9} = \dfrac{11}{9}$

67. $-47.36 + 24.28 = -23.08$

69. $-0.000617 + (-0.0015) = -0.002117$

71. To add two numbers with different signs, subtract the smaller absolute value from the larger absolute value and apply the sign of the number with the larger absolute value.

73. $x + y + \sqrt{z} = -3 + (-2) + \sqrt{16} = -5 + 4 = -1$

75. $y + 3\sqrt{z} = -2 + 3\sqrt{16}$
$\qquad\qquad = -2 + 3 \cdot 4$
$\qquad\qquad = -2 + 12$
$\qquad\qquad = 10$

77. $|x| + |y| = |-3| + |-2| = 3 + 2 = 5$

79. $-x + y = -(-3) + (-2) = 3 + (-2) = 1$

81. $-6 + (-10); -16$

83. $-3 + 8; 5$

85. $-21 + 17; -4$

87. $3(-14 + 20); 18$

89. $(-7 + (-2)) + 5; -4$

91. $-5 + 13 + (-11); -3°F$

93. $-2 + 6 + (-5); -1$ yd or 1-yd loss

95. (a) $52.23 + (-52.95) = -\$0.72$

(b) Yes

97. (a) $1 + (-3) + (-1) + 2$

(b) -1

Calculator Exercises

1.

```
-8+( -5)
            -13
```

3.

```
627-( -84)
            711
```

5.

```
-3.2-( -14.5)
            11.3
```

7.

```
-12-9+4
            -17
```

Section 1.5 Practice Exercises

1. Answers will vary.

3. x^2

5. $-b + 2$

7. $1 + 36 \div 9 \cdot 2 = 1 + 4 \cdot 2 = 1 + 8 = 9$

9. -3

11. -12

13. 4

15. $3 - 5 = 3 + (-5) = -2$

17. $3 - (-5) = 3 + 5 = 8$

19. $-3 - 5 = -3 + (-5) = -8$

21. $-3 - (-5) = -3 + 5 = 2$

23. $23 - 17 = 6$

25. $23 - (-17) = 23 + 17 = 40$

27. $-23 - 17 = -23 + (-17) = -40$

29. $-23 - (-23) = 0$

31. $-6 - 14 = -6 + (-14) = -20$

33. $-7 - 17 = -7 + (-17) = -24$

35. $13 - (-12) = 13 + 12 = 25$

37. $-14 - (-9) = -14 + 9 = -5$

39. $-\dfrac{6}{5} - \dfrac{3}{10} = -\dfrac{12}{10} + \left(-\dfrac{3}{10}\right) = -\dfrac{15}{10} = -\dfrac{3}{2}$

41. $\dfrac{3}{8} - \left(-\dfrac{4}{3}\right) = \dfrac{9}{24} + \dfrac{32}{24} = \dfrac{41}{24}$

43. $\dfrac{1}{2} - \dfrac{1}{10} = \dfrac{5}{10} - \dfrac{1}{10} = \dfrac{4}{10} = \dfrac{2}{5}$

45. $-\dfrac{11}{12} - \left(-\dfrac{1}{4}\right) = -\dfrac{11}{12} + \dfrac{3}{12} = -\dfrac{8}{12} = -\dfrac{2}{3}$

47. $6.8 - (-2.4) = 6.8 + 2.4 = 9.2$

49. $3.1 - 8.82 = 3.10 + (-8.82) = -5.72$

51. $-4 - 3 - 2 - 1 = -4 + (-3) + (-2) + (-1) = -10$

53. $6 - 8 - 2 - 10 = 6 + (-8) + (-2) + (-10) = -14$

55. $-36.75 - 14.25 = -51$

57. $-112.846 + (-13.03) - 47.312 = -173.188$

59. $0.085 - (-3.14) + (0.018) = 3.243$

61. $6 - (-7); \ 13$

63. $3 - 18; \ -15$

65. $-5 - (-11); \ 6$

67. $-1 - (-13); \ 12$

69. $-32 - 20; \ -52$

71. $200 + 400 + 600 + 800 - 1000; \ \$1000$

73. $113° - (-39°) = 152°F$

75. $8848 - (-11,033 \text{ m}) = 19,881 \text{ m}$

77. $6 + 8 - (-2) - 4 + 1 = 14 + 2 - 4 + 1$
$\qquad\qquad\qquad\quad = 16 - 4 + 1$
$\qquad\qquad\qquad\quad = 13$

79. $-1 - 7 + (-3) - 8 + 10 = -8 + (-3) - 8 + 10$
$\qquad\qquad\qquad\qquad\qquad = -9$

81. $2 - (-8) + 7 + 3 - 15 = 2 + 8 + 7 + 3 - 15$
$\qquad\qquad\qquad\qquad\quad = 17 + 3 - 15$
$\qquad\qquad\qquad\qquad\quad = 5$

83. $-6 + (-1) + (-8) + (-10) = -7 + (-8) + (-10)$
$\qquad\qquad\qquad\qquad\qquad\quad = -25$

85. $-4 - \{11 - [4 - (-9)]\} = -4 - \{11 - [4 + 9]\}$
$\qquad\qquad\qquad\qquad\quad = -4 - \{11 - 13\}$
$\qquad\qquad\qquad\qquad\quad = -4 - (-2)$
$\qquad\qquad\qquad\qquad\quad = -2$

87. $-\dfrac{13}{10} + \dfrac{8}{15} - \left(-\dfrac{2}{5}\right) = -\dfrac{39}{30} + \dfrac{16}{30} + \dfrac{12}{30} = -\dfrac{11}{30}$

89. $\left(\dfrac{2}{3} - \dfrac{5}{9}\right) - \left(\dfrac{4}{3} - (-2)\right)$
$= \left(\dfrac{6}{9} - \dfrac{5}{9}\right) - \left(\dfrac{4}{3} + \dfrac{6}{3}\right)$
$= \dfrac{1}{9} - \dfrac{10}{3}$
$= \dfrac{1}{9} - \dfrac{30}{9}$
$= -\dfrac{29}{9}$

91. $\sqrt{29 + (-4)} - 7 = \sqrt{25} - 7 = 5 - 7 = -2$

93. $|10 + (-3)| - |-12 + (-6)| = |7| - |-18|$
$\qquad\qquad\qquad\qquad\qquad = 7 - 18$
$\qquad\qquad\qquad\qquad\qquad = -11$

95. $\dfrac{3 - 4 + 5}{4 + (-2)} = \dfrac{4}{2} = 2$

97. $(a + b) - c = (-2 + (-6)) - (-1) = -8 + 1 = -7$

99. $a - (b + c) = -2 - (-6 + (-1))$
$\qquad\qquad\qquad = -2 - (-7)$
$\qquad\qquad\qquad = -2 + 7$
$\qquad\qquad\qquad = 5$

101. $(a - b) - c = (-2 - (-6)) - (-1) = (4) + 1 = 5$

103. $a - (b - c) = -2 - (-6 - (-1))$
$\qquad\qquad\qquad = -2 - (-5)$
$\qquad\qquad\qquad = -2 + 5$
$\qquad\qquad\qquad = 3$

Problem Recognition Exercises

1. Add their absolute values and apply a negative sign.

3. $65 - 24 = 41$

5. $13 - (-18) = 13 + 18 = 31$

7. $4.8 - 6.1 = 4.8 + (-6.1) = -1.3$

9. $4 + (-20) = -16$

11. $\dfrac{1}{3} - \dfrac{5}{12} = \dfrac{4}{12} + \left(-\dfrac{5}{12}\right) = -\dfrac{1}{12}$

13. $-32 - 4 = -32 + (-4) = -36$

15. $-6 + (-6) = -12$

17. $-4 - \left(-\dfrac{5}{6}\right) = -\dfrac{24}{6} + \dfrac{5}{6} = -\dfrac{19}{6}$

19. $-60 + 55 = -5$

21. $-18 - (-18) = -18 + 18 = 0$

23. $-3.5 - 4.2 = -3.5 + (-4.2) = -7.7$

25. $-\dfrac{9}{5} + \left(-\dfrac{1}{3}\right) = -\dfrac{27}{15} + \left(-\dfrac{5}{15}\right) = -\dfrac{32}{15}$

27. $-14 + (-2) - 16 = -16 + (-16) = -32$

29. $-4.2 + 1.2 + 3.0 = 0$

31. $-10 - 8 - 6 - 4 - 2$
$= -10 + (-8) + (-6) + (-4) + (-2)$
$= -30$

Calculator Exercises

1.
```
-6*5
                -30
```

3.
```
( -5)( -5)( -5)( -5)
                625
```

5.
```
-5^4
                -625
```

7.
```
( -2.4)²
                5.76
```

9.
```
-8.4/-2.1
                    4
```

Section 1.6 Practice Exercises

1. Answers will vary.

2. The **reciprocal of a real number** a is $\dfrac{1}{a}$.

3. True; $4 > 1$

5. False; $0 > 0$

7. -56

9. 143

11. -12.76

13. $\left(-\dfrac{2}{3}\right)\left(-\dfrac{9}{8}\right) = \dfrac{18}{24} = \dfrac{3}{4}$

15. $(-6)^2 = 36$

17. $-6^2 = -36$

19. $\left(-\dfrac{3}{5}\right)^3 = \left(-\dfrac{3}{5}\right)\left(-\dfrac{3}{5}\right)\left(-\dfrac{3}{5}\right) = -\dfrac{27}{125}$

21. $(-0.2)^4 = 0.0016$

23. $\dfrac{54}{-9} = -6$

25. $\dfrac{-15}{-17} = \dfrac{15}{17}$

27. $\dfrac{-14}{-7} = 2$

29. $\dfrac{13}{-65} = -\dfrac{1}{5}$

31. $(-2)(-7) = 14$

33. $-5 \cdot 0 = 0$

35. No number multiplied by 0 equals 6.

37. $(-6)(4) = -24$

39. $2 \cdot 3 = 6$

41. $2(-3) = -6$

43. $(-24) \div 3 = -8$

45. $(-24) \div (-3) = 8$

47. $-6 \cdot 0 = 0$

49. Undefined

51. $0\left(-\dfrac{2}{5}\right) = 0$

53. $0 \div \left(-\dfrac{1}{10}\right) = 0$

55. $\dfrac{-9}{6} = -\dfrac{3}{2}$

57. $\dfrac{-250}{-1000} = \dfrac{1}{4}$

59. $\dfrac{52}{-4} = -13$

61. $(1.72)(-4.6) = -7.912$

63. $-0.02(-4.6) = 0.092$

65. $\dfrac{14.4}{-2.4} = -6$

67. $\dfrac{-5.25}{-2.5} = 2.1$

69. $(-3)^2 = 9$

71. $-3^2 = -9$

73. $\left(-\dfrac{4}{3}\right)^3 = \left(-\dfrac{4}{3}\right)\left(-\dfrac{4}{3}\right)\left(-\dfrac{4}{3}\right) = -\dfrac{64}{27}$

75. $2.8(-5.1) = -14.28$

77. $(-6.8) \div (-0.02) = 340$

79. $\left(-\dfrac{2}{15}\right)\left(\dfrac{25}{3}\right) = -\dfrac{50}{45} = -\dfrac{\cancel{5} \cdot 10}{\cancel{5} \cdot 9} = -\dfrac{10}{9}$

81. $\left(-\dfrac{7}{8}\right) \div \left(-\dfrac{9}{16}\right) = \left(-\dfrac{7}{8}\right) \cdot \left(-\dfrac{16}{9}\right)$

$= \dfrac{112}{72}$

$= \dfrac{\cancel{8} \cdot 14}{\cancel{8} \cdot 9}$

$= \dfrac{14}{9}$

83. $(-2)(-5)(-3) = (10)(-3) = -30$

85. $(-8)(-4)(-1)(-3) = (32)(3) = 96$

87. $100 \div (-10) \div (-5) = (-10) \div (-5) = 2$

89. $-12 \div (-6) \div (-2) = 2 \div (-2) = -1$

91. $\dfrac{2}{5} \cdot \dfrac{1}{3} \cdot \left(-\dfrac{10}{11}\right) = \dfrac{2}{15} \cdot \left(-\dfrac{10}{11}\right) = -\dfrac{20}{165} = -\dfrac{4}{33}$

93. $\left(1\dfrac{1}{3}\right) \div 3 \div \left(-\dfrac{7}{9}\right) = \dfrac{4}{3} \cdot \dfrac{1}{3} \div \left(-\dfrac{7}{9}\right)$

$= \dfrac{4}{9} \cdot \left(-\dfrac{9}{7}\right)$

$= -\dfrac{4}{7}$

95. $12 \div (-2)(4) = (-6)(4) = -24$

97. $\left(-\dfrac{12}{5}\right) \div (-6) \cdot \left(-\dfrac{1}{8}\right) = \left(-\dfrac{12}{5}\right) \cdot \left(-\dfrac{1}{6}\right) \cdot \left(-\dfrac{1}{8}\right)$

$\qquad = \dfrac{12}{30} \cdot \left(-\dfrac{1}{8}\right)$

$\qquad = \dfrac{2}{5} \cdot \left(-\dfrac{1}{8}\right)$

$\qquad = -\dfrac{2}{40}$

$\qquad = -\dfrac{1}{20}$

99. $8 - 2^3 \cdot 5 + 3 - (-6) = 8 - 8 \cdot 5 + 3 + 6$

$\qquad = 8 - 40 + 3 + 6$

$\qquad = -23$

101. $-(2-8)^2 \div (-6) \cdot 2 = -36 \div (-6) \cdot 2$

$\qquad = 6 \cdot 2$

$\qquad = 12$

103. $\dfrac{6(-4) - 2(5-8)}{-6 - 3 - 5} = \dfrac{-24 + 6}{-14} = \dfrac{-18}{-14} = \dfrac{9}{7}$

105. $\dfrac{-4 + 5}{(-2) \cdot 5 + 10} = \dfrac{1}{-10 + 10} = \dfrac{1}{0}$ is undefined

107. $-4 - 3[2 - (-5+3)] - 8 \cdot 2^2$

$\qquad = -4 - 3[2 - (-2)] - 8 \cdot 4$

$\qquad = -4 - 3[4] - 32$

$\qquad = -4 - 12 - 32$

$\qquad = -48$

109. $-|-1| - |5| = -1 - 5 = -6$

111. $\dfrac{|2-9| - |5-7|}{10 - 15} = \dfrac{7-2}{-5} = \dfrac{5}{-5} = -1$

113. $\dfrac{6 - 3[2 - (6-8)]^2}{-2|2-5|} = \dfrac{6 - 3[2 - (-2)]^2}{-2 \cdot 3}$

$\qquad = \dfrac{6 - 3 \cdot 16}{-6}$

$\qquad = \dfrac{6 - 48}{-6}$

$\qquad = \dfrac{-42}{-6}$

$\qquad = 7$

115. $-x^2 = -(-2)^2 = -4$

117. $4(2x - z) = 4(2(-2) - 6)$

$\qquad = 4(-4 - 6)$

$\qquad = 4(-10)$

$\qquad = -40$

119. $\dfrac{3x + 2y}{y} = \dfrac{3(-2) + 2(-4)}{-4}$

$\qquad = \dfrac{-6 + (-8)}{-4}$

$\qquad = \dfrac{-14}{-4}$

$\qquad = \dfrac{7}{2}$

121. No, the first expression equals $10 \div (5x) = 2 \div x$, and the second equals $10 \div 5 \cdot x = 2x$.

123. $-3.75(0.3) = -1.125$

125. $\left(\dfrac{16}{5}\right) \div \left(-\dfrac{8}{9}\right) = \dfrac{16}{5} \cdot \left(-\dfrac{9}{8}\right) = -\dfrac{144}{40} = -\dfrac{18}{5}$

126. $-\dfrac{3}{14} \div \dfrac{1}{7} = -\dfrac{3}{14} \cdot \dfrac{7}{1} = -\dfrac{21}{14} = -\dfrac{3}{2}$

127. $-0.4 + 6(-0.42) = -2.92$

128. $0.5 + (-2)(0.125) = 0.25$

129. $-\dfrac{1}{4} - 6\left(-\dfrac{1}{3}\right) = -\dfrac{1}{4} + 2 = -\dfrac{1}{4} + \dfrac{8}{4} = \dfrac{7}{4}$

131. $-2(3) + 3 = -3$; a loss of \$3

133. **(a)** $-4 - 3 - 2 - 1 = -4 + (-3) + (-2) + (-1)$
$= -10$

    (b) $-4(-3)(-2)(-1) = 12(2) = 24$

    (c) Part (a) is subtraction; part (b) is multiplication.

Problem Recognition Exercises

1. **a.** $-8 - (-4) = -4$

    b. $-8(-4) = 32$

    c. $-8 + (-4) = -12$

    d. $-8 \div (-4) = 2$

3. **a.** $-36 + 9 = -27$

    b. $-36(9) = -324$

    c. $-36 \div 9 = -4$

    d. $-36 - 9 = -45$

5. **a.** $-5(-10) = 50$

    b. $-5 + (-10) = -15$

    c. $-5 \div (-10) = \dfrac{1}{2}$

    d. $-5 - (-10) = 5$

7. **a.** $-4(-16) = 64$

    b. $-4 - (-16) = 12$

    c. $-4 \div (-16) = \dfrac{1}{4}$

    d. $-4 + (-16) = -20$

9. **a.** $80(-5) = -400$

    b. $80 - (-5) = 85$

    c. $80 \div (-5) = -16$

    d. $80 + (-5) = 75$

Section 1.7 Practice Exercises

1. Answers will vary.

3. $(-6) + 14 = 8$

5. $-13 - (-5) = -13 + 5 = -8$

7. $18 \div (-4) = -\dfrac{18}{4} = -\dfrac{9}{2} = -4.5$

9. $-3 \cdot 0 = 0$

11. $\dfrac{1}{2} + \dfrac{3}{8} = \dfrac{4}{8} + \dfrac{3}{8} = \dfrac{7}{8}$

13. $\left(-\dfrac{3}{5}\right)\left(\dfrac{4}{27}\right) = -\dfrac{12}{135} = -\dfrac{4}{45}$

15. $-8 + 5$

17. $x + 8$

19. $4(5)$

21. $-12x$

23. $x + (-3)$; $-3 + x$

25. $4p + (-9)$; $-9 + 4p$

27. $(x + 4) + 9 = x + (4 + 9) = x + 13$

29. $-5(3x) = (-5 \cdot 3)x = -15x$

31. $\dfrac{6}{11}\left(\dfrac{11}{6}x\right) = \left(\dfrac{6}{11} \cdot \dfrac{11}{6}\right)x = x$

33. $-4\left(-\dfrac{1}{4}t\right) = \left(-4 \cdot -\dfrac{1}{4}\right)t = t$

35. $-8 + (2 + y) = (-8 + 2) + y = -6 + y$

37. $-5(2x) = (-5 \cdot 2)x = -10x$

39. Reciprocal

41. Zero

43. $6(5x + 1) = 6(5x) + 6(1) = 30x + 6$

45. $-2(a + 8) = -2a + (-2)(8) = -2a - 16$

47. $3(5c - d) = 3(5c) - 3d = 15c - 3d$

49. $-7(y - 2) = -7y - (-7)(2) = -7y + 14$

51. $-\dfrac{2}{3}(x - 6) = -\dfrac{2}{3}x - \left(-\dfrac{2}{3}\right)(6)$

$\qquad = -\dfrac{2}{3}x + \dfrac{12}{3}$

$\qquad = -\dfrac{2}{3}x + 4$

53. $\dfrac{1}{3}(m - 3) = \dfrac{1}{3}m - \dfrac{1}{3} \cdot 3 = \dfrac{1}{3}m - 1$

55. $-(2p + 10) = -2p - 10$

57. $-2(-3w - 5z + 8) = -2(-3w) - 2(-5z) - 2(8)$

$\qquad = 6w + 10z - 16$

59. $4(x + 2y - z) = 4(x) + 4(2y) - 4(z)$

$\qquad\qquad = 4x + 8y - 4z$

61. $-(-6w + x - 3y) = 6w - x + 3y$

63. $2(3 + x) = 6 + 2x$

65. $4(6z) = 24z$

67. $-2(7x) = -14x$

69. $-4(1 + x) = -4 - 4x$

71. b

73. i

75. g

77. d

79. h

81. Term: $2x$, coefficient 2;
Term: $-y$, coefficient -1;
Term: $18xy$, coefficient 18;
Term: 5, coefficient 5.

83. Term: $-x$, coefficient -1;
Term: $8y$, coefficient 8;
Term: $-9x^2 y$, coefficient -9;
Term: -3, coefficient -3.

85. The variable factors are different

87. The variables are the same *and* raised to the same power.

89. Answers vary: $5y, -2x, 6$

91. $-4p - 2p = -6p$

93. $2y^2 - 5y^2 - 3y^2 = -6y^2$

95. $8x^3 y + 3 - 7 - x^3 y = 7x^3 y - 4$

97. $\dfrac{2}{5} + 2t - \dfrac{3}{5} + t - \dfrac{6}{5} = 3t - \dfrac{7}{5}$

99. $-3(2x - 4) + 10 = -6x + 12 + 10 = -6x + 22$

101. $4(w + 3) - 12 = 4w + 12 - 12 = 4w$

103. $5 - 3(x - 4) = 5 - 3x + 12 = -3x + 1$

105. $-3(2t + 4) + 8(2t - 4) = -6t - 12 + 16t - 32$

$\qquad\qquad\qquad\qquad = -6t + 16t - 12 - 32$

$\qquad\qquad\qquad\qquad = 10t - 44$

107. $2(w - 5) - (2w + 8) = 2w - 10 - 2w - 8 = -18$

109. $-\dfrac{1}{3}(6t + 9) + 10 = -2t - 3 + 10 = -2t + 7$

111. $10(5.1a - 3.1) + 4 = 51a - 31 + 4 = 51a - 27$

113. $-4m + 2(m - 3) + 2m = -4m + 2m - 6 + 2m$
$$= -6$$

115. $\dfrac{1}{2}(10q - 2) + \dfrac{1}{3}(2 - 3q) = 5q - 1 + \dfrac{2}{3} - q$
$$= 5q - q - 1 + \dfrac{2}{3}$$
$$= 4q - \dfrac{1}{3}$$

117. $7n - 2(n - 3) - 6 + n = 7n - 2n + 6 - 6 + n$
$$= 6n$$

119. $\quad 6(x + 3) - 12 - 4(x - 3)$
$$= 6x + 18 - 12 - 4x + 12$$
$$= 2x + 18$$

121. $\quad 6.1(5.3z - 4.1) - 5.8 = 32.33z - 25.01 - 5.8$
$$= 32.33z - 30.81$$

123. $\quad 6 + 2[-8 - 3(2x + 4)] + 10x$
$$= 6 + 2[-8 - 6x - 12] + 10x$$
$$= 6 + 2[-6x - 20] + 10x$$
$$= 6 - 12x - 40 + 10x$$
$$= -2x - 34$$

125. $\quad 1 - 3[2(z + 1) - 5(z - 2)]$
$$= 1 - 3[2z + 2 - 5z + 10]$$
$$= 1 - 3[-3z + 12]$$
$$= 1 + 9z - 36$$
$$= 9z - 35$$

127. Equivalent

129. Not equivalent. The terms are not *like* terms and cannot be combined.

131. Not equivalent. Subtraction is not commutative.

133. Equivalent

135. (a) $10 + (1 + 9) + (2 + 8) + (3 + 7)$
$\quad + (4 + 6) + 5$
$= 55$

(b) $(1 + 19) + (2 + 18) + (3 + 17) + (4 + 16)$
$\quad + (5 + 15) + (6 + 14) + (7 + 13)$
$\quad + (8 + 12) + (9 + 11) + 10 + 20 = 210$

Group Activity

1. Substitute $C = 35$.
$$F = \dfrac{9}{5}C + 32$$
$$= \dfrac{9}{5}(35) + 32$$
$$= 63 + 32$$
$$= 95$$

3. Substitute $k = 0.05$, $L = 200$, $r = 0.5$.
$$R = k\left(\dfrac{L}{r^2}\right)$$
$$= 0.05\left(\dfrac{200}{0.5^2}\right)$$
$$= 0.05(800)$$
$$= 40$$

5. Substitute $\bar{x} = 69$, $\mu = 55$, $\sigma = 20$, $n = 25$
$$z = \dfrac{\bar{x} - \mu}{\dfrac{\sigma}{\sqrt{n}}}$$
$$= \dfrac{69 - 55}{\dfrac{20}{\sqrt{25}}}$$
$$= \dfrac{14}{\dfrac{20}{5}}$$
$$= \dfrac{14}{4}$$
$$= 3.5$$

7. Substitute $a = 2$, $b = -7$, $c = -15$

$$x = \frac{-b + \sqrt{b^2 - 4ac}}{2a}$$

$$= \frac{-(-7) + \sqrt{(-7)^2 - 4(2)(-15)}}{2(2)}$$

$$= \frac{7 + \sqrt{49 + 120}}{4}$$

$$= \frac{7 + \sqrt{169}}{4}$$

$$= \frac{7 + 13}{4}$$

$$= \frac{20}{4}$$

$$= 5$$

Chapter 1 Review Exercises

Section 1.1

1. $\frac{14}{5}$; *improper*

3. $\frac{3}{3}$; *improper*

5. $2 \times 2 \times 2 \times 2 \times 7$

7. $\frac{2}{9} + \frac{3}{4} = \frac{8}{36} + \frac{27}{36} = \frac{35}{36}$

9. $\frac{{}^{3}\cancel{21}}{{}_{3}\cancel{24}} \times \frac{\cancel{16}^{2}}{\cancel{49}_{7}} = \frac{6}{21} = \frac{2}{7}$

11. $5\frac{1}{3} \div 1\frac{7}{9} = \frac{16}{3} \div \frac{16}{9} = \frac{{}^{1}\cancel{16}}{{}_{1}\cancel{3}} \times \frac{\cancel{9}^{3}}{\cancel{16}_{1}} = \frac{3}{1} = 3$

13. $\frac{7}{10} \times 510{,}000{,}000\,km = 357{,}000{,}000\,km$

Section 1.2

15. $\left|\frac{1}{2}\right| = \frac{1}{2}$

17. $\left|-\sqrt{7}\right| = \sqrt{7}$

19. False

21. True

23. True

25. False

27. True

Section 1.3

29. $\frac{7}{y}$ or $7 \div y$

31. $a - 5$

33. $13z - 7$

35. $(8)^2 - 4 = 64 - 4 = 60$

37. $\sqrt{(8) + 2(4)} = \sqrt{8 + 8} = \sqrt{16} = 4$

39. $15^2 = 225$

41. $\frac{1}{\sqrt{100}} = \frac{1}{10}$

43. $\left(\frac{3}{2}\right)^3 = \frac{27}{8}$

45. $\left|-11\right| + \left|5\right| - (7 - 2) = 11 + 5 - 5 = 11$

47. $22 - 3(8 \div 4)^2 = 22 - 3(2)^2 = 22 - 12 = 10$

Section 1.4

49. $14 + (-10) = 4$

51. $-12 + (-5) = -17$

53. $-\frac{8}{11} + \frac{1}{2} = -\frac{16}{22} + \frac{11}{22} = -\frac{5}{22}$

55. $\left(-\dfrac{5}{2}\right)+\left(-\dfrac{1}{5}\right)=-\dfrac{25}{10}+\left(-\dfrac{2}{10}\right)=-\dfrac{27}{10}$

57. $2.9+(-7.18)=-4.28$

59. $-5+(-7)+20=-12+20=8$

61. When a and b are both negative or when a and b have different signs and the number with the larger absolute value is negative.

Section 1.5

63. $13-25=-12$

65. $-8-(-7)=-8+7=-1$

67. $\left(-\dfrac{7}{9}\right)-\dfrac{5}{6}=-\dfrac{14}{18}-\dfrac{15}{18}=-\dfrac{29}{18}$

69. $7-8.2=-1.2$

71. $-16.1-(-5.9)=-16.1+5.9=-10.2$

73. $\dfrac{11}{2}-\left(-\dfrac{1}{6}\right)-\dfrac{7}{3}=\dfrac{33}{6}+\dfrac{1}{6}-\dfrac{14}{6}=\dfrac{20}{6}=\dfrac{10}{3}$

75. $6-14-(-1)-10-(-21)-5$
$=6-14+1-10+21-5$
$=-8-9+16$
$=-17+16$
$=-1$

77. $-7-(-18);$
$-7-(-18)=11$

79. $7-13;$
$7-13=-6$

81. $(6+(-12))-21;$
$(6+(-12))-21=-6-21=-27$

Section 1.6

83. $10(-17)=-170$

85. $(-52)\div26=-2$

87. $\dfrac{7}{4}\div\left(-\dfrac{21}{2}\right)=\dfrac{7}{4}\cdot\left(-\dfrac{2}{21}\right)=-\dfrac{14}{84}=-\dfrac{1}{6}$

89. $-\dfrac{21}{5}\cdot0=0$

91. $0\div(-14)=0$

93. $-\dfrac{21}{14}=-\dfrac{3\cdot7}{2\cdot7}=-\dfrac{3}{2}$

95. $(5)(-2)(3)=(-10)(3)=-30$

97. $\left(-\dfrac{1}{2}\right)\left(\dfrac{7}{8}\right)\left(-\dfrac{4}{7}\right)=\left(-\dfrac{7}{16}\right)\left(-\dfrac{4}{7}\right)=\dfrac{7\cdot4}{16\cdot7}=\dfrac{1}{4}$

99. $40\div4\div(-5)=10\div(-5)=-2$

101. $9-4[-2(4-8)-5(3-1)]$
$=9-4[-2(-4)-5(2)]$
$=9-4[8-10]$
$=9-4[-2]$
$=9+8$
$=17$

103. $\dfrac{2}{3}-\left(\dfrac{3}{8}+\dfrac{5}{6}\right)\div\dfrac{5}{3}=\dfrac{2}{3}-\left(\dfrac{9}{24}+\dfrac{20}{24}\right)\cdot\dfrac{3}{5}$
$=\dfrac{16}{24}-\dfrac{29}{24}\cdot\dfrac{3}{5}$
$=\dfrac{16}{24}-\dfrac{29}{40}$
$=\dfrac{80}{120}-\dfrac{87}{120}$
$=-\dfrac{7}{120}$

105. $\dfrac{5-[3-(-4)^2]}{36\div(-2)(3)}$
$=\dfrac{5-[3-16]}{(-18)(3)}$
$=\dfrac{5-[-13]}{-54}$
$=\dfrac{18}{-54}$
$=-\dfrac{1}{3}$

107. $3(x+2) \div y = 3(4+2) \div (-9)$
$$= 18 \div (-9)$$
$$= -2$$

109. $-xy = -(4)(-9) = 36$

111. $x = \mu + z\sigma$
$x = (100) + (-1.96)(15)$
$x = 70.6$

113. False; any nonzero real number raised to an even power is positive.

115. True

117. True

Section 1.7

119. $2 + 3 = 3 + 2$

121. $5 + (-5) = 0$

123. $5 \cdot 2 = 2 \cdot 5$

125. $3 \cdot \dfrac{1}{3} = 1$

127. $5x - 2y = 5x + (-2y)$; then use commutative property of addition..

129. $3y, 10x, -12, xy$

131. $3a + 3b - 4b + 5a - 10$
$$= 3a + 5a + 3b - 4b - 10$$
$$= 8a - b - 10$$

133. $-2(4z + 9) = -8z - 18$

135. $2p - (p+5) + 3 = 2p - p - 5 + 3 = p - 2$

139. $-4[2(x+1) - (3x+8)] = -4[2x + 2 - 3x - 8]$
$$= -4[-x - 6]$$
$$= 4x + 24$$

140. $5[(7y-3) + 3(y+8)] = 5[7y - 3 + 3y + 24]$
$$= 5[10y + 21]$$
$$= 50y + 105$$

Chapter 1 Test

1. $\dfrac{135}{36} = \dfrac{15}{4}$

3. $4\dfrac{1}{12} \div 1\dfrac{1}{3} = \dfrac{49}{12} \div \dfrac{4}{3} = \dfrac{49}{\cancel{12}_4} \times \dfrac{\cancel{3}^1}{4} = \dfrac{49}{16} = 3\dfrac{1}{16}$

5. Rational; all repeating decimals are rational numbers.

7. (a) False

(b) True

(c) True

(d) True

9. (a) Twice the difference of a and b

(b) The difference of twice a and b

11. $18 + (-12) = 6$

13. $21 - (-7) = 21 + 7 = 28$

15. $-10.06 - (-14.72) = -10.06 + 14.72 = 4.66$

17. $-84 \div 7 = -12$

19. $7(-4) = -28$

21. $(-16)(-2)(-1)(-3) = (32)(3) = 96$

23. $(8-10)\dfrac{3}{2} + (-5) = (-2)\dfrac{3}{2} + (-5)$
$$= -3 + (-5)$$
$$= -8$$

25. $\dfrac{\sqrt{5^2 - 4^2}}{|-12 + 3|} = \dfrac{\sqrt{25 - 16}}{|-9|} = \dfrac{\sqrt{9}}{9} = \dfrac{3}{9} = \dfrac{1}{3}$

27. a. $5 + 2 + (-10) + 4$

b. He gained 1 yd.

29. $-5x - 4y + 3 - 7x + 6y - 7$
$= -5x - 7x - 4y + 6y + 3 - 7$
$= -12x + 2y - 4$

31. $3k - 20 + (-9k) + 12 = -6k - 8$

33. $\frac{1}{2}(12p - 4) + \frac{1}{3}(2 - 6p) = 6p - 2 + \frac{2}{3} - 2p$
$$= 4p - \frac{4}{3}$$

35. $3x - 2y = 3(4) - 2(-3)$
$= 12 - (-6)$
$= 12 + 6$
$= 18$

37. $-y^2 - 4x + z = -(-3)^2 - 4(4) + (-7)$
$= -9 - 4(4) + (-7)$
$= -9 - 16 + (-7)$
$= -9 + (-16) + (-7)$
$= -32$

39. $6 - 8;$
$6 - 8 = -2$

Chapter 2

Chapter 2 Opener

$$8 \cdot \left(\frac{3}{8}\right) = \text{three}$$

$$6 \cdot \left(\frac{2}{3}\right) = \text{four}$$

$$100(0.17) = \text{seventeen}$$

$$100(0.09) = \text{nine}$$

$$\text{five} \cdot \left(\frac{2}{5}\right) = 2$$

$$\text{seven} \cdot \left(\frac{6}{7}\right) = 6$$

$$\text{eight} \cdot \left(\frac{3}{4}\right) = 6$$

$$\text{twelve} \cdot \left(\frac{5}{6}\right) = 10$$

$$\text{ten} \cdot (0.4) = 4$$

Section 2.1 Practice Exercises

1. Writing exercises, exercise keyed to video, calculator exercises, and translating expressions exercises.

3. Expression

5. Equation

7. Substitute the value into the equation and determine if the right-hand side is equal to the left-hand side.

9. No; $4 - 1 \neq 5$
$$3 \neq 5$$

11. Yes; $5(-2) = -10$
$$-10 = -10$$

13. Yes; $3(-2) + 9 = 3$
$$-6 + 9 = 3$$
$$3 = 3$$

15. $$x + 6 = 5$$
$$x + 6 + (-6) = 5 + (-6)$$
$$x = -1$$

17. $$q - 14 = 6$$
$$q - 14 + 14 = 6 + 14$$
$$q = 20$$

19. $$2 + m = -15$$
$$-2 + 2 + m = -15 - 2$$
$$m = -17$$

21. $$-23 = y - 7$$
$$-23 + 7 = y - 7 + 7$$
$$-16 = y \text{ or } y = -16$$

23. $$4 + c = 4$$
$$-4 + 4 + c = 4 - 4$$
$$c = 0$$

25. $$4.1 = 2.8 + a$$
$$4.1 - 2.8 = -2.8 + 2.8 + a$$
$$1.3 = a \quad \text{or} \quad a = 1.3$$

27.
$$5 = z - \frac{1}{2}$$
$$5 + \frac{1}{2} = z - \frac{1}{2} + \frac{1}{2}$$
$$\frac{11}{2} = z \text{ or } z = \frac{11}{2}$$
$$\text{or } z = 5\frac{1}{2}$$

29.
$$x + \frac{5}{2} = \frac{1}{2}$$
$$x + \frac{5}{2} - \frac{5}{2} = \frac{1}{2} - \frac{5}{2}$$
$$x = -\frac{4}{2} = -2$$

31.
$$-6.02 + c = -8.15$$
$$6.02 - 6.02 + c = -8.15 + 6.02$$
$$c = -2.13$$

33.
$$3.245 + t = -0.0225$$
$$3.245 - 3.245 + t = -0.0225 - 3.245$$
$$t = -3.2675$$

35.
$$6x = 54$$
$$\frac{6x}{6} = \frac{54}{6}$$
$$x = 9$$

37.
$$12 = -3p$$
$$\frac{12}{-3} = \frac{-3p}{-3}$$
$$-4 = p \text{ or } p = -4$$

39.
$$-5y = 0$$
$$\frac{-5y}{-5} = \frac{0}{5}$$
$$y = 0$$

41.
$$-\frac{y}{5} = 3$$
$$-\frac{y}{5} \cdot (-5) = 3(-5)$$
$$y = -15$$

43.
$$\frac{4}{5} = -t$$
$$\frac{4}{5}(-1) = -t(-1)$$
$$-\frac{4}{5} = t \quad \text{or} \quad t = -\frac{4}{5}$$

45.
$$\frac{2}{5}a = -4$$
$$\frac{5}{2} \cdot \frac{2}{5}a = \frac{5}{2}(-4) = -\frac{20}{2}$$
$$a = -10$$

47.
$$-\frac{1}{5}b = -\frac{4}{5}$$
$$(-5)\left(-\frac{1}{5}b\right) = (-5)\left(-\frac{4}{5}\right)$$
$$b = 4$$

49.
$$-41 = -x$$
$$(-1)(-41) = (-1)(-x)$$
$$x = 41$$

51.
$$3.81 = -0.03p$$
$$\frac{3.81}{-0.03} = \frac{-0.03p}{-0.03}$$
$$p = -127$$

53.
$$5.82y = -15.132$$
$$\frac{5.82y}{5.82} = \frac{-15.132}{5.82}$$
$$y = -2.6$$

55.
Let x = the number. $-8 + x = 42$;
$$-8 + x = 42$$
$$8 - 8 + x = 42 + 8$$
$$x = 50$$

57. Let x = the number. $x - (-6) = 18$;
$$x - (-6) = 18$$
$$x + 6 - 6 = 18 - 6$$
$$x = 12$$

59. Let $x =$ the number. $x \cdot 7 = -63$ or $7x = -63$

$$\frac{7x}{7} = \frac{-63}{7}$$

$$x = -9$$

61. Let $x =$ the number. $x - 3.2 = 2.1$

$$x - 3.2 + 3.2 = 2.1 + 3.2$$

$$x = 5.3$$

63. Let $x =$ the number. $\dfrac{x}{12} = \dfrac{1}{3}$

$$12 \cdot \frac{x}{12} = 12 \cdot \frac{1}{3}$$

$$x = 4$$

65. Let $x =$ the number. $x + \dfrac{5}{8} = \dfrac{13}{8}$;

$$x + \frac{5}{8} = \frac{13}{8}$$

$$x + \frac{5}{8} - \frac{5}{8} = \frac{13}{8} - \frac{5}{8}$$

$$x = \frac{8}{8} = 1$$

67. $\quad a - 9 = 1$

$$a - 9 + 9 = 1 + 9$$

$$a = 10$$

69. $-9x = 1$

$$\frac{-9x}{-9} = \frac{1}{-9}$$

$$-\frac{1}{9} = x$$

71. $\qquad -\dfrac{2}{3}h = 8$

$$\left(-\frac{3}{2}\right)\left(-\frac{2}{3}h\right) = \left(-\frac{3}{2}\right) \cdot 8$$

$$h = -\frac{24}{2} = -12$$

73. $\qquad \dfrac{2}{3} + t = 8$

$$-\frac{2}{3} + \frac{2}{3} + t = -\frac{2}{3} + 8$$

$$t = \frac{22}{3} \text{ or } 7\frac{1}{3}$$

75. $\qquad \dfrac{r}{3} = -12$

$$3 \cdot \frac{r}{3} = 3(-12)$$

$$r = -36$$

77. $\qquad k + 16 = 32$

$$k + 16 - 16 = 32 - 16$$

$$k = 16$$

79. $16k = 32$

$$\frac{16k}{16} = \frac{32}{16}$$

$$k = 2$$

81. $\quad 7 = -4q$

$$\frac{7}{-4} = \frac{-4q}{-4}$$

$$q = -\frac{7}{4} \text{ or } -1\frac{3}{4}$$

83. $\qquad -4 + q = 7$

$$-4 + 4 + q = 4 + 7$$

$$q = 11$$

85. $\qquad -\dfrac{1}{3}d = 12$

$$(-3)\left(-\frac{1}{3}d\right) = (-3)(12)$$

$$d = -36$$

87. $\qquad 4 = \dfrac{1}{2} + z$

$$4 - \frac{1}{2} = \frac{1}{2} - \frac{1}{2} + z$$

$$z = \frac{7}{2} \text{ or } 3\frac{1}{2}$$

89. $1.2y = 4.8$

$$\frac{1.2y}{1.2} = \frac{4.8}{1.2}$$

$$y = 4$$

91. $4.8 = 1.2 + y$

$$4.8 - 1.2 = 1.2 - 1.2 + y$$

$$y = 3.6$$

93. $0.0034 = y - 0.405$

$$0.0034 + 0.405 = y - 0.405 + 0.405$$

$$y = 0.4084$$

95. Yes

97. No

99. Yes

101. Yes

103. For example: $y + 9 = 15$

105. For example: $2p = -8$

107. For example: $5a + 5 = 5$

109. $5x - 4x + 7 = 8 - 2$

$$x + 7 = 6$$

$$x = -1$$

111. $6p - 3p = 15 + 6$

$$3p = 21$$

$$p = \frac{21}{3} = 7$$

Section 2.2 Practice Exercises

1. Answers will vary.

3. $5z + 2 - 7z - 3z = 5z - 10z + 2 = -5z + 2$

4. $10 - 4w + 7w - 2 + w = 10 + 3w + w - 2$
$$= 4w + 8$$

5. $-(-7p + 9) + (3p - 1) = 7p - 9 + 3p - 1$
$$= 10p - 10$$

7. To simplify an expression, clear parentheses and combine *like* terms. To solve an equation, use the addition, subtraction, multiplication, and division properties of equality to isolate the variable.

9. $-7y = 21$

$$\frac{-7y}{-7} = \frac{21}{-7}$$

$$y = -3$$

11. $z - 23 = -28$

$$z - 23 + 23 = -28 + 23$$

$$z = -5$$

13. $6z + 1 = 13$

$$6z + 1 - 1 = 13 - 1$$

$$\frac{6z}{6} = \frac{12}{6}$$

$$z = 2$$

15. $3y - 4 = 14$

$$3y - 4 + 4 = 4 + 14$$

$$\frac{3y}{3} = \frac{18}{3}$$

$$y = 6$$

17. $-2p + 8 = 3$

$$-2p + 8 - 8 = 3 - 8$$

$$\frac{-2p}{-2} = \frac{-5}{-2}$$

$$p = \frac{5}{2} \text{ or } 2\frac{1}{2}$$

19. $0.2x + 3.1 = -5.3$

$$0.2x + 3.1 - 3.1 = -5.3 - 3.1$$

$$\frac{0.2x}{0.2} = \frac{-8.4}{0.2}$$

$$x = -42$$

21.
$$\frac{5}{8} = \frac{1}{4} - \frac{1}{2}p$$
$$\frac{5}{8} - \frac{1}{4} = -\frac{1}{4} + \frac{1}{4} - \frac{1}{2}p$$
$$(-2)\left(\frac{3}{8}\right) = (-2)\left(-\frac{1}{2}p\right)$$
$$p = -\frac{6}{8} = -\frac{3}{4}$$

23. $7w - 6w + 1 = 10 - 4$
$$w + 1 = 6$$
$$w + 1 - 1 = 6 - 1$$
$$w = 5$$

25. $11h - 8 - 9h = -16$
$$2h - 8 + 8 = -16 + 8$$
$$\frac{2h}{2} = \frac{-8}{2}$$
$$h = -4$$

27. $3a + 7 = 2a - 19$
$$3a - 2a + 7 - 7 = 2a - 2a - 19 - 7$$
$$a = -26$$

29. $-4r - 28 = -58 - r$
$$-4r + r - 28 + 28 = -58 + 28 - r + r$$
$$\frac{-3r}{-3} = \frac{-30}{-3}$$
$$r = \frac{30}{3} = 10$$

31. $-2z - 8 = -z$
$$-2z + 2z - 8 = -z + 2z$$
$$-8 = z \text{ or } z = -8$$

33.
$$\frac{5}{6}x + \frac{2}{3} = -\frac{1}{6}x - \frac{5}{3}$$
$$\frac{5}{6}x + \frac{1}{6}x + \frac{2}{3} - \frac{2}{3} = -\frac{1}{6}x + \frac{1}{6}x - \frac{5}{3} - \frac{2}{3}$$
$$x = -\frac{7}{3} \text{ or } -2\frac{1}{3}$$

35. $3y - 2 = 5y - 2$
$$3y - 5y - 2 + 2 = 5y - 5y - 2 + 2$$
$$\frac{-2y}{-2} = \frac{0}{-2}$$
$$y = 0$$

37 $4q + 14 = 2$
$$4q + 14 - 14 = 2 - 14$$
$$\frac{4q}{4} = \frac{-12}{4}$$
$$q = -3$$

39. $-9 = 4n - 1$
$$-9 + 1 = 4n - 1 + 1$$
$$\frac{-8}{4} = \frac{4n}{4}$$
$$n = -2$$

41. $3(2p - 4) = 15$
$$6p - 12 = 15$$
$$6p - 12 + 12 = 15 + 12$$
$$\frac{6p}{6} = \frac{27}{6}$$
$$p = \frac{9}{2} \text{ or } 4\frac{1}{2}$$

43. $6(3x + 2) - 10 = -4$
$$18x + 12 - 10 = -4$$
$$18x + 2 = -4$$
$$18x + 2 - 2 = -4 - 2$$
$$\frac{18x}{18} = \frac{-6}{18}$$
$$x = -\frac{1}{3}$$

45, $3.4x - 2.5 = 2.8x + 3.5$
$$3.4x - 2.8x - 2.5 = 2.8x - 2.8x + 3.5$$
$$0.6x - 2.5 + 2.5 = 3.5 + 2.5$$
$$\frac{0.6x}{0.6} = \frac{6}{0.6}$$
$$x = 10$$

47. $17(s+3) = 4(s-10)+13$
$17s+51 = 4s-40+13$
$17s-4s = -27-51$
$\dfrac{13s}{13} = \dfrac{-78}{13}$
$s = -6$

49. $6(3t-4)+10 = 5(t-2)-(3t+4)$
$18t-24+10 = 5t-10-3t-4$
$18t-14 = 2t-14$
$16t = 0$
$t = 0$

51. $5-3(x+2) = 5$
$5-3x-6 = 5$
$-3x-1 = 5$
$-3x = 6$
$x = -2$

53. $3(2z-6)-4(3z+1) = 5-2(z+1)$
$6z-18-12z-4 = 5-2z-2$
$-6z-22 = -2z+3$
$-4z = 25$
$z = -\dfrac{25}{4}$

55. $-2[(4p+1)-(3p-1)] = 5(3-p)-9$
$-2[4p+1-3p+1] = 15-5p-9$
$-8p-2+6p-2 = 6-5p$
$-2p-4 = 6-5p$
$3p = 10$
$p = \dfrac{10}{3}$ or $3\dfrac{1}{3}$

57. $3(-0.9n+0.5) = -3.5n+1.3$
$-2.7n+1.5 = -3.5n+1.3$
$0.8n = -0.2$
$n = -0.25$

59. $2(k-7) = 2k-13$
$2k-14 = 2k-13$
$-14 = -13$
Contradiction; $\{\}$

61. Conditional equation; $\{-15\}$
$7x+3 = 6x-12$
$x = -15$

63. $3-5.2p = -5.2p+3$
$3 = 3$
Identity; the set of real numbers

65. One solution

67. Infinitely many solutions

69. $4p-6 = 8+2p$
$4p-2p-6 = 8+2p-2p$
$2p-6+6 = 8+6$
$2p = 14$
$\dfrac{2p}{2} = \dfrac{14}{2}$
$p = 7$

71. $2k-9 = -8$
$2k-9+9 = -8+9$
$2k = 1$
$\dfrac{2k}{2} = \dfrac{1}{2}$
$k = \dfrac{1}{2}$

73. $7(w-2) = -14-3w$
$7w-14 = -14-3w$
$10w = 0$
$w = 0$

75. $2(x+2)-3 = 2x+1$
$2x+4-3 = 2x+1$
$2x+1 = 2x+1$
$2x-2x+1 = 2x-2x+1$
$1 = 1$
All real numbers are solutions.

77. $0.5b = -23$
$\dfrac{0.5b}{0.5} = \dfrac{-23}{0.5}$
$b = -46$

79.
$$8 - 2q = 4$$
$$8 - 8 - 2q = 4 - 8$$
$$-2q = -4$$
$$\frac{-2q}{-2} = \frac{-4}{-2}$$
$$q = 2$$

81.
$$2 - 4(y - 5) = -4$$
$$2 - 4y + 20 = -4$$
$$-4y + 22 = -4$$
$$-4y = -26$$
$$y = \frac{-26}{-4}$$
$$y = \frac{13}{2}$$

83.
$$0.4(a + 20) = 6$$
$$0.4 + 8 = 6$$
$$0.4a = -2$$
$$\frac{0.4a}{0.4} = \frac{-2}{0.4}$$
$$a = -5$$

85.
$$10(2n + 1) - 6 = 20(n - 1) + 12$$
$$20n + 10 - 6 = 20n - 20 + 12$$
$$20n + 4 = 20n - 8$$
$$20n - 20n + 4 = 20n - 20n - 8$$
$$4 \neq -8$$
No solution

87.
$$c + 0.123 = 2.328$$
$$c + 0.123 - 0.123 = 2.328 - 0.123$$
$$c = 2.205$$

89.
$$\frac{4}{5}t - 1 = \frac{1}{5}t + 5$$
$$\frac{3}{5}t = 6$$
$$\left(\frac{^1\cancel{5}}{_1\cancel{3}}\right)\frac{\cancel{3}^1}{\cancel{5}_1}t = {^2}\cancel{6}\left(\frac{5}{\cancel{3}_1}\right)$$
$$t = 10$$

91.
$$6w - (8 + 2w) = 2(w - 4)$$
$$6w - 8 - 2w = 2w - 8$$
$$4w - 8 = 2w - 8$$
$$2w = 0$$
$$w = 0$$

93.
$$x + a = 10$$
$$-5 + a = 10$$
$$a = 15$$

95.
$$ax = 12$$
$$a(3) = 12$$
$$a = 4$$

97. For example: $5x + 2 = 2 + 5x$

Section 2.3 Practice Exercises

1. Answers will vary.

3.
$$5(x + 2) - 3 = 4x + 5$$
$$5x + 10 - 3 = 4x + 5$$
$$5x + 7 = 4x + 5$$
$$x + 7 = 5$$
$$x = -2$$

5.
$$3(2y + 3) - 4(-y + 1) = 7y - 10$$
$$6y + 9 + 4y - 4 = 7y - 10$$
$$10y + 5 = 7y - 10$$
$$3y + 5 = -10$$
$$3y = -15$$
$$y = -5$$

7.
$$7x + 2 = 7(x - 12)$$
$$7x + 2 = 7x - 84$$
$$2 \neq -84$$
No solution

9. 18, 36

11. 100; 1000; 10,000

13. 30, 60

15.
$$\frac{1}{2}x + 3 = 5$$
$$2\left(\frac{1}{2}x + 3\right) = 2(5)$$
$$x + 6 = 10$$
$$x = 4$$

17.
$$\frac{2}{15}z + 3 = \frac{7}{5}$$
$$15\left(\frac{2}{15}z + 3\right) = 15\left(\frac{7}{5}\right)$$
$$2z + 45 = 21$$
$$\frac{2z}{2} = \frac{-24}{2}$$
$$z = -12$$

19.
$$\frac{1}{3}q + \frac{3}{5} = \frac{1}{15}q - \frac{2}{5}$$
$$15\left(\frac{1}{3}q + \frac{3}{5}\right) = 15\left(\frac{1}{15}q - \frac{2}{5}\right)$$
$$5q + 9 = q - 6$$
$$4q = -15$$
$$q = -\frac{15}{4}$$

21.
$$\frac{12}{5}w + 7 = 31 - \frac{3}{5}w$$
$$5\left(\frac{12}{5}w + 7\right) = 5\left(31 - \frac{3}{5}w\right)$$
$$12w + 35 = 155 - 3w$$
$$15w = 120$$
$$w = 8$$

23.
$$\frac{1}{4}(3m - 4) - \frac{1}{5} = \frac{1}{4}m + \frac{3}{10}$$
$$20\left[\frac{1}{4}(3m - 4) - \frac{1}{5}\right] = 20\left(\frac{1}{4}m + \frac{3}{10}\right)$$
$$5(3m - 4) - 4 = 5m + 6$$
$$15m - 20 - 4 = 5m + 6$$
$$15m - 24 = 5m + 6$$
$$10m = 30$$
$$m = 3$$

25.
$$\frac{1}{6}(5s + 3) = \frac{1}{2}(s + 11)$$
$$6\left[\frac{1}{6}(5s + 3)\right] = 6\left[\frac{1}{2}(s + 11)\right]$$
$$5s + 3 = 3(s + 11)$$
$$5s + 3 = 3s + 33$$
$$2s = 30$$
$$s = 15$$

27.
$$\frac{2}{3}x + 4 = \frac{2}{3}x - 6$$
$$3\left(\frac{2}{3}x + 4\right) = 3\left(\frac{2}{3}x - 6\right)$$
$$2x + 12 = 2x - 18$$
$$12 \neq -18$$
No solution

29.
$$\frac{1}{6}(2c - 1) = \frac{1}{3}c - \frac{1}{6}$$
$$6\left(\frac{1}{6}(2c - 1)\right) = 6\left(\frac{1}{3}c - \frac{1}{6}\right)$$
$$2c - 1 = 2c - 1$$
$$-1 = -1$$
All real numbers

31.
$$\frac{2x + 1}{3} + \frac{x - 1}{3} = 5$$
$$3\left(\frac{2x + 1}{3} + \frac{x - 1}{3}\right) = 3(5)$$
$$2x + 1 + x - 1 = 15$$
$$3x = 15$$
$$x = 5$$

33.
$$\frac{3w - 2}{6} = 1 - \frac{w - 1}{3}$$
$$6\left(\frac{3w - 2}{6}\right) = 6\left(1 - \frac{w - 1}{3}\right)$$
$$3w - 2 = 6 - 2(w - 1)$$
$$3w - 2 = 8 - 2w$$
$$5w = 10$$
$$w = 2$$

35.
$$\frac{x+3}{3} - \frac{x-1}{2} = 4$$
$$6\left(\frac{x+3}{3}\right) - 6\left(\frac{x-1}{2}\right) = 6(4)$$
$$2(x+3) - 3(x-1) = 24$$
$$2x + 6 - 3x + 3 = 24$$
$$-x + 9 = 24$$
$$-x = 15$$
$$x = -15$$

37.
$$9.2y - 4.3 = 50.9$$
$$10\,(9.2y - 4.3) = 10\,(50.9)$$
$$92y = 552$$
$$y = 6$$

39.
$$21.1w + 4.6 = 10.9w + 35.2$$
$$10\,(21.1w + 4.6) = 10\,(10.9w + 35.2)$$
$$102w = 306$$
$$w = 3$$

41.
$$0.2p - 1.4 = 0.2(p - 7)$$
$$10\,(0.2p - 1.4) = 10\,(0.2(p - 7))$$
$$2p - 14 = 2p - 14$$
$$0 = 0$$
All real numbers

43.
$$0.20x + 53.60 = x$$
$$100\,(0.20x + 53.60) = 100\,(x)$$
$$20x + 5360 = 100x$$
$$5360 = 80x$$
$$67 = x \quad \text{or} \quad x = 67$$

45.
$$0.15(90) + 0.05p = 0.10(90 + p)$$
$$100\,(0.15(90) + 0.05p) = 100\,(0.10(90 + p))$$
$$1350 + 5p = 900 + 10p$$
$$-5p = -450$$
$$p = 90$$

47.
$$0.40(y + 10) - 0.60(y + 2) = 2$$
$$100\,(0.40(y + 10) - 0.60(y + 2)) = 100\,(2)$$
$$40y + 400 - 60y - 120 = 200$$
$$-20y + 280 = 200$$
$$-20y = -80$$
$$y = 4$$

49.
$$0.4x + 0.2 = -3.6 - 0.6x$$
$$10(0.4x + 0.2) = 10(-3.6 - 0.6x)$$
$$4x + 2 = -36 - 6x$$
$$10x + 2 = -36$$
$$10x = -38$$
$$x = -3.8$$

51.
$$0.06(x - 0.5) = 0.06x + 0.01$$
$$0.06x - 0.03 = 0.06x + 0.01$$
$$-0.03 \neq 0.01$$
No solution

53.
$$-3.5x + 1.3 = -0.3(9x - 5)$$
$$10(-3.5x + 1.3) = 10(-0.3(9x - 5))$$
$$-35x + 13 = -3(9x - 5)$$
$$-35x + 13 = -27x + 15$$
$$-8x + 13 = 15$$
$$-8x = 2$$
$$x = -0.25$$

55.
$$0.2x - 1.8 = -3$$
$$0.2x = -1.2$$
$$x = -6$$

57.
$$\frac{1}{4}(x + 4) = \frac{1}{5}(2x + 3)$$
$$20\left[\frac{1}{4}(x + 4)\right] = 20\left[\frac{1}{5}(2x + 3)\right]$$
$$5(x + 4) = 4(2x + 3)$$
$$5x + 20 = 8x + 12$$
$$-3x = -8$$
$$x = \frac{8}{3}$$

59.
$$0.3(x + 6) - 0.7(x + 2) = 4$$
$$10\,(0.3(x + 6) - 0.7(x + 2)) = 10\,(4)$$
$$3x + 18 - 7x - 14 = 40$$
$$-4x + 4 = 40$$
$$-4x = 36$$
$$x = -9$$

61.
$$\frac{2k+5}{4} = 2 - \frac{k+2}{3}$$
$$12\left(\frac{2k+5}{4}\right) = 12\left(2 - \frac{k+2}{3}\right)$$
$$3(2k+5) = 24 - 4(k+2)$$
$$6k+15 = 24 - 4k - 8$$
$$6k+15 = -4k + 16$$
$$10k = 1$$
$$k = \frac{1}{10}$$

63.
$$\frac{1}{8}v + \frac{2}{3} = \frac{1}{6}v + \frac{3}{4}$$
$$24\left(\frac{1}{8}v + \frac{2}{3}\right) = 24\left(\frac{1}{6}v + \frac{3}{4}\right)$$
$$3v + 16 = 4v + 18$$
$$-v = 2$$
$$v = -2$$

65.
$$\frac{1}{2}a + 0.4 = -0.7 - \frac{3}{5}a$$
$$10\left(\frac{1}{2}a + 0.4\right) = 10\left(-0.7 - \frac{3}{5}a\right)$$
$$5a + 4 = -7 - 6a$$
$$11a = -11$$
$$a = -1$$

66.
$$\frac{3}{4}c - 0.11 = 0.23(c-5)$$
$$100\left(\frac{3}{4}c - 0.11\right) = 100(0.23(c-5))$$
$$75c - 11 = 23(c-5)$$
$$75c - 11 = 23c - 115$$
$$52c = -104$$
$$c = \frac{-104}{52} = -2$$

67.
$$0.8 + \frac{7}{10}b = \frac{3}{2}b - 0.8$$
$$10\left(0.8 + \frac{7}{10}b\right) = 10\left(\frac{3}{2}b - 0.8\right)$$
$$8 + 7b = 15b - 8$$
$$-8b = -16$$
$$b = \frac{-16}{-8} = 2$$

Problem Recognition Exercises

1. Expression: $-4b + 18$

3. Equation: $\frac{y}{4} = -2$
$$4 \cdot \frac{y}{4} = 4(-2)$$
$$y = -8$$

5. Equation:
$$3(4h-2) - (5h-8) = 8 - (2h+3)$$
$$12h - 6 - 5h + 8 = 8 - 2h - 3$$
$$7h + 2 = -2h + 5$$
$$9h = 3$$
$$h = \frac{1}{3}$$

7. Expression:
$$3(8z-1) + 10 - 6(5+3z)$$
$$= 24z - 3 + 10 - 30 - 18z$$
$$= 6z - 23$$

9. Equation: $6c + 3(c+1) = 10$
$$6c + 3c + 3 = 10$$
$$9c = 7$$
$$c = \frac{7}{9}$$

11. Equation:
$$0.5(2a-3)-0.1 = 0.4(6+2a)$$
$$10\ 0.5(2a-3)-0.1 = 10\ 0.4(6+2a)$$
$$10a-15-1 = 24+8a$$
$$10a-16 = 24+8a$$
$$2a = 40$$
$$a = 20$$

13. Equation:
$$-\frac{5}{9}w+\frac{11}{12}=\frac{23}{36}$$
$$36\left(-\frac{5}{9}w+\frac{11}{12}\right)=36\left(\frac{23}{36}\right)$$
$$-20w+33 = 23$$
$$-20w = -10$$
$$w = \frac{-10}{-20}=\frac{1}{2}$$

15. Expression:
$$\frac{7}{3}(6-12t)+\frac{1}{2}(4t+8)$$
$$=14-28t+2t+4$$
$$=-26t+18$$

17. Equation: no solution

19. Equation:
$$\frac{w-4}{6}-\frac{3w-1}{2}=-1$$
$$6\left(\frac{w-4}{6}-\frac{3w-1}{2}\right)=-1(6)$$
$$w-4-3(3w-1)=-6$$
$$w-4-9w+3=-6$$
$$-8w-1=-6$$
$$-8w=-5$$
$$w=\frac{5}{8}$$

21. Equation:
$$-k-41-2-k=-2(20+k)-3$$
$$-2k-43=-40-2k-3$$
$$-2k-43=-2k-43$$
all real numbers

23. Equation: $\frac{1}{2}(2c-4)+3=\frac{1}{3}(6c+3)$
$$c-2+3=2c+1$$
$$c+1=2c+1$$
$$c=0$$

25. Expression:
$$-10(2k+1)-4(4-5k)+25$$
$$=-20k-10-16+20k+25$$
$$=-1$$

27. Expression: $-9-4[3-2(q+3)]$
$$=-9-4[3-2q-6]$$
$$=-9-4[-3-2q]$$
$$=-9+12+8q$$
$$=8q+3$$

29. Equation:
$$-1-5[2+3(w-2)]=5(w+4)$$
$$-1-5[2+3w-6]=5w+20$$
$$-1-5[3w-4]=5w+20$$
$$-1-15w+20=5w+20$$
$$-15w+19=5w+20$$
$$-20w=1$$
$$w=-\frac{1}{20}$$

Section 2.4 Practice Exercises

1. Answers may vary.

3. $x+5$

5. $3x$

7. $3x+20$

9. Let x represent the number.
6 less than $x = -10$
$$x-6=-10$$
$$x=-4$$
The number is -4.

11. Let x represent the unknown number.

Twice(sum of x and 7) = 8

$$2(x+7)=8$$
$$2x+14=8$$
$$2x=-6$$
$$x=-3$$

The number is -3.

13. Let x represent the unknown number.

(x added to 5) = Twice x

$$x+5=2x$$
$$x=5$$

The number is 5.

15. Let x represent the unknown number.

(Sum of $6x$ and 10) = (difference of x and 15)

$$6x+10=x-15$$
$$5x=-25$$
$$x=-5$$

The number is -5.

17. Let x represent the unknown number.

Triple(difference of x and 4) = 6 more than x

$$3(x-4)=x+6$$
$$3x-12=x+6$$
$$2x=18$$
$$x=9$$

The number is 9.

19. **(a)** Let x represent the smallest of three consecutive integers. The next two consecutive integers are $x+1$ and $x+2$.

(b) Let x represent the largest of three consecutive integers. The next two consecutive integers are $x-1$ and $x-2$.

21. Let x = first integer. Then, $x+1$ is the next integer.

(1st integer) + (2nd integer) = -67

$$x+x+1=-67$$
$$2x+1=-67$$
$$2x=-68$$
$$x=-34$$

The integers are -34 and -33.

23. Let x = first odd integer. Then, $x+2$ is the next odd integer.

(1st integer) + (2nd integer) = 28

$$x+x+2=28$$
$$2x+2=28$$
$$2x=26$$
$$x=13$$

The integers are 13 and 15.

25. Let x, $x+1$, $x+2$, $x+3$, $x+4$ be the lengths of the sides of the pentagon.

$$\text{Perimeter}=\begin{pmatrix}\text{sum of the}\\ \text{lengths of the}\\ \text{five sides}\end{pmatrix}$$

$$80=x+x+1+x+2+x+3+x+4$$
$$80=5x+10$$
$$70=5x$$
$$14=x \quad \text{or} \quad x=14$$

The sides are 14 in., 15 in., 16 in., 17 in., and 18 in.

27. Let x = first even integer. Then, $x+2$ and $x+4$ are the next two even integers.

sum of three integers = 48 + 2(smallest integer)

$$x+x+2+x+4=48+2(x)$$
$$3x+6=48+2x$$
$$x=42$$

The integers are 42, 44, and 46.

29. Let x = first odd integer. Then, $x+2$ and $x+4$ are the next two odd integers.

8(sum of three integers) = 210 + 10(middle integer)

$$8(x+x+2+x+4)=210+10(x+2)$$
$$8(3x+6)=210+10x+20$$
$$24x+48=10x+230$$
$$14x=182$$
$$x=13$$

The integers are 13, 15, and 17.

31. Let x = the length of the first piece. Then, the length of the second piece is $x + 20$.

$$\left(\begin{array}{c}\text{length of}\\ \text{the 1st piece}\end{array}\right) + \left(\begin{array}{c}\text{length of}\\ \text{2nd piece}\end{array}\right) = 86 \text{ cm}$$
$$x + (x + 20) = 86$$
$$2x = 66$$
$$x = 33$$

The lengths of the pieces are 33 cm and 53 cm.

33. Let x = Clarann's age. Then, $x + 12$ is Karen's age.

$$(\text{Clarann's age}) + (\text{Karen's age}) = 58$$
$$x + x + 12 = 58$$
$$2x + 12 = 58$$
$$2x = 46$$
$$x = 23$$

Clarann's age is 23, and Karen's age is 35.

35. Let x = Democrats. Then, $x - 31$ is Republicans.

$$(\text{Democrats}) + (\text{Republicans}) = 433$$
$$x + x - 31 = 433$$
$$2x - 31 = 433$$
$$2x = 464$$
$$x = 232$$
$$x - 31 = 201$$

There were 201 Republicans and 232 Democrats.

37. Let x = number of people who watch *The Dr. Phil Show*.

$$(\text{Dr. Phil viewers}) + 1.118 = (\text{Oprah viewers})$$
$$x + 1.118 = 5.816$$
$$x = 4.698$$

4.698 million people watch *The Dr. Phil Show*.

39. Let x = length of the Congo River. Then, the length of the Nile is $x + 2455$.

$$\left(\begin{array}{c}\text{length of}\\ \text{Congo}\end{array}\right) + \left(\begin{array}{c}\text{length of}\\ \text{Nile}\end{array}\right) = 11,195 \text{ km}$$
$$x + (x + 2455) = 11195$$
$$2x = 8740$$
$$x = 4370$$

The length of the Congo is 4370 km; the length of the Nile is 6825 km.

41. Let x = the land area of Africa. Then, the land area of Asia is $x + 14,514,000$.

$$\left(\begin{array}{c}\text{area of}\\ \text{Africa}\end{array}\right) + \left(\begin{array}{c}\text{area of}\\ \text{Asia}\end{array}\right) = 74,644,000 \text{ km}^2$$
$$x + x + 14,514,000 = 74,644,000$$
$$2x = 60,130,000$$
$$x = 30,065,000$$

The area of Africa is 30,065,000 km^2. The area of Asia is 44,579,000 km^2.

43. Let x = Money Angie made. Then, $x - 10$ is Money Marie made and $x - 10 - 25$ is Money Gwen made.

$$(\text{Angie's}) + (\text{Marie's}) + (\text{Gwen's}) = 120$$
$$x + (x - 10) + (x - 10 - 25) = 120$$
$$3x - 45 = 120$$
$$3x = 165$$
$$x = 55$$
$$x - 10 = 45$$
$$x - 10 - 25 = 20$$

Angie made $55, Marie made $45, and Gwen made $20.

45. Let x = length of middle piece. Then the length of the smallest piece is $(x - 16)$. The longest piece is $(2x)$ long.

$$\text{(Middle pc)} + \text{(Small pc)} + \text{(Long pc)} = 72$$
$$x + (x - 16) + (2x) = 72$$
$$4x - 16 = 72$$
$$4x = 88$$
$$x = 22$$
$$(x - 16) = 22 - 16$$
$$= 6$$
$$2x = 2(22)$$
$$= 44$$

The pieces are 6 in., 22 in., and 44 in.

47. Let x = smallest integer. Then, $x + 1$ is the next integer and $x + 2$ is the largest.

$$(3 \text{ times the largest}) = \left(\begin{array}{c} 47 + \text{the sum} \\ \text{of the two smaller} \end{array} \right)$$
$$3(x + 2) = 47 + x + x + 1$$
$$3x + 6 = 2x + 48$$
$$x = 42$$

The numbers are 42, 43, and 44.

49. Let x = earnings for U2. Then,
$0.5x + 2.5$ = earnings for Jennifer Lopez.

$$\text{Total earnings} = 106$$
$$x + 0.5x + 2.5 = 106$$
$$1.5x + 2.5 = 106$$
$$2.5x = 103.5$$
$$x = 69$$

U2 made \$69 million and Jennifer Lopez made \$37 million.

51. Let x represent the unknown number.

$$5(\text{the difference of } x \text{ and } 3) = 4 \text{ less than } 4 \cdot x$$
$$5(x - 3) = 4x - 4$$
$$5x - 15 = 4x - 4$$
$$x = 11$$

The number is 11.

53. Let x = the first page number and $x + 1$ be the next page number.

$$\left(\begin{array}{c} \text{1st page} \\ \text{number} \end{array} \right) + \left(\begin{array}{c} \text{2nd page} \\ \text{number} \end{array} \right) = 941$$
$$x + x + 1 = 941$$
$$2x = 940$$
$$x = 470$$

The page numbers are 470 and 471.

55. Let x represent the unknown number.

$$(3 \text{ added to } 5x) = (43 \text{ more than } x)$$
$$3 + 5x = 43 + x$$
$$4x = 40$$
$$x = 10$$

The number is 10.

57. Let x = the deepest point in the Arctic Ocean. Then, the deepest point in the Pacific Ocean is $2x + 676$.

$$\left(\begin{array}{c} \text{Deepest point} \\ \text{in Pacific} \end{array} \right) = 10,920 \text{ m}$$
$$2x + 676 = 10,920$$
$$2x = 10,244$$
$$x = 5122$$

The deepest point in the Arctic Ocean is 5122 m.

59. Let x = number.

$$\left(\begin{array}{c} \text{twice} \\ \text{a number} \end{array} \right) + \frac{3}{4} = \left(\begin{array}{c} \text{four times} \\ \text{the number} \end{array} \right) - \frac{1}{8}$$
$$2x + \frac{3}{4} = 4x - \frac{1}{8}$$
$$-2x = -\frac{1}{8} - \frac{3}{4}$$
$$-2x = -\frac{7}{8}$$
$$x = \frac{7}{16}$$

The number is $\frac{7}{16}$.

61. Let x = number.

$$\begin{pmatrix} \text{product of} \\ \text{a number} \\ \text{and } 3.86 \end{pmatrix} = \begin{pmatrix} 7.15 \\ \text{more than} \\ \text{the number} \end{pmatrix}$$

$$3.86x = x + 7.15$$
$$2.86x = 7.15$$
$$x = 2.5$$

The number is 2.5.

Section 2.5 Practice Exercises

1. Individual Activity

3. Let x = first integer. Then, $x + 1$ is the next integer.

$$\begin{pmatrix} 3 \text{ times the} \\ \text{larger} \end{pmatrix} = \begin{pmatrix} 45 \text{ more than} \\ \text{the smaller} \end{pmatrix}$$

$$3(x+1) = x + 45$$
$$3x + 3 = x + 45$$
$$2x + 3 = 45$$
$$2x = 42$$
$$x = 21$$

The numbers are 21 and 22.

5. Let x = the percent.

$$45 = x(360)$$
$$360x = 45$$
$$x = 0.125$$
$$x = 12.5\%$$

7. Let x = the percent.

$$544 = x(640)$$
$$640x = 544$$
$$x = 0.85$$
$$x = 85\%$$

9. Let x = the number.

$$0.5\% \text{ of } 150 = x$$
$$0.005(150) = x$$
$$x = 0.75$$

11. Let x = the number.

$$142\% \text{ of } 740 = x$$
$$1.42(740) = x$$
$$x = 1050.8$$

13. Let x = the number.

$$177 = 20\% \text{ of } x$$
$$177 = 0.20x$$
$$x = \frac{177}{0.20} = 885$$

15. Let x = the number.

$$275 = 12.5\% \text{ of } x$$
$$275 = 0.125x$$
$$x = \frac{275}{0.125} = 2200$$

17. Let x = the amount of tax.

$$\begin{pmatrix} \text{Sales} \\ \text{tax} \end{pmatrix} = \begin{pmatrix} \text{tax} \\ \text{rate} \end{pmatrix}\begin{pmatrix} \text{price} \\ \text{of the drill} \end{pmatrix}$$

$$x = 7\% \text{ of } 99.99$$
$$x = 0.07(99.99)$$
$$x = 6.9993$$

$$\begin{pmatrix} \text{total} \\ \text{price} \end{pmatrix} = \begin{pmatrix} \text{sale} \\ \text{price} \end{pmatrix} + \begin{pmatrix} \text{sales} \\ \text{tax} \end{pmatrix}$$

$$= 99.99 + 6.9993$$
$$= 106.9893$$
$$\approx 106.99$$

Molly will have to pay $106.99.

$$= 317.9576$$
$$\approx 317.96$$

Patrick will have to pay $317.96.

19. Let x = number of cases of prostate cancer.

$$x = 33\% \text{ of } 7000000$$

$$x = 0.33(7000000)$$

$$x = 231000$$

There are approximately 231,000 cases of prostate cancer.

21. Let x = percent of cases of pancreas cancer.

$$x = \frac{14000}{700000} = 0.02 = 2\%$$

2% of cancer cases were diagnosed as pancreas cancer.

23. Let x = Javon's taxtable income.

$$\left(\begin{array}{l}\text{federal}\\\text{income}\\\text{tax}\end{array}\right) = \begin{array}{l}\text{tax}\\\text{rate}\end{array}\begin{array}{l}\text{taxable}\\\text{income}\end{array}$$

$$23520 = 28\% \text{ of } x$$
$$23520 = 0.28\,x$$
$$x = \frac{23520}{0.28}$$
$$x = 84000$$

Javon's taxable income was $84,000.

25. $I = Prt$
$I = (\$1800)(2.75\%)(1 \text{ year})$
$I = \$49.50$

$I = Prt$
$I = (\$1800)(4.25\%)(1 \text{ year})$
$I = \$76.50$

$76.50-\$49.50=\$27.00$ more would be earned in the CD

27. Let P = amount borrowed.
Total paid = $P + Prt$
$$\$1260 = P + P(5\%)(1)$$
$$1260 = P + 0.05P$$
$$1.05P = 1260$$
$$P = \$1200$$
Bob borrowed $1200.

29. Interest = $1950 - \$1500 = \$450$
$$I = Prt$$
$$450 = 1500(r)(5)$$
$$450 = 7500r$$
$$r = 0.06 = 6\%$$
The rate is 6%.

31. Let P = amount invested.
Total saved = $P + Prt$
$$3500 = P + P(3\%)(2)$$
$$3500 = P + 0.06P$$
$$3500 = 1.06P$$
$$P \approx 3302$$
Perry needs to invest $3302.

33. (a) Let x = discount on the CD/MP3 player.

$$\text{Discount} = \left(\begin{array}{l}\text{Percent}\\\text{off}\end{array}\right)\text{cost}$$

$$x = 12\% \text{ of } 170$$
$$x = 0.12(170)$$
$$x = 20.4$$

The discount on the CD/MP 3 player is $20.40.

(b) sale price = cost − discount
$$= 170 - 20.40$$
$$= 149.60$$
The sale price is $149.60.

35. Let x = original price of the Sony digital camera.

$$\left(\begin{array}{l}\text{Original}\\\text{price}\end{array}\right) - \text{Discount} = \left(\begin{array}{l}\text{Sale}\\\text{price}\end{array}\right)$$

$$x - 15\% \text{ of } x = 400.00$$
$$x - 0.15x = 400.00$$
$$0.85x = 400.00$$
$$x = 470.5882353$$
$$x \approx 470.59$$

The original price of the Sony digital camera is approximately $470.59.

37. Let x = percent discount.

$$\left(\begin{array}{l}\text{Original}\\\text{price}\end{array}\right) - \text{Discount} = \left(\begin{array}{l}\text{Sale}\\\text{price}\end{array}\right)$$

$$250 - x(250) = 220$$
$$-250x = -30$$
$$x = 0.12$$
$$x = 12\%$$
The percent discount is 12%.

39. Let x = the cost before the increase.

$$\begin{pmatrix} \text{Cost before} \\ \text{the increase} \end{pmatrix} + \text{ Markup } = \begin{pmatrix} \text{New} \\ \text{cost} \end{pmatrix}$$

$$x + 6\% \text{ of } x = 63.60$$
$$x + 0.06x = 63.60$$
$$1.06x = 63.60$$
$$x = 60$$

The original cost was $60.

41. Let x = tax rate.

$$(\text{price}) + (\text{tax rate of price}) = \$1890$$
$$1800 + x(1800) = 1890$$
$$1800x = 90$$
$$x = \frac{90}{1800}$$
$$= 0.05$$

The tax rate is 5%.

43. Let x = original price before the new tax.

$$(original) + (32\% \text{ increase}) = 6.86$$
$$x + 0.32x = 6.86$$
$$1.32x = 6.86$$
$$x = 5.20$$

The original ticket price before taxes was $5.20.

45. Let x = original purchase price.

$$(\text{price}) + (24\% \text{ of price}) = 260400$$
$$x + 0.24x = 260400$$
$$1.24x = 260400$$
$$x = 210000$$

The original purchase price was $210,000.

47. Let x = Alina's salary.

salary = 1600 + (12% commission)
$$x = 1600 + 0.12(25000)$$
$$x = 4600$$

Alina made $4600 that month.

49. Let x = amount sold over $200.

$$\begin{pmatrix} 4\% \text{ on amount} \\ \text{sold over } \$200 \end{pmatrix} = \$25.80$$
$$0.04x = 25.80$$
$$x = \frac{25.80}{0.04} = 645$$

Diane sold $645 over $200 worth of merchandise.

Calculator Exercises

1.

```
880/(2π)
          140.0563499
```

3.

```
20/(5π)
     1.273239545
```

Section 2.6 Practice Exercises

1. Answers will vary.

3.
$$3(2y + 3) - 4(-y + 1) = 7y - 10$$
$$6y + 9 + 4y - 4 = 7y - 10$$
$$10y + 5 = 7y - 10$$
$$3y = -15$$
$$y = -5$$

5.
$$\frac{1}{2}(x - 3) + \frac{3}{4} = 3x - \frac{3}{4}$$
$$(4)\left[\frac{1}{2}(x - 3) + \frac{3}{4}\right] = (4)\left[3x - \frac{3}{4}\right]$$
$$2(x - 3) + 3 = 12x - 3$$
$$2x - 3 = 12x - 3$$
$$-10x = 0$$
$$x = 0$$

7.
$$0.5(y+2)-0.3=0.4y+0.5$$
$$10\left[0.5(y+2)-0.3\right]=10\left[0.4y+0.5\right]$$
$$5y+10-3=4y+5$$
$$5y+7=4y+5$$
$$y=-2$$

9.
$$P=a+b+c$$
$$P-b-c=a+b+c-b-c$$
$$a=P-b-c$$

11.
$$x=y-z$$
$$y=x+z$$

13.
$$p=250+q$$
$$p-250=250-250+q$$
$$q=p-250$$

15.
$$A=bh$$
$$\frac{A}{h}=\frac{bh}{h}$$
$$b=\frac{A}{h}$$

17.
$$PV=nrt$$
$$\frac{PV}{nr}=t$$

19.
$$x-y=5$$
$$x=5+y$$

21.
$$3x+y=-19$$
$$y=-3x-19$$

23.
$$2x+3y=6$$
$$3y=-2x+6$$
$$y=\frac{-2x+6}{3}=-\frac{2}{3}x+2$$

25.
$$-2x-y=9$$
$$-2x=y+9$$
$$x=\frac{y+9}{-2}=-\frac{1}{2}y-\frac{9}{2}$$

27.
$$4x-3y=12$$
$$-3y=-4x+12$$
$$y=\frac{-4x+12}{-3}=\frac{4}{3}x-4$$

29.
$$ax+by=c$$
$$by=-ax+c$$
$$y=\frac{-ax+c}{b}\ \text{ or }\ y=-\frac{a}{b}x+\frac{c}{b}$$

31.
$$A=P(1+rt)$$
$$A=P+Prt$$
$$A-P=Prt$$
$$t=\frac{A-P}{Pr}=\frac{A}{Pr}-\frac{1}{r}$$

33.
$$a=2(b+c)$$
$$a=2b+2c$$
$$a-2b=2c$$
$$c=\frac{a-2b}{2}\ \text{ or }\ c=\frac{a}{2}-b$$

35.
$$Q=\frac{x+y}{2}$$
$$2Q=x+y$$
$$y=2Q-x$$

37.
$$M=\frac{a}{S}$$
$$a=MS$$

39.
$$P=I^2R$$
$$R=\frac{P}{I^2}$$

41. Let $x=$ width. Then, length equals $x+2$.
$$P=2w+2l$$
$$24=2x+2(x+2)$$
$$24=2x+2x+4$$
$$4x=20$$
$$x=5$$
The width is 5 feet; the length is 7 feet.

43. Let x = width. Then, the length is $4x$.
$$P = 2w + 2l$$
$$300 = 2x + 2(4x)$$
$$300 = 2x + 8x$$
$$10x = 300$$
$$x = 30$$
The width is 30 yd. and the length is 120 yd.

45. Let x = width. Then, the length is $2x - 5$.
$$P = 2w + 2l$$
$$590 = 2x + 2(2x - 5)$$
$$590 = 2x + 4x - 10$$
$$6x = 600$$
$$x = 100$$
The width is 100 m; the length is 195 m.

47. Let x = length of the two sides that are the same. Then, the length of the third side is $x + 5$.
$$P = a + b + c$$
$$71 = x + x + x + 5$$
$$71 = 3x + 5$$
$$3x = 66$$
$$x = 22$$
The sides are 22 m, 22 m, and 27 m.

49. Adjacent supplementary angles form a straight angle. The words *supplementary* and *straight* both begin with the same letter.

51. Let x = one angle. Then, $3x - 4°$ is the other angle.
$$(\text{sum of the angles}) = 90°$$
$$x + 3x - 4 = 90$$
$$4x = 94$$
$$x = 23.5$$
The angles are 23.5° and 66.5°.

53 Let x = one angle. Then $4x + 6$ is the other angle.
$$(\text{sum of the angles}) = 180°$$
$$x + 4x + 6 = 180$$
$$5x = 174$$
$$x = 34.8$$

55. Vertical angles are equal.
$$x + 17 = 2x - 3$$
$$x = 20$$
The angles are $20 + 17 = 37°$ and $2(20) - 3 = 37°$.

57. Let x = smallest angle. Then the middle angle is $2x$ and the largest angle is $3x$.
$$(\text{sum of angles of a triangle}) = 180°$$
$$x + 2x + 3x = 180$$
$$6x = 180$$
$$x = 30°$$
The angles are 30°, 60°, and 90°.

59. Let x = largest angle. Then, the middle angle is $x - 30°$, and the smallest angle is $\frac{1}{2}$ of $x = \frac{1}{2}x$.
$$(\text{sum of angles of a triangle}) = 180°$$
$$x + x - 30 + \frac{1}{2}x = 180$$
$$\frac{5}{2}x = 210$$
$$x = 210 \cdot \frac{2}{5} = 84°$$
The angles are 84°, $84° - 30° = 54°$, and $\frac{1}{2}(84°) = 42°$.

61. The sum of complementary angles is 90°.
$$(3x + 5) + (2x) = 90$$
$$5x = 85$$
$$x = 17$$
The angles are $3(17) + 5 = 56°$, $2(17) = 34°$.

63. **(a)** $A = lw$

(b) $A = lw$
$$w = \frac{A}{l}$$

(c) $w = \frac{A}{l}$
$$w = \frac{1740.5}{59} = 29.5 \text{ feet}$$

65. (a) $P = l + l + w + w = 2l + 2w$

(b)
$$P = 2l + 2w$$
$$P - 2w = 2l$$
$$\frac{P - 2w}{2} = \frac{2l}{2}$$
$$l = \frac{P - 2w}{2}$$

(c) $l = \dfrac{P - 2w}{2}$

$$l = \frac{338 - 2(66)}{2} = \frac{206}{2}$$
$$l = 103$$
The length is 103 m.

67. (a) $C = 2\pi r$

(b)
$$C = 2\pi r$$
$$\frac{C}{2\pi} = \frac{2\pi r}{2\pi}$$
$$r = \frac{C}{2\pi}$$

(c) $r = \dfrac{C}{2\pi}$

$$r = \frac{880}{2(3.14)} = \frac{880}{6.28}$$
$$r \approx 140$$
The radius is approximately 140 ft.

69. (a) $A = \pi r^2$

$$A = \pi(11.5)^2$$
$$A = 132.25\pi$$
$$A \approx 415.48 \text{ m}^2$$

(b) $V = \pi r^2 h$

$$V = \pi(11.5)^2(25)$$
$$V = 3306.25\pi$$
$$V \approx 10,386.89 \text{ m}^3$$

Section 2.7 Practice Exercises

1. Answers will vary.

3. $cd = r$

$$c = \frac{r}{d}$$

5.
$$3(2y + 5) - 8(y - 1) = 3y + 3$$
$$6y + 15 - 8y + 8 = 3y + 3$$
$$-2y + 23 = 3y + 3$$
$$-5y = -20$$
$$y = 4$$

7. $200 - t$

9. $100 - x$

11. $3000 - y$

13. Let x = number of $3 tickets. Then, the number of $2 tickets is $81 - x$.

	$3 Tickets	$2 Tickets	Total
Number of tickets	x	$81 - x$	81
Cost of tickets	$3x	$2(81 - x)$	$215

$$3x + 2(81 - x) = 215$$
$$3x + 162 - 2x = 215$$
$$x + 162 = 215$$
$$x = 53$$
$$81 - x = 81 - 53 = 28$$
The church sold 53 tickets at $3 and 28 tickets at $2.

15. Let x = the number of songs costing $0.90 each. Then, the number of songs costing $1.50 each is $25 - x$.

$$\begin{pmatrix} \text{cost} \\ \text{of songs} \\ \text{at \$0.90} \\ \text{each} \end{pmatrix} + \begin{pmatrix} \text{cost} \\ \text{of songs} \\ \text{at \$1.50} \\ \text{each} \end{pmatrix} = \begin{pmatrix} \text{Total} \\ \text{cost} \end{pmatrix}$$

$$0.90x + 1.50(25 - x) = 27.30$$
$$0.90x + 37.50 - 1.50x = 27.30$$
$$-0.60x = -10.2$$
$$x = 17$$

$25 - x = 25 - 17 = 8$

Josh downloaded 17 songs for $0.90 each and 8 songs at $1.50 each.

17. Let x = the number of Nintendo Wii games. Then, the number of Nintendo DS games is $3x$.

$$\begin{pmatrix} \text{Number of} \\ \text{Nintendo Wii} \\ \text{games at \$50} \\ \text{each} \end{pmatrix} + \begin{pmatrix} \text{Number of} \\ \text{Nintendo DS} \\ \text{games at \$30} \\ \text{each} \end{pmatrix} = \$700$$

$$50x + 30(3x) = 700$$
$$50x + 90x = 700$$
$$140x = 700$$
$$x = 5$$

Christopher has 5 Wii games and 15 DS games.

19. $x + 7$ or $7 + x$

21. $d + 2000$

23. Let x = number of ounces of 50% antifreeze solution. Then, the number of ounces of 60% antifreeze solution is $x + 10$.

	50% Anti-freeze	80% Anti-freeze	Final Mixture: 60% Anti-freeze
Number of ounces of solution	x oz	10 oz	$x + 10$ oz
Number of ounces of pure anti-freeze	$0.50x$	$0.80(10)$	$0.60(x + 10)$

$$0.50x + 0.80(10) = 0.60(x + 10)$$
$$0.50x + 8 = 0.60x + 6$$
$$-0.10x = -2$$
$$x = 20$$

20 oz of 50% antifreeze solution

25. Let x = number of mL of the 1% saline solution. Then, the number of mL of the 9% of saline solution is $x + 24$.

$$\begin{pmatrix} \text{Number} \\ \text{of mL of} \\ \text{pure} \\ \text{saline} \\ \text{in 1\%} \\ \text{solution} \end{pmatrix} + \begin{pmatrix} \text{Number} \\ \text{of mL of} \\ \text{pure} \\ \text{saline} \\ \text{in 16\%} \\ \text{solution} \end{pmatrix} = \begin{pmatrix} \text{Number} \\ \text{of mL of} \\ \text{pure} \\ \text{saline} \\ \text{in 9\%} \\ \text{solution} \end{pmatrix}$$

$$0.01x + 0.16(24) = 0.09(x + 24)$$
$$0.01x + 3.84 = 0.09x + 2.16$$
$$-0.08x = -1.68$$
$$x = 21$$

The pharmacist needs to use 21 mL of the 1% saline solution.

27. Let x = number of ounces of 50% acid solution. Then, the number of ounces of 30% of acid solution is $x + 15$.

$$\begin{pmatrix} \text{Number} \\ \text{of ounces} \\ \text{of pure} \\ \text{acid} \\ \text{in 50\%} \\ \text{solution} \end{pmatrix} + \begin{pmatrix} \text{Number} \\ \text{of ounces} \\ \text{of pure} \\ \text{acid} \\ \text{in 21\%} \\ \text{solution} \end{pmatrix} = \begin{pmatrix} \text{Number} \\ \text{of ounces} \\ \text{of acid} \\ \text{in 30\%} \\ \text{solution} \end{pmatrix}$$

$$0.50x + 0.21(15) = 0.30(x + 15)$$
$$0.50x + 3.15 = 0.30x + 4.5$$
$$0.20x = 1.35$$
$$x = 6.75$$

The contractor needs to mix 6.75 ounces of 50% acid solution.

29. **(a)** $d = rt = (60)(5) = 300$ mi

(b) $d = rt = 5x$

(c) $d = 5(x + 12) = 5x + 60$

31. Let x mph = speed walking down to the lake. Then, the speed walking uphill is $x - 2$.

	Distance	Rate	Time
Downhill to the lake	$2x$ mi	x mph	2 hours
Uphill from the lake	$4(x - 2)$ mi	$x - 2$ mph	4 hours

$$2x = 4(x - 2)$$
$$2x = 4x - 8$$
$$-2x = -8$$
$$x = 4$$

She walks 4 mph to the lake.

33. Let x mph = speed hiking uphill. Then, speed hiking downhill is $x + 1$ mph.

$$\begin{pmatrix} \text{Distance} \\ \text{hiking} \\ \text{uphill} \end{pmatrix} = \begin{pmatrix} \text{Distance} \\ \text{hiking} \\ \text{downhill} \end{pmatrix}$$

$$3x = 2(x + 1)$$
$$3x = 2x + 2$$
$$x = 2$$
$$d = rt = 2(3) = 6$$

Bryan hiked 6 mi up the canyon.

35. Let x mph = speed of the plane in still air. Then, the speed of the plane with the wind is $x + 40$ mph and the speed of the plane against the wind is $x - 40$ mph.

$$\begin{pmatrix} \text{Distance} \\ \text{traveled} \\ \text{with the wind} \end{pmatrix} = \begin{pmatrix} \text{Distance} \\ \text{traveled} \\ \text{against} \\ \text{the wind} \end{pmatrix}$$

$$3.5(x + 40) = 4(x - 40)$$
$$3.5x + 140 = 4x - 160$$
$$-0.5x = -300$$
$$x = 600$$

The plane travels 600 mph in still air.

37. Let x mph = speed of slower car. Then, the speed of the faster car is $x + 4$ mph.

$$\begin{pmatrix} \text{Distance} \\ \text{traveled} \\ \text{by slower} \\ \text{car} \end{pmatrix} + \begin{pmatrix} \text{Distance} \\ \text{traveled} \\ \text{by faster} \\ \text{car} \end{pmatrix} = \begin{pmatrix} \text{total} \\ \text{distance} \end{pmatrix}$$

$$2x + 2(x + 4) = 200$$
$$2x + 2x + 8 = 200$$
$$4x + 8 = 200$$
$$4x = 192$$
$$x = 48$$

$x + 4 = 48 + 4 = 52$

The slower car travels 48 mph and the faster car travels 52 mph.

39. Let x mph = speed of the 1st vehicle. Then, the speed of the 2nd vehicle is $x + 10$ mph. Time taken by the 1st vehicle is 4 hours and by the 2nd vehicle is 3 hours.

$$\begin{pmatrix} \text{Distance} \\ \text{traveled} \\ \text{by the } 1^{st} \\ \text{vehicle} \end{pmatrix} - \begin{pmatrix} \text{Distance} \\ \text{traveled} \\ \text{by the } 2^{nd} \\ \text{vehicel} \end{pmatrix} = \begin{pmatrix} \text{distance} \\ \text{between} \\ \text{them} \end{pmatrix}$$

$$4x - 3(x + 10) = 10$$
$$4x - 3x - 30 = 10$$
$$x - 30 = 10$$
$$x = 40$$

$x + 10 = 40 + 10 = 50$
The speeds of the vehicles are 40 mph and 50 mph.

41. Let x mph = speed of the slower boat. Then, the speed of the faster boat is $2x$ mph.

$$\begin{pmatrix} \text{Distance} \\ \text{traveled} \\ \text{by the} \\ \text{faster} \\ \text{boat} \end{pmatrix} - \begin{pmatrix} \text{Distance} \\ \text{traveled} \\ \text{by the} \\ \text{slower} \\ \text{boat} \end{pmatrix} = \begin{pmatrix} \text{distance} \\ \text{between} \\ \text{them} \end{pmatrix}$$

$$2(2x) - 2x = 40$$
$$4x - 2x = 40$$
$$2x = 40$$
$$x = 20$$

$2x = 2(20) = 40$
The rates of the boats are 20 mph and 40 mph.

43. (a) 10% of peanuts = $0.10(20) = 2$
There are 2 lb of peanuts.

(b) $0.10x$

(c) $0.10(x + 3) = 0.10x + 0.30$

45. Let x = number of pounds of the $12 coffee. Then, the number of pounds of the $8 coffee is $50 - x$.

	$12 coffee	$8 coffee	Total
Number of pounds	x	$50 - x$	50
Value of coffee	$12x$	$8(50 - x)$	$8.80(50)$

$$12x + 8(50 - x) = 8.80(50)$$
$$12x + 400 - 8x = 440$$
$$4x = 40$$
$$x = 10$$

$50 - x = 50 - 10 = 40$
10 lb of coffee sold at $12 per pound and 40 lb of coffee sold at $8 per pound

47. Let x hours = time that it will take for the boats to reach each other.

$$\begin{pmatrix} \text{Distance} \\ \text{traveled} \\ \text{by the} \\ \text{distress} \\ \text{boat} \end{pmatrix} + \begin{pmatrix} \text{Distance} \\ \text{traveled} \\ \text{by the} \\ \text{guard} \\ \text{cruiser} \end{pmatrix} = \begin{pmatrix} \text{total} \\ \text{distance} \end{pmatrix}$$

$$3x + 25x = 21$$
$$28x = 21$$
$$x = \frac{21}{28}$$
$$x = \frac{3}{4}$$

$x = \frac{3}{4}$ hr $= \frac{3}{4}(60) = 45$ min

The boats will meet in $\frac{3}{4}$ hr or 45 min.

49. Let x = number of packages of wax. Then, the number of bottles of sunscreen is $21 - x$.

$$\begin{pmatrix} \text{Cost} \\ \text{of} \\ \text{packages} \\ \text{of} \\ \text{wax} \end{pmatrix} + \begin{pmatrix} \text{Cost} \\ \text{of} \\ \text{bottles} \\ \text{of} \\ \text{sunscreen} \end{pmatrix} = \begin{pmatrix} \text{Total} \\ \text{cost} \end{pmatrix}$$

$$3.00x + 8.00(21 - x) = 88.00$$
$$3.00x + 168 - 8.00x = 88.00$$
$$-5.00x = -80$$
$$x = 16$$

$21 - x = 21 - 16 = 5$

Sam purchased 16 packages of wax and 5 bottles of sunscreen.

51. Let x = number of quarts of 85% chlorine solution. Then, the number of quarts of 45% chlorine solution is $x + 5$.

$$\begin{pmatrix} \text{Number} \\ \text{of quarts} \\ \text{of pure} \\ \text{chlorine} \\ \text{in 85\%} \\ \text{solution} \end{pmatrix} + \begin{pmatrix} \text{Number} \\ \text{of quarts} \\ \text{of pure} \\ \text{chlorine} \\ \text{in 25\%} \\ \text{solution} \end{pmatrix} = \begin{pmatrix} \text{Number} \\ \text{of quarts} \\ \text{of pure} \\ \text{chlorine} \\ \text{in 45\%} \\ \text{solution} \end{pmatrix}$$

$$0.85x + 0.25(5) = 0.45(x + 5)$$
$$0.85x + 1.25 = 0.45x + 2.25$$
$$0.40x = 1$$
$$x = 2.5$$

2.5 quarts of 85% chlorine solution

53. Let x = number of L of pure water. Then, the number of L of 15% alcohol solution is $x + 12$.

$$\begin{pmatrix} \text{Number} \\ \text{of L of} \\ \text{alcohol} \\ \text{in pure} \\ \text{water} \end{pmatrix} + \begin{pmatrix} \text{Number} \\ \text{of L} \\ \text{of pure} \\ \text{alcohol} \\ \text{in 40\%} \\ \text{solution} \end{pmatrix} = \begin{pmatrix} \text{Number} \\ \text{of L} \\ \text{of pure} \\ \text{alcohol} \\ \text{in 15\%} \\ \text{solution} \end{pmatrix}$$

$$0x + 0.40(12) = 0.15(x + 12)$$
$$4.8 = 0.15x + 1.8$$
$$3.0 = 0.15x$$
$$x = 20$$

20 L of pure water

55. Let x km/hr = speed of the Acela Express. Then, the speed of the Japanese bullet train is $x + 60$ km/r.

$$\begin{pmatrix} \text{Distance} \\ \text{traveled} \\ \text{by the} \\ \text{Acela} \\ \text{Express} \end{pmatrix} = \begin{pmatrix} \text{Distance} \\ \text{traveled} \\ \text{by the} \\ \text{Bullet} \\ \text{train} \end{pmatrix}$$

$$3.375x = 2.7(x + 60)$$
$$3.375x = 2.7x + 162$$
$$0.675x = 162$$
$$x = 240$$

$x + 60 = 240 + 60 = 300$

The Acela Express travels 240 km/hr and the Japanese bullet train travels 300 km/hr.

Section 2.8 Practice Exercises

1. Answers will vary.

3. $3(x + 2) - (2x - 7) = -(5x - 1) - 2(x + 6)$
$$x + 13 = -7x - 11$$
$$8x = -24$$
$$x = -3$$

5. $x > 5$

7. $x \le \dfrac{5}{2}$

9. $13 > p$

11. $2 \le y \le 6.5$

13. $0 < x < 4$

15. $1 < p \leq 8$

17. $[6, \infty)$

19. $(-\infty, 2.1]$

21. $(-2, 7]$

23. $\left\{ x \middle| x > \dfrac{3}{4} \right\}$

$\left(\dfrac{3}{4}, \infty \right)$

25. $\{x | -1 < x < 8\}$

$(-1, 8)$

27. $\{x | x < -14\}$

$(-\infty, -14)$

29. $\{x | x \geq 18\}$

31. $\{x | x < -0.6\}$

33. $\{x | -3.5 \leq x < 7.1\}$

35. (a) $x + 3 - 3 = 6 - 3$

$x = 3$

(b) $x + 3 - 3 > 6 - 3$

$x > 3$

$x | x > 3$

$3, \infty$

37. (a) $p - 4 + 4 = 9 + 4$

$p = 13$

(b) $p - 4 + 4 \leq 9 + 4$

$p \leq 13$

$p | p \leq 13$

$-\infty, 13$

39. (a) $\dfrac{4c}{4} = \dfrac{-12}{4}$

$c = -3$

(b) $\dfrac{4c}{4} < \dfrac{-12}{4}$

$c < -3$

$c | c < -3$

$-\infty, -3$

41. (a) $\dfrac{-10z}{-10} = \dfrac{15}{-10}$

$z = -\dfrac{15}{10} = -\dfrac{3}{2}$

(b) $-10z \leq 15$

$\dfrac{-10z}{-10} \geq \dfrac{15}{-10}$

$z \geq -\dfrac{3}{2}$

$\left\{ z \middle| z \geq -\dfrac{3}{2} \right\}$

$\left[-\dfrac{3}{2}, \infty \right)$

43.

$-1, 4$

45. $\quad 0 < x + 3 < 8$
$0 - 3 < x + 3 - 3 < 8 - 3$
$\qquad -3 < x < 5$

$-3, 5$

47. $\quad 8 \le 4x \le 24$
$\dfrac{8}{4} \le \dfrac{4x}{4} \le \dfrac{24}{4}$
$\qquad 2 \le x \le 6$

$2, 6$

49. $\quad x + 5 - 5 \le 6 - 5$
$\qquad x \le 1$
$(-\infty, 1]$

51. $\quad 3q - 7 > 2q + 3$
$\qquad q > 10$
$(10, \infty)$

53. $\qquad 4 < 1 + z$
$1 - 1 + z > 4 - 1$
$\qquad z > 3$
$(3, \infty)$

55. $\qquad 2 \ge a - 6$
$2 + 6 \ge a - 6 + 6$
$\qquad 8 \ge a \text{ or } a \le 8$
$(-\infty, 8]$

57. $\quad 3c > 6$
$\dfrac{3c}{3} > \dfrac{6}{3}$
$\quad c > 2$
$(2, \infty)$

59. $\quad -3c > 6$
$\dfrac{-3c}{-3} < \dfrac{6}{-3}$
$\quad c < -2$
$(-\infty, -2)$

61. $\qquad -h \le -14$
$(-1)(-h) \ge (-1)(-14)$
$\qquad h \ge 14$
$[14, \infty)$

63. $\qquad 12 \ge -\dfrac{x}{2}$
$(-2)(12) \le (-2)\left(-\dfrac{x}{2}\right)$
$\qquad -24 \le x \text{ or } x \ge -24$
$[-24, \infty)$

65. $\qquad -2 \le p + 1 < 4$
$-2 - 1 \le p + 1 - 1 < 4 - 1$
$\qquad -3 \le p < 3$
$[-3, 3)$

67. $\quad -3 < 6h - 3 < 12$
$\qquad 0 < 6h < 15$
$\qquad 0 < h < \dfrac{15}{6}$
$\qquad 0 < h < \dfrac{5}{2}$
$\left(0, \dfrac{5}{2}\right)$

69.

$$5 < \frac{1}{2}x < 6$$

$$2(5) < 2\left(\frac{1}{2}x\right) < 2(6)$$

$$10 < x < 12$$

$$(10, 12)$$

71. $-5 \le 4x - 1 < 15$

$$-4 \le 4x < 16$$

$$-1 \le x < 4$$

$$[-1, 4)$$

73. $0.6z \ge 54$

$$\frac{0.6z}{0.6} \ge \frac{54}{0.6}$$

$$z \ge 90$$

$$[90, \infty)$$

75.

$$-\frac{2}{3}y < 6$$

$$\left(-\frac{3}{2}\right)\left(-\frac{2}{3}y\right) > \left(-\frac{3}{2}\right)(6)$$

$$y > -9$$

$$(-9, \infty)$$

77. $-2x - 4 \le 11$

$$-2x \le 15$$

$$\frac{-2x}{-2} \ge \frac{15}{-2}$$

$$x \ge -\frac{15}{2}$$

$$\left[-\frac{15}{2}, \infty\right)$$

79. $-12 > 7x + 9$

$$-21 > 7x$$

$$\frac{7x}{7} < \frac{-21}{7}$$

$$x < -3$$

$$-\infty, -3$$

81. $-7b - 3 \le 2b$

$$-9b \le 3$$

$$b \ge -\frac{1}{3}$$

$$\left[-\frac{1}{3}, \infty\right)$$

83. $4n + 2 < 6n + 8$

$$-2n < 6$$

$$n > -3$$

$$(-3, \infty)$$

85. $8 - 6(x - 3) > -4x + 12$

$$8 - 6x + 18 > -4x + 12$$

$$-2x > -14$$

$$x < 7$$

$$(-\infty, 7)$$

87. $3(x + 1) - 2 \le \frac{1}{2}(4x - 8)$

$$3x + 3 - 2 \le 2x - 4$$

$$3x + 1 \le 2x - 4$$

$$x + 1 \le -4$$

$$x \le -5$$

$$(-\infty, -5]$$

89.
$$\frac{7}{6}p + \frac{4}{3} \geq \frac{11}{6}p - \frac{7}{6}$$
$$6\left(\frac{7}{6}p + \frac{4}{3}\right) \geq 6\left(\frac{11}{6}p - \frac{7}{6}\right)$$
$$7p + 8 \geq 11p - 7$$
$$-4p \geq -15$$
$$p \leq \frac{15}{4}$$
$$\left(-\infty, \frac{15}{4}\right]$$

91.
$$\frac{y-6}{3} > y + 4$$
$$y - 6 > 3y + 12$$
$$-2y > 18$$
$$y < -9$$
$$(-\infty, -9)$$

93.
$$-1.2a - 0.4 < -0.4a + 2$$
$$-0.8a < 2.4$$
$$a > -3$$
$$(-3, \infty)$$

95.
$$-2x + 5 \geq -x + 5$$
$$-x \geq 0$$
$$x \leq 0$$
$$(-\infty, 0]$$

97.
$$-2(-2) + 5 < 4$$
$$9 < 4; \text{ No}$$

99.
$$4(1+7) - 1 > 2 + 1$$
$$31 > 3; \text{ Yes}$$

101. $L \geq 10$

103. $w > 75$

105. $t \leq 72$

107. $L \geq 8$

109. $2 < h < 5$

111. Let x = August rainfall.
$$\left(\begin{array}{c}\text{Average summer}\\\text{rainfall}\end{array}\right) \geq (7.4 \text{ inches})$$
$$\left(\frac{5.9 + 6.1 + x}{3}\right) \geq 7.4$$
$$12 + x \geq 22.2$$
$$x \geq 10.2$$
More than 10.2 inches of rain is needed.

113. (a) Let x = number of birdhouses ordered.
$$(\text{original price}) - \left(\begin{array}{c}\text{percent}\\\text{discount}\end{array}\right) = \left(\begin{array}{c}\text{total}\\\text{cost}\end{array}\right)$$
$$\left(\begin{array}{c}\$9 \text{ of}\\\text{number}\\\text{ordered}\end{array}\right) - \left(\begin{array}{c}10\% \text{ of}\\\text{original cost}\end{array}\right) = \left(\begin{array}{c}\text{total}\\\text{cost}\end{array}\right)$$
$$9x - 0.10(9x) = \left(\begin{array}{c}\text{total}\\\text{cost}\end{array}\right)$$
$$9(190) - 0.10(9)(190) = 1539$$
The total cost is $1539.

(b) Total cost for 200 birdhouses is $9(200) - 0.20(9)(200) = 1440$, or $1440. The cost of 190 is $1539. Therefore, it is cheaper to purchase 200 birdhouses because the discount is greater.

115. Let x = the number of text messages

Per text plan $\geq$ Unlimited text plan

$$4.95 + 0.09x \geq 18$$
$$0.09x \geq 13.05$$
$$x \geq 145$$
If more than 145 text messages were sent, the unlimited plan would be a better deal.

117. Let x = the number of hours babysitting

Money saved + potential earnings $\geq$ the cost of the trip

$$700 + 10x \geq 475 + 5(54) + 350$$
$$700 + 10x \geq 1095$$
$$10x \geq 395$$
$$x \geq 39.5$$

Madison would need to babysit for a minimum of 39.5 hours.

119. $3(x+2) - (2x-7) \leq (5x-1) - 2(x+6)$
$$3x + 6 - 2x + 7 \leq 5x - 1 - 2x - 12$$
$$x + 13 \leq 3x - 13$$
$$-2x \leq -26$$
$$x \geq 13$$

$[13, \infty)$

121. $-2 - \dfrac{w}{4} \leq \dfrac{1+w}{3}$

$$12\left(-2 - \dfrac{w}{4}\right) \leq 12\left(\dfrac{1+w}{3}\right)$$
$$-24 - 3w \leq 4(1+w)$$
$$-7w \leq 28$$
$$w \geq -4$$

$[-4, \infty)$

123. $-0.703 < 0.122p - 2.472$
$$1.769 < 0.122p$$
$$0.122p > 1.769$$
$$p > 14.5$$
$(14.5, \infty)$

Group Activity

1. $\text{BMI} = \dfrac{703W}{h^2}$

$$= \dfrac{703(160 \text{ lb})}{(5'4")^2}$$
$$= \dfrac{703(160 \text{ lb})}{(64")^2}$$
$$= \dfrac{112480}{4096}$$
$$= 27.4609375$$
$$\approx 27.5$$

No, the person is considered overweight.

3. $18.5 \leq \dfrac{703W}{72^2} \leq 24.9$

$$72^2(18.5) \leq 703W \leq 72^2(24.9)$$
$$\dfrac{72^2(18.5)}{703} \leq W \leq \dfrac{72^2(24.9)}{703}$$
$$136.4 \leq W \leq 183.6$$

The person's ideal weight range is $136.4 \leq W \leq 183.6$.

Chapter 2 Review Exercises

Section 2.1

1. (a) Equation

   (b) Expression

   (c) Equation

   (d) Equation

3. (a) Nonlinear

   (b) Linear

   (c) Nonlinear

   (d) Linear

5.
$$a + 6 = -2$$
$$a + 6 - 6 = -2 - 6$$
$$a = -8$$

7.
$$-\frac{3}{4} + k = \frac{9}{2}$$
$$k = \frac{9}{2} + \frac{3}{4} = \frac{18}{4} + \frac{3}{4} = \frac{21}{4}$$

9.
$$-5x = 21$$
$$x = \frac{21}{-5} = -\frac{21}{5}$$

11.
$$-\frac{2}{5}k = \frac{4}{7}$$
$$-\frac{5}{2}\left(-\frac{2}{5}k\right) = -\frac{5}{2} \cdot \frac{4}{7}$$
$$k = -\frac{20}{14} = -\frac{10}{7}$$

13. Let x = the number.
$$\left(\begin{array}{c}\text{quotient of}\\ x \text{ and } -6\end{array}\right) = -10$$
$$\frac{x}{-6} = -10$$
$$x = (-10)(-6) = 60$$
The number is 60.

15. Let x = the number.
$$x - 4 = -12$$
$$x = -8$$
The number is -8..

Section 2.2

17.
$$4d + 2 = 6$$
$$4d = 4$$
$$d = 1$$

19.
$$-7c = -3c - 8$$
$$-4c = -8$$
$$c = 2$$

21.
$$\frac{b}{3} + 1 = 0$$
$$\frac{b}{3} = -1$$
$$b = (-1)(3) = -3$$

23.
$$-3p + 7 = 5p + 1$$
$$-8p = -6$$
$$p = \frac{-6}{-8} = \frac{3}{4}$$

25.
$$4a - 9 = 3(a - 3)$$
$$4a - 9 = 3a - 9$$
$$a = 0$$

27.
$$7b + 3(b - 1) + 16 = 2(b + 8)$$
$$7b + 3b - 3 + 16 = 2b + 16$$
$$10b + 13 = 2b + 16$$
$$8b = 3$$
$$b = \frac{3}{8}$$

29. A contradiction has no solution and an identity is true for all real numbers.

31.
$$3x - 19 = 2x + 1$$
$$x = 20; \text{ conditional}$$

33.
$$2x - 8 = 2(x - 4)$$
$$0 = 0; \text{ identity}$$

35.
$$4x - 4 = 3x - 2$$
$$x = 2; \text{ conditional}$$

Section 2.3

37.
$$\frac{y}{15} - \frac{2}{3} = \frac{4}{5}$$
$$15\left(\frac{y}{15} - \frac{2}{3}\right) = 15\left(\frac{4}{5}\right)$$
$$y - 10 = 12$$
$$y = 22$$

39.
$$\frac{x-6}{3} - \frac{2x+8}{2} = 12$$
$$6\left(\frac{x-6}{3} - \frac{2x+8}{2}\right) = 12(6)$$
$$2(x-6) - 3(2x+8) = 72$$
$$2x - 12 - 6x - 24 = 72$$
$$-4x - 36 = 72$$
$$-4x = 108$$
$$x = -27$$

41.
$$\frac{1}{4}y - \frac{3}{4} = \frac{1}{2}y + 1$$
$$4\left(\frac{1}{4}y - \frac{3}{4}\right) = 4\left(\frac{1}{2}y + 1\right)$$
$$y - 3 = 2y + 4$$
$$-y = 7$$
$$y = -7$$

43.
$$\frac{2}{7}(w+4) = \frac{1}{2}$$
$$14 \cdot \frac{2}{7}(w+4) = 14 \cdot \frac{1}{2}$$
$$4(w+4) = 7$$
$$4w = -9$$
$$w = -\frac{9}{4}$$

45.
$$4.9z + 4.6 = 3.2z - 2.2$$
$$1.7z = -6.8$$
$$z = -4$$

47.
$$62.84t - 123.66 = 4(2.36 + 2.4t)$$
$$62.84t - 123.66 = 9.44 + 9.6t$$
$$53.24t = 133.10$$
$$t = 2.5$$

49.
$$0.20(x+4) + 0.65x = 0.20(854)$$
$$0.20x + 0.8 + 0.65x = 170.8$$
$$0.85x = 170$$
$$x = 200$$

51.
$$3 - (x+4) + 5 = 3x + 10 - 4x$$
$$3 - x - 4 + 5 = -x + 10$$
$$4 \neq 10$$
No solution

53.
$$9 - 6(2z+1) = -3(4z-1)$$
$$9 - 12z - 6 = -12z + 3$$
$$-12z + 3 = -12z + 3$$
$$0 = 0$$
Identity; all real numbers

Section 2.4

55. Let x = the number.
$$20 + (x+6) = 37$$
$$26 + x = 37$$
$$x = 11$$
The number is 11.

57. Let x = the number.
$$5x - 8 = x - 48$$
$$4x = -40$$
$$x = -10$$
The number is -10..

59. Let x = 1st integer. Then, $x + 1$ is the next and $x + 2$ is the largest.

$$\left(\begin{array}{c}\text{10 times} \\ \text{the smallest}\end{array}\right) = 213 + \left(\begin{array}{c}\text{sum of} \\ \text{other two} \\ \text{integers}\end{array}\right)$$
$$10x = 213 + (x+1) + (x+2)$$
$$10x = 216 + 2x$$
$$8x = 216$$
$$x = 27$$
The numbers are 27, 28, and 29.

61. Let x = 1st integer. Then, the next four integers are $x + 1, x + 2, x + 3, x + 4$.
$$P = (\text{sum of the sides})$$
$$190 = x + x + 1 + x + 2 + x + 3 + x + 4$$
$$190 = 5x + 10$$
$$180 = 5x$$
$$x = 36$$
Sides are 36 cm, 37 cm, 38 cm, 39 cm, and 40 cm.

63. Let x = population of Kentucky (in millions of people). Then, $x + 2.1$ is the population of Indiana.

$$\left(\begin{array}{c}\text{population}\\\text{of Indiana}\end{array}\right) + \left(\begin{array}{c}\text{population}\\\text{of Kentucky}\end{array}\right) = 10.3$$

$$x + x + 2.1 = 10.3$$
$$2x = 8.2$$
$$x = 4.1$$

Kentucky has 4.1 million people; Indiana has 6.2 million people.

Section 2.5

65. Let x = the number.
$$x = (4\% \text{ of } 720)$$
$$x = 0.04(720)$$
$$x = 28.8$$

67. Let x = the percent.
$$68.4 = x\% \text{ of } 72$$
$$68.4 = x(72)$$
$$x = \frac{68.4}{72} = 0.95 = 95\%$$

69. Let x = a number.
$$8.75 = 0.5\% \text{ of } x$$
$$8.75 = 0.005x$$
$$x = \frac{8.75}{0.005} = 1750$$

71. (a) $I = Prt$
$$I = (3000)(0.08)(3.5)$$
$$I = 840$$
Anna Tsao earned $840.

(b) Total amount $= P + I$
Total amount $= 3000 + 840 = 3840$
Her balance will be $3840.

73. Let x = original price.
$$\left(\begin{array}{c}\text{Sale}\\\text{price}\end{array}\right) = \left(\begin{array}{c}\text{original}\\\text{price}\end{array}\right) - \text{discount}$$
$$20.65 = x - 30\% \text{ of } x$$
$$20.65 = x - 0.30x$$
$$20.65 = 0.70x$$
$$x = 29.50$$
The Novel originally was $29.50.

Section 2.6

75. $K = C + 273$
$$K - 273 = C \text{ or } C = K - 273$$

77. $P = 3s$
$$\frac{P}{3} = s \text{ or } s = \frac{P}{3}$$

79. $a + bx = c$
$$bx = c - a$$
$$x = \frac{c - a}{b}$$

81. $4(a + b) = Q$
$$4a + 4b = Q$$
$$4b = Q - 4a$$
$$b = \frac{Q - 4a}{4} \text{ or } b = \frac{Q}{4} - a$$

83. (a) $V = \dfrac{1}{3}\pi r^2 h$
$$3V = \pi r^2 h$$
$$h = \frac{3V}{\pi r^2}$$

(b) $h = \dfrac{3V}{\pi r^2}$
$$h = \frac{3(47.8)}{\pi(3)^2}$$
$$h = \frac{143.4}{9\pi}$$
$$h \approx 5.1 \text{ in.}$$

85. Let x = the first angle. Then, $x - 10$ is the second angle.
$$(\text{complementary angles sum}) = 90°$$
$$x + (x - 10) = 90$$
$$2x - 10 = 90$$
$$2x = 100$$
$$x = 50$$
The angles are 50° and 40°.

87. $2x + 25 = 4x - 15$

$25 = 2x - 15$

$40 = 2x$

$x = 20$

$(2x + 25)° = [2(20) + 25]°$

$= (40 + 25)°$

$= 65°$

The angle measure is 65°.

Section 2.7

89. Let x km/hr = speed in stormy weather. Then, the speed in good weather is $x + 15$.

	Distance	Rate	Time
stormy weather	$14x$ km	x km/hr	14 hr
good weather	$10.5(x + 15)$ km	$x + 15$ km/hr	10.5 hr

$14x = 10.5(x + 15)$

$14x = 10.5x + 157.5$

$3.5x = 157.5$

$x = 45$

$x + 15 = 45 + 15 = 60$

The truck travels 45 km/hr in stormy weather and 60 km/hr in good weather.

91. Let x hours = time that it will take for the cars to be 327.6 mi apart.

$$\begin{pmatrix} \text{Distance} \\ \text{traveled} \\ \text{by the} \\ \text{car heading} \\ \text{east} \end{pmatrix} + \begin{pmatrix} \text{Distance} \\ \text{traveled} \\ \text{by the} \\ \text{car heading} \\ \text{west} \end{pmatrix} = \begin{pmatrix} \text{total} \\ \text{distance} \\ \text{between} \\ \text{them} \end{pmatrix}$$

$55x + 62x = 327.6$

$117x = 327.6$

$x = 2.8$

$x = 2.8$ hr $= 2$ hr and $0.8(60) = 2$ hr 48 min

Two cars will be 327.6 mi apart after 2.8 hr or 2 hr and 48 min.

93. Let x = number of lb of ground beef. Then, the number of lb of a mixture is $x + 8$.

$$\begin{pmatrix} \text{Number} \\ \text{of lb of} \\ \text{fat in} \\ \text{ground} \\ \text{beef} \end{pmatrix} + \begin{pmatrix} \text{Number} \\ \text{of lb of} \\ \text{fat in} \\ \text{ground} \\ \text{sirloin} \end{pmatrix} = \begin{pmatrix} \text{Number} \\ \text{of lb of} \\ \text{fat in} \\ \text{the} \\ \text{mixture} \end{pmatrix}$$

$0.24x + 0.06(8) = 0.096(x + 8)$

$0.24x + 0.48 = 0.096x + 0.768$

$0.144x = 0.288$

$x = 2$

2 lb of ground beef with 24% fat

Section 2.8

95. $(-2, \infty)$

97. $(-1, 4]$

99. $c + 6 < 23$

$c < 17$

$c|c < 17$

$(-\infty, 17)$

101. $-2x - 7 \geq 5$

$-2x \geq 12$

$\dfrac{-2x}{-2} \geq \dfrac{12}{-2}$

$x \leq -6$

$x|x \leq -6$

$(-\infty, -6]$

103.
$$-\frac{3}{7}a \le -21$$
$$\left(-\frac{7}{3}\right)\left(-\frac{3}{7}a\right) \ge \left(-\frac{7}{3}\right)(-21)$$
$$a \ge 49$$
$$a \,|\, a \ge 49$$
$$[49, \infty)$$

105.
$$4k + 23 < 7k - 31$$
$$-3k < -54$$
$$k > 18$$
$$k \,|\, k > 18$$
$$(18, \infty)$$

107.
$$-6 < 2b \le 14$$
$$\frac{-6}{2} \le \frac{2b}{2} \le \frac{14}{2}$$
$$-3 < b \le 7$$
$$b \,|\, -3 < b \le 7$$
$$(-3, 7]$$

109. Let x = rain in August.
(average summer rainfall) > 5.3 inches
$$\left(\frac{6.3 + 7.1 + x}{3}\right) > 5.3$$
$$6.3 + 7.1 + x > 15.9$$
$$x > 2.5$$
More than 2.5 in. is required.

Chapter 2 Test

1. (a) No; $4(-3) + 1 = 10$
$$-12 + 1 = 10$$
$$-11 \ne 10$$

(b) Yes; $6(-3 - 1) = -3 - 21$
$$6(-4) = -24$$
$$-24 = -24$$

(c) No; $5(-3) - 2 = 2(-3) + 1$
$$-15 - 2 = -6 + 1$$
$$-17 \ne -5$$

(d) Yes; $\frac{1}{3}(-3) + 1 = 0$
$$-1 + 1 = 0$$
$$0 = 0$$

3.
$$t + 3 = -13$$
$$t + 3 - 3 = -13 - 3$$
$$t = -16$$

5.
$$\frac{t}{8} = -\frac{2}{9}$$
$$(8)\frac{t}{8} = (8)\left(-\frac{2}{9}\right)$$
$$t = -\frac{16}{9}$$

7.
$$2(p - 4) = p + 7$$
$$2p - 8 = p + 7$$
$$p = 15$$

9.
$$\frac{3}{7} + \frac{2}{5}x = -\frac{1}{5}x + 1$$
$$35\left(\frac{3}{7} + \frac{2}{5}x\right) = 35\left(-\frac{1}{5}x + 1\right)$$
$$15 + 14x = -7x + 35$$
$$21x = 20$$
$$x = \frac{20}{21}$$

11.
$$\frac{3x + 1}{2} - \frac{4x - 3}{3} = 1$$
$$6\left(\frac{3x + 1}{2} - \frac{4x - 3}{3}\right) = 6(1)$$
$$3(3x + 1) - 2(4x - 3) = 6$$
$$9x + 3 - 8x + 6 = 6$$
$$x + 9 = 6$$
$$x = -3$$

13.
$$-5(x + 2) + 8x = -2 + 3x - 8$$
$$-5x - 10 + 8x = -10 + 3x$$
$$3x - 10 = 3x - 10$$
$$0 = 0$$
Identity; all real numbers

15. $C = 2\pi r$

$$\frac{C}{2\pi} = \frac{2\pi r}{2\pi}$$

$$r = \frac{C}{2\pi}$$

17. Let x = the first number. Then, $4 + \frac{1}{2}x$ is the second number.

$$(\text{1st number}) + (\text{2nd number}) = 31$$

$$x + 4 + \frac{1}{2}x = 31$$

$$\frac{3}{2}x + 4 = 31$$

$$\frac{3}{2}x = 27$$

$$x = 18$$

The numbers are 18 and 13.

19. Let x = cost of shoes before tax.

$$(\text{cost of shoes}) + (\text{sales tax}) = \$87.74$$

$$x + (0.07x) = 87.74$$

$$1.07 = 87.74$$

$$x = 82$$

The cost was \$82.00.

21. Let x = original amount borrowed.

$$A = P + Prt$$

$$8000 = x + x(6\%)(10)$$

$$8000 = x + 0.60x$$

$$8000 = 1.60x$$

$$x = 5000$$

Clarita originally borrowed \$5000.

23. Let y = one angle.

$$(\text{sum of angles in a triangle}) = 180°$$

$$y + y + 9 + 4y - 9 = 180$$

$$6y = 180$$

$$y = 30$$

$$y + 9 = 30 + 9 = 39$$

$$4y - 9 = 4(30) - 9 = 111$$

The measures of the angles are 30°, 39°, and 111°.

25. Let x mph = speed of one family. Then, the speed of the other family is $x - 5$ mph.

$$\begin{pmatrix} \text{distance} \\ \text{traveled} \\ \text{by one} \\ \text{family} \end{pmatrix} + \begin{pmatrix} \text{distance} \\ \text{traveled} \\ \text{by the} \\ \text{other} \\ \text{family} \end{pmatrix} = \begin{pmatrix} \text{distance} \\ \text{between} \\ \text{them} \end{pmatrix}$$

$$\begin{pmatrix} \text{speed} \\ \text{of one} \\ \text{family} \end{pmatrix}(2) + \begin{pmatrix} \text{speed} \\ \text{of the} \\ \text{other} \\ \text{family} \end{pmatrix}(2) = 210 \text{ mi.}$$

$$2x + 2(x - 5) = 210$$

$$2x + 2x - 10 = 210$$

$$4x = 220$$

$$x = 55$$

One family travels at 55 mph and the other family travels at 50 mph.

27. (a) $(-\infty, 0)$

(b) $[-2, 5)$

29. $2(3 - x) \geq 14$

$$6 - 2x \geq 14$$

$$-2x \geq 8$$

$$x \leq -4$$

$$x \mid x \leq -4$$

$$(-\infty, -4]$$

31. $-13 \leq 3p + 2 \leq 5$

$$-15 \leq 3p \leq 3$$

$$\frac{-15}{3} \leq \frac{3p}{3} \leq \frac{3}{3}$$

$$-5 \leq p \leq 1$$

$$p \mid -5 \leq p \leq 1$$

$$[-5, 1]$$

Cumulative Review Exercises
Chapters 1–2

1. $\left|-\dfrac{1}{5}+\dfrac{7}{10}\right|=\left|-\dfrac{2}{10}+\dfrac{7}{10}\right|=\left|\dfrac{5}{10}\right|=\dfrac{1}{2}$

3. $-\dfrac{2}{3}+\left(\dfrac{1}{2}\right)^2=-\dfrac{2}{3}+\dfrac{1}{4}=-\dfrac{8}{12}+\dfrac{3}{12}=-\dfrac{5}{12}$

5. $\sqrt{5-(-20)-3^2}=\sqrt{5+20-9}=\sqrt{16}=4$

7. $-14+12=-2$

9. $\quad-4[2x-3(x+4)]+5(x-7)$
$=-4[2x-3x-12]+5x-35$
$=4x+48+5x-35$
$=9x+13$

11. $-2.5x-5.2=12.8$
$\qquad-2.5x=18$
$\qquad\quad x=-7.2$

13. $\qquad\dfrac{x+3}{5}-\dfrac{x+2}{2}=2$
$10\left(\dfrac{x+3}{5}-\dfrac{x+2}{2}\right)=10(2)$
$2(x+3)-5(x+2)=20$
$2x+6-5x-10=20$
$\qquad\quad-3x-4=20$
$\qquad\qquad-3x=24$
$\qquad\qquad\quad x=-8$

15. $-0.6w=48$
$\qquad w=-80$

17. Let $x=$ cost before tax.
$\left(\begin{array}{c}\text{Cost of}\\\text{suit}\end{array}\right)+\left(\begin{array}{c}7\%\ \text{tax}\\\text{on cost}\end{array}\right)=\$374.50$
$\qquad x+0.07x=374.50$
$\qquad\qquad 1.07x=374.50$
$\qquad\qquad\quad x=350$
The cost before tax is \$350.

19. $-3x-3(x+1)<9$
$\quad-3x-3x-3<9$
$\qquad\quad-6x-3<9$
$\qquad\qquad-6x<12$
$\qquad\qquad\quad x>-2$
$\qquad\qquad x\,|\,x>-2$
$\qquad\qquad(-2,\infty)$

Chapter 3

Chapter 3 Opener

1. $y = -\dfrac{3}{2}x + 3 \, (THE)$

2. $y = -4x - 7 \, (EQUATION)$

3. $y = \dfrac{1}{2}x + \dfrac{3}{2} \, (IS)$

4. $y = -2x + 9 \, (WRITTEN)$

5. $y = \dfrac{1}{2}x - \dfrac{5}{2} \, (IN)$

6. $y = -\dfrac{2}{3}x + 3 \, (SLOPE)$

7. $y = -2x - \dfrac{5}{3} \, (INTERCEPT)$

8. $y = \dfrac{1}{3}x - \dfrac{1}{3} \, (FORM)$

Section 3.1 Practice Exercises

1. Answers will vary.

3. **(a)** Month 10

   (b) 30

   (c) Between months 3 and 5; also between months 10 and 12

   (d) Between months 8 and 9

   (e) Month 3

   (f) 80 patients

5. **(a)** On day 1 the price per share of the stock was $89.25.

   (b) $93.00 − $90.25 = $1.75

   (c) $90.25 − $93.00 = −$2.75

7.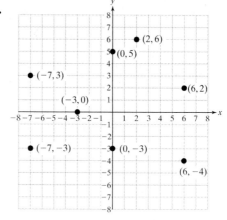

9.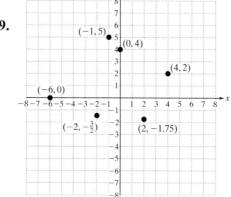

11. Quadrant IV

13. Quadrant II

15. Quadrant III

17. Quadrant I

19. $(0, -5)$ lies on the y-axis.

21. $\left(\dfrac{7}{8}, 0\right)$ is located on the x-axis.

23. $A(-4, 2)$, $B\left(\dfrac{1}{2}, 4\right)$, $C(3, -4)$, $D(-3, -4)$, $E(0, -3)$, $F(5, 0)$

25. (a) $A(400, 200)$, $B(200, -150)$,
$C(-300, -200)$, $D(-300, 250)$, $E(0, 450)$

(b) 250 m − (−200 m) = 450 m

27. (a) (250, 225), (175, 193), (315, 330),
(220, 209), (450, 570), (400, 480),
(190, 185); the first ordered pair
represents 250 people in attendance
produces $225 in popcorn sales.

(b)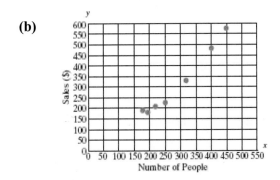

29. (a) (1, −10.2), (2, −9.0), (3, −2.5), (4, 5.7),
(5, 13.0), (6, 18.3), (7, 20.9), (8, 19.6),
(9, 14.8), (10, 8.7), (11, 2.0), (12, −6.9)

(b)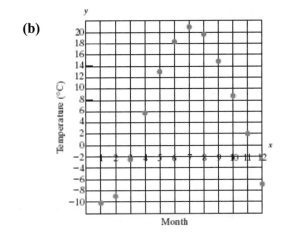

31.(a)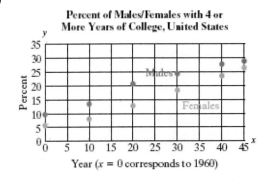

(b) Increasing

(c) Increasing

32. (a) 1980

(b) 2005

(c) Yes

Calculator Exercises

1. Set the viewing window at

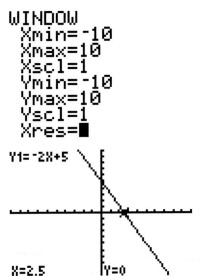

3.   Set the viewing window at

```
WINDOW
 Xmin=-3
 Xmax=10
 Xscl=1
 Ymin=-6
 Ymax=3
 Yscl=■
 Xres=1
```

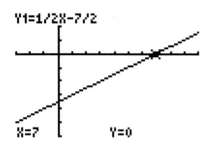

5.   Set the viewing window at

```
WINDOW
 Xmin=-10
 Xmax=10
 Xscl=1
 Ymin=-10
 Ymax=10
 Yscl=1
 Xres=1
```

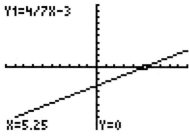

7.   Set the viewing window at

```
WINDOW
 Xmin=-10
 Xmax=10
 Xscl=1
 Ymin=-10
 Ymax=10
 Yscl=1
 Xres=■
```

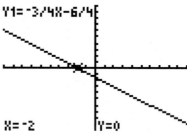

9.

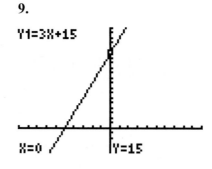

11.

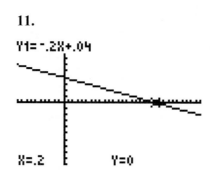

Section 3.2 Practice Exercises

1. Answers will vary.

3. (2, 4); quadrant I

5. (0, −1); y-axis

7. (3, −4); quadrant IV

9. Yes; 8 − 2 = 6

11. Yes; $4 = -\dfrac{1}{3}(-3) + 3$

13. No; $4\left(\dfrac{1}{4}\right) + 5\left(-\dfrac{2}{5}\right) \neq 1$

15. No; 6 ≠ −2

17. Yes; −5 = −5

19.

x	y
1	−3
−2	0
−3	1
−4	2

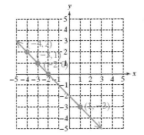

21.

x	y
−2	3
−1	0
−4	9

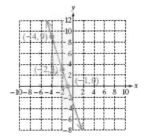

23.

x	y
0	4
2	0
3	−2

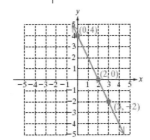

25.

x	y
0	−2
5	−5
10	−8

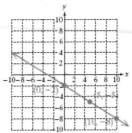

27.

x	y
0	−2
−3	−2
5	−2

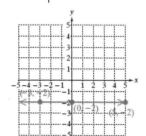

29.

x	y
$\frac{3}{2}$	−1
$\frac{3}{2}$	2
$\frac{3}{2}$	−3

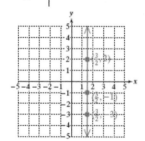

31.

x	y
0	4.6
1	3.4
2	2.2

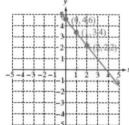

33. $x - y = 4$

x	y
2	−2
0	−4
−2	−6

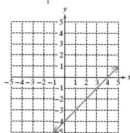

35. $2x - 5y = 10$

x	y
−5	−4
0	−2
5	0

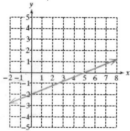

36. $y = 4x$

x	y
−1	−4
0	0
1	4

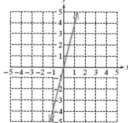

37. $y = -2x$

x	y
-2	4
0	0
2	-4

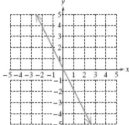

39. $y = \dfrac{1}{4}x - 2$

x	y
-4	-3
0	-2
4	-1

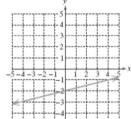

41. $-x + y = 0$

x	y
-10	-10
-5	-5
0	0

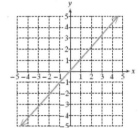

43. $-30x - 20y = 60$

x	y
0	-3
-4	3
-2	0

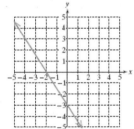

45. Since the y-intercept is the point with x-coordinate $= 0$, it is on the y-axis.

47. x-intercept: $(-1, 0)$
y-intercept: $(0, -3)$

49. x-intercept: $(-4, 0)$
y-intercept: $(0, 1)$

51. $4x - 3y = -9$

x-intercept: $4x - 3(0) = -9$

$$4x = -9$$

$$x = -\frac{9}{4} \qquad \left(-\frac{9}{4}, 0\right)$$

y-intercept: $4(0) - 3y = -9$

$$-3y = -9$$

$$y = 3 \qquad (0, 3)$$

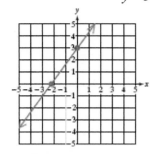

53. $y = -\frac{3}{4}x + 2$

x-intercept: $0 = -\frac{3}{4}x + 2$

$$-2 = -\frac{3}{4}x$$

$$\frac{8}{3} = x \qquad \left(\frac{8}{3}, 0\right)$$

y-intercept: $y = -\frac{3}{4}(0) + 2$

$$y = 2 \qquad (0, 2)$$

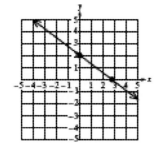

55. $2x + 8 = y$

x-intercept: $2x + 8 = 0$

$$2x = -8$$

$$x = -4 \qquad (-4, 0)$$

y-intercept: $2(0) + 8 = y$

$$8 = y \qquad (0, 8)$$

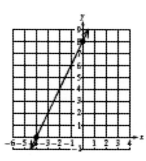

57. $2x - 2y = 0$

x-intercept: $2x - 2(0) = 0$

$$2x = 0$$

$$x = 0 \qquad (0, 0)$$

y-intercept: $2(0) - 2y = 0$

$$-2y = 0$$

$$y = 0 \qquad (0, 0)$$

Because the x-intercept and y-intercept are the same point, we need one additional point to graph the line. We arbitrarily let $x = 1$.

$$2(1) - 2y = 0$$

$$2 - 2y = 0$$

$$2 = 2y$$

$$1 = y \qquad (1, 1)$$

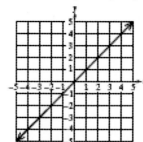

59. $20x = -40y + 200$

x-intercept: $20x = -40(0) + 200$
$$20x = 200$$
$$x = 10 \qquad (10, 0)$$

y-intercept: $20(0) = -40y + 200$
$$40y = 200$$
$$y = 5 \qquad (0, 5)$$

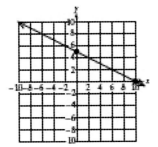

61. $x = -5y$

x-intercept: $x = -5(0)$
$$x = 0 \qquad (0, 0)$$

y-intercept: $\begin{array}{l} 0 = -5y \\ 0 = y \end{array} \qquad (0, 0)$

Because the x-intercept and y-intercept are the same point, we need one additional point to graph the line. We arbitrarily let $x = 5$.

$$5 = -5y$$
$$-1 = y \qquad (5, -1)$$

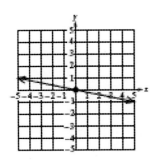

63. True

65. True

67. $y = -1$

(a) Horizontal

(b)

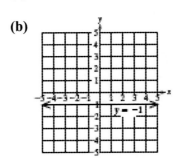

(c) no x-intercept; y-intercept: $(0, -1)$

69. $5x = 20$
$$x = 4$$

(a) Vertical

(b)

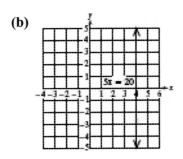

(c) x-intercept: $(4, 0)$; no y-intercept

71. $y + 8 = 11$
$y = 3$

(a) Horizontal

(b)

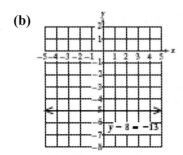

(c) no x-intercept; y-intercept: $(0, 3)$

73. $5x = 0$
$x = 0$

(a) Vertical

(b)

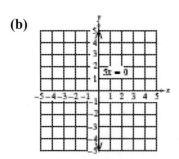

(c) All points on the y-axis are y-intercepts; x-intercept: $(0, 0)$

75. A horizontal line may not have an x-intercept. A vertical line may not have a y-intercept.

77. a,b,d

79. (a) $y = -1025(1) + 12{,}215 = 11{,}190$

(b) $9140 = -1025x + 12{,}215$
$-3075 = -1025x$
$$\frac{-3075}{-1025} = x$$
$x = 3$

(c) $(1, 11{,}190)$ One year after purchase the value of the car is \$11,190.
$(3, 9140)$ Three years after purchase the value of the car is \$9,140.

Section 3.3 Practice Exercises

1. Answers will vary.

3. x-intercept $\qquad$ y-intercept
$x - 3(0) = 6 \qquad\quad 0 - 3y = 6$
$x = 6 \qquad\qquad\quad y = -2$
$(6, 0) \qquad\qquad\quad (0, -2)$

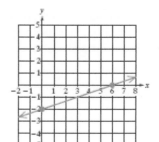

5. x-intercept $\qquad$ y-intercept
$0 = \dfrac{2}{3}x \qquad\qquad y = \dfrac{2}{3}(0)$
$x = 0 \qquad\qquad\quad y = 0$
$(0, 0) \qquad\qquad\quad (0, 0)$

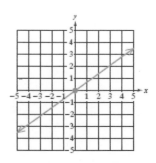

7. *x*-intercept   *y*-intercept

$$4x + 0 = 8 \qquad 4(0) + y = 8$$
$$x = 2 \qquad\qquad y = 8$$
$$(2, 0) \qquad\qquad (0, 8)$$

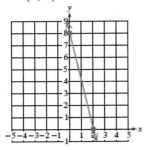

9. $m = \dfrac{8}{24} = \dfrac{1}{3}$

11. $m = \dfrac{3}{5.5} = \dfrac{3(2)}{5.5(2)} = \dfrac{6}{11}$

13. Undefined

15. Positive

17. Slope is negative because the line falls from left to right

19. Slope is zero because the line is horizontal

21. Slope is undefined because the line is vertical

23. Slope is positive because the line rises from left to right

25. Slope is negative because the line falls from left to right

27. (0, 1) and (2, 2) are on the line.

$$m = \dfrac{2-1}{2-0} = \dfrac{1}{2}$$

29. (0, 0) and (1, −3) are on the line.

$$m = \dfrac{-3-0}{1-0} = \dfrac{-3}{1} = -3$$

31. (0, −3) and (1, −3) are on the line.

$$m = \dfrac{-3-(-3)}{1-0} = \dfrac{-3+3}{1} = \dfrac{0}{1} = 0$$

33. (−2, 0) and (−2, 1) are on the line.

$$m = \dfrac{1-0}{-2-(-2)} = \dfrac{1}{-2+2} = \dfrac{1}{0}$$

The slope is undefined.

35. $m = \dfrac{2-4}{-4-2} = \dfrac{-2}{-6} = \dfrac{1}{3}$

37. $m = \dfrac{-6-3}{1-(-2)} = \dfrac{-9}{3} = -3$

39. $m = \dfrac{2-5}{(-4)-1} = \dfrac{-3}{-5} = \dfrac{3}{5}$

41. $m = \dfrac{3-3}{-2-5} = \dfrac{0}{-7} = 0$

43. $m = \dfrac{5-(-7)}{2-2} = \dfrac{12}{0}$ is undefined

45. $m = \dfrac{-\frac{4}{5}-\frac{3}{5}}{\frac{1}{4}-\frac{1}{2}} = \dfrac{-\frac{7}{5}}{-\frac{1}{4}} = \dfrac{28}{5}$

47. $m = \dfrac{6-(-1)}{-5-3} = \dfrac{7}{-8} = -\dfrac{7}{8}$

49. $m = \dfrac{1.1-(-3.4)}{-3.2-6.8} = \dfrac{4.5}{-10} = -0.45$ or $-\dfrac{9}{20}$

51. $m = \dfrac{2.6-3.5}{2000-1994} = \dfrac{-0.9}{6} = -0.15$ or $-\dfrac{3}{20}$

53. **(a)** $m = -2$

   (b) $m = -\dfrac{1}{-2} = \dfrac{1}{2}$

55. **(a)** $m = 0$

   (b) $m = -\dfrac{1}{0}$ is undefined

57. (a) $m = \dfrac{4}{5}$

(b) $m = -\dfrac{1}{\frac{4}{5}} = -\dfrac{5}{4}$

59. (a) m is undefined

(b) m is 0

61. $m_1 m_2 = -2\left(\dfrac{1}{2}\right) = -1$

The lines are perpendicular.

63. $m_1 = m_2 = 1$

The two lines are parallel.

65. $m_1 = \dfrac{2}{7} \neq m_2 = -\dfrac{2}{7}$

$m_1 m_2 = \dfrac{2}{7}\left(-\dfrac{2}{7}\right) = -\dfrac{4}{49} \neq -1$

The lines are neither parallel nor perpendicular.

67. $m_1 = \dfrac{-2-4}{-1-2} = \dfrac{-6}{-3} = 2$

$m_2 = \dfrac{5-7}{0-1} = \dfrac{-2}{-1} = 2$

Since $m_1 = m_2 = 2$, the two lines are parallel.

69. $m_1 = \dfrac{4-9}{0-1} = \dfrac{-5}{-1} = 5$

$m_2 = \dfrac{1-2}{10-5} = \dfrac{-1}{5}$

$m_1 m_2 = 5\left(-\dfrac{1}{5}\right) = -1$

The two lines are perpendicular.

71. $m_1 = \dfrac{3-4}{0-4} = \dfrac{1}{4}$

$m_2 = \dfrac{-1-7}{-1-1} = \dfrac{-8}{-2} = 4$

$m_1 \neq m_2$

$m_1 m_2 = \dfrac{1}{4}(4) = 1 \neq -1$

The lines are neither parallel nor perpendicular.

73. $m = \dfrac{32{,}000 - 29{,}600}{0 - 15} = \dfrac{2400}{-15} = 160$

The average rate of change is $160 per year

75. (a) We use the ordered pairs (1980, 304) and (2009, 1609) to find the slope.

$m = \dfrac{1609 - 304}{2009 - 1980} = \dfrac{1305}{29} = 45$

(b) The slope $m = 45$ means that the number of male prisoners increased at a rate of 45 thousand per year during this time period.

77. (a) $d = 0.2t = 0.2(5 \text{ sec}) = 1$ mile

(b) $d = 0.2t = 0.2(10 \text{ sec}) = 2$ miles

(c) $d = 0.2t = 0.2(15 \text{ sec}) = 3$ miles

(d) $m = \dfrac{(2 \text{ miles}) - (1 \text{ mile})}{(10 \text{ sec}) - (5 \text{ sec})} = \dfrac{1}{5} = 0.2$

The slope $m = 0.2$ means that the distance between a lightning strike and an observer increases by 0.2 miles for every additional second between seeing lightning and hearing thunder.

79. $m = \dfrac{3 \text{ units up}}{4 \text{ units right}} = \dfrac{3}{4}$

81. $m = \dfrac{0 \text{ units up}}{5 \text{ units right}} = \dfrac{0}{5} = 0$

83.

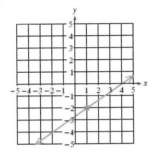

From (1, –2) going 2 units up and 3 units to the right yields the point (4, 0). Or, going 2 units down and 3 units to the left yields the point (–2, –4).

85.

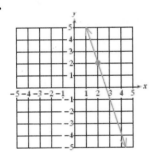

From (2, 2) going 3 units down and 1 unit to the right yields the point (3, –1). Or, going 3 units up and 1 unit to the left yields the point (1, 5).

For Exercises 85-90, answers will vary.

87.

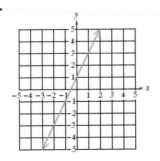

89.

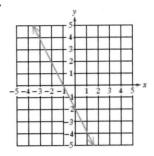

91.

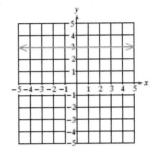

93. Label the points.

$(x_1, y_1) = (a + b, 4m - n)$

$(x_2, y_2) = (a - b, m + 2n)$

Now substitute into the slope formula.

$$m = \dfrac{(m + 2n) - (4m - n)}{(a - b) - (a + b)}$$
$$= \dfrac{m + 2n - 4m + n}{a - b - a - b}$$
$$= \dfrac{m - 4m + 2n + n}{a - a - b - b}$$
$$= \dfrac{-3m + 3n}{-2b} \text{ or } \dfrac{3m - 2n}{2b}$$

95. To find the x-intercept, substitute $y = 0$.

$$ax + b(0) = c$$
$$ax = c$$
$$x = \frac{c}{a}$$

$$\left(\frac{c}{a}, 0\right)$$

97. From $(2, -1)$ going 2 units up and 5 units to the right yields the point $(7, 1)$. Or, going 2 units down and 5 units to the left yields the point $(-3, -3)$.

Calculator Exercises

1. l_1: $y = -x + 1$ $m_1 = -1$

l_2: $y = x + 3$ $m_2 = 1$

$m_1 m_2 = -1(1) = -1$

The lines are perpendicular.

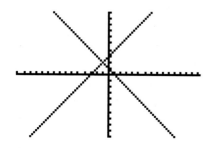

3. l_1: $y = 2x - 4$ $m_1 = 2$

l_2: $y = -\dfrac{3}{2}x + 2$ $m_2 = -\dfrac{3}{2}$

$m_1 m_2 = 2\left(-\dfrac{3}{2}\right) = -3 \neq -1$

The lines are neither parallel nor perpendicular.

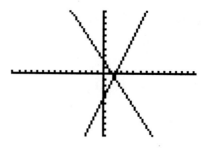

5.

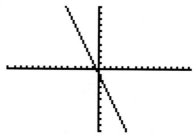

The lines may appear to coincide on a graph; however, they are not the same line because their y-intercepts are different.

l_1: $y = -2x - 1$ y-intercept is $(0, -1)$

l_2: $y = -2x - 0.99$ y-intercept is $(0, -0.99)$

The lines are not the same.

6.

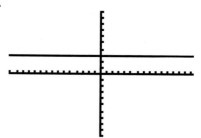

The line may appear to be horizontal; but it is not. The slope is 0.001 and is not zero.

Section 3.4 Practice Exercises

1. Answers will vary.

3. x-intercept: $y = 0$ y-intercept: $x = 0$
$x - 5(0) = 10$ $0 - 5y = 10$
      $x = 10$ $y = -2$
(10, 0)   (0, −2)

5. x-intercept: $y = 0$ y-intercept: $x = 0$
none $3y = -9$
              $y = -3$
             (0, −3)

7. x-intercept: $y = 0$ y-intercept: $x = 0$
$-4x = 6(0)$ $-4(0) = 6y$
     $x = 0$ $y = 0$
(0, 0)   (0, 0)

9. x-intercept: $y = 0$ y-intercept: $x = 0$
$5x = 20$ none
    $x = 4$

(4, 0)

11. $y = -2x + 3$
$m = -2$; y-intercept $= (0, 3)$

13. $y = x - 2$
$m = 1$; y-intercept $= (0, -2)$

15. $y = -x$
$m = -1$; y-intercept $= (0, 0)$

17. $y = \dfrac{3}{4}x - 1$

$m = \dfrac{3}{4}$; y-intercept $= 0, -1$

19. $2x - 5y = 4$
   $-5y = -2x + 4$
      $y = \dfrac{-2}{-5}x + \dfrac{4}{-5}$
      $y = \dfrac{2}{5}x - \dfrac{4}{5}$

$m = \dfrac{2}{5}$; y-intercept $= \left(0, -\dfrac{4}{5}\right)$

21. $3x - y = 5$
     $y = 3x - 5$
$m = 3$; y-intercept $= (0, -5)$

23. $x + y = 6$
    $y = -x + 6$
$m = -1$; y-intercept $= (0, 6)$

25. $x + 6 = 8$
     $x = 2$

It is a vertical line at $x = 2$; slope is undefined and no y-intercept.

27. $-8y = 2$
    $y = -\dfrac{1}{4}$
It is a horizontal line; $m = 0$, y-intercept $=$
$\left(0, -\dfrac{1}{4}\right)$

29. $3y - 2x = 0$
     $3y = 2x$
      $y = \dfrac{2}{3}x$

$m = \dfrac{2}{3}$; y-intercept $= (0, 0)$

31.

33.

35. The slope is positive and the y-intercept is positive, so the equation matches graph b.

37. The slope is negative and the y-intercept is positive, so the equation matches graph e.

39. The slope is positive and the y-intercept is $(0, 0)$, so the equation matches graph c.

41. $x - 2y = 6$

$$-2y = -x + 6$$

$$y = \frac{1}{2}x - 3$$

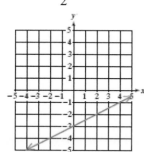

43. $2x + y = 9$

$$y = -2x + 9$$

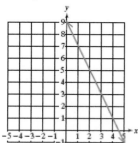

45. $2x = -4y + 6$

$$-4y = 2x - 6$$

$$y = -\frac{1}{2}x + \frac{3}{2}$$

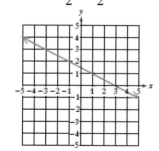

47. $x + y = 0$

$$y = -x$$

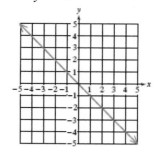

49. $5y = 4x$

$$y = \frac{4}{5}x$$

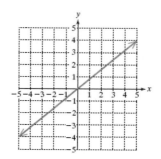

51. $3y + 2 = 0$

$$y = -\frac{2}{3}$$

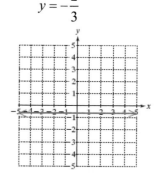

53. $l_1: m_1 = -2$

$$l_2: m_2 = \frac{1}{2}$$

$$m_1 m_2 = -2\left(\frac{1}{2}\right) = -1$$

The lines are perpendicular.

55. $l_1: m_1 = \dfrac{4}{5}$

$l_2: m_2 = \dfrac{5}{4}$

$m_1 m_2 = \dfrac{4}{5}\left(\dfrac{5}{4}\right) = 1 \neq -1$

$m_1 \neq m_2$

The lines are neither parallel nor perpendicular.

57. $l_1: m = -9$

$l_2: m = -9$

parallel

59. Vertical and horizontal lines; they are perpendicular.

61. Both are vertical lines and are parallel.

63. $l_1: 2x + 3y = 6$

$3y = -2x + 6$

$y = -\dfrac{2}{3}x + 2$

$m_1 = -\dfrac{2}{3}$

$l_2: 3x - 2y = 12$

$-2y = -3x + 12$

$y = \dfrac{3}{2}x - 6$

$m_2 = \dfrac{3}{2}$

$m_1 m_2 = -\dfrac{2}{3}\left(\dfrac{3}{2}\right) = -1$

The lines are perpendicular.

65. $l_1: 4x + 2y = 6$

$2y = -4x + 6$

$y = -2x + 3$

$m_1 = -2$

$l_2: 4x + 8y = 16$

$8y = -4x + 16$

$y = -\dfrac{1}{2}x + 2$

$m_2 = -\dfrac{1}{2}$

$m_1 m_2 = -2\left(-\dfrac{1}{2}\right) = 1 \neq -1$

$m_1 \neq m_2$

The lines are neither parallel nor perpendicular.

67. $l_1: m = \dfrac{1}{5}$

$l_2: 2x - 10y = 20$

$-10y = -2x + 20$

$y = \dfrac{1}{5}x - 2$

$m_2 = \dfrac{1}{5}$

$m_1 = m_2$

The lines are parallel.

69. $y = mx + b$

$y = -\dfrac{1}{3}x + 2$

71. $y = mx + b$
$y = 10x - 19$

73. $y = 6x - 8$

75. $y = \dfrac{1}{2}x - 3$ or $x - 2y = 6$

77. $y = -11$

79. $y = 5x$

81. (a) $m = 49.95$; the cost increases $49.95 per day.

(b) (0, $31.95); the base fee for renting the car is $31.95.

(c) $C = 49.95(7) + 31.95 = 381.6$; $381.60

83. $Ax + By = C$
$$By = -Ax + C$$
$$y = \frac{-A}{B}x + \frac{C}{B}$$
$$m = \frac{-A}{B}$$

85. $A = 6, B = 7$
$$m = -\frac{A}{B} = -\frac{6}{7}$$

87. $A = 11, B = -8$
$$m = -\frac{A}{B} = -\frac{11}{-8} = \frac{11}{8}$$

Problem Recognition Exercises

a. $y = 5x$: $m = 5$, passes through the origin

b. $2x + 3y = 12$: $m = -\frac{2}{3}$; y-intercept = (0, 4);

x-intercept = (6, 0)

c. $y = \frac{1}{2}x - 5$: $m = \frac{1}{2}$; y-intercept = (0, -5);

x-intercept = (10, 0)

d. $3x - 6y = 10$: $m = \frac{1}{2}$;

y-intercept = $\left(0, -\frac{5}{3}\right)$; x-intercept = $\left(\frac{10}{3}, 0\right)$

e. $2y = -8$: $m = 0$; y-intercept = (0, -4);

no x-intercept

f. $y = -2x + 4$: $m = -2$; y-intercept = (0, 4);

x-intercept = (2, 0)

g. $3x = 1$; slope is undefined; no y-intercept;

x-intercept = $\left(\frac{1}{3}, 0\right)$

h. $x + 2y = 6$: $m = -\frac{1}{2}$; y-intercept = (0,3);

x-intercept = (6, 0)

1. Line whose slope is positive: a, c, d

3. Line that passes through the origin: a

5. Line whose y-intercept is (0, 4): b, f

7. Line whose slope is $\frac{1}{2}$: c, d

9. Line whose slope is 0: e

11. Line that is parallel to the line with the equation $y = -\frac{2}{3}x + 4$: b

13. Line that is vertical: g

15. Line whose x-intercept is (10, 0): c

17. Line that is parallel to the x-axis: e

19. Line with a negative slope and positive y-intercept: b, f, h

Section 3.5 Practice Exercises

1. Answers will vary.

3. $2x - 3y = -3$

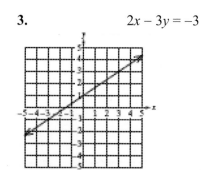

5. $3 - y = 9$

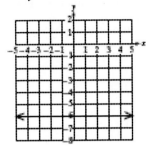

7. $m = \dfrac{-3-6}{1-2} = \dfrac{-9}{-1} = 9$

9. $m = \dfrac{5-5}{-2-5} = \dfrac{0}{-7} = 0$

11. $y - y_1 = m(x - x_1)$
$y - 1 = 3(x - (-2))$
$y - 1 = 3(x + 2)$
$y - 1 = 3x + 6$
$y = 3x + 7 \text{ or } 3x - y = -7$

13. $y - y_1 = m(x - x_1)$
$y - (-2) = -4[x - (-3)]$
$y + 2 = -4(x + 3)$
$y + 2 = -4x - 12$
$y = -4x - 14 \text{ or } 4x + y = -14$

15. $y - y_1 = m(x - x_1)$
$y - 0 = -\dfrac{1}{2}[x - (-1)]$
$y = -\dfrac{1}{2}(x + 1)$
$y = -\dfrac{1}{2}x - \dfrac{1}{2}$

$Or, \dfrac{1}{2}x + y = -\dfrac{1}{2}$
$x + 2y = -1$

17. $m = \dfrac{-6-0}{-2-1} = \dfrac{-6}{-3} = 2$
$y - y_1 = m(x - x_1)$
$y - (-6) = 2(x - (-2))$
$y + 6 = 2(x + 2)$
$y + 6 = 2x + 4$
$y = 2x - 2 \text{ or } 2x - y = 2$

19. $m = \dfrac{-4-(-3)}{0-(-1)} = \dfrac{-1}{1} = -1$
$y - y_1 = m(x - x_1)$
$y - (-4) = -1(x - 0)$
$y + 4 = -x$
$y = -x - 4 \text{ or } x + y = -4$

21. $m = \dfrac{-3.3-(-5.3)}{2.2-12.2} = \dfrac{2}{-10} = -0.2$
$y - y_1 = m(x - x_1)$
$y - (-3.3) = -0.2(x - 2.2)$
$y + 3.3 = -0.2x + 0.44$
$y = -0.2x - 2.86$

$Or, 0.2x + y = -2.86$
$20x + 100y = -286$

23. Two points $(-2, 5)$ and $(-1, 3)$

$m = \dfrac{5-3}{-2-(-1)} = \dfrac{2}{-1} = -2$
$y - y_1 = m(x - x_1)$
$y - 3 = -2[x - (-1)]$
$y - 3 = -2(x + 1)$
$y - 3 = -2x - 2$
$y = -2x + 1$

25. Two points $(-2, 0)$ and $(0, 4)$

$$m = \frac{0-4}{-2-0} = \frac{-4}{-2} = 2$$
$$y - y_1 = m(x - x_1)$$
$$y - 4 = 2(x - 0)$$
$$y - 4 = 2x$$
$$y = 2x + 4$$

27. Two points $(-4, -3)$ and $(4, 1)$

$$m = \frac{-3-1}{-4-4} = \frac{-4}{-8} = \frac{1}{2}$$
$$y - y_1 = m(x - x_1)$$
$$y - 1 = \frac{1}{2}(x - 4)$$
$$y - 1 = \frac{1}{2}x - 2$$
$$y = \frac{1}{2}x - 1$$

29. $l: y = 4x + 3$: slope = 4

Since the two lines are parallel, $m = 4$.

$$y - y_1 = m(x - x_1)$$
$$y - 1 = 4[x - (-3)]$$
$$y - 1 = 4(x + 3)$$
$$y - 1 = 4x + 12$$
$$y = 4x + 13 \text{ or } 4x - y = -13$$

31. $3x + 2y = 8$
$$2y = -3x + 8$$
$$y = -\frac{3}{2}x + 4$$

$$\text{Slope} = -\frac{3}{2}$$

Since the two lines are parallel, $m = -\frac{3}{2}$

$$y - y_1 = m(x - x_1)$$
$$y - 0 = -\frac{3}{2}(x - 4)$$
$$y = -\frac{3}{2}x + 6$$

33. The slope of the given line is $\frac{1}{2}$. The slope of a line perpendicular to the given line is the negative reciprocal of $\frac{1}{2}$ or -2.

$$y - y_1 = m(x - x_1)$$
$$y - 2 = -2(x - (-5))$$
$$y - 2 = -2(x + 5)$$
$$y - 2 = -2x - 10$$
$$y = -2x - 8 \text{ or } 2x + y = -8$$

35. Write the given line in slope-intercept form to determine the slope of the line.
$$-5x + y = 4$$
$$y = 5x + 4$$

The slope of the given line is 5. The slope of a line perpendicular to the given line is the negative reciprocal of 5 or $-\frac{1}{5}$.

$$y - y_1 = m(x - x_1)$$
$$y - (-6) = -\frac{1}{5}(x - 0)$$
$$y + 6 = -\frac{1}{5}x$$
$$y = -\frac{1}{5}x - 6$$

$$Or, \frac{1}{5}x + y = -6$$
$$x + 5y = -30$$

37. iv Vertical line

39. vi Slope formula

41. iii Horizontal line

43. A line parallel to a horizontal line is a horizontal line and its equation has the form y equal to a constant. $y = 1$

45. A line perpendicular to a horizontal line is a vertical line and its equation has the form x equal to a constant. $x = 2$

47. A line perpendicular to $x = 0$, a vertical line, is a horizontal line and its equation has the form y equal to k, a constant. $y = 2$

49. $y - y_1 = m(x - x_1)$

$y - (6) = \dfrac{1}{4}(x - (-8))$

$y - 6 = \dfrac{1}{4}(x + 8)$

$y - 6 = \dfrac{1}{4}x + 2$

$y = \dfrac{1}{4}x + 8$ or x-4y=-32

51. $m = 3$

$y - y_1 = m(x - x_1)$

$y - (4) = 3(x - (4))$

$y - 4 = 3(x - 4)$

$y - 4 = 3x - 12$

$y = 3x - 8$ or 3x-y=8

53. $y - y_1 = m(x - x_1)$

$y - (-2.2) = 4.5(x - (-5.2))$

$y + 2.2 = 4.5(x + 5.2)$

$y + 2.2 = 4.5x - 23.4$

$y = 4.5x - 25.6$ or 45x-10y=256

55. Undefined slope; vertical line $x = -6$

57. Zero slope; horizontal line $y = -2$

59. Vertical line $x = -4$

Calculator Exercises

1.

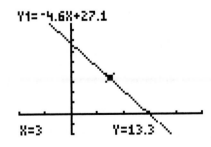

3.

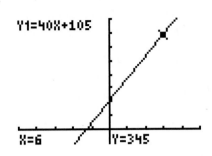

Section 3.6 Practice Exercises

1. Answers may vary.

3. $5x + 6y = 30$

x-intercept: $5x + 6(0) = 30$

$5x = 30$

$x = 6$ (6, 0)

y-intercept: $5(0) + 6y = 30$

$6y = 30$

$y = 5$ (0, 5)

5. $y = -2x - 4$

x-intercept: $0 = -2x - 4$

$2x = -4$

$x = -2$ (–2, 0)

y-intercept: (0, –4)

7. $y = -9$

x-intercept: none

y-intercept: (0, –9)

9. (a) 1980 corresponds to $x = 1980 - 1970 = 10$

$y = 0.14(10) + 1.60 = 3.00$

Minimum wage in the year 1980 was $3.00 per hour.

(b) 2010 corresponds to $x = 40$

$y = 0.14x + 1.60$

$y = 0.14(40) + 1.60$

$y = 7.20$

$7.20 per hour

(c) The y-intercept is $(0, 1.6)$. This indicates that the minimum hourly wage was $1.60 per hour in the year 1970.

(d) The slope is 0.14. This indicates that the minimum wage has risen approximately $0.14 per year during this period.

11. (a) Using the points $(70, 42)$ and $(84, 46)$ the slope can be found.

$$m = \frac{46-42}{84-70} = -\frac{4}{14} = \frac{2}{7} \approx 0.3$$

(b) Using the points $(70, 40)$ and $(84, 48)$ the slope can be found.

$$m = \frac{48-40}{84-70} = -\frac{8}{14} = \frac{4}{7} \approx 0.6$$

(c) $m = \dfrac{2}{7}$ means that Grindel"s weight is increasing at a rate of 2 oz in 7 days. $m = \dfrac{4}{7}$ means that Frisco's weight is increasing at a rate of 4 oz. in 7 days.

(d) Frisco is gaining weight more rapidly.

13. $y = 0.095x + 11.95 \qquad x \geq 0$

(a) $y = 0.095(1000) + 11.95$
$y = \$106.95$

(b) $y = 0.095(2000) + 11.95$
$y = \$201.95$

(c) y-intercept: $y = 4.20(0)$
$\qquad\qquad y = 0 \qquad (0, 0)$
For 0 kilowatt-hours used, the cost is $0 plus a fixed monthly tax of $11.95.

(d) $m = 0.095$
The cost increases by $0.095 for each kilowatt-hour used.

15. (a) Using the points $(0, 7.6)$ and $(25, 5.6)$ the slope of the equation can be found.

$$m = \frac{976-902}{75-150} = -\frac{74}{75} \approx -1.0$$

(b) Use this slope, the point $(0, 7.6)$, and the point-slope formula the equation can be determined.
$$y - 976 = -1.0(x - 75)$$
$$y - 976 = -x + 75$$
$$y = -x + 1051$$

(c) The minimum pressure was approximately 921 mb

$$y = -x + 1051$$
$$y = -130 + 1051$$
$$y = 921$$

17. (a) Use the points $(0, 57)$ and $(4, 143)$ to determine the slope.

$$m = \frac{143-57}{4-0} = \frac{86}{4} = 21.5$$

(b) The slope means that the consumption of wind energy in the United States increased by 21.5 trillions of Btu per year.

(c) $y - y_1 = m(x - x_1)$

$$y - 57 = 21.5(x - 0)$$
$$y - 57 = 21.5x$$
$$y = 21.5x + 57$$

(d) Year 2010 corresponds to $x = 10$.

$$y = 21.5(10) + 57 = 272$$

The consumption of wind energy will be 272 trillion Btu in the year 2010.

19. (a) $y = 0.20x + 39.99$

(b) $y = 0.20(40) + 39.99$
$y = 8.00 + 39.99$
$y = 47.99$
His bill would be $47.99

21. (a) $y = 90x + 105$

(b) $y = 90(12) + 105$
$y = 1080 + 105$
$y = 1185$
It will cost $1185 to rent the unit for
1 year.

23. (a) $y = 0.8x + 100$

(b) $y = 0.8(200) + 100$
$y = 160 + 100$
$y = 260$
It will cost $260 to produce 200 loaves
of bread in one day.

Group Activity

Answers will vary throughout this exercise.

Chapter 3 Review Exercises

Section 3.1

1.

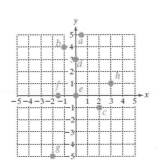

3. III

4. II

5. IV

7. IV

9. x-axis

11. (a) On day 1, the price per share of a stock
was $26.25.

(b) Day 2

(c) $28.50 − $26.25 = $2.25

Section 3.2

13. $5(0) − 3(4) = 12$
$-12 \neq 12$
No

15. $1 = \dfrac{1}{3}(9) − 2$
$1 = 3 − 2 = 1$
Yes

17.

x	y
2	1
3	4
1	−2

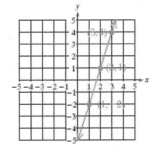

19.

x	y
0	−1
3	1
−6	−5

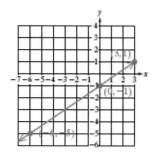

27. Horizontal

29.
x-intercept
$$-4x + 8(0) = 12$$
$$-4x = 12$$
$$x = -3$$
$$(-3, 0)$$

y-intercept
$$-4(0) + 8y = 12$$
$$8y = 12$$
$$y = \frac{12}{8} = \frac{3}{2}$$
$$\left(0, \frac{3}{2}\right)$$

21.

31.
x-intercept
$$0 = 8x$$
$$x = 0$$
$$(0, 0)$$

y-intercept
$$y = 8(0)$$
$$y = 0$$
$$(0, 0)$$

33.
x-intercept
none

y-intercept
$$6y = -24$$
$$y = -4$$
$$(0, -4)$$

23.

35.
x-intercept
$$2x + 5 = 0$$
$$x = -\frac{5}{2}$$
$$\left(-\frac{5}{2}, 0\right)$$

y-intercept
none

Section 3.3

37. $m = \dfrac{12 \text{ ft}}{5 \text{ ft}} = \dfrac{12}{5}$

25. Vertical

39. $m = \dfrac{-1 - (-9)}{-5 - 7} = \dfrac{8}{-12} = -\dfrac{2}{3}$

41. $m = \dfrac{-7 - 0}{3 - 3} = \dfrac{-7}{0}$ is undefined

42. $m = 0$

43. **(a)** $m = -5$

(b) $m = -\dfrac{1}{-5} = \dfrac{1}{5}$

45. $m_1 = \dfrac{5-7}{0-3} = \dfrac{-2}{-3} = \dfrac{2}{3}$

$m_2 = \dfrac{-3-3}{-3-6} = \dfrac{-6}{-9} = \dfrac{2}{3}$

Since $m_1 = m_2$, the two lines are parallel.

47. $m_1 = \dfrac{0-\frac{5}{6}}{2-0} = \dfrac{-\frac{5}{6}}{2} = -\dfrac{5}{12}$

$m_2 = \dfrac{0-\frac{6}{5}}{-\frac{1}{2}-0} = \dfrac{-\frac{6}{5}}{-\frac{1}{2}} = \dfrac{12}{5}$

Since $m_1 m_2 = -1$, the two lines are perpendicular.

49. **(a)** Using the ordered pairs (1, 35955) and (31, 37005) the slope can be found.

$m = \dfrac{37005-35955}{31-1} = \dfrac{1050}{30} = 35$

(b) The number of kilowatt-hours increased at a rate of 35 kilowatt-hours per day.

Section 3.4

51. $5x - 2y = 10$

$-2y = -5x + 10$

$y = \dfrac{5}{2}x - 5$

$m = \dfrac{5}{2}$ y-intercept $(0, -5)$

53. $x - 3y = 0$

$3y = x$

$y = \dfrac{1}{3}x$

$m = \dfrac{1}{3}$ y-intercept $(0, 0)$

55. $2y = -5$

$y = -\dfrac{5}{2}$

$m = 0$ y-intercept $\left(0, -\dfrac{5}{2}\right)$

57. $m_1 = \dfrac{3}{5}$

$m_2 = \dfrac{5}{3}$

$m_1 \ne m_2$

$m_1 m_2 = 1 \ne -1$

The lines are neither parallel nor perpendicular.

59. $m_1 = -\dfrac{3}{2}$

$m_2 = -\dfrac{3}{2}$

Since $m_1 = m_2$, the lines are parallel.

61. m_1 is undefined.

$m_2 = 0$

Since one line is vertical and the other one is horizontal, they are perpendicular.

63. $y = -\dfrac{4}{3}x - 1$ or $4x + 3y = -3$

65. $y - y_1 = m(x - x_1)$

$y - 2 = -\dfrac{4}{3}(x - (-6))$

$y - 2 = -\dfrac{4}{3}x - 8$

$y = -\dfrac{4}{3}x - 6$

or $4x + 3y = -18$

Section 3.5

67. Answers may vary. For example: $y = 3x + 2$

69. $m = \dfrac{y_1 - y_2}{x_1 - x_2} = \dfrac{y_2 - y_1}{x_2 - x_1}$

71. Answers may vary. For example: $x = 6$

73. $y - 8 = -6(x - (-1))$
$y - 8 = -6(x + 1)$
$y - 8 = -6x - 6$
$\quad y = -6x + 2$ or $6x + y = 2$

75. First, use the points to determine the slope.
$$m = \frac{-4 - (-2)}{0 - 8} = \frac{-2}{-8} = \frac{1}{4}$$
Use this value, one of the points, and the point-slope formula to determine the equation of the line.
$$y - (-4) = \frac{1}{4}(x - 0)$$
$$y + 4 = \frac{1}{4}x$$
$$y = \frac{1}{4}x - 4$$

Or, $\dfrac{1}{4}x - y = 4$

$x - 4y = 16$

77. The slope of the given line is $-\dfrac{5}{6}$. The slope of a perpendicular line is the negative reciprocal, $\dfrac{6}{5}$. Use this value, the point, and the point-slope formula to determine the equation.
$$y - 12 = \frac{6}{5}(x - 5)$$
$$y - 12 = \frac{6}{5}x - 6$$
$$y = \frac{6}{5}x + 6$$

Or, $\dfrac{6}{5}x - y = -6$

$6x - 5y = -30$

Section 3.6

79. (a) $y = 2.4x + 31$
$y = 2.4(7) + 31$
$y = 47.8$ inches

(b) The slope is 2.4 and indicates that the average height for girls increases at a rate of 2.4 in. per year.

81. (a) $y = 20x + 55$

(b) $y = 20(9) + 55$
$y = 180 + 55$
$y = 235$
The total cost of renting the system for nine months is $235.

Chapter 3 Test

1. (a) II

   (b) IV

   (c) III

3. 0

5. (a) $2(0) - 6 = 6$
       $-6 \neq 6$
       No

   (b) $2(4) - 2 = 6$
           $6 = 6$
           Yes

   (c) $2(3) - 0 = 6$
           $6 = 6$
           Yes

   (d) $2\left(\dfrac{9}{2}\right) - 3 = 6$
           $6 = 6$
           Yes

7. $y = 3x + 2$

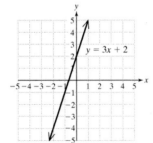

9. $3x + 2y = 8$

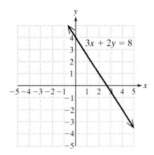

11. $x = \dfrac{7}{5}$; vertical

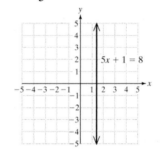

13. x-intercept y-intercept
        $2(0) = 6x$ $2y = 6(0)$
        $0 = 6x$ $2y = 0$
        $x = 0$ $y = 0$
        $0, 0$ $(0, 0)$

15. x-intercept y-intercept
        none $y = 3$
                           $(0, 3)$

17. (a) $m = \dfrac{-1 - 0}{-5 - (-2)} = \dfrac{-1}{-3} = \dfrac{1}{3}$

   (b) $4x - 3y = 9$
           $y = \dfrac{4}{3}x - 3$
           $m = \dfrac{4}{3}$

19. (a) m is undefined

   (b) $m = 0$

21. First, use the points to determine the slopes.

$$m_1 = \frac{-2-4}{-1-1} = \frac{-6}{-2} = 3$$

$$m_2 = \frac{-11-(-5)}{-2-0} = \frac{-6}{-2} = 3$$

Because the slopes are the same, the lines are parallel.

23. $y = \dfrac{1}{4}x + \dfrac{1}{2}$

Or, $\dfrac{1}{4}x - y = -\dfrac{1}{2}$

$x - 4y = -2$

25. First, use the points to determine the slope of the line.

$$m = \frac{8-1}{2-4} = \frac{7}{-2} = -\frac{7}{2}$$

Use this value, one of the points, and the point-slope formula to determine the equation.

$$y - 8 = -\frac{7}{2}(x - 2)$$

$$y - 8 = -\frac{7}{2}x + 7$$

$$y = -\frac{7}{2}x + 15$$

Or, $\dfrac{7}{2}x + y = 15$

$7x + 2y = 30$

27. First, write the given equation in slope-intercept form to determine the slope of the given line.

$$2x + 6y = -5$$

$$6y = -2x - 5$$

$$y = -\frac{1}{3}x - \frac{5}{6}$$

The slope of the given line is $-\dfrac{1}{3}$. The slope of a parallel line is also $-\dfrac{1}{3}$. Use this value, the point, and the point-slope formula to determine the equation of the parallel line.

$$y - 0 = -\frac{1}{3}(x - 3)$$

$$y = -\frac{1}{3}x + 1$$

Or, $\dfrac{1}{3}x + y = 1$

$x + 3y = 3$

29. **(a)** $y = 1.5x + 10$

(b) $y = 1.5(10) + 10$
$y = 15 + 10$
$y = 25$
The cost of attending the State Fair and going on 10 rides is $25.

Cumulative Review Exercises

Chapters 1-3

1. **(a)** Rational

   (b) Rational

   (c) Irrational

   (d) Rational

3. $32 \div 2 \cdot 4 + 5 = 16 \cdot 4 + 5 = 69$

5. $16 - 5 - (-7) = 16 - 5 + 7 = 18$

7. $(-2.1)(-6); (-2.1)(-6) = 12.6$

9. $6x - 10 = 14$
   $6x = 24$
   $x = 4$

11. $\dfrac{2}{3}y - \dfrac{1}{6} = y + \dfrac{4}{3}$
    $6\left(\dfrac{2}{3}y - \dfrac{1}{6}\right) = 6\left(y + \dfrac{4}{3}\right)$
    $4y - 1 = 6y + 8$
    $-2y = 9$
    $y = -\dfrac{9}{2}$

13. Let x = the area of Maine.
    712 less than $29x = 267,277$
    $29x - 712 = 267,277$
    $29x = 267,989$
    $x = 9241$
    The area of Maine is 9241 mi^2.

15.

17. $3x + 2y = -12$
    $2y = -3x - 12$
    $y = -\dfrac{3}{2}x - 6$
    $m = -\dfrac{3}{2}$ y-intercept $(0, -6)$

19. $y - y_1 = m(x - x_1)$
    $y - (-5) = -3(x - 2)$
    $y + 5 = -3x + 6$
    $y = -3x + 1 \text{ or } 3x + y = 1$

Chapter 4

Calculator Exercises

1.

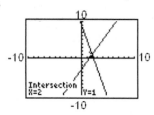

The solution is (2, 1).

3.

Equation 1	Equation 2
$x + y = 4$	$-2x + y = -5$
$y = -x + 4$	$y = 2x - 5$

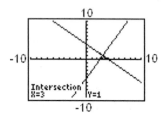

The solution is (3, 1).

5.

Equation 1	Equation 2
$-x + 3y = -6$	$6y = 2x + 6$
$3y = x - 6$	
$y = \dfrac{1}{3}x - 2$	$y = \dfrac{1}{3}x + 1$

Since the two lines have the same slopes but different y-intercept, they are parallel. The system has no solution. The system is inconsistent.

Section 4.1 Practice Exercises

1. Answers will vary..

3. $3x - y = 7$
$x - 2y = 4$ point: $(2, -1)$
Substitute the given point into both equations.
$3(2) - (-1) \overset{?}{=} 7$ ✓
$2 - 2(-1) \overset{?}{=} 4$ ✓

Because the given point is a solution to each equation, it is a solution to the system of equations.   Yes

5. $4y = -3x + 12$
$y = \dfrac{2}{3}x - 4$ point: $(0, 4)$

Substitute the given point into both equations.
$4(4) \overset{?}{=} -3(0) + 12$
$4 \overset{?}{=} \dfrac{2}{3}(0) - 4$

Because the given point is not a solution of either equation it is not a solution of the system of equations.   No

7. $3x - 6y = 9$
$x - 2y = 3$ point: $\left(4, \dfrac{1}{2}\right)$
Substitute the given point into both equations.
$3(4) - 6\left(\dfrac{1}{2}\right) \overset{?}{=} 9$ ✓
$4 - 2\left(\dfrac{1}{2}\right) \overset{?}{=} 3$ ✓

Because the given point is a solution to each equation, it is a solution to the system of equations.   Yes

9. $\dfrac{1}{3}x = \dfrac{2}{5}y - \dfrac{4}{5}$

$\dfrac{3}{4}x + \dfrac{1}{2}y = 2$ point: (0, 2)

Substitute the given point into both equations.

$\dfrac{1}{3}(0) \overset{?}{=} \dfrac{2}{5}(2) - \dfrac{4}{5}$ ✓

$\dfrac{3}{4}(0) + \dfrac{1}{2}(2) \overset{?}{=} 2$

Because the given point is not a solution to the second equation, it is not a solution to the system of equations.   No

11. b   Since parallel lines do not intersect, parallel lines represent a system with no solution.

13. d   The lines intersect at the origin or (0, 0).

15. (a) $y = 2x - 3$
$y = 2x + 5$

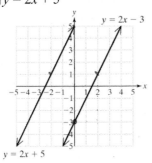

(b) $y = 2x + 1$
$y = 4x - 5$

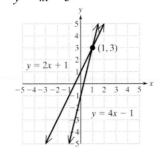

(c) $y = 3x - 5$
$y = 3x - 5$

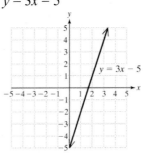

17. c   Coinciding lines have the same slope and the same y-intercept.

19. a   An inconsistent system graphs as parallel lines.

21. a   The graph of the system is parallel lines.

23. b   Distinct intersecting lines always have different slopes.

25. c   Coinciding lines with the same slopes and same y-intercept have infinitely many solutions.

27. $y = -x + 4$
$y = x - 2$

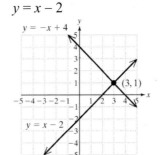

(3, 1); consistent; independent system

29. $2x + y = 0$
$3x + y = 1$
Rewrite in slope-intercept form.
$y = -2x$
$y = -3x + 1$

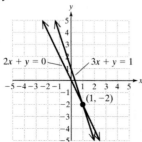

$(1, -2)$; consistent; independent system

31. $2x + y = 6$
$x = 1$
Rewrite the first equation in slope-intercept form. The second equation is a vertical line through the point $(1, 0)$.
$y = -2x + 6$

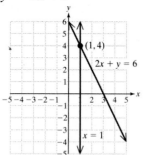

$(1, 4)$; consistent; independent system

33. $-6x - 3y = 0$
$4x + 2y = 4$
Rewrite both equations in slope-intercept form.
$y = -2x$
$y = -2x + 2$

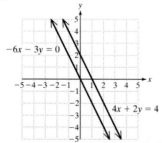

No solution; inconsistent; independent

35. $-2x + y = 3$
$6x - 3y = -9$
Rewrite both equations in slope-intercept form.
$y = 2x + 3$
$y = 2x + 3$

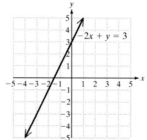

Infinitely many solutions
$\{(x, y) | y = 2x + 3\}$;
consistent; dependent system

37. $\quad y = 6$
$2x + 3y = 12$
Rewrite the second equation in slope-intercept form. The first equation is a horizontal line through the point $(0, 6)$.
$y = -\dfrac{2}{3}x + 4$

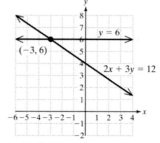

$(-3, 6)$; consistent; independent system

39. $x = 4 + y$

$3y = -3x$

Rewrite both equations in slope-intercept form.

$y = x - 4$

$y = -x$

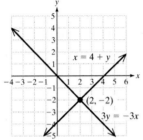

(2, −2); consistent; independent system

41. $-x + y = 3$

$4y = 4x + 6$

Rewrite both equations in slope-intercept form.

$y = x + 3$

$y = x + \dfrac{3}{2}$

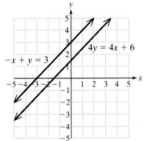

No solution; inconsistent; independent system

43. $x = 4$

$2y = 4$

Solve the second equation for y.

$x = 4$

$y = 2$

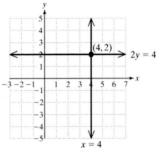

(4, 2); consistent; independent system

45. $2x + y = 4$

$4x - 2y = 0$

Rewrite both equations in slope-intercept form.

$y = -2x + 4$

$y = 2x$

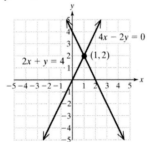

1, 2 ; consistent; independent system

47. $y = 0.5x + 2$
$-x + 2y = 4$

Rewrite the second equation in slope-intercept form.
$y = 0.5x + 2$
$y = 0.5x + 2$

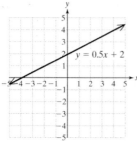

Infinitely many solutions
$\{(x, y)|y = 0.5x + 2\}$;
consistent; dependent system

49. $x - 3y = 0$
$y = -x - 4$

Rewrite the first equation in slope-intercept form.
$y = -x + 1$
$y = \dfrac{1}{3}x$

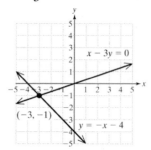

$-3, -1$; consistent; independent sys

51. The point of intersection gives the answer, (2500, 50). The same cost occurs when $2500 in merchandise is purchased.

53. The point of intersection is below the x-axis and cannot have a positive y-coordinate.

55. Answers may vary. For example:
$4x + y = 9$
$-2x - y = -5$

These equations were found by simply putting together some combination of x and y and substituting $x = 2$ and $y = 1$ into them to determine the constant value.

57. Answers may vary. For example:
$2x + 2y = 1$
This equation was found by multiplying each side of the given equation by a different value.

Section 4.2 Practice Exercises

1. $2x - y = 4$
$-2y = -4x + 8$

Rewrite both equations in slope-intercept form.
$y = 2x - 4$
$y = 2x - 4$
Since the slopes and the y-intercepts are equal, they are coinciding lines..

3. $2x + 3y = 6$
$x - y = 5$

Rewrite both equations in slope-intercept form.

$y = -\dfrac{2}{3}x + 2$
$y = x - 5$
Since the slopes are unequal, the lines intersect.

5. $2x = \dfrac{1}{2}y + 2$
$4x - y = 13$

Rewrite both equations in slope-intercept form.
$y = 4x - 4$
$y = 4x - 13$
Since the slopes are equal but the y-intercepts are different, the lines are parallel.

7. $3x + 2y = -3$
$\qquad y = 2x - 12$

The second equation is solved for y. Substitute this value for y into the first equation.
$$3x + 2y = -3$$
$$3x + 2(2x - 12) = -3$$
$$3x + 4x - 24 = -3$$
$$7x - 24 = -3$$
$$7x = 21$$
$$x = 3$$

Substitute $x = 3$ into the second equation to solve for y.

$y = 2x - 12$
$y = 2(3) - 12$
$y = -6$
Solution: $(3, -6)$

9. $\qquad x = -4y + 16$
$3x + 5y = 20$

The first equation is solved for x. Substitute this value for x into the second equation.
$$3x + 5y = 20$$
$$3(-4y + 16) + 5y = 20$$
$$-12y + 48 + 5y = 20$$
$$-7y + 48 = 20$$
$$-7y = -28$$
$$y = 4$$

Substitute $y = 4$ into the second equation to solve for x.

$x = -4y + 16$
$x = -4(4) + 16$
$x = 0$
Solution: $(0, 4)$

11. (a) y in the second equation is easier to solve for because its coefficient is 1.

(b) $4x - 2y = -6$
$\qquad 3x + y = 8$

Solving the second equation for y gives $y = -3x + 8$. Substitute this value for y into the first equation.
$$4x - 2y = -6$$
$$4x - 2(-3x + 8) = -6$$
$$4x + 6x - 16 = -6$$
$$10x - 16 = -6$$
$$10x = 10$$
$$x = 1$$
$$3x + y = 8$$
$$3(1) + y = 8$$
$$3 + y = 8$$
$$y = 5$$
Solution: $(1, 5)$

13. $\qquad x = 3y - 1$
$\quad 2x - 4y = 2$

The first equation is solved for x. Substitute this value for x into the second equation.
$$2x - 4y = 2$$
$$2(3y - 1) - 4y = 2$$
$$6y - 2 - 4y = 2$$
$$2y - 2 = 2$$
$$2y = 4$$
$$y = 2$$
$x = 3y - 1$
$x = 3(2) - 1$
$x = 5$
Solution: $(5, 2)$

15. $-2x + 5y = 5$
$\quad\quad x = 4y - 10$

The second equation is solved for x. Substitute this value for x into the first equation.

$$-2x + 5y = 5$$
$$-2(4y - 10) + 5y = 5$$
$$-8y + 20 + 5y = 5$$
$$-3y + 20 = 5$$
$$-3y = -15$$
$$y = 5$$

$x = 4y - 10$
$x = 4(5) - 10$
$x = 10$
Solution: (10, 5)

17. $4x - y = -1$
$\quad\quad 2x + 4y = 13$

Solving the first equation for y gives $y = 4x + 1$. Substitute this value for y into the second equation.

$$2x + 4y = 13$$
$$2x + 4(4x + 1) = 13$$
$$2x + 16x + 4 = 13$$
$$18x + 4 = 13$$
$$18x = 9$$
$$x = \frac{1}{2}$$

$$4x - y = -1$$
$$4\left(\frac{1}{2}\right) - y = -1$$
$$2 - y = -1$$
$$-y = -3$$
$$y = 3$$

Solution: $\left(\dfrac{1}{2}, 3\right)$

19. $4x - 3y = 11$
$\quad\quad x = 5$

The second equation is solved for x. Substitute this value for x into the first equation.

$$4(5) - 3y = 11$$
$$20 - 3y = 11$$
$$-3y = -9$$
$$y = 3$$
Solution: (5, 3)

21. $\quad\quad 4x = 8y + 4$
$\quad\quad 5x - 3y = 5$

Solving the first equation for x gives $x = 2y + 1$. Substitute this value for x into the second equation.

$$5x - 3y = 5$$
$$5(2y + 1) - 3y = 5$$
$$10y + 5 - 3y = 5$$
$$7y + 5 = 5$$
$$7y = 0$$
$$y = 0$$

$4x = 8y + 4$
$4x = 8(0) + 4$
$4x = 4$
$x = 1$
Solution: (1, 0)

23. $x - 3y = -11$
$\quad\quad 6x - y = 2$

Solving the first equation for x gives $x = 3y - 11$. Substitute this value for x into the second equation.

$$6x - y = 2$$
$$6(3y - 11) - y = 2$$
$$18y - 66 - y = 2$$
$$17y - 66 = 2$$
$$17y = 68$$
$$y = 4$$

$x - 3y = -11$
$x - 3(4) = -11$
$x - 12 = -11$
$x = 1$
Solution: (1, 4)

25. $3x + 2y = -1$

$\dfrac{3}{2}x + y = 4$

Solving the second equation for y gives

$y = -\dfrac{3}{2}x + 4$. Substitute this value for y into

the first equation.

$3x + 2y = -1$

$3x + 2\left(-\dfrac{3}{2}x + 4\right) = -1$

$3x - 3x + 8 = -1$

$8 \neq -1$

No solution; inconsistent system

27. $10x - 30y = -10$

$2x - 6y = -2$

None of the variables in either equation have a coefficient of 1. You may choose either equation to solve for either variable. Solving the first equation for x gives $x = 3y - 1$. Substitute this value for x into the second equation.

$2x - 6y = -2$

$2(3y - 1) - 6y = -2$

$6y - 2 - 6y = -2$

$-2 = -2$ Identity

Infinitely may solutions

Solution: $\{(x, y) | 2x - 6y = -2\}$; dependent system

29. $2x + y = 3$

$y = -7$

A value for y has been determined. To find a value for x, substitute $y = -7$ into the first equation.

$2x + y = 3$

$2x - 7 = 3$

$2x = 10$

$x = 5$

Solution: $(5, -7)$

31. $x + 2y = -2$

$4x = -2y - 17$

Solving the first equation for x gives $x = -2y - 2$. Substitute the value for x into the second equation.

$4x = -2y - 17$

$4(-2y - 2) = -2y - 17$

$-8y - 8 = -2y - 17$

$-6y - 8 = -17$

$-6y = -9$

$y = \dfrac{3}{2}$

$x + 2y = -2$

$x + 2\left(\dfrac{3}{2}\right) = -2$

$x + 3 = -2$

$x = -5$

Solution: $\left(-5, \dfrac{3}{2}\right)$

33. $y = -\dfrac{1}{2}x - 4$

$y = 4x - 13$

The first equation is solved for y. Substitute this value into the second equation.

$y = 4x - 13$

$-\dfrac{1}{2}x - 4 = 4x - 13$

$-x - 8 = 8x - 26$

$-9x - 8 = -26$

$-9x = -18$

$x = 2$

$y = -\dfrac{1}{2}x - 4$

$y = -\dfrac{1}{2}(2) - 4$

$y = -5$

Solution: $(2, -5)$

35.
$$y = 6$$
$$y - 4 = -2x - 6$$

A value for y has been determined. To find a value for x, substitute $y = 6$ into the second equation.

$$y - 4 = -2x - 6$$
$$6 - 4 = -2x - 6$$
$$2 = -2x - 6$$
$$2x = -8$$
$$x = -4$$

Solution: $(-4, 6)$

37.
$$3x + 2y = 4$$
$$2x - 3y = -6$$

None of the variables in either equation have a coefficient of 1. You may choose either equation to solve for either variable. Solving the first equation for x gives $x = -\dfrac{2}{3}y + \dfrac{4}{3}$. Substitute this value for x into the second equation.

$$2x - 3y = -6$$
$$2\left(-\frac{2}{3}y + \frac{4}{3}\right) - 3y = -6$$
$$-\frac{4}{3}y + \frac{8}{3} - 3y = -6$$
$$-4y + 8 - 9y = -18$$
$$-13y + 8 = -18$$
$$-13y = -26$$
$$y = 2$$

$$3x + 2y = 4$$
$$3x + 2(2) = 4$$
$$3x = 0$$
$$x = 0$$

Solution: $(0, 2)$

39.
$$y = 0.25x + 1$$
$$-x + 4y = 4$$

The first equation is solved for y. Substitute this value into the second equation.

$$-x + 4y = 4$$
$$-x + 4(0.25x + 1) = 4$$
$$-x + x + 4 = 4$$
$$4 = 4 \quad \text{Identity}$$

Infinitely many solutions
Solution: $\{(x, y) | y = 0.25x + 1\}$; dependent system

41.
$$11x + 6y = 17$$
$$5x - 4y = 1$$

None of the variables in either equation has a coefficient of 1. You may choose either equation to solve for either variable. Solving the second equation for x gives $x = \dfrac{4}{5}y + \dfrac{1}{5}$.

Substitute this value for x into the first equation.

$$11x + 6y = 17$$
$$11\left(\frac{4}{5}y + \frac{1}{5}\right) + 6y = 17$$
$$\frac{44}{5}y + \frac{11}{5} + 6y = 17$$
$$44y + 11 + 30y = 85$$
$$74y + 11 = 85$$
$$74y = 74$$
$$y = 1$$

$$5x - 4y = 1$$
$$5x - 4(1) = 1$$
$$5x = 5$$
$$x = 1$$

Solution: $(1, 1)$

43. $x + 2y = 4$
$\qquad 4y = -2x - 8$

Solving the first equation for x gives $x = -2y + 4$. Substitute the value for x into the second equation.

$4y = -2x - 8$
$4y = -2(-2y + 4) - 8$
$4y = 4y - 8 - 8$
$4y = 4y - 16$
$\quad 0 \neq -16$

Contradiction; no solution; inconsistent system

45. $\quad 2x = 3 - y$
$\quad x + y = 4$

Solving the second equation for y gives $y = -x + 4$. Substitute the value for y into the first equation.

$2x = 3 - y$
$2x = 3 - (-x + 4)$
$2x = 3 + x - 4$
$2x = x - 1$
$\quad x = -1$
$\quad x + y = 4$
$-1 + y = 4$
$\quad\quad y = 5$

Solution: $(-1, 5)$

47. $\dfrac{x}{3} + \dfrac{y}{2} = -4$
$x - 3y = 6$

Solving the second equation for x gives $x = 3y + 6$. Substitute the value for x into the first equation.

$$\frac{x}{3} + \frac{y}{2} = -4$$
$$\frac{3y + 6}{3} + \frac{y}{2} = -4$$
$$2(3y + 6) + 3y = -24$$
$$6y + 12 + 3y = -24$$
$$9y + 12 = -24$$
$$9y = -36$$
$$y = -4$$
$$x - 3y = 6$$
$$x - 3(-4) = 6$$
$$x = -6$$

Solution: $(-6, -4)$

49. Let x represent one number. Let y represent the other number. The statement "two numbers have a sum of 106" translates to the equation $x + y = 106$. The statement "one number is 10 less than the other" translates to the equation $x = y - 10$.

$x + y = 106$
$\quad x = y - 10$

The second equation is solved for x. Substitute this value into the first equation.

$x + y = 106$
$y - 10 + y = 106$
$2y - 10 = 106$
$2y = 116$
$y = 58$

$x = y - 10$
$x = 58 - 10$
$x = 48$

The numbers are 48 and 58.

51. Let x represent one positive number. Let y represent the other positive number. The statement "the difference between two positive numbers is 26" translates to the equation $x - y = 26$. The statement "the larger number is three times the smaller" translates to the equation $x = 3y$.

$$x - y = 26$$
$$x = 3y$$

The second equation is solved for x. Substitute this value into the first equation.

$$3y - y = 26$$
$$2y = 26$$
$$y = 13$$
$$x = 3(13)$$
$$x = 39$$

The numbers are 13 and 39.

53. Let x represent the measure of one angle. Let y represent the measure of the second angle. The statement "two angles are supplementary" translates to the equation $x + y = 180$. The statement "one angle is 15° more than 10 times the other angle" translates to the equation $x = 10y + 15$.

$$x + y = 180$$
$$x = 10y + 15$$

The second equation is solved for x. Substitute this value into the first equation.

$$x + y = 180$$
$$10y + 15 + y = 180$$
$$11y + 15 = 180$$
$$11y = 165$$
$$y = 15$$
$$x = 10y + 15$$
$$x = 10(15) + 15$$
$$x = 165$$

The measures of the angles are 165° and 15°.

55. Let x represent the measure of the first angle. Let y represent the measure of the second angle. The statement "two angles are complementary" translates to the equation $x + y = 90$. The statement "one angle is 10° more than 3 times the other angle" translates to the equation $x = 3y + 10$.

$$x + y = 90$$
$$x = 3y + 10$$

The second equation is solved for x. Substitute this value into the first equation.

$$x + y = 90$$
$$3y + 10 + y = 90$$
$$4y = 80$$
$$y = 20$$
$$x = 3y + 10$$
$$x = 3(20) + 10$$
$$x = 70$$

The measures of the angles are 70° and 20°.

57. Let x represent the measure of one of the acute angles. Let y represent the measure of the other acute angle. The sum of the measures of the angles of a triangle is 180°. In a right triangle one of the angles is a right angle measuring 90°. Thus the sum of the measures of the other two angles is 90°. From this information comes the first equation: $x + y = 90$. The statement "one of the acute angles is 6° less than the other acute angle" translates to the equation $x = y - 6$.

$$x + y = 90$$
$$x = y - 6$$

The second equation is solved for x. Substitute this value into the first equation.

$$x + y = 90$$
$$y - 6 + y = 90$$
$$2y - 6 = 90$$
$$2y = 96$$
$$y = 48$$
$$x = y - 6$$
$$x = 48 - 6$$
$$x = 42$$

The measures of the angles are 42° and 48°.

59.
$$y = 2x + 3$$
$$-4x + 2y = 6$$

Answers may vary. It is stated that the system is dependent. Therefore, x can equal any real number. Pick a value for x, substitute that value into one of the equations and determine a corresponding value for y.

If $x = 0$, then $y = 2(0) + 3 = 3$. (0, 3)
If $x = 1$, then $y = 2(1) + 3 = 5$. (1, 5)
If $x = -1$, then $y = 2(-1) + 3 = 1$. (-1, 1)

Section 4.3 Practice Exercises

1. $2x + y = -7$
$$x - 10 = 4y$$

Graphing method: Rewrite both equations in slope-intercept form.
$$y = -2x - 7$$
$$y = \frac{1}{4}x - \frac{5}{2}$$

The x- and y-intercepts of $2x + y = -7$ are (-3.5, 0) and (0, -7). The x- and y-intercepts of $x - 10 = 4y$ are (10, 0) and (0, -2.5). Use these points to graph the equations.
Point of intersection: (-2, -3).

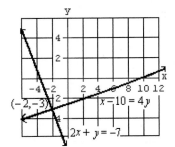

(b) Substitution method: Solving the first equation for y gives $y = -2x - 7$.
$$2x + y = -7$$
$$x - 10 = 4y$$

Substitute this value of y into the second equation and solve the resulting equation for x.
$$x - 10 = 4y$$
$$x - 10 = 4(-2x - 7)$$
$$x - 10 = -8x - 28$$
$$9x = -18$$
$$x = -2$$

$$2(-2) + y = -7$$
$$-4 + y = -7$$
$$y = -3$$
Solution: (-2, -3

(c) $2x + y = -7$
$$x - 10 = 4y$$

Writing the second equation in standard form gives $x - 4y = 10$. Neither set of coefficients are opposites. Multiplying the first equation by 4 will result in opposite coefficients on y.
$$8x + 4y = -28$$
$$\underline{x - 4y = 10}$$
$$9x = -18$$
$$x = -2$$

$$2x + y = -7$$
$$2(-2) + y = -7$$
$$-4 + y = -7$$
$$y = -3$$
Solution: (-2, -3)

3.
$$x = y + 1$$
$$-x + 2y = 0 \quad \text{Ordered pair: (3, 2)}$$

$$3 \overset{?}{=} 2 + 1 \quad \checkmark$$

$$-3 + 2(2) \overset{?}{=} 0 \quad \text{Not a solution}$$

No; since the ordered pair is not a solution to the second equation, it is not a solution of the system.

5.
$$x = 2y - 11$$
$$-x + 5y = 23 \quad \text{Ordered pair: } (-3, 4)$$

$$-3 \overset{?}{=} 2(4) - 11 \ \checkmark$$
$$-(-3) + 5(4) \overset{?}{=} 23 \ \checkmark \quad \text{A solution}$$

Yes; since the ordered pair is a solution to both equations, it is a solution of the system.

7. (a) True. This will create opposite coefficients on the x-variable.

(b) False. Remember, the goal is to create opposite coefficients on the y-variable. Multiply the first equation by 8 and the second equation by 5.

9. (a) x-variable is easier, because one coefficient is a multiple of the other

(b) $-2x + 5y = -15$
$$6x - 7y = 21$$

Both equations are already written in standard form. There are no fractions or decimals. Neither set of coefficients is opposites. Multiplying the first equation by 3 will create opposite coefficients on x.

$$-6x + 15y = -45$$
$$\underline{6x - 7y = 21}$$
$$8y = -24$$
$$y = -3$$

$$-2x + 5(-3) = -15$$
$$-2x - 15 = -15$$
$$-2x = 0$$
$$x = 0$$
Solution: $(0, -3)$

11. $2x - 3y = 11$
$$-4x + 3y = -19$$

Both equations are already written in standard form. Coefficients on y are opposites. Add the two equations and then solve the resulting equation.

$$2x - 3y = 11$$
$$\underline{-4x + 3y = -19}$$
$$-2x = -8$$
$$x = 4$$

$$2(4) - 3y = 11$$
$$8 - 3y = 11$$
$$-3y = 3$$
$$y = -1$$
Solution: $(4, -1)$

13. $-2u + 6v = 10$
$$-2u + v = -5$$

Both equations are already written in standard form. Neither set of coefficients are opposites. Multiplying the first equation by -1 will result in opposite coefficients on u.

$$2u - 6v = -10$$
$$\underline{-2u + v = -5}$$
$$-5v = -15$$
$$v = 3$$

$$-2u + 6(3) = 10$$
$$-2u + 18 = 10$$
$$-2u = -8$$
$$u = 4$$
Solution: $(4, 3)$

15. $5m - 2n = 4$
$3m + n = 9$
Both equations are already written in standard form. Neither set of coefficients is opposites. Multiplying the second equation by 2 will result in opposite coefficients on n.
$5m - 2n = 4$
$\underline{6m + 2n = 18}$
$11m = 22$
$m = 2$

$5(2) - 2n = 4$
$10 - 2n = 4$
$-2n = -6$
$n = 3$
Solution: $(2, 3)$

17. $7a + 2b = -1$
$3a - 4b = 19$
Both equations are already written in standard form. Neither set of coefficients is opposites. Multiplying the first equation by 2 will result in opposite coefficients on b.
$14a + 4b = -2$
$\underline{3a - 4b = 19}$
$17a = 17$
$a = 1$

$7(1) + 2b = -1$
$7 + 2b = -1$
$2b = -8$
$b = -4$
Solution: $(1, -4)$

19. $2s + 3t = -1$
$5s = 2t + 7$
Writing the second equation in standard form yields $5s - 2t = 7$.

$2s + 3t = -1$
$5s - 2t = 7$

Neither set of coefficients is opposites. Multiplying the first equation by 2 and the second equation by 3 will result in opposite coefficients on t.
$4s + 6t = -2$
$\underline{15s - 6t = 21}$
$19s = 19$
$s = 1$

$2s + 3t = -1$
$2(1) + 3t = -1$
$2 + 3t = -1$
$3t = -3$
$t = -1$
Solution: $(1, -1)$

21. $4k - 2r = -4$
$3k - 5r = 18$
Both equations are already written in standard form. Neither set of coefficients is opposites. Multiplying the first equation by 5 and the second equation by -2 will result in opposite coefficients on r.
$20k - 10r = -20$
$\underline{-6k + 10r = -36}$
$14k = -56$
$k = -4$

$4k - 2r = -4$
$4(-4) - 2r = -4$
$-16 - 2r = -4$
$-2r = 12$
$r = -6$
Solution: $(-4, -6)$

23. $6x + 6y = 8$

$9x - 18y = -3$

Both equations are already written in standard form. Neither set of coefficients is opposites. Multiplying the first equation by 3 will result in opposite coefficients on y.

$18x + 18y = 24$

$\underline{9x - 18y = -3}$

$27x = 21$

$x = \dfrac{21}{27}$

$x = \dfrac{7}{9}$

$6x + 6y = 8$

$6\left(\dfrac{7}{9}\right) + 6y = 8$

$\dfrac{14}{3} + 6y = 8$

$6y = \dfrac{10}{3}$

$y = \dfrac{10}{18}$

$y = \dfrac{5}{9}$

Solution: $\left(\dfrac{7}{9}, \dfrac{5}{9}\right)$

25. Since the statement is a contradiction, the system will have no solutions. The lines are parallel.

27. Since the statement is an identity, the system will have infinitely many solutions. The lines coincide.

29. The system will have one solution. The lines intersect at a point whose x-coordinate is 0.

31. $-2x + y = -5$

$8x - 4y = 12$

Both equations are already written in standard form. Neither set of coefficients is opposites. Multiplying the first equation by 4 will result in opposite coefficients on y.

$-8x + 4y = -20$

$\underline{8x - 4y = 12}$

$0 = -8$

No solution; inconsistent system

33. $x + 2y = 2$

$-3x - 6y = -6$

Both equations are already written in standard form. Neither set of coefficients is opposites. Multiplying the first equation by 3 will result in opposite coefficients on x.

$3x + 6y = 6$

$\underline{-3x - 6y = -6}$

$0 = 0$ Identity

Infinitely many solutions

Solution: $(x, y) | x + 2y = 2$; dependent system

35. $3a + 2b = 11$

$7a - 3b = -5$

Both equations are already written in standard form. Neither set of coefficients is opposites. However, the signs of the coefficients on b are opposites. Choose to eliminate b by multiplying the first equation by 3 and the second equation by 2 to obtain opposite coefficients on b.

$9a + 6b = 33$

$\underline{14a - 6b = -10}$

$23a = 23$

$a = 1$

$3(1) + 2b = 11$

$3 + 2b = 11$

$2b = 8$

$b = 4$

Solution: $(1, 4)$

37. $3x - 5y = 7$
$5x - 2y = -1$

Both equations are already written in standard form. Neither set of coefficients is opposites. Neither set of coefficients has opposite signs. Choose either variable to eliminate. x will be the chosen variable in this solution. To obtain opposite coefficients on x multiply the first equation by 5 and the second equation by -3.

$15x - 25y = 35$
$\underline{-15x + 6y = 3}$
$-19y = 38$
$y = -2$

$3x - 5(-2) = 7$
$3x + 10 = 7$
$3x = -3$
$x = -1$
Solution: $(-1, -2)$

39. $2x + 2 = -3y + 9$
$3x - 10 = -4y$

Write both equations in standard form.
$2x + 3y = 7$
$3x + 4y = 10$

Neither set of coefficients are opposites of each other. Neither variable has coefficients with opposite signs. Choose either variable to eliminate. x will be the chosen variable in this solution. To obtain opposite coefficients on x multiply the first equation by -3 and the second equation by 2.

$-6x - 9y = -21$
$\underline{6x + 8y = 20}$
$-y = -1$
$y = 1$

$3x - 10 = -4(1)$
$3x - 10 = -4$
$3x = 6$
$x = 2$
Solution: $(2, 1)$

41. $4x - 5y = 0$
$8(x - 1) = 10y$

Write the second equation in standard form.
$4x - 5y = 0$
$8x - 10y = 8$

The coefficient on x in the second equation is a multiple of the coefficient on x in the first equation. Multiply the first equation by -2 to obtain opposite coefficients on x.

$-8x + 10y = 0$
$\underline{8x - 10y = 8}$
$0 = 8$

No solution; inconsistent system

43. $5x - 2y = 4$
$y = -3x + 9$

Since the second equation is solved for y, use the substitution method by substituting this value for y into the first equation and solving this new equation for x.
$5x - 2(-3x + 9) = 4$
$5x + 6x - 18 = 4$
$11x - 18 = 4$
$11x = 22$
$x = 2$

$y = -3(2) + 9$
$y = 3$
Solution: $(2, 3)$

45. $0.1x + 0.1y = 0.6$

$0.1x - 0.1y = 0.1$

Both equations are written in standard form. The coefficients on y are opposites. Use the addition method. Add the equations and solve the resulting equation.

$0.1x + 0.1y = 0.6$

$\underline{0.1x - 0.1y = 0.1}$

$0.2x \qquad = 0.7$

$\qquad x = 3.5$

$0.1x + 0.1y = 0.6$

$0.1(3.5) + 0.1y = 0.6$

$0.35 + 0.1y = 0.6$

$0.1y = 0.25$

$y = 2.5$

Solution: $(3.5, 2.5)$

47. $3x = 5y - 9$

$2y = 3x + 3$

Since neither equation is solved for x or y, consider using the addition method. Write both equations in standard form.

$3x - 5y = -9$

$-3x + 2y = 3$

The coefficients on x are opposites. Add the two equations and then solve the resulting equation.

$3x - 5y = -9$

$\underline{-3x + 2y = 3}$

$-3y = -6$

$y = 2$

$3x = 5(2) - 9$

$3x = 1$

$x = \dfrac{1}{3}$

Solution: $\left(\dfrac{1}{3}, 2\right)$

49. $y = -5x - 5$

$6x - 3 = -3y$

Since the first equation is solved for y, use the substitution method. Substitute the value of y into the second equation and solve the resulting equation for x.

$6x - 3 = -3(-5x - 5)$

$6x - 3 = 15x + 15$

$-9x = 18$

$x = -2$

$y = -5x - 5$

$y = -5(-2) - 5$

$y = 5$

Solution: $(-2, 5)$

51. $x = -\dfrac{1}{2}$

$6x - 5y = -8$

Since the first equation is solved for x, use the substitution method by substituting this value for x into the second equation and solving this new equation for y.

$6\left(-\dfrac{1}{2}\right) - 5y = -8$

$-3 - 5y = -8$

$-5y = -5$

$y = 1$

Solution: $\left(-\dfrac{1}{2}, 1\right)$

53. $0.02x + 0.04y = 0.12$
$0.03x - 0.05y = -0.15$

Both equations are written in standard form. Neither set of coefficients are opposites of each other. Multiplying the first equation by 5 and the second equation by 4 will result in opposite coefficients on y.

$\begin{array}{r} 0.1x + 0.2y = 0.6 \\ 0.12x - 0.2y = -0.6 \\ \hline 0.22x = 0 \\ x = 0 \end{array}$

$0.02x + 0.04y = 0.12$
$0.02(0) + 0.04y = 0.12$
$y = 3$

Solution: (0, 3)

55. $8x - 16y = 24$
$2x - 4y = 0$

Since both equations are in standard form, use the addition method. The coefficient on x in the first equation is a multiple of the coefficient on x in the second equation. Multiply the second equation by -4 to obtain opposite coefficients on x.

$\begin{array}{r} 8x - 16y = 24 \\ -8x + 16y = 0 \\ \hline 0 = 24 \end{array}$

No solution; inconsistent system

57. $\dfrac{m}{2} + \dfrac{n}{5} = \dfrac{13}{10}$
$3m - 3n = m - 10$

Since neither equation is solved for m and n, consider using the addition method. Write both equations in standard form.

$5m + 2n = 13$
$2m - 3n = -10$

Neither set of coefficients are opposites of each other. The n-variable has coefficients with opposite signs. To obtain opposite coefficients on n multiply the first equation by 3 and the second equation by 2.

$\begin{array}{r} 15m + 6n = 39 \\ 4m - 6n = -20 \\ \hline 19m = 19 \\ m = 1 \end{array}$

$3(1) - 3n = 1 - 10$
$3 - 3n = -9$
$-3n = -12$
$n = 4$

Solution: (1, 4)

59. $2m - 6n = m + 4$
$3m + 8 = 5m - n$

Since neither equation is solved for m or n, consider using the addition method. Write both equations in standard form.

$m - 6n = 4$
$-2m + n = -8$

The signs of the m-variable are opposite. Multiply the first equation by 2 to obtain opposite coefficients on m.

$\begin{array}{r} 2m - 12n = 8 \\ -2m + n = -8 \\ \hline -11n = 0 \\ n = 0 \end{array}$

$3m + 8 = 5m - 0$
$-2m + 8 = 0$
$-2m = -8$
$m = 4$

Solution: (4, 0)

61. $9a - 2b = 8$

$18a + 6 = 4b + 22$

Since neither equation is solved for a or b, consider using the addition method. Write both equations in standard form.

$9a - 2b = 8$

$18a - 4b = 16$

Neither variable has opposite signs nor opposite coefficients. The coefficient on a in the second equation is a multiple of the coefficient in the first equation. Multiply the first equation by -2 to obtain opposite coefficients on a.

$-18a + 4b = -16$

$\underline{18a - 4b = 16}$

$0 = 0 \qquad$ Identity

Infinitely many solutions

Solution: $(a, b) | 9a - 2b = 8$; dependent system

63. $6x - 5y = 7$

$4x - 6y = 7$

Both equations are already written in standard form. Neither set of coefficients is opposites. Multiplying the first equation by 2 and the second equation by -3 will result in opposite coefficients on x.

$12x - 10y = 14$

$\underline{-12x + 18y = -21}$

$8y = -7$

$y = -\dfrac{7}{8}$

$6x - 5y = 7$

$6x - 5\left(-\dfrac{7}{8}\right) = 7$

$6x + \dfrac{35}{8} = 7$

$6x = \dfrac{21}{8}$

$x = \dfrac{21}{48}$

$x = \dfrac{7}{16}$

Solution: $\left(\dfrac{7}{16}, -\dfrac{7}{8}\right)$

65. Let x represent the first positive number. Let y represent the second positive number. The statement "difference of two positive numbers is 2" translates to the equation $x - y = 2$. The statement "sum of the numbers is 36" translates to the equation $x + y = 36$.

$x - y = 2$

$x + y = 36$

The coefficients on y are opposites. Add the two equations and solve the resulting equation.

$x - y = 2$

$\underline{x + y = 36}$

$2x = 38$

$x = 19$

$19 + y = 36$

$y = 17$

The two positive numbers are 19 and 17.

67. Let x represent the smaller number. Let y represent the larger number. The statement "six times the smaller of two numbers minus the larger number is -9" translates to the equation $6x - y = -9$. The statement "ten times the smaller number plus five times the larger number is 5" translates to the equation $10x + 5y = 5$.

$6x - y = -9$

$10x + 5y = 5$

Since the signs on y are opposites, multiply the first equation by 5 to obtain opposite coefficients on y.

$30x - 5y = -45$

$\underline{10x + 5y = 5}$

$40x = -40$

$x = -1$

$6(-1) - y = -9$

$-y = -3$

$y = 3$

The two numbers are -1 and 3.

69. Let x represent the first angle. Let y represent the second angle. The statement "the difference of an angle and twice another angle is 42" translates to the equation $x - 2y = 42$. If x and y are supplementary, it is understood that $x + y = 180$.

$$x - 2y = 42$$
$$x + y = 180$$

Since the signs on y are opposites, multiply the second equation by 2 to obtain opposite coefficients on y.

$$x - 2y = 42$$
$$\underline{2x + 2y = 360}$$
$$3x = 402$$
$$x = 134$$
$$134 + y = 180$$
$$y = 46$$

The angles are 134 and 46 degrees.

71. $\quad 3x + y = 6$
$\quad\quad -2x + 2y = 4$

(a) Graphing Method: Write the equations in slope-intercept form.

$$y = -3x + 6$$
$$y = x + 2$$

The two lines have unequal slopes and they intersect.

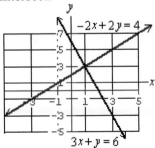

Solution: 1,3

(b) $\quad 3x + y = 6$
$\quad\quad -2x + 2y = 4$

Substitution method: Solving the first equation for y gives $y = -3x + 6$.

Substitute this value of y into the second equation and solve the resulting equation for x.

$$-2x + 2y = 4$$
$$-2x + 2(-3x + 6) = 4$$
$$-2x - 6x + 12 = 4$$
$$-8x = -8$$
$$x = 1$$

Substitute this value of x into the first equation and solve for y.

$$3x + y = 6$$
$$3(1) + y = 6$$
$$3 + y = 6$$
$$y = 3$$

Solution: 1,3

(c) $\quad 3x + y = 6$
$\quad\quad -2x + 2y = 4$

Multiply the first equation by -2 to obtain opposite coefficients on y. Solve for x.

$$-6x - 2y = -12$$
$$\underline{-2x + 2y = 4}$$
$$-8x = -8$$
$$x = 1$$

Substitute this value of x into the first equation and solve for y.

$$3x + y = 6$$
$$3(1) + y = 6$$
$$3 + y = 6$$
$$y = 3$$

Solution: 1,3

73. One line within the system would have to "bend" for the system to have exactly two points of intersection. This is not possible.

75. $4x + Ay = -32$
$Bx + 6y = 18$

If $(-3, 4)$ is a solution to the system then substitute $x = -3$ and $y = 4$ into the equations and solve for A and B.

First equation:
$4(-3) + A(4) = -32$
$-12 + 4A = -32$
$4A = -20$
$A = -5$

Second equation:
$B(-3) + 6(4) = 18$
$-3B + 24 = 18$
$-3B = -6$
$B = 2$

Problem Recognition Exercises

1. Since the equations represent the same line, there are infinitely many solutions.

3. Since the equations represent intersecting lines, there is one solution.

5. Since the equations represent two parallel lines, there is no solution.

7. $\quad\quad x = -2y + 5$
$2x - 4y = 10$

Substitute the value of x into the second equation and solve the resulting equation.

$2x - 4y = 10$
$2(-2y + 5) - 4y = 10$
$-4y + 10 - 4y = 10$
$-8y + 10 = 10$
$-8y = 0$
$y = 0$
$x = -2y + 5$
$x = -2(0) + 5$
$x = 5$
Solution: $(5, 0)$

9. $3x - 2y = 22$
$5x + 2y = 10$

Add the two equations and solve the resulting equation.
$\begin{array}{r} 3x - 2y = 22 \\ 5x + 2y = 10 \\ \hline 8x \quad\quad = 32 \\ x \quad\quad = 4 \end{array}$

$3(4) - 2y = 22$
$12 - 2y = 22$
$-2y = 10$
$y = -5$
Solution: $(4, -5)$

11. $\dfrac{1}{3}x + \dfrac{1}{2}y = \dfrac{2}{3}$
$-\dfrac{2}{3}x + \quad y = -\dfrac{4}{3}$

Rewrite the equations in standard form. Clear the fractions in the first equation by multiplying by 6, in the second equation by multiplying by 3.
$\begin{array}{r} 2x + 3y = 4 \\ -2x + 3y = -4 \\ \hline 6y = 0 \\ y = 0 \end{array}$

$-\dfrac{2}{3}x + y = -\dfrac{4}{3}$
$-\dfrac{2}{3}x + 0 = -\dfrac{4}{3}$
$-\dfrac{2}{3}x = -\dfrac{4}{3}$
$x = 2$
Solution: $(2, 0)$

13. $2c + 7d = -1$
$\qquad c = 2$

A value for c has been determined. To find a value for d, substitute $c = 2$ into the first equation.

$2c + 7d = -1$
$2(2) + 7d = -1$
$4 + 7d = -1$
$7d = -5$
$d = -\dfrac{5}{7}$

Solution: $\left(2, -\dfrac{5}{7}\right)$

15. $y = 0.4x - 0.3$
$-4x + 10y = 20$

Substitute the value for y into the second equation and solve the resulting equation.

$-4x + 10(0.4x - 0.3) = 20$
$-4x + 4x - 3 = 20$
$-3 \neq 20$

No solution; inconsistent system

17. $3a + 7b = -3$
$-11a + 3b = 11$

Either method is appropriate. Since the equations are in standard form, the addition method will be used. To obtain opposite coefficients on a, multiply the first equation by 11 and the second equation by 3.

$33a + 77b = -33$
$-33a + 9b = 33$
$\overline{\qquad 86b = 0}$
$b = 0$

$3a + 7b = -3$
$3a + 7(0) = -3$
$3a = -3$
$a = -1$

Solution: $-1, 0$

19. $y = 2x - 14$
$4x - 2y = 28$

Rewrite the equations in standard form,

$-2x + y = -14$
$4x - 2y = 28$

To obtain opposite coefficients on x, multiply the first equation by 2.

$-4x + 2y = -28$
$4x - 2y = 28$
$\overline{\qquad 0 = 0} \qquad$ Identity

Infinitely many solutions

Solution: $\{(x, y) | y = 2x - 14\}$; dependent system

21. $x + y = 3200$
$0.06x + 0.04y = 172$

Rewrite the equations in standard form. Clear the decimals in the second equation by multiplying it by 100.

$x + y = 3200$
$6x + 4y = 17,200$

To obtain opposite coefficients on x, multiply the first equation by -6.

$-6x - 6y = -19,200$
$6x + 4y = 17,200$
$\overline{\qquad -2y = -2000}$
$y = 1000$

$x + y = 3200$
$x + 1000 = 3200$
$x = 2200$

Solution: $(2200, 1000)$

23. $3x + y - 7 = x - 4$
$3x - 4y + 4 = -6y + 5$

Rewrite the equations in standard form.

$2x + y = 3$
$3x + 2y = 1$

To obtain opposite coefficients on y, multiply the first equation by -2.

$-4x - 2y = -6$
$\underline{3x + 2y = 1}$
$-x = -5$
$x = 5$

$3x + y - 7 = x - 4$
$3(5) + y - 7 = 5 - 4$
$y + 8 = 1$
$y = -7$

Solution: $(5, -7)$

25. $3x - 6y = -1$
$9x + 4y = 8$

Either method is appropriate. Since the equations are in standard form, the addition method will be used. To obtain opposite coefficients on x, multiply the first equation by -3.

$-9x + 18y = 3$
$\underline{9x + 4y = 8}$
$22y = 11$
$y = \dfrac{1}{2}$

$3x - 6y = -1$
$3x - 6\left(\dfrac{1}{2}\right) = -1$
$3x - 3 = -1$
$3x = 2$
$x = \dfrac{2}{3}$

Solution: $\left(\dfrac{2}{3}, \dfrac{1}{2}\right)$

Section 4.4 Practice Exercises

1. $-2x + y = 6$
$2x + y = 2$

(a) Graphing Method: The x- and y-intercepts of $-2x + y = 6$ are $(-3, 0)$ and $(0, 6)$. The x- and y-intercepts of $2x + y = 2$ are $(1, 0)$ and $(0, 2)$. Use these points to graph the equations.

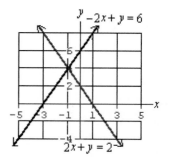

Point of intersection: $(-1, 4)$

(b) $-2x + y = 6$
$2x + y = 2$

Substitution method: Solving the first equation for y gives $y = 2x + 6$.

Substitute this value of y into the second equation and solve the resulting equation for x.

$2x + y = 2$
$2x + 2x + 6 = 2$
$4x + 6 = 2$
$4x = -4$
$x = -1$

$-2(-1) + y = 6$
$2 + y = 6$
$y = 4$

Solution: $(-1, 4)$

(c) $-2x + y = 6$
$2x + y = 2$

Addition method: The equations of the system are written in standard form. The coefficients on x are opposites. Add the two equations together and solve the resulting equation.

$$\begin{array}{r} -2x + y = 6 \\ 2x + y = 2 \\ \hline 2y = 8 \\ y = 4 \end{array}$$

$-2x + y = 6$
$-2x + 4 = 6$
$-2x = 2$
$x = -1$
Solution: $(-1, 4)$

3. $y = -2x + 6$
$4x - 2y = 8$

(a) Graphing method: The x- and y-intercepts of $y = -2x + 6$ are $(3, 0)$ and $(0, 6)$. the x- and y-intercepts of $4x - 2y = 8$ are $(2, 0)$ and $(0, -4)$. Use these points to graph the equations.

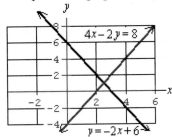

Point of intersection: $\left(\dfrac{5}{2}, 1\right)$

(b) Substitution method: Since the first equation is solved for y, substitute this value into the second equation and solve the resulting equation for x.

$$4x - 2y = 8$$
$$4x - 2(-2x + 6) = 8$$
$$4x + 4x - 12 = 8$$
$$8x - 12 = 8$$
$$8x = 20$$
$$x = \frac{20}{8} = \frac{5}{2}$$

$y = -2x + 6$
$y = -2\left(\dfrac{5}{2}\right) + 6$
$y = 1$

Solution: $\left(\dfrac{5}{2}, 1\right)$

(c) Addition method: Rewrite the equations in standard form.

$2x + y = 6$
$4x - 2y = 8$

Since the y-variables have opposite signs, multiply the first equation by 2 to obtain opposite coefficients on y.

$$\begin{array}{r} 4x + 2y = 12 \\ 4x - 2y = 8 \\ \hline 8x = 20 \\ x = \frac{20}{8} = \frac{5}{2} \end{array}$$

$4x - 2y = 8$
$4\left(\dfrac{5}{2}\right) - 2y = 8$
$10 - 2y = 8$
$-2y = -2$
$y = 1$

Solution: $\left(\dfrac{5}{2}, 1\right)$

5. Let x represent one number. Let y represent the other number. The statement "one number is eight more than twice another" translates to the equation $x = 2y + 8$. The statement "their sum is 20" translates to the equation $x + y = 20$.

$x = 2y + 8$
$x + y = 20$

Since one equation is solved for x, use the substitution method. Substitute this value for x into the second equation and solve the resulting equation for y.

$$x + y = 20$$
$$2y + 8 + y = 20$$
$$3y + 8 = 20$$
$$3y = 12$$
$$y = 4$$

$x = 2y + 8$
$x = 2(4) + 8$
$x = 8 + 8$
$x = 16$

The numbers are 4 and 16.

7. Let x represent the measure of one of the angles. Let y represent the measure of the other angle. The statement "two angles are complementary" translates to the equation $x + y = 90$. The statement "one angle is 10° less than 9 times the other" translates to the equation $x = 9y - 10$.

$x + y = 90$
$x = 9y - 10$

Since one equation is solved for x, use the substitution method. Substitute this value for x into the first equation and solve the resulting equation for y.

$$x + y = 90$$
$$9y - 10 + y = 90$$
$$10y - 10 = 90$$
$$10y = 100$$
$$y = 10$$

$x = 9y - 10$
$x = 9(10) - 10$
$x = 80$

The measures of the angles are 80° and 10°.

9. Let v represent the cost of renting one video game. Let d represent the cost of renting one DVD.

$$\begin{pmatrix} \text{Cost of} \\ \text{two} \\ \text{video games} \end{pmatrix} + \begin{pmatrix} \text{Cost of} \\ \text{three} \\ \text{DVD's} \end{pmatrix} = \begin{pmatrix} \text{Total} \\ \text{cost} \end{pmatrix}$$

$$\begin{pmatrix} \text{Cost of} \\ \textit{one} \\ \text{video games} \end{pmatrix} + \begin{pmatrix} \text{Cost of} \\ \text{two} \\ \text{DVDs} \end{pmatrix} = \begin{pmatrix} \text{Total} \\ \text{cost} \end{pmatrix}$$

$2v + 3d = 34.10$
$v + 2d = 19.80$

Since the equations are in standard form and the coefficient on v in the second equation is one, use the addition method by multiplying the second equation by -2.

$$2v + 3d = 34.10$$
$$\underline{-2v - 4d = -39.60}$$
$$-d = -5.50$$
$$d = 5.50$$

$$v + 2d = 19.80$$
$$v + 2(5.50) = 19.80$$
$$v + 11.00 = 19.80$$
$$v = 8.80$$

It costs \$8.80 to rent a video game and \$5.50 to rent a DVD.

11. Let t represent the cost of one share of technology stock. Let m represent the cost of one share of mutual fund.

$$\begin{pmatrix} \text{Cost of} \\ \text{100 shares} \\ \text{technology} \\ \text{stock} \end{pmatrix} + \begin{pmatrix} \text{Cost of} \\ \text{200 shares} \\ \text{mutual} \\ \text{fund} \end{pmatrix} = \begin{pmatrix} \text{Total} \\ \text{cost} \end{pmatrix}$$

$$\begin{pmatrix} \text{Cost of} \\ \text{300 shares} \\ \text{technology} \\ \text{stock} \end{pmatrix} + \begin{pmatrix} \text{Cost of} \\ \text{50 shares} \\ \text{mutual} \\ \text{fund} \end{pmatrix} = \begin{pmatrix} \text{Total} \\ \text{cost} \end{pmatrix}$$

$$100t + 200m = 3800$$
$$300t + 50m = 5350$$

Since the equations are written in standard form, use the addition method. To obtain opposite coefficients on t, multiply the first equation by -3.

$$\begin{aligned} -300t - 600m &= -11400 \\ \underline{300t + 50m} &= \underline{5350} \\ -550m &= -6050 \\ m &= 11 \end{aligned}$$

$$100t + 200m = 3800$$
$$100t + 200(11) = 3800$$
$$100t + 2200 = 3800$$
$$100t = 1600$$
$$t = 16$$

Technology stock costs $16 per share and the mutual fund costs $11 per shar

13. Let x represent the number of 44¢ stamps. Let y represent the number of 61¢ stamps.

$$\begin{pmatrix} \text{Number of} \\ 44¢ \\ \text{stamps} \end{pmatrix} + \begin{pmatrix} \text{Number of} \\ 61¢ \\ \text{stamps} \end{pmatrix} = \begin{pmatrix} \text{Total number} \\ \text{of stamps} \end{pmatrix}$$

$$\begin{pmatrix} \text{Cost of} \\ \text{x} \\ 44¢ \text{ stamps} \end{pmatrix} + \begin{pmatrix} \text{Cost of} \\ \text{y} \\ 61¢ \text{ stamps} \end{pmatrix} = \begin{pmatrix} \text{Total} \\ \text{cost} \end{pmatrix}$$

$$0.44x + 0.61y = 22.70$$
$$x + y = 50$$

Since the equations are in standard form and the coefficient on x in the second equation is one, use the addition method by multiplying the second equation by -0.44.

$$\begin{aligned} 0.44x + 0.61y &= 23.70 \\ \underline{-0.44x - 0.44y} &= \underline{-22.0} \\ 0.17y &= 1.70 \\ y &= 10 \end{aligned}$$

$$x + y = 50$$
$$x + 10 = 50$$
$$x = 40$$

Patricia bought forty 44¢ stamps and ten 61¢ stamps.

15. Let x represent the amount Shanelle invested in the 10% account. Let y represent the amount Shanelle invested in the 7% account.

	10% Account	7% Account	Total
Principal invested	x	y	$10,000
Interest earned	0.10x	0.07y	$805

$$x + y = 10,000$$
$$0.1x + 0.07y = 805$$

Since the equations are in standard form and the coefficient on x in the first equation is one, use the addition method by multiplying the second equation by -0.1.

$$\begin{aligned} -0.1x - 0.1y &= -1000 \\ \underline{0.1x + 0.07y} &= \underline{805} \\ -0.03y &= -195 \\ y &= 6500 \end{aligned}$$

$$x + 6500 = 10,000$$
$$x = 3500$$

Shanelle invested $3500 in the 10% account and $6500 in the 7% account.

17. Let x represent the amount borrowed at 9%. Let y represent the amount borrowed at 6%.

	9% account	6% account	Total
Amount borrowed	x	Y	$12,000
Interest charged	$0.09x$	$0.06y$	$810

$$x + y = 12,000$$
$$0.09x + 0.06y = 810$$

Since the equations are in standard form and the coefficient on x in the first equation is 1, use the addition method by multiplying the first equation by −0.09.

$$-0.09x + (-0.09y) = -1080$$
$$\underline{0.09x + 0.06y = 810}$$
$$-0.03y = -270$$
$$y = 9000$$

$$x + 9000 = 12,000$$
$$x = 3000$$

$9000 is borrowed at 6%, and $3000 is borrowed at 9%.

19. Let x represent the amount you invest in the bond fund that returns 8%. Let y represent the amount you invest in the stock fund that will return 12%.

	8% bond fund	12% stock fund	Total
Principle invested	x	y	$30000
Interest earned	$0.08x$	$0.12y$	$3120

$$x + y = 30000$$
$$0.08x + 0.12y = 3120$$

Since the equations are in standard form and the coefficient on x in the first equation is 1, use the addition method by multiplying the first equation by −0.08.

$$-0.08x - 0.08y = -2400$$
$$\underline{0.08x + 0.12y = 3120}$$
$$0.04y = 720$$
$$y = 18000$$

$$x + 18000 = 30000$$
$$x = 12000$$

$12000 must be invested in the bond fund that returns 8% and $18000 invested in the stock fund that returns 12%.

21. Let x represent the amount of 50% disinfectant solution. Let y represent the amount of 40% disinfectant solution.

	50% Mixture	40% Mixture	46% Mixture
Amount of solution	x	y	25
Amount of disinfectant	$0.50x$	$0.40y$	$0.46(25)$

$$x + y = 25$$
$$0.5x + 0.4y = 11.5$$

Since the equations are in standard form and the coefficient on x is one, use the addition method by multiplying the first equation by −0.5.

$$-0.5x - 0.5y = -12.5$$
$$\underline{0.5x + 0.4y = 11.5}$$
$$-0.1y = -1$$
$$y = 10$$

$$x + 10 = 25$$
$$x = 15$$

15 gallons of 50% mixture should be mixed with 10 gallons of 40% mixture.

23. Let x represent the amount of 45% disinfectant solution. Let y represent the amount of 30% disinfectant solution.

	45% Mixture	30% Mixture	39% Mixture
Amount of solution	x	Y	20
Amount of disinfectant	$0.45(x)$	$0.30(y)$	$0.39(20)$

$$x + y = 20$$
$$0.45x + 0.3y = 7.8$$

Since the equations are in standard from and the coefficient on x is one, use the addition method by multiplying the first equation by -0.45.

$$
\begin{aligned}
-0.45x - 0.45y &= -9.0 \\
0.45x + 0.3y &= 7.8 \\
\hline
-0.15y &= -1.2 \\
y &= 8
\end{aligned}
$$

$$x + 8 = 20$$
$$x = 12$$

12 gallons of the 45% disinfectant solution should be mixed with 8 gallons of the 30% disinfectant mixture.

25. Let x represent the amount of 13% salt solution. Let y represent the amount of 18% salt solution.

	13% Mixture	18% Mixture	16% Mixture
Amount of solution	x	y	50
Amount of salt	$0.13x$	$0.18y$	$50(0.16)$

$$x + y = 50$$
$$0.13x + 0.18y = 8$$

Since the equations are in standard form and the coefficient on x is one, use the addition method by multiplying the first equation by -0.13.

$$
\begin{aligned}
-0.13x - 0.13y &= -6.5 \\
0.13x + 0.18y &= 8 \\
\hline
0.05y &= 1.5 \\
y &= 30
\end{aligned}
$$

$$x + 30 = 50$$
$$x = 20$$

20 mL of the 13% salt solution should be mixed with 30 mL of the 18% salt solution.

27. Let x represent the speed of the boat in still water. Let y represent the speed of the current.

	Distance	Rate	Time
Downstream	16	$x + y$	2
Return	16	$x - y$	4

$$2x + 2y = 16$$
$$4x - 4y = 16$$

Since the equations are in standard form and the coefficients on y have opposite signs, use the addition method by multiplying the first equation by 2.

$$
\begin{aligned}
4x + 4y &= 32 \\
4x - 4y &= 16 \\
\hline
8x &= 48 \\
x &= 6
\end{aligned}
$$

$$2(6) + 2y = 16$$
$$2y = 4$$
$$y = 2$$

The speed of the boat in still water is 6 mph and the speed of the current is 2 mph.

29. Let x represent the speed of the plane in still air. Let y represent the speed of the wind.

	Distance	Rate	Time
Flying with the wind	960	$x + y$	3
Flying against the wind	840	$x - y$	3

$3x + 3y = 960$
$3x - 3y = 840$

Since the equations are in standard form and the coefficients on y are opposites, use the addition method.

$$\begin{array}{l} 3x + 3y = 960 \\ \underline{3x - 3y = 840} \\ 6x \quad\quad = 1800 \\ \quad x \quad\quad = 300 \end{array}$$

$3(300) + 3y = 960$
$900 + 3y = 960$
$3y = 60$
$y = 20$

The speed of the plane in still air is 300 mph, and the wind is 20 mph.

31. Let p represent the speed of the plane in still air. Let w represent the speed of the wind.

	Distance	Rate	Time
With the wind	3600	$p + w$	6
Against the wind	3600	$p - w$	8

$3600 = 6(p + w)$
$3600 = 8(p - w)$

$3600 = 6p + 6w$
$3600 = 8p - 8w$

Multiply the first equation by 4. Multiply the second equation by -3.

$$\begin{array}{l} 14400 = 24p + 24w \\ \underline{-10800 = -24p + 24w} \\ 3600 = 48w \\ \quad 75 = w \end{array}$$

$3600 = 6p + 6(75)$
$3600 = 6p + 450$
$3150 = 6p$
$525 = p$

The speed of the plane in still air is 525 mph. The speed of the wind is 75 mph

33. Let x represent the number of dimes. Let y represent the number of nickels.

$$\left(\begin{array}{c} \text{number} \\ \text{of nickels} \end{array}\right) = \left(\begin{array}{c} \text{number} \\ \text{of dimes} \end{array}\right) + 5$$

$$\left(\begin{array}{c} \text{value of} \\ \text{dimes} \end{array}\right) + \left(\begin{array}{c} \text{value of} \\ \text{nickels} \end{array}\right) = \left(\begin{array}{c} \text{total} \\ \text{value} \end{array}\right)$$

$y = x + 5$
$0.10x + 0.05y = 2.80$

Since the first equation is solved for y, use the substitution method by substituting this value into the second equation.

$0.10x + 0.05(x + 5) = 2.80$
$0.10x + 0.05x + 0.25 = 2.80$
$0.15x + 0.25 = 2.80$
$0.15x = 2.55$
$x = 17$

$y = x + 5$
$y = 17 + 5$
$y = 22$

There are 17 dimes and 22 nickels.

35. (a) Let x represent the number of free throws. Let y represent the number of field goals. The statement "made 2432 baskets...some were free throws and some were field goals" translates to the equation $x + y = 2432$. The statement "the number of field goals was 762 more than the number of free throws" translates to the equation $y = x + 762$.

$$x + y = 2432$$
$$y = x + 762$$

Since the second equation is solved for y, use the substitution method substituting this value into the first equation.

$$x + x + 762 = 2432$$
$$2x + 762 = 2432$$
$$2x = 1670$$
$$x = 835$$

$$y = x + 762$$
$$y = 835 + 762$$
$$y = 1597$$

He made 835 free throws and 1597 field goals.

(b) $835(1) + 1597(2) = 835 + 3194 = 4029$
He scored 4029 points.

(c) $\dfrac{4029}{80} = 50.3625$

He averaged approximately 50 points per game.

37. Let x represent the speed of the plane in still air. Let y represent the speed of the wind.

	Distance	Rate	Time
Flying with a tailwind	350	$x + y$	$1\frac{3}{4}$
Flying with a headwind	210	$x - y$	$1\frac{3}{4}$

$$\frac{7}{4}x + \frac{7}{4}y = 350$$
$$\frac{7}{4}x - \frac{7}{4}y = 210$$

Clear fractions by multiplying both equations by 4.

$$7x + 7y = 1400$$
$$7x - 7y = 840$$

Since the equations are in standard form and the coefficients on y are opposites, use the addition method.

$$7x + 7y = 1400$$
$$\underline{7x - 7y = 840}$$
$$14x = 2240$$
$$x = 160$$

$$\frac{7}{4}x + \frac{7}{4}y = 350$$
$$\frac{7}{4}(160) + y = 350$$

$$1120 + 7y = 1400$$
$$7y = 280$$
$$y = 40$$

The speed of the plane in still air is 160 mph and the wind is 40 mph.

39. Let x represent the amount invested in the first account. Let y represent the amount invested in the second account.

	First Account	Second Account	Total
Principal	x	y	60,000
Interest	$0.055x$	$0.065y$	3750

$$x + y = 60,000$$
$$0.055x + 0.065y = 3750$$

Since the equations are written in standard form, use the addition method by multiplying the first equation by -0.055.

$$-0.055x - 0.055y = -3300$$
$$\underline{0.055x + 0.065y = 3750}$$
$$0.010y = 450$$
$$y = 45,000$$

$$x + y = 60,000$$
$$x + 45,000 = 60,000$$
$$x = 15,000$$

$15,000 is invested in the 5.5% account and $45,000 is invested in the 6.5% account.

41. Let x represent the number of pounds of candy needed. Let y represent the number of pounds of nuts needed.

	Candy	Nuts	Total
Number of	x	Y	20
Value of	$1.80x$	$1.20y$	$1.56(20)$

$$x + y = 20$$
$$1.80x + 1.20y = 31.20$$

Since the equations are written in standard form, use the addition method by multiplying the first equation by -1.20.

$$-1.20x - 1.20y = -24.00$$
$$\underline{1.80x + 1.20y = 31.20}$$
$$0.60x = 7.20$$
$$x = 12$$

$$x + y = 20$$
$$12 + y = 20$$
$$y = 8$$

12 pounds of candy should be mixed with 8 pounds of nuts.

43. Let d represent the number of points scored by the Dallas Cowboys. Let b represent the number of points scored by the Buffalo Bills. The statement "the Dallas Cowboys scored four more than twice the number of points scored by the Buffalo Bills" translates to the equation $d = 2b + 4$. The statement "total number of points scored by both teams was 43" translates to the equation $d + b = 43$.

$$d = 2b + 4$$
$$d + b = 43$$

Since one equation is solved for d, use the substitution method. Substitute this value for d into the first equation and solve the resulting equation for b.

$$d + b = 43$$
$$2b + 4 + b = 43$$
$$3b + 4 = 43$$
$$3b = 39$$
$$b = 13$$

$$d = 2b + 4$$
$$d = 2(13) + 4$$
$$d = 30$$

Dallas scored 30 points, and Buffalo scored 13 points.

45. Let x represent the number of women college students. Let y represent the number of men college students. The statement "500 college students" translates to the equation $x + y = 500$. The statement "340 said that the campus lacked adequate lighting" together with "$\frac{4}{5}$ of the women and $\frac{1}{2}$ of the men said that they thought the campus lacked adequate lighting" translates to the equation $\frac{4}{5}x + \frac{1}{2}y = 340$.

$$x + y = 500$$
$$\frac{4}{5}x + \frac{1}{2}y = 340$$

Clear fractions from the second equation by multiplying it by 10.
$$x + y = 500$$
$$8x + 5y = 3400$$

Since the equations are written in standard form, use the addition method by multiplying the first equation by -5.
$$-5x - 5y = -2500$$
$$\underline{8x + 5y = 3400}$$
$$3x = 900$$
$$x = 300$$

$$x + y = 500$$
$$300 + y = 500$$
$$y = 200$$

There were 300 women and 200 men in the survey.

Section 4.5 Practice Exercises

1. (a) A **linear inequality in two variables** x and y is an inequality that can be written in one of the following forms: $ax + by < c$, $ax + by > c$, $ax + by \leq c$, or $ax + by \geq c$.

(b) A **test point method** is a process to graph a linear inequality in two variables. First graph the related equation. Then choose a test point *not* on the lien to determine which side of the line to shade.

3. Graph the line $y = \frac{3}{5}x + 2$ using the point-slope form.

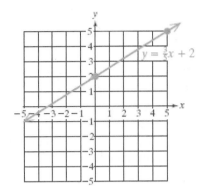

5. When the inequality symbol is $\leq$ or $\geq$, a solid line is used in the graph of a linear inequality in two variables.

7. All of the points in the shaded region are solutions to the inequality..

9. (a) $-2x - y \leq 2$

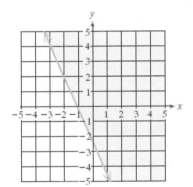

11. $3(3) + 2(-1) > 1$
$$9 - 2 > 1$$
$$7 > 1$$

True

13. $0 < -2(2) + 4$
$$0 < -4 + 4$$
$$0 < 0$$

False

15. $-3 + 10(0) < 1$

$\quad -3 + 0 < 1$

$\quad\quad -3 < 1$

True

17. $y \geq -x + 5$

Using the slope-intercept method of graphing, graph the related equation $y = -x + 5$ with a solid line. Using $(0, 0)$ as a test point, a false statement is obtained. Shade the region not containing $(0, 0)$.

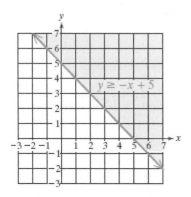

Answers may vary. For example: $(0, 5)$, $(2, 7)$, $(-1, 8)$

19. $y < 4x$

Using the slope-intercept method of graphing, graph the related equation $y = 4x$ with a dashed line. Using $(1, 1)$ as a test point, a true statement is obtained. Shade the region containing $(1, 1)$.

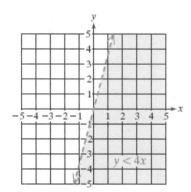

Answers may vary. For example: $(1, -1)$, $(3, 0)$, $(-2, -9)$

21. $3x + 7y \leq 14$

Using the intercepts method of graphing, graph the related equation $3x + 7y = 14$ with a solid line. Using $(0, 0)$ as a test point, a true statement is obtained. Shade the region containing $(0, 0)$.

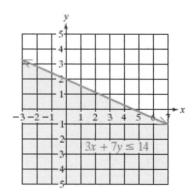

Answers may vary. For example: $(0, 0)$, $(0, 2)$, $(-1, -3)$

23. $x - y > 6$

Using the intercepts method of graphing, graph the related equation $x - y = 6$ with a dashed line. Using $(0, 0)$ as a test point, a false statement is obtained. Shade the region not containing $(0, 0)$.

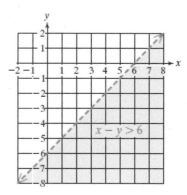

25. $x \geq -1$

Graph the related equation $x = -1$ with a solid vertical line. Using $(0, 0)$ as a test point, a true statement is obtained. Shade the region containing $(0, 0)$.

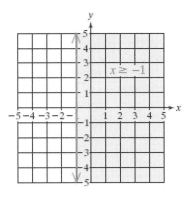

27. $y < 3$

Graph the related equation $y = 3$ with a dashed horizontal line. Using $(0, 0)$ as a test point, a true statement is obtained. Shade the region containing $(0, 0)$.

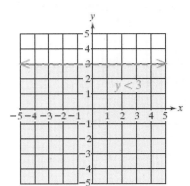

29. $y \leq -\dfrac{3}{4}x + 2$

Using the slope-intercept method of graphing, graph the related equation $y = -\dfrac{3}{4}x + 2$ with a solid line. Using $(0, 0)$ as a test point, a true statement is obtained. Shade the region containing $(0, 0)$.

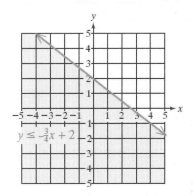

31. $y - 2x > 0$

Using the slope-intercept method of graphing, graph the related equation $y = 2x$ with a dashed line. Using $(1, 1)$ as a test point, a false statement is obtained. Shade the region not containing $(1, 1)$.

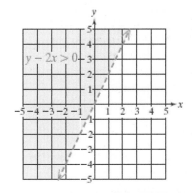

33. $x \leq 0$

Graph the related equation $x = 0$ or the y-axis with a solid vertical line. Using $(1, 1)$ as a test point, a false statement is obtained. Shade the region not containing $(1, 1)$.

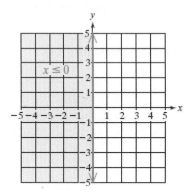

35. $y \geq 0$

Graph the related equation $y = 0$ or the x-axis with a solid horizontal line. Using $(1, 1)$ as a test point, a true statement is obtained. Shade the region containing $(1, 1)$.

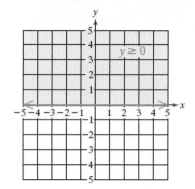

37. $-x \leq \dfrac{1}{2}y - 2$

$-x + 2 \leq \dfrac{1}{2}y$
$-2x + 4 \leq y$
$y \geq -2x + 4$

Using the slope-intercept method of graphing, graph the related equation $y = -2x + 4$ with a solid line. Using $(0, 0)$ as a test point, a false statement is obtained. Shade the region not containing $(0, 0)$.

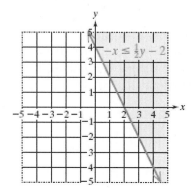

39. $2x > 3y$

$\dfrac{2}{3}x > y$

$y < \dfrac{2}{3}x$

Using the slope-intercept method of graphing, graph the related equation $y = \dfrac{2}{3}x$ with a dashed line. Using $(1, 0)$ as a test point, a true statement is obtained. Shade the region containing $(1, 0)$.

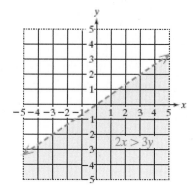

41. (a) $x + y > 4$

The graph of the inequality is a set of ordered pairs above the dashed line $x + y = 4$, for example, (6, 3), (–2, 8), (0, 5). Answers will vary.

(b) $x + y = 4$

The graph of the equation is a set of ordered pairs on the line $x + y = 4$, for example (0, 4), (4, 0), (2, 2). Answers will vary.

(c) $x + y < 4$

The graph of the inequality is a set of ordered pairs below the dashed line $x + y = 4$, for example, (0, 0), (–2, 1), (3, 0). Answers will vary.

43. $2x + y < 3$

Using the intercepts method of graphing, graph the related equation $2x + y = 3$ with a dashed line. Substituting the test point (0, 0) into the inequality results in a true statement. Shade the region below the dashed line.

$y \geq x + 3$

Using the slope-intercept method of graphing, graph the related equation $y = x + 3$ with a solid line. Substituting the test point (0, 0) into the inequality results in a false statement. Shade the region above the solid line.

Putting the two regions on the same graph, the intersection is the solution to the system of inequalities.

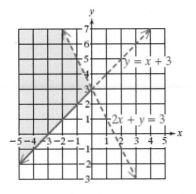

45. $x + y \geq -3$

Using the intercepts method of graphing, graph the related equation $x + y = -3$ with a solid line. Substituting the test point (0, 0) into the inequality results in a true statement. Shade the region above the solid line.

$x - 2y \geq 6$

Using the intercepts method of graphing, graph the related equation $x - 2y = 6$ with a solid line. Substituting the test point (0, 0) into the inequality results in a false statement. Shade the region below the solid line.

Putting the two regions on the same graph, the intersection is the solution to the system of inequalities

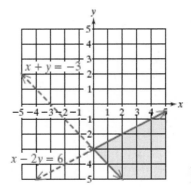

47. $2x + 3y < 6$

Using the intercepts method of graphing, graph the related equation $2x + 3y = 6$ with a dashed line. Substituting the test point (0, 0) into the inequality results in a true statement. Shade the region below the dashed line.

$3x + y > -5$

Using the intercepts method of graphing, graph the related equation $3x + y = -5$ with a dashed line. Substituting the test point (0, 0) into the inequality results in a true statement. Shade the region above the dashed line.

Putting the two regions on the same graph, the intersection is the solution to the system of inequalities.

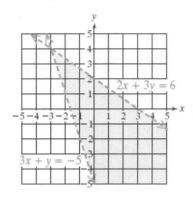

49. $y > 2x$

Using the slope-intercept method of graphing, graph the related equation $y = 2x$ with a dashed line. Substituting the test point (1, 1) into the inequality results in a false statement. Shade the region above the dashed line.

$y > -4x$

Using the slope-intercept method of graphing, graph the related equation $y = -4x$ with a dashed line. Substituting the test point (1, 1) into the inequality results in a true statement. Shade the region above the dashed line.

Putting the two regions on the same graph, the intersection is the solution to the system of inequalities.

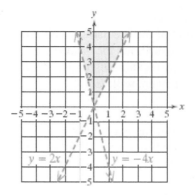

51. $y < \frac{1}{2}x - 1$

Using the slope-intercept method of graphing, graph the related equation

$y = \frac{1}{2}x - 1$ with a dashed line. Substituting the test point (0, 0) into the inequality results in a false statement. Shade the region below the solid line.

$5x + y \leq -12$

Using the intercepts method of graphing, graph the related equation $5x + y = -12$ with a solid line. Substituting the test point (0, 0) into the inequality results in a false statement. Shade the region below the solid line.

Putting the two regions on the same graph, the intersection is the solution to the system of inequalities.

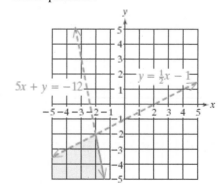

53. $y < 4$

Graph the related equation $y = 4$ with a dashed horizontal line. Substituting the test point $(0, 0)$ into the inequality results in a true statement. Shade the region below the dashed line.

$4x + 3y \geq 12$
Using the intercepts method of graphing, graph the related equation $4x + 3y = 12$ with a solid line. Substituting the test point $(0, 0)$ into the inequality results in a false statement. Shade the region above the solid line.

Putting the two regions on the same graph, the intersection is the solution to the system of inequalities.

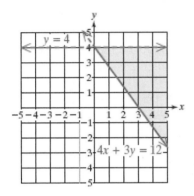

55. $x > -4$

Graph the related equation $x = -4$ with a dashed vertical line. Substituting the test point $(0, 0)$ into the inequality results in a true statement. Shade the region to the right of the dashed vertical line.

$y \leq 3$
Graph the related equation $y = 3$ with a solid horizontal line. Substituting the test point $(0, 0)$ into the inequality results in a true statement. Shade the region below the solid line.

Putting the two regions on the same graph, the intersection is the solution to the system of inequalities.

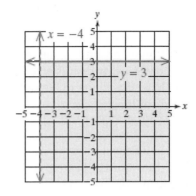

57. $2x \geq 5$

Graph the related equation $x = 2.5$ with a solid vertical line. Substituting the test point $(0, 0)$ into the inequality results in a false statement. Shade the region to the right of the solid vertical line.

$6 > 3y$

Graph the related equation $2 = y$ with a dashed horizontal line. Substituting the test point $(0, 0)$ into the inequality results in a true statement. Shade the region below the dashed horizontal line.

Putting the two regions on the same graph, the intersection is the solution to the system of inequalities.

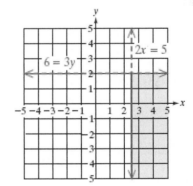

59. $x \geq -4$

Graph the related equation $x = -4$ with a solid vertical line. Substituting the test point $(0, 0)$ into the inequality results in a true statement. Shade the region to the right of the solid vertical line.

$x \leq 1$

Graph the related equation $x = 1$ with a solid vertical line. Substituting the test point $(0, 0)$ into the inequality results in a true statement. Shade the region to the left of the solid line.

Putting the two regions on the same graph, the intersection is the solution to the system of inequalities.

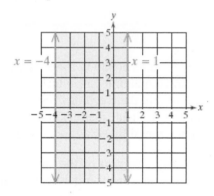

Group Activity

Answers will vary throughout this exercise.

Chapter 4 Review Exercises

Section 4.1

1. $x - 4y = -4$
$x + 2y = 8$ ordered pair: (4, 2)

$(4) - 4(2) \overset{?}{=} -4$ ✓

$(4) + 2(2) \overset{?}{=} 8$ ✓

The ordered pair (4, 2) is a solution

3. $3x + y = 9$
$y = 3$ ordered pair: (1, 3)

$3(1) + 3 \overset{?}{=} 9$ No

$3 \overset{?}{=} 3$ ✓

The ordered pair (1, 3) is not a solution.

5. $y = -\dfrac{1}{2}x + 4$
$y = x - 1$

Since the slopes are different, the lines intersect.

7. $y = -\dfrac{4}{7}x + 3$
$y = -\dfrac{4}{7}x - 5$

Since the lines have the same slope but different y-intercepts, the lines are parallel.

9. $y = 9x - 2$
$9x - y = 2$

Rewrite the second equation in slope-intercept form.
$y = 9x - 2$
$y = 9x - 2$

Since the lines have the same slope and same y-intercept, the lines coincide.

11.
$$y = -\frac{2}{3}x - 2$$
$$-x + 3y = -6$$

Rewrite the second equation in slope-intercept form.
$$y = -\frac{2}{3}x - 2$$
$$y = \frac{1}{3}x - 2$$

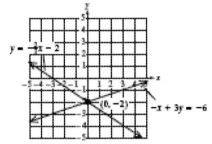

$(0, -2)$ consistent and independent system

13.
$$4x = -2y + 10$$
$$2x + y = 5$$

Rewrite the equations in slope-intercept form.
$$y = -2x + 5$$
$$y = -2x + 5$$

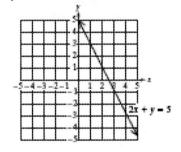

Infinitely many solutions
$\{(x, y)|y = -2x + 5\}$
consistent and dependent system

15.
$$6x - 3y = 9$$
$$y = -1$$

Rewrite the first equation in slope-intercept form.
$$y = 2x - 3$$
$$y = -1$$

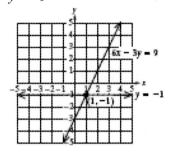

$(1, -1)$ consistent and independent system

17.
$$x - 7y = 14$$
$$-2x + 14y = 14$$

Rewrite the equations in slope-intercept form.
$$y = \frac{1}{7}x - 2$$
$$y = \frac{1}{7}x + 1$$

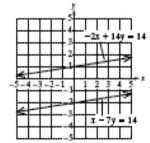

No solution; inconsistent and independent system

19.
$$y_1 = y_2$$
$$0.15x + 3.90 = 0.25x$$
$$3.90 = 0.10x$$
$$39 = x$$

$$y_2 = 0.25x$$
$$y_2 = 0.25(39)$$
$$y_2 = 9.75$$

Cost would be the same ($9.75) after 39 minutes.

Section 4.2

21. $2x + 3y = -5$
$$x = y - 5$$

Substitute the value for x into the first equation and solve for y.
$$2(y - 5) + 3y = -5$$
$$2y - 10 + 3y = -5$$
$$5y - 10 = -5$$
$$5y = 5$$
$$y = 1$$

$$x = y - 5$$
$$x = 1 - 5$$
$$x = -4$$
Solution: $(-4, 1)$

23. $4x + 2y = 4$
$$y = -2x + 2$$

Substitute the value for y into the first equation and solve for x.
$$4x + 2(-2x + 2) = 4$$
$$4x - 4x + 4 = 4$$
$$4 = 4 \qquad \text{Identity}$$
Infinitely many solutions
$$\{(x, y) \mid y = -2x + 2\}; \text{ dependent system}$$

25. (a) y in the second equation is easiest to isolate for because its coefficient is 1.

(b) $4x - 3y = 9$
$$2x + y = 12$$

Solving the second equation for y gives $y = -2x + 12$. Substitute this value into the first equation and solve for x.
$$4x - 3(-2x + 12) = 9$$
$$4x + 6x - 36 = 9$$
$$10x - 36 = 9$$
$$10x = 45$$
$$x = \frac{45}{10} = \frac{9}{2}$$
$$2x + y = 12$$
$$2\left(\frac{9}{2}\right) + y = 12$$
$$9 + y = 12$$
$$y = 3$$

Solution: $\left(\frac{9}{2}, 3\right)$

27. $x + 5y = 20$
$$3x + 2y = 8$$

Solving the first equation for x gives $x = -5y + 20$. Substitute this value into the second equation and solve for y.
$$3(-5y + 20) + 2y = 8$$
$$-15y + 60 + 2y = 8$$
$$-13y + 60 = 8$$
$$-13y = -52$$
$$y = 4$$
$$x + 5y = 20$$
$$x + 5(4) = 20$$
$$x + 20 = 20$$
$$x = 0$$
Solution: $(0, 4)$

29. $-3x + y = 15$
$6x - 2y = 12$

Solving the first equation for y gives
$y = 3x + 15$. Substitute this value into the
second equation and solve for y.
$6x - 2(3x + 15) = 12$
$6x - 6x - 30 = 12$
$-30 = 12$

No solution; inconsistent and independent
system

31. Let x represent the measure of one of the
acute angles. Let y represent the measure of
the second acute angle. The sum of the
acute angles in a right triangle is 90°. This
translates to the equation $x + y = 90$. The
statement "one of the acute angles is 6°
more than the other acute angle" translates
to the equation $y = x + 6$.

$x + y = 90$
$y = x + 6$

Since the second equation is solved for y,
use the substitution method by substituting
the value for y into the first equation and
solving for x.
$x + (x + 6) = 90$
$x + x + 6 = 90$
$2x + 6 = 90$
$2x = 84$
$x = 42$
$y = x + 6$
$y = 42 + 6$
$y = 48$
The measures of the angles are 42° and 48°.

Section 4.3

33. 1. Write both equations in standard form.

2. Multiply one or both equations by a
constant to create opposite coefficients
for one of the variables.

3. Add the equations to eliminate the
variable.

4. Solve for the remaining variable.

5. Substitute the known variable value into
an original equation to solve for the
other variable.

35. (a) Answers may vary. For example, y is
easier to eliminate because the signs are
opposite.

(b) $9x - 2y = 14$
$4x + 3y = 14$

Multiply the first equation by 3 and the
second equation by 2 to obtain opposite
coefficients on y.
$27x - 6y = 42$
$8x + 6y = 28$
$\overline{35x = 70}$
$x = 2$
$9x - 2y = 14$
$9(2) - 2y = 14$
$18 - 2y = 14$
$-2y = -4$
$y = 2$
Solution: $(2, 2)$

37.
$$x + 3y = 0$$
$$-3x - 10y = -2$$

Multiply the first equation by 3 to obtain opposite coefficients on x.
$$3x + 9y = 0$$
$$\underline{-3x - 10y = -2}$$
$$-y = -2$$
$$y = 2$$
$$x + 3y = 0$$
$$x + 3(2) = 0$$
$$x + 6 = 0$$
$$x = -6$$
Solution: $(-6, 2)$

39.
$$12x = 5y + 5$$
$$5y = -1 - 4x$$

Rewrite the equations in standard form.
$$12x - 5y = 5$$
$$\underline{4x + 5y = -1}$$
$$16x = 4$$
$$x = \frac{1}{4}$$
$$5y = -1 - 4x$$
$$5y = -1 - 4\left(\frac{1}{4}\right)$$
$$5y = -1 - 1$$
$$5y = -2$$
$$y = -\frac{2}{5}$$
Solution: $\left(\frac{1}{4}, -\frac{2}{5}\right)$

41.
$$-8x - 4y = 16$$
$$10x + 5y = 5$$

Multiply the first equation by 5 and the second equation by 4 to obtain opposite coefficients on y.
$$-40x - 20y = 80$$
$$\underline{40x + 20y = 20}$$
$$0 = 100 \qquad \text{Contradiction}$$

No solution; inconsistent and independent system

43.
$$0.5x - 0.2y = 0.5$$
$$0.4x + 0.7y = 0.4$$

Multiply both equations by 10 to clear the decimals.
$$5x - 2y = 5$$
$$4x + 7y = 4$$

Multiply the first equation by 7 and the second equation by 2 to obtain opposite coefficients on y.
$$35x - 14y = 35$$
$$\underline{8x + 14y = 8}$$
$$43x = 43$$
$$x = 1$$

$$0.5x - 0.2y = 0.5$$
$$0.5(1) - 0.2y = 0.5$$
$$0.5 - 0.2y = 0.5$$
$$-0.2y = 0$$
$$y = 0$$
Solution: $(1, 0)$

45. (a) Answers may vary. For example, use the addition method because the equations are written in standard form.

(b)
$$5x - 8y = -2$$
$$3x - 7y = 1$$

Multiply the first equation by 3 to obtain opposite coefficients on x.
$$15x - 24y = -6$$
$$\underline{-15x + 35y = 5}$$
$$11y = -11$$
$$y = -1$$
$$5x - 8(-1) = -2$$
$$5x + 8 = -2$$
$$5x = -10$$
$$x = -2$$

Solution: $(-2, -1)$

Section 4.4

47. Let x represent the amount of money invested at 12%. Let y represent the amount of money invested at 4%.

	12% Account	4% Account	Total
Principal	x	y	600,000
Interest	$0.12x$	$0.04y$	30000

$$x + y = 600,000$$
$$0.12x + 0.04y = 30,000$$

Multiply the second equation by 100 to eliminate the decimals.
$$x + y = 600,000$$
$$12x + 4y = 3,000,000$$

Multiply the first equation by -12 to obtain opposite coefficients on x.
$$-12x - 12y = -7,200,000$$
$$\underline{12x + 4y = 3,000,000}$$
$$-8y = -4,200,000$$
$$y = 525,000$$
$$x + y = 600,000$$
$$x + 525,500 = 600,000$$
$$x = 75,000$$
He invested $75,000 in the 12% account and $525,000 in the 4% account.

49. Let b represent the speed of the boat in still water. Let c represent the speed of the current.

	Distance	Rate	Time
Downstream	80	$b + c$	4
Upstream	80	$b - c$	5

$$4b + 4c = 80$$
$$5b - 5c = 80$$

Multiply the first equation by 5 and the second equation by 4 to obtain opposite coefficients on c.
$$20b + 20c = 400$$
$$\underline{20b - 20c = 320}$$
$$40b = 720$$
$$b = 18$$
$$4(b + c) = 80$$
$$4b + 4c = 80$$
$$4(18) + 4c = 80$$
$$72 + 4c = 80$$
$$4c = 8$$
$$c = 2$$
The speed of the boat in still water is 18 mph and the speed of the current is 2 mph.

51. Let x represent the cost of a soft drink. Let y represent the cost of a hot dog. The statement "the total cost of a soft drink and a hot dog is $8.00" translates to the equation $x + y = 8.00$. The statement "the price of the hot dog is $1.00 more than the cost of the soft drink" translates to the equation $y = x + 1$.

$$x + y = 8.00$$
$$y = x + 1$$

Since the second equation is solved for y, use the substitution method by substituting the value for y into the first equation and solving for x.
$$x + x + 1 = 8.00$$
$$2x + 1 = 8.00$$
$$2x = 7.00$$
$$x = 3.50$$
$$y = x + 1$$
$$y = 3.50 + 1$$
$$y = 4.50$$
A hot dog costs $4.50 and a drink costs $3.50.

53. Let x represent Ray's score in the first round. Let y represent his score in the second round. The statement "total score of 154" translates to the equation $x + y = 154$. The statement "his score in the second round is 10 more than his score in the first round" translates to the equation $y = x + 10$.

$x + y = 154$
$\quad y = x + 10$

Since the second equation is solved for y, use the substitution method by substituting the value for y into the first equation and solving for x.

$x + x + 10 = 154$
$\quad 2x + 10 = 154$
$\qquad 2x = 144$
$\qquad\quad x = 72$

$y = x + 10$
$y = 72 + 10$
$y = 82$

The scores were 72 on the first round and 82 on the second round.

Section 4.5

55. $y > -2x + 6$

The related equation is in slope-intercept form with a slope of -2 and y-intercept of $(0, 6)$. Since the sign of inequality does not include an equal sign, the line will be dashed. Using $(0, 0)$ as a test point, a false statement is obtained. Using $(4, 0)$ as a test point, a true statement is obtained. Shade the region containing $(4, 0)$.

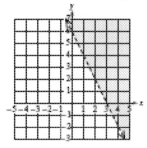

Answers may vary. Three possible solutions are: $(5, 5)$, $(4, 0)$, $(0, 7)$

57. $4x - 2y \le 10$

Rewriting the related equation in slope-intercept form gives $y = 2x - 5$ with a slope of 2 and a y-intercept of $(0, -5)$. Since the sign of inequality includes an equal sign, the line will be solid. Using $(0, 0)$ as a test point, a true statement is obtained. Using $(3, 0)$ as a test point, a false statement is obtained. Shade the region containing $(0, 0)$.

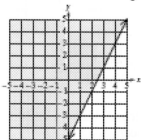

Answers may vary. Three possible solutions are: $(0, 0)$, $(0, -5)$, $(-1, 1)$

59. $7x - y \le 0$

Rewriting the related equation in slope-intercept form gives $y = 7x$ with a slope of 7 and a y-intercept of $(0, 0)$. Since the sign of inequality includes an equal sign, the line will be solid. Using $(-2, 0)$ as a test point, a true statement is obtained. Using $(2, 0)$ as a test point a false statement is obtained. Shade the region containing $(-2, 0)$.

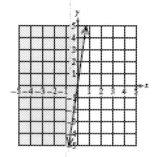

61. $y < -4$

The related equation, $y = -4$, is a horizontal line through the point $(0, -4)$. Since the sign of inequality does not include an equal sign, the line will be dashed. Using $(0, 0)$ as a test point, a false statement is obtained. Using $(0, -6)$ as a test point, a true statement is obtained. Shade the region containing $(0, -6)$.

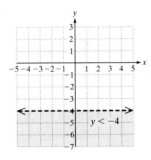

63. $x \geq 0$

The related equation, $x = 5$, is a vertical line through the point $(0, 0)$. Since the sign of inequality includes an equal sign, the line will be solid. Using $(-1, 0)$ as a test point, a false statement is obtained. Using $(0, 1)$ as a test point, a true statement is obtained. Shade the region containing $(0, 1)$.

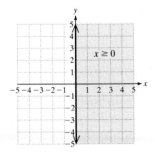

65.

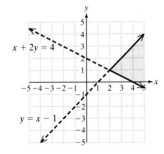

67.

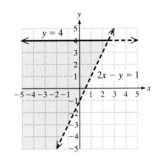

Chapter 4 Test

1. $5x + 2y = -6$

$-\dfrac{5}{2}x - y = -3$

Rewriting each equation in slope-intercept form gives

$y = -\dfrac{5}{2}x - 3$

$y = -\dfrac{5}{2}x + 3$

Since the slopes of the two lines are equal and their y-intercepts are unequal, the lines are parallel.

3. Graph each line using the slope-intercept method.

$$y = -\frac{1}{2}x + 3$$

$$y = -\frac{1}{2}x + 3$$

Since the equations of the two lines are equal, the lines are the same.

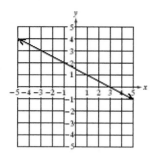

Infinitely many solutions;
$\{(x, y) | 2x + 4y = 12\}$; dependent system.

5. Let x represent the number of points scored by Sheryl Swoopes. Let y represent the number of points scored by Lauren Jackson. The statement "together they scored a total 1211 points" translates to the equation $x + y = 1211$. The statement "Swoopes ... scored 17 points more than ... Jackson" translates to the equation $x = y + 17$.

$$x + y = 1211$$
$$x = y + 17$$

Since the second equation is solved for x, substitute this value for x into the first equation and solve for y.

$$x + y = 1211$$
$$y + 17 + y = 1211$$
$$2y + 17 = 1211$$
$$2y = 1194$$
$$y = 597$$
$$x = y + 17$$
$$x = 597 + 17$$
$$x = 614$$

Swoopes scored 614 points and Jackson scored 597 points.

7. Let x represent the number of milliliters of 50% acid solution. Let y represent the number of milliliters of 20% acid solution.

	50% Solution	20% Solution	30% Solution
Amount of solution	x	y	36
Amount of acid	$0.5x$	$0.2y$	$0.3(36)$

$$x + y = 36$$
$$0.5x + 0.2y = 10.8$$

Since the equations are written in standard form, use the addition method. Multiply the first equation by -0.5 to obtain opposite coefficients on x.

$$-0.5x - 0.5y = -18$$
$$\underline{0.5x + 0.2y = 10.8}$$
$$-0.3y = -7.2$$
$$y = 24$$

$$x + y = 36$$
$$x + 24 = 36$$
$$x = 12$$

12 milliliters of the 50% acid solution should be mixed with 24 milliliters of the 20% acid solutions.

9. $\dfrac{1}{3}x + y = \dfrac{7}{3}$

$$x = \frac{3}{2}y - 11$$

Since the second equation is solved for x, use the substitution method by substituting this value for x into the first equation and solving for y.

$$\frac{1}{3}x + y = \frac{7}{3}$$
$$\frac{1}{3}\left(\frac{3}{2}y - 11\right) + y = \frac{7}{3}$$
$$\frac{1}{2}y - \frac{11}{3} + y = \frac{7}{3}$$

Clear the fractions by multiplying both sides of the equation by 6.

$$3y - 22 + 6y = 14$$
$$9y - 22 = 14$$
$$9y = 36$$
$$y = 4$$

$$x = \frac{3}{2}y - 11$$
$$x = \frac{3}{2}(4) - 11$$
$$x = 6 - 11$$
$$x = -5$$

Solution: $(-5, 4)$

11. $3x - 4y = 29$
$2x + 5y = -19$

Since the equations are in standard form and the signs on y are opposite, use the addition method. Multiply the second equation by 4 and the first equation by 5 to obtain opposite coefficients on y. Add these equations together and solve for x.

$$15x - 20y = 145$$
$$\underline{8x + 20y = -76}$$
$$23x = 69$$
$$x = 3$$

$$3x - 4y = 29$$
$$3(3) - 4y = 29$$
$$9 - 4y = 29$$
$$-4y = 20$$
$$y = -5$$

Solution: $3, -5$

13. $-0.25 - 0.05y = 0.2$
$10x + 2y = -8$

Clear the decimals from the first equation by multiplying it by 100.

$$-25x - 5y = 20$$
$$10x + 2y = -8$$

The equations are now in standard form. Use the addition method by multiplying the first equation by 2 and the second equation by 5 to obtain opposite coefficients on x. Add the equations and solve for y.

$$-50x - 10y = 40$$
$$\underline{50x + 10y = -40}$$
$$0 = 0 \qquad \text{Identity}$$

Infinitely many solutions
$\{(x, y) \mid 10x + 2y = -8\}$; dependent system

15. Let x represent the price of a CD. Let y represent the price of a DVD.

	Number of CDs	Number of DVDs	Total cost
Latrell's purchase	4	2	54
Kendra's purchase	2	3	49

$$4x + 2y = 54$$
$$2x + 3y = 49$$

Multiply the second equation by -2 to obtain opposite coefficients on x.

$$4x + 2y = 54$$
$$\underline{-4x - 6y = -98}$$
$$-4y = -44$$
$$y = 11$$

$$4x + 2y = 54$$
$$4x + 2(11) = 54$$
$$4x + 22 = 54$$
$$4x = 32$$
$$x = 8$$

CDs cost \$8 each and DVDs cost \$11 each.

17. Let x represent the amount borrowed at 10%. Let y represent the amount borrowed at 8%.

	10% account	8% account	Total
Amount borrowed	x	y	$5000
Interest	$0.10x$	$0.08y$	$424

$$x + y = 5000$$
$$0.10x + 0.08y = 424$$

Multiply the second equation by -10 to obtain opposite coefficients on x.

$$x + y = 5000$$
$$\underline{-x - 0.8y = -4240}$$
$$0.2y = 760$$
$$y = 3800$$

$$x + y = 5000$$
$$x + 3800 = 5000$$
$$x = 1200$$

$1200 was borrowed at 10%, and $3800 was borrowed at 8%.

19. Let p represent the speed of the plane in still air. Let w represent the speed of the wind.

	Rate	Time	Distance
With the wind	$p + w$	2	1090
Against the wind	$p - w$	2	910

$$2(p + w) = 1090$$
$$2(p - w) = 910$$

Rewrite the equations in standard form.
$$2p + 2w = 1090$$
$$2p - 2w = 910$$

Since the coefficients on w are opposites, add the equations and solve for p.

$$2p + 2w = 1090$$
$$\underline{2p - 2w = 910}$$
$$4p = 2000$$
$$p = 500$$

$$2(p + w) = 1090$$
$$2p + 2w = 1090$$
$$2(500) + 2w = 1090$$
$$1000 + 2w = 1090$$
$$2w = 90$$
$$w = 45$$

The speed of the plane in still air is 500 mph and the speed of the wind is 45 mph.

21. Let x represent the number of mL of 10% acid. Let y represent the number of mL of 25% acid.

	10% Solution	25% Solution	16% Solution
Amount of solution	x	y	100
Amount of antifreeze	$0.10x$	$0.25y$	$0.16(100)$

$$x + y = 100$$
$$0.10x + 0.25y = 16$$

Since the equations are written in standard form, use the addition method by multiplying the first equation by -0.10 to obtain opposite coefficients on x. Add the equations and solve for y.

$$-0.10x - 0.10y = -10$$
$$\underline{0.10x + 0.25y = 16}$$
$$0.15y = 6$$
$$y = 40$$

$$x + y = 100$$
$$x + 40 = 100$$
$$x = 60$$

60 mL of the 10% acid solution should be mixed with 40 mL of the 25% acid solution.

23. $2x + y > 1$
$x + y < 2$

The solution region for $2x + y > 1$ is the region "above" a dashed line passing through the points $(0, 1)$ and $(-1, 3)$. It contains the point $(2, -2)$.

The solution region for $x + y < 2$ is the region "below" a dashed line passing through the points $(2, 0)$ and $(0, 2)$. It contains the point $(2, -2)$.

The region bounded by these inequalities is triangular in shape with a leftmost vertex at $(-1, 3)$. It has no sides.

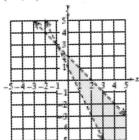

Cumulative Review Exercises, Chapters 1–4

1. $\dfrac{|2-5| + 10 \div 2 + 3}{\sqrt{10^2 - 8^2}} = \dfrac{|2-5| + 10 \div 2 + 3}{\sqrt{100 - 64}}$

$= \dfrac{|-3| + 5 + 3}{\sqrt{36}}$

$= \dfrac{3 + 5 + 3}{6}$

$= \dfrac{11}{6}$

3. $-4(a+3) + 2 = -5(a+1) + a$
$-4a - 12 + 2 = -5a - 5 + a$
$-4a - 10 = -4a - 5$
$\qquad -10 = -5 \qquad$ Contradiction
No solution

5. $z = \dfrac{x - m}{5}$

$5z = x - m$
$5z + m = x$
$\qquad x = 5z + m$

7. Let x represent the measure of one of the remaining angles. Let y represent the measure of the other remaining angle. The sum of the angles in a triangle is 180. Thus the equation is $110 + x + y = 180$ or $x + y = 70$. The statement "one is 4° less than the other angle" translates to the equation $y = x - 4$.

$x + y = 70$
$\qquad y = x - 4$

Since the second equation is solved for y, use the substitution method by substituting this value into the first equation and solving for x.

$\qquad x + y = 70$
$x + x - 4 = 70$
$\quad 2x - 4 = 70$
$\qquad 2x = 74$
$\qquad\quad x = 37$

$y = x - 4$
$y = 37 - 4$
$y = 33$

The measures of the angles are 37°, 33°, and 110°.

9. 37% of 2,060,000 votes
$0.37(2,060,000) = 762,200$
Jesse Ventura received 762,200 votes.

11. Let x represent the measure of one angle. Let y represent the measure of the other angle. The statement "two angles are complementary" translates to the equation $x + y = 90$.

The statement "one angle measures 17° larger than the other angle" translates to the equation $x = y + 17$.

$x + y = 90$
$x = y + 17$

Since the second equation is solved for x, substitute this value for x in the first equation and solve for y.

$$x + y = 90$$
$$y + 17 + y = 90$$
$$2y + 17 = 90$$
$$2y = 73$$
$$y = 36.5$$

$x = y + 17$
$x = 36.5 + 17$
$x = 53.5$

The angles are 36.5° and 53.5°.

13. (a) The slope of a line parallel to the given line is the same as the given line: $-\dfrac{2}{3}$.

(b) The slope of a line perpendicular to the given line is the negative reciprocal of the given line: $\dfrac{3}{2}$

15. (a) & (b)

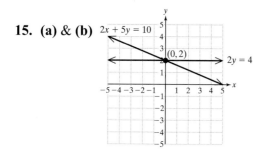

(c) Point of intersection: $(0, 2)$

$$2(0) + 5(2) \overset{?}{=} 10 \ \checkmark$$
$$2(2) \overset{?}{=} 4 \ \checkmark$$

17. (a) $2x + y = 3$ Use the intercepts method to graph. Substituting $x = 0$ into the equation gives $y = 3$. The y-intercept is $(0, 3)$. Substituting $y = 0$ into the equation gives $x = \dfrac{3}{2}$. The x-intercept is $\left(\dfrac{3}{2}, 0\right)$.

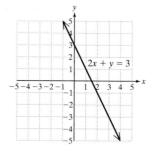

(b) Using the intercept method of graphing, graph the related equation $2x + y = 3$ with a dashed line. Using $(0, 0)$ as a test point, a true statement is obtained. Shade the region containing the point $(0, 0)$.

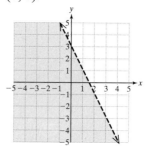

(c) Part (a) represents the solutions to an equation. Part (b) represents the solutions to a strict inequality.

19. Since $x°$ and $y°$ are complementary angles, we have x + y = 90. Since $x°$ and $(3y - 36)°$ are supplementary angles, we have

$$x° + (3y° - 36°) = 180°$$
$$x + y = 90$$
$$x + (3y - 36) = 180$$

Solving the first equation for x gives $x = 90 - y$. Use the substitution method by substituting this value into the second equation to solve for y.

$$90 - y + 3y - 36 = 180$$
$$2y + 54 = 180$$
$$2y = 126$$
$$y = 63$$

$$x + y = 90$$
$$x + 63 = 90$$
$$x = 27$$

x is 27° and y is 63°.

Chapter 5

Chapter 5 Opener

1. $6x - (4x + 2) - 7 = 2x - 9$ (Y)

2. $2x + 3(x - 5) + x = 6x - 15$ (D)

3. $5 + 2(4x - 1) + 2x = 10x + 3$ (K)

4. $5(x - 6) - 3(2x + 1) = -x - 33$ (P)

5. $3(8 - x) + 5x = 2x + 24$ (E)

6. $7(2 + 3x) - 8 = 21x - 6$ (T)

A polynomial that has two terms is called a BINOMIAL.

Calculator Exercises

1.

```
1.06^5
          1.338225578
```

3.

```
5000(1.06)^5
          6691.127888
```

5.

```
3000(1+0.06)²
          3370.8
```

Section 5.1 Practice Exercises

1. (a) An **exponent** is used to show repeated multiplication.

   (b) The **base** of an expression with an exponent is the value multiplied by itself repeatedly, according to the exponent.

   (c) **Simple interest** is the amount I due on a loan in addition to the principal P according to the formula $I = Prt$, where r is the interest rate and t is the time in years.

   (d) **Compound interest** is computed on the original principal and on the interest already accrued.

3. Base: x; exponent: 4

5. Base: 3; exponent: 5

7. Base: -1; exponent: 4

9. Base: 13; exponent: 1

11. v

13. 1

15. $(-6b)(-6b) = (-6b)^2$

17. $-6 \cdot b \cdot b = -6b^2$

19. $(y+2)(y+2)(y+2)(y+2) = (y+2)^4$

21. $\dfrac{-2}{t \cdot t \cdot t} = \dfrac{-2}{t^3}$

23. No; $-5^2 = -25$ and $(-5)^2 = 25$

25. Yes; $-2^5 = -32$ and $(-2)^5 = -32$

27. Yes; $\left(\dfrac{1}{2}\right)^3 = \dfrac{1}{8}$ and $\dfrac{1}{2^3} = \dfrac{1}{8}$

29. Yes; $\left(\dfrac{3}{10}\right)^2 = \dfrac{9}{100}$ and $(0.3)^2 = 0.09$

31. $16^1 = 16$

33. $(-1)^{21} = (-1)(-1)^{20} = (-1)(1) = -1$

35. $\left(-\dfrac{1}{3}\right)^2 = \left(-\dfrac{1}{3}\right)\left(-\dfrac{1}{3}\right) = \dfrac{1}{9}$

37. $-\left(\dfrac{2}{5}\right)^2 = -\left(\dfrac{2}{5}\right)\left(\dfrac{2}{5}\right) = -\dfrac{4}{25}$

39. $3 \cdot 2^4 = 3 \cdot 16 = 48$

41. $-4(-1)^7 = -4(-1) = 4$

43. $6^2 - 3^3 = 36 - 27 = 9$

45. $2 \cdot 3^2 + 4 \cdot 2^3 = 2 \cdot 9 + 4 \cdot 8 = 18 + 32 = 50$

47. $-4b^2 = -4(5)^2 = -4(25) = -100$

49. $(-4b)^2 = (-4 \cdot 5)^2 = (-20)^2 = 400$

51. $(a+b)^2 = [-4+5]^2 = (1)^2 = 1$

53. $a^2 + 2ab + b^2 = (-4)^2 + 2(-4)(5) + 5^2$
$$= 16 + (-40) + 25$$
$$= 1$$

55. $-10ab^2 = -10(-4)(5^2)$
$$= -10(-4)(25)$$
$$= 1000$$

57. $-10a^2b = -10(-4)^2(5) = -10(16)(5) = -800$

59. (a) $x^4 \cdot x^3 = (x \cdot x \cdot x \cdot x)(x \cdot x \cdot x) = x^7$

(b) $5^4 \cdot 5^3 = (5 \cdot 5 \cdot 5 \cdot 5)(5 \cdot 5 \cdot 5) = 5^7$

61. $z^5 z^3 = z^{5+3} = z^8$

63. $a \cdot a^8 = a^{1+8} = a^9$

65. $4^5 \cdot 4^9 = 4^{5+9} = 4^{14}$

67. $\left(\dfrac{2}{3}\right)^3 \left(\dfrac{2}{3}\right) = \left(\dfrac{2}{3}\right)^4$

69. $c^5 c^2 c^7 = c^{5+2+7} = c^{14}$

71. $x \cdot x^4 \cdot x^{10} \cdot x^3 = x^{1+4+10+3} = x^{18}$

73. (a) $\dfrac{p^8}{p^3} = \dfrac{p \cdot p \cdot p \cdot p \cdot p \cdot \cancel{p} \cdot \cancel{p} \cdot \cancel{p}}{\cancel{p} \cdot \cancel{p} \cdot \cancel{p}} = p^5$

(b) $\dfrac{8^8}{8^3} = \dfrac{8 \cdot 8 \cdot 8 \cdot 8 \cdot 8 \cdot \cancel{8} \cdot \cancel{8} \cdot \cancel{8}}{\cancel{8} \cdot \cancel{8} \cdot \cancel{8}} = 8^5$

75. $\dfrac{x^8}{x^6} = x^{8-6} = x^2$

77. $\dfrac{a^{10}}{a} = a^{10-1} = a^9$

79. $\dfrac{7^{13}}{7^6} = 7^{13-6} = 7^7$

81. $\dfrac{5^8}{5} = 5^{8-1} = 5^7$

83. $\dfrac{y^{13}}{y^{12}} = y^{13-12} = y$

85. $\dfrac{h^3 h^8}{h^7} = \dfrac{h^{3+8}}{h^7} = h^{11-7} = h^4$

87. $\dfrac{7^2 \cdot 7^6}{7} = \dfrac{7^{2+6}}{7} = 7^{8-1} = 7^7$

89. $\dfrac{10^{20}}{10^3 \cdot 10^8} = \dfrac{10^{20}}{10^{3+8}} = 10^{20-11} = 10^9$

91. $(2x^3)(3x^4) = 2 \cdot 3 \cdot x^3 x^4 = 6x^{3+4} = 6x^7$

93. $(5a^2b)(8a^3b^4) = 8 \cdot 5 \cdot a^2 a^3 b b^4 = 40a^5 b^5$

95. $(r^6 s^4)(13r^2 s) = 13r^6 r^2 s^4 s = 13r^8 s^5$

97. $s^3 \cdot t^5 \cdot t \cdot t^{10} \cdot s^6 = s^3 \cdot s^6 \cdot t^5 \cdot t \cdot t^{10} = s^9 t^{16}$

99. $(-2v^2)(3v)(5v^5) = -2 \cdot 3 \cdot 5 v^2 v v^5 = -30v^8$

101. $\left(\dfrac{2}{3}m^{13}n^8\right)(24m^7 n^2) = \dfrac{2}{3} \cdot 24m^{13}m^7 n^8 n^2$
$$= 16m^{20}n^{10}$$

103. $\dfrac{14c^4 d^5}{7c^3 d} = 2c^{4-3}d^{5-1} = 2cd^4$

105. $\dfrac{z^3 z^{11}}{z^4 z^6} = \dfrac{z^{3+11}}{z^{4+6}} = \dfrac{z^{14}}{z^{10}} = z^{14-10} = z^4$

107. $\dfrac{25h^3 jk^5}{12h^2 k} = \dfrac{25}{12} \cdot \dfrac{h^3}{h^2} \cdot j \cdot \dfrac{k^5}{k}$

$= \dfrac{25h^{3-2} jk^{5-1}}{12} = \dfrac{25hjk^4}{12}$

109. $(-4p^6 q^8 r^4)(2pqr^2) = -4 \cdot 2 p^6 pq^8 qr^4 r^2$

$= -8p^{6+1} q^{8+1} r^{4+2}$

$= -8p^7 q^9 r^6$

111. $\dfrac{-12s^2 tu^3}{4su^2} = \dfrac{-12}{4} \cdot \dfrac{s^2}{s} \cdot t \cdot \dfrac{u^3}{u^2}$

$= -3s^{2-1} tu^{3-2} = -3stu$

113. Substitute $P = 5000$, $t = 2$, and $r = 7\% = 0.07$ into the formula.

$A = P(1+r)^t$

$= \$5000(1+0.07)^2$

$= 5000(1.07)^2$

$= \$5724.50$

115. Substitute $P = 4000$, $t = 3$, and $r = 6\% = 0.06$ into the formula.

$A = P(1+r)^t$

$= \$4000(1+0.06)^3$

$= 4000(1.06)^3$

$= \$4764.06$

117. Substitute $r = 16$ and $\pi = 3.14$ into the formula.

$A = \pi r^2$

$= (3.14)(8 \text{ in.})^2$

$= 3.14(64)$

$= 200.96$

$\approx 201 \text{ in.}^2$　　　Round to the nearest in^2

119. Since the radius of a sphere is half of its diameter, $r = \dfrac{d}{2} = \dfrac{8}{2} = 4$ in. Substitute $r = 4$ and $\pi = 3.14$ into the formula.

$V = \dfrac{4}{3}\pi r^3$

$= \dfrac{4}{3}(3.14)(4)^3$

$= 267.9466667$

$\approx 268 \text{ in.}^3$　　　Round to the nearest in^3

121. $x^n x^{n+1} = x^{n+n+1} = x^{2n+1}$

123. $p^{3m+5} p^{-m-2} = p^{3m+5-m-2} = p^{2m+3}$

125. $\dfrac{z^{b+1}}{z^b} = z^{b+1-b} = z$

127. $\dfrac{r^{3a+3}}{r^{3a}} = r^{3a+3-3a} = r^3$

Section 5.2 Practice Exercises

1. $4^2 \cdot 4^7 = 4^{2+7} = 4^9$

3. $a^{13} \cdot a \cdot a^6 = a^{13+1+6} = a^{20}$

5. $\dfrac{d^{13} d}{d^5} = d^{14-5} = d^9$

7. $\dfrac{7^{11}}{7^5} = 7^{11-5} = 7^6$

9. When multiplying expressions with the same base, add the exponents. When raising an expression with an exponent to a power, multiply the exponents.

11. $(5^3)^4 = 5^{3 \cdot 4} = 5^{12}$

13. $(12^3)^2 = 12^{3 \cdot 2} = 12^6$

15. $(y^7)^2 = y^{7 \cdot 2} = y^{14}$

17. $(w^5)^5 = w^{5 \cdot 5} = w^{25}$

19. $(a^2 a^4)^6 = (a^6)^6 = a^{6 \cdot 6} = a^{36}$

21. $(y^3 y^4)^2 = (y^7)^2 = y^{7 \cdot 2} = y^{14}$

23. $(2^2)^3 = 2^6$; $(2^3)^2 = 2^6$, they are both equal to 2^6.

25. $4^{(3^2)} = 4^9$ and $(4^3)^2 = 4^6$; the expression $4^{(3^2)}$ is greater than $(4^3)^2$.

27. $(5w)^2 = 5^2 w^2 = 25w^2$

29. $(srt)^4 = s^4 r^4 t^4$

31. $\left(\dfrac{2}{r}\right)^4 = \dfrac{2^4}{r^4} = \dfrac{16}{r^4}$

33. $\left(\dfrac{x}{y}\right)^5 = \dfrac{x^5}{y^5}$

35. $(-3a)^4 = (-3)^4 a^4 = 81a^4$

37. $(-3abc)^3 = (-3)^3 a^3 b^3 c^3 = -27a^3 b^3 c^3$

39. $\left(-\dfrac{4}{x}\right)^3 = (-1)^3 \dfrac{4^3}{x^3} = -\dfrac{64}{x^3}$

41. $\left(-\dfrac{a}{b}\right)^2 = (-1)^2 \dfrac{a^2}{b^2} = \dfrac{a^2}{b^2}$

43. $(6u^2 v^4)^3 = 6^3 (u^2)^3 (v^4)^3$
$= 6^3 u^6 v^{12}$ or $216u^6 v^{12}$

45. $5(x^2 y)^4 = 5(x^2)^4 (y)^4 = 5x^8 y^4$

47. $(-h^4)^7 = (-1)^7 h^{28} = -h^{28}$

49. $(-m^2)^6 = (-1)^6 m^{12} = m^{12}$

51. $\left(\dfrac{4}{rs^4}\right)^5 = \dfrac{4^5}{(rs^4)^5}$

$= \dfrac{4^5}{(r)^5 (s^4)^5}$

$= \dfrac{4^5}{r^5 s^{20}}$ or $\dfrac{1024}{r^5 s^{20}}$

53. $\left(\dfrac{3p}{q^3}\right)^5 = \dfrac{(3p)^5}{(q^3)^5}$

$= \dfrac{3^5 p^5}{q^{3 \cdot 5}}$

$= \dfrac{3^5 p^5}{q^{15}}$ or $\dfrac{243 p^5}{q^{15}}$

55. $\dfrac{y^8 (y^3)^4}{(y^2)^3} = \dfrac{y^8 y^{12}}{y^6} = \dfrac{y^{20}}{y^6} = y^{14}$

57. $(x^2)^5 (x^3)^7 = x^{10} x^{21} = x^{31}$

59. $(2a^2 b)^3 (5a^4 b^3)^2$
$= 2^3 (a^2)^3 b^3 \cdot 5^2 (a^4)^2 (b^3)^2$
$= 8a^6 b^3 \cdot 25a^8 b^6$
$= 8 \cdot 25 a^{6+8} b^{3+6}$
$= 200 a^{14} b^9$

61. $(-2p^2 q^4)^4 = (-2)^4 (p^2)^4 (q^4)^4 = 16 p^8 q^{16}$

63. $(-m^7 n^3)^5 = (-1)^5 (m^7)^5 (n^3)^5 = -m^{35} n^{15}$

65. $\dfrac{(5a^3 b)^4 (a^2 b)^4}{(5ab)^2} = \dfrac{5^4 a^{12} b^4 a^8 b^4}{5^2 a^2 b^2}$

$= \dfrac{5^4 a^{20} b^8}{5^2 a^2 b^2}$

$= 5^2 a^{18} b^6$

$= 25 a^{18} b^6$

67. $\left(\dfrac{2c^3 d^4}{3c^2 d}\right)^2 = \dfrac{2^2 c^6 d^8}{3^2 c^4 d^2} = \dfrac{4}{9} c^2 d^6$

68. $\left(\dfrac{x^3 y^5 z}{5xy^2}\right)^2 = \dfrac{x^6 y^{10} z^2}{25 x^2 y^4} = \dfrac{1}{25} x^4 y^6 z^2$

70. $\left(\dfrac{s^5 t^6}{2s^2 t}\right)^2 (10s^3 t^3)^2 = \dfrac{s^{10} t^{12}}{2^2 s^4 t^2} (10^2 s^6 t^6)$

$= \dfrac{s^{10} t^{12} \cdot 100 s^6 t^6}{4 s^4 t^2}$

$= \dfrac{100 s^{16} t^{18}}{4 s^4 t^2}$

$= 25 s^{12} t^{16}$

74. $\dfrac{(-6a^2)^2 (a^3)^4}{9a} = \dfrac{(-6)^2 a^4 a^{12}}{9a}$

$= \dfrac{36 a^{16}}{9a}$

$= 4a^{16-1}$

$= 4a^{15}$

76. $(y^3)^n = y^{3n}$

78. $(3b^4)^m = 3^m (b^4)^m = 3^m b^{4m}$

80. $\left(\dfrac{x^5}{y^3}\right)^m = \dfrac{x^{5m}}{y^{3m}}$

82. $\left(\dfrac{4m^6}{3n^2}\right)^b = \dfrac{4^b (m^6)^b}{3^b (n^2)^b} = \dfrac{4^b m^{6b}}{3^b n^{2b}}$

Section 5.3 Practice Exercises

1. Answers may vary

3. $c^7 c^2 = c^{7+2} = c^9$

5. $\dfrac{y^9}{y^8} = y^{9-8} = y^1 = y$

7. $\dfrac{3^{14}}{3^3 \cdot 3^5} = \dfrac{3^{14}}{3^8} = 3^6$ or 729

9. $(7w^7 z^2)^4 = 7^4 (w^7)^4 (z^2)^4$

$= 7^4 w^{28} z^8$ or $2401 w^{28} z^8$

11. (a) $d^0 = 1$

(b) $\dfrac{d^3}{d^3} = d^{3-3} = d^0 = 1$

13. $p^0 = 1$

15. $5^0 = 1$

17. $-4^0 = -(4^0) = -1$

19. $(-6)^0 = 1$

21. $(8x)^0 = 8^0 x^0 = 1$

23. $-7x^0 = -7 \cdot 1 = -7$

25. (a) $t^{-5} = \dfrac{1}{t^5}$

(b) $\dfrac{t^3}{t^8} = t^{3-8} = t^{-5} = \dfrac{1}{t^5}$

27. $\left(\dfrac{2}{7}\right)^{-3} = \left(\dfrac{7}{2}\right)^3 = \dfrac{7^3}{8^3} = \dfrac{343}{8}$

29. $\left(-\dfrac{1}{5}\right)^{-2} = (-5)^2 = 25$

31. $a^{-3} = \dfrac{1}{a^3}$

33. $12^{-1} = \dfrac{1}{12}$

35. $(4b)^{-2} = \dfrac{1}{(4b)^2} = \dfrac{1}{16b^2}$

37. $6x^{-2} = 6 \cdot \dfrac{1}{x^2} = \dfrac{6}{x^2}$

39. $(-8)^{-2} = \dfrac{1}{(-8)^2} = \dfrac{1}{64}$

41. $-3y^{-4} = -3 \cdot \dfrac{1}{y^4} = -\dfrac{3}{y^4}$

43. $(-t)^{-3} = \dfrac{1}{(-t)^3} = -\dfrac{1}{t^3}$

45. $\dfrac{1}{a^{-5}} = a^5$

47. Subtract (-6). $\dfrac{x^4}{x^{-6}} = x^{4-(-6)} = x^{10}$

49. The exponent is only on the variable a.

$2a^{-3} = a \cdot \dfrac{1}{a^3} = \dfrac{2}{a^3}$

51. $x^{-8}x^4 = x^{-8+4} = x^{-4} = \dfrac{1}{x^4}$

53. $a^{-8}a^8 = a^{-8+8} = a^0 = 1$

55. $y^{17}y^{-13} = y^{17+(-13)} = y^4$

57. $(m^{-6}n^9)^3 = (m^{-6})^3(n^9)^3 = m^{-18}n^{27} = \dfrac{n^{27}}{m^{18}}$

59. $(-3j^{-5}k^6)^4 = (-3)^4(j^{-5})^4(k^6)^4$

$\qquad = 81j^{-20}k^{24}$

$\qquad = \dfrac{81k^{24}}{j^{20}}$

61. $\dfrac{p^3}{p^9} = p^{3-9} = p^{-6} = \dfrac{1}{p^6}$

63. $\dfrac{r^{-5}}{r^{-2}} = r^{-5-(-2)} = r^{-3} = \dfrac{1}{r^3}$

65. $\dfrac{a^2}{a^{-6}} = a^{2-(-6)} = a^8$

67. $\dfrac{y^{-2}}{y^6} = y^{-2-6} = y^{-8} = \dfrac{1}{y^8}$

69. $\dfrac{7^3}{7^2 \cdot 7^8} = \dfrac{7^3}{7^{10}} = 7^{3-10} = 7^{-7} = \dfrac{1}{7^7}$

71. $\dfrac{a^2 a}{a^3} = \dfrac{a^{2+1}}{a^3} = \dfrac{a^3}{a^3} = 1$

73. $\dfrac{a^{-1}b^2}{a^3 b^8} = a^{-1-3}b^{2-8} = a^{-4}b^{-6} = \dfrac{1}{a^4 b^6}$

75. $\dfrac{w^{-8}(w^2)^{-5}}{w^3} = \dfrac{w^{-8}w^{-10}}{w^3}$

$\qquad = \dfrac{w^{-18}}{w^3}$

$\qquad = w^{-21}$

$\qquad = \dfrac{1}{w^{21}}$

77. $\dfrac{3^{-2}}{3} = 3^{-2-1} = 3^{-3} = \dfrac{1}{3^3} = \dfrac{1}{27}$

79. $\left(\dfrac{p^{-1}q^5}{p^{-6}}\right)^0 = 1$

81. $(8x^3 y^0)^{-2} = 8^{-2}x^{-6}y^0 = \dfrac{1}{8^2} \cdot \dfrac{1}{x^6} \cdot 1 = \dfrac{1}{64x^6}$

83. $(-8y^{-12})(2y^{16}z^{-2}) = (-8)(2)y^{-12+16}z^{-2}$

$\qquad = -16y^4 z^{-2}$

$\qquad = \dfrac{-16y^4}{z^2}$

85. $\dfrac{-18a^{10}b^6}{108a^{-2}b^6} = \dfrac{-18}{108}a^{10-(-2)}b^{6-6}$

$\qquad = -\dfrac{1}{6}a^{12}b^0$

$\qquad = -\dfrac{a^{12}}{6}$

87. $\dfrac{(-4c^{12}d^7)^2}{(5c^{-3}d^{10})^{-1}} = \dfrac{(-4)^2(c^{12})^2(d^7)^2}{(5)^{-1}(c^{-3})^{-1}(d^{10})^{-1}}$

$= \dfrac{16c^{24}d^{14}}{5^{-1}c^3d^{-10}}$

$= 16(5)c^{24-3}d^{14-(-10)}$

$= 80c^{21}d^{24}$

89.

$\dfrac{2x^3y^2{}^{-3}}{3x^2y^4{}^{-2}} = \dfrac{3x^2y^4{}^{2}}{2x^3y^2{}^{3}}$

$= \dfrac{3^{\,2}\;x^2{}^{2}\;y^4{}^{2}}{2^{\,3}\;x^3{}^{3}\;y^2{}^{3}}$

$= \dfrac{9x^4y^8}{8x^9y^6}$

$= \dfrac{9}{8}x^{4-9}y^{8-6}$

$= \dfrac{9}{8}x^{-5}y^2$

$= \dfrac{9y^2}{8x^5}$

91. $\left(\dfrac{5cd^{-3}}{10d^5}\right)^{-2} = \left(\dfrac{1}{2}cd^{-3-5}\right)^{-2}$

$= \left(\dfrac{1}{2}\right)^{-2} c^{-2}(d^{-8})^{-2}$

$= 2^2 \cdot \dfrac{1}{c^2}d^{16}$

$= \dfrac{4d^{16}}{c^2}$

93. $(2xy^3)\left(\dfrac{9xy}{4x^3y^2}\right) = \dfrac{18x^2y^4}{4x^3y^2}$

$= \dfrac{18}{4}x^{2-3}y^{4-2}$

$= \dfrac{9}{2}x^{-1}y^2$

$= \dfrac{9y^2}{2x}$

95. $5^{-1} + 2^{-2} = \dfrac{1}{5} + \dfrac{1}{2^2} = \dfrac{1}{5} + \dfrac{1}{4} = \dfrac{4}{20} + \dfrac{5}{20} = \dfrac{9}{20}$

97. $10^0 - 10^{-1} = 1 - \dfrac{1}{10} = \dfrac{10}{10} - \dfrac{1}{10} = \dfrac{9}{10}$

99. $2^{-2} + 1^{-2} = \dfrac{1}{2^2} + \dfrac{1}{1^2} = \dfrac{1}{4} + 1 = \dfrac{5}{4}$

101. $4 \cdot 5^0 - 2 \cdot 3^{-1} = 4 \cdot 1 - 2 \cdot \dfrac{1}{3}$

$= 4 - \dfrac{2}{3}$

$= \dfrac{12}{3} - \dfrac{2}{3}$

$= \dfrac{10}{3}$

Calculator Exercises

1.

```
(5.2E6)*(4.6E-3)
                23920
```

3.

```
(4.76E-5)/(2.38E
9)
               2E-14
```

5.

```
(9.6E7)*(4.0E-3)
/(2.0E-2)
             19200000
```

Section 5.4 Practice Exercises

1. To write a positive number in **scientific notation** is to express the positive number in the form: $a \times 10^n$, where $1 \leq a < 10$ and n is an integer. To write a negative number in **scientific notation** is to express the negative number in the form: $a \times 10^n$, where $-10 < a \leq -1$ and n is an integer.

3. $b^5 b^8 = b^{5+8} = b^{13}$

5. $10^5 \cdot 10^8 = 10^{5+8} = 10^{13}$

7. $\dfrac{y^2}{y^7} = y^{2-7} = y^{-5} = \dfrac{1}{y^5}$

9. $(x^5 y^{-3})^4 = (x^5)^4 (y^{-3})^4 = x^{20} y^{-12} = \dfrac{x^{20}}{y^{12}}$

11. $\dfrac{w^{-2} w^5}{w^{-1}} = \dfrac{w^3}{w^{-1}} = w^{3-(-1)} = w^4$

13. $\dfrac{10^{-2} \cdot 10^5}{10^{-1}} = \dfrac{10^3}{10^{-1}} = 10^{3-(-1)} = 10^4$

15. Move the decimal point between 2 and 3 and multiply by 10^{-10}; 2.3×10^{-10}

17. Move the decimal point between 5 and 0 and multiply by 10^4; $50,000 = 5 \times 10^4$

19. Move the decimal point between 2 and 0 and multiply by 10^5; $208,000 = 2.08 \times 10^5$

21. Move the decimal point between 6 and 0 and multiply by 10^6; $6,010,000 = 6.01 \times 10^6$

23. Move the decimal point between 8 and 0 and multiply by 10^{-6}; $0.000008 = 8 \times 10^{-6}$

25. Move the decimal point between 1 and 2 and multiply by 10^{-4}; $0.000125 = 1.25 \times 10^{-4}$

27. Move the decimal point between 6 and 7 and multiply by 10^{-3}; $0.006708 = 6.708 \times 10^{-3}$

29. Move the decimal point between 1 and 7 and multiply by 10^{-24}; 1.7×10^{-24} g

31. Move the decimal point between 2 and 7 and multiply by 10^{10}; $\$2.7 \times 10^{10}$

33. Move the decimal point between 6 and 8 and multiply by 10^7; 6.8×10^7 gal
Move the decimal point between 1 and 0 and multiply by 10^2; 1.0×10^2 mi

35. Move the decimal point nine places to the left; 0.0000000031

37. Move the decimal point five places to the left; 0.00005

39. Move the decimal point three places to the right; 2800

41. Move the decimal point four places to the left; 0.000603

43. Move the decimal point six places to the right; 2,400,000

45. Move the decimal point two places to the left; 0.019

47. Move the decimal point three places to the right; 7032

49. Move the decimal point twelve places to the left; 0.000000000001 g

51. Move the decimal point three places to the right; 1600 calories; move the decimal point three places to the right; 2800 calories

53. $(2.5 \times 10^6)(2.0 \times 10^{-2}) = 2.5(2.0) \times 10^6 \cdot 10^{-2}$
$= 5.0 \times 10^4$

55. $(1.2 \times 10^4)(3 \times 10^7) = 1.2(3) \times 10^4 \cdot 10^7$
$= 3.6 \times 10^{11}$

57. $\dfrac{7.7 \times 10^6}{3.5 \times 10^2} = \dfrac{7.7}{3.5} \times 10^{6-2} = 2.2 \times 10^4$

59. $\dfrac{9.0 \times 10^{-6}}{4.0 \times 10^7} = \dfrac{9.0}{4.0} \times 10^{-6-7} = 2.25 \times 10^{-13}$

61. $(8.0 \times 10^{10})(4.0 \times 10^3) = 8(4) \times 10^{10} \cdot 10^3$
$= 32 \times 10^{13}$
$= 3.2 \times 10^1 \times 10^{13}$
$= 3.2 \times 10^{14}$

63. $(3.2 \times 10^{-4})(7.6 \times 10^{-7})$
$= 3.2(7.6) \times 10^{-4} \cdot 10^{-7}$
$= 24.32 \times 10^{-11}$
$= 2.432 \times 10^1 \times 10^{-11}$
$= 2.432 \times 10^{-10}$

65. $\dfrac{2.1 \times 10^{11}}{7.0 \times 10^{-3}} = \dfrac{2.1}{7} \times 10^{11-(-3)}$
$= 0.3 \times 10^{14}$
$= 3.0 \times 10^{-1} \times 10^3$
$= 3.0 \times 10^{13}$

67. $\dfrac{5.7 \times 10^{-2}}{9.5 \times 10^{-8}} = \dfrac{5.7}{9.5} \times 10^{-2-(-8)}$
$= 0.6 \times 10^6$
$= 6.0 \times 10^{-1} \times 10^6$
$= 6.0 \times 10^5$

69. $6,000,000,000 \times 0.0000000023$
$= (6 \times 10^9)(2.3 \times 10^{-9})$
$= 13.8 \times 10^{9+(-9)}$
$= 1.38 \times 10^1 \times 10^0$
$= 1.38 \times 10^1$

71. $\dfrac{0.0000000003}{6000} = \dfrac{3.0 \times 10^{-10}}{6.0 \times 10^3}$
$= 0.5 \times 10^{-10-3}$
$= 5.0 \times 10^{-1} \times 10^{-13}$
$= 5.0 \times 10^{-14}$

73. (thickness of paper)(no. of pieces)
$= (3 \times 10^{-3})(1.25 \times 10^3)$
$= 3(1.25) \times 10^{-3+3}$
$= 3.75 \times 10^0$
$= 3.75$ inches

75. (number of shares)(price per share)
$= (1,100,000,000)(27)$
$= (1.1 \times 10^9)(27)$
$= 29.7 \times 10^9$
$= 2.97 \times 10^1 \times 10^9$
$= \$2.97 \times 10^{10}$ or $\$29,700,000,000$

77. (a) 65 million $= 65,000,000 = 6.5 \times 10^7$

(b) 6.5×10^7 years
$= (6.5 \times 10^7 \text{ years})(365 \text{ days})$
$= (6.5 \times 10^7 \text{ years})(3.65 \times 10^2 \text{ days})$
$= 23.725 \times 10^9$
$= 2.3725 \times 10^1 \times 10^9$
$= 2.3725 \times 10^{10}$ days

(c) 6.5×10^7 years
$= (2.3725 \times 10^{10} \text{ days})(24 \text{ hours})$
$= (2.3725 \times 10^{10} \text{ days})(2.4 \times 10^1 \text{ hours})$
$= 5.694 \times 10^{11}$ hours

(d) 6.5×10^7 years
$= (5.694 \times 10^{11} \text{ hours})(3600 \text{ seconds})$
$= (5.694 \times 10^{11} \text{ hours})(3.6 \times 10^3 \text{ seconds})$
$= 20.4984 \times 10^{14}$
$= 2.04984 \times 10^1 \times 10^{14}$
$= 2.04984 \times 10^{15}$ seconds

Problem Recognition Exercises

1. $t^3 t^5 = t^{3+5} = t^8$

3. $\dfrac{y^7}{y^2} = y^{7-2} = y^5$

5. $(r^2 s^4)^2 = (r^2)^2 (s^4)^2 = r^4 s^8$

7. $\dfrac{w^4}{w^{-2}} = w^{4-(-2)} = w^6$

9. $\dfrac{y^{-7} x^4}{z^{-3}} = \dfrac{x^4 z^3}{y^7}$

11. $\begin{aligned}(2.5 \times 10^{-3})(5.0 \times 10^5) &= 2.5(5.0) \times 10^{-3+5} \\ &= 12.5 \times 10^2 \\ &= 1.25 \times 10^1 \times 10^2 \\ &= 1.25 \times 10^3\end{aligned}$

13. $\begin{aligned}\dfrac{4.8 \times 10^7}{6.0 \times 10^{-2}} &= \dfrac{4.8}{6.0} \times 10^{7-(-2)} \\ &= 0.8 \times 10^9 \\ &= 8.0 \times 10^{-1} \times 10^9 \\ &= 8.0 \times 10^8\end{aligned}$

15. $\dfrac{1}{p^{-6} p^{-8} p^{-1}} = \dfrac{1}{p^{-6+(-8)+(-1)}} = \dfrac{1}{p^{-15}} = p^{15}$

17. $\dfrac{v^9}{v^{11}} = v^{9-11} = v^{-2} = \dfrac{1}{v^2}$

19. $\left(\dfrac{1}{2}\right)^{-1} + \left(\dfrac{1}{3}\right)^0 = \left(\dfrac{2}{1}\right)^1 + 1 = 2 + 1 = 3$

21. $(2^5 b^{-3})^{-3} = 2^{5(-3)} b^{(-3)(-3)} = 2^{-15} b^9 = \dfrac{b^9}{2^{15}}$

23. $\left(\dfrac{3x}{2y}\right)^{-4} = \left(\dfrac{2y}{3x}\right)^4 = \dfrac{2^4 y^4}{3^4 x^4} = \dfrac{16 y^4}{81 x^4}$

25. $\begin{aligned}(3ab^2)(a^2 b)^3 &= (3ab^2)(a^{2(3)} b^3) \\ &= (3ab^2)(a^6 b^3) \\ &= 3aa^6 b^2 b^3 \\ &= 3a^7 b^5\end{aligned}$

27. $\begin{aligned}\left(\dfrac{xy^2}{x^3 y}\right)^4 &= (x^{1-3} y^{2-1})^4 \\ &= (x^{-2} y)^4 \\ &= x^{-2(4)} y^4 \\ &= x^{-8} y^4 \\ &= \dfrac{y^4}{x^8}\end{aligned}$

29. $\dfrac{(t^{-2})^3}{t^{-4}} = \dfrac{t^{-6}}{t^{-4}} = t^{-6-(-4)} = t^{-2} = \dfrac{1}{t^2}$

31. $\begin{aligned}\left(\dfrac{2w^2 x^3}{3y^0}\right)^3 &= \dfrac{2^3 w^{2(3)} x^{3(3)}}{3^3 y^{0(3)}} \\ &= \dfrac{8 w^6 x^9}{27 y^0} \\ &= \dfrac{8 w^6 x^9}{27}\end{aligned}$

33. $\dfrac{q^3 r^{-2}}{s^{-1} t^5} = \dfrac{q^3 s}{r^2 t^5}$

35. $\begin{aligned}\dfrac{(y^{-3})^2 (y^5)}{(y^{-3})^{-4}} &= \dfrac{(y^{-6})(y^5)}{y^{12}} \\ &= \dfrac{y^{-1}}{y^{12}} \\ &= y^{-1-12} \\ &= y^{-13} \\ &= \dfrac{1}{y^{13}}\end{aligned}$

37. $\left(\dfrac{-2a^2b^{-3}}{a^{-4}b^{-5}}\right)^{-3} = (-2a^{2-(-4)}b^{-3-(-5)})^{-3}$

$= (-2a^6b^2)^{-3}$

$= \dfrac{1}{(-2a^6b^2)^3}$

$= \dfrac{1}{(-2)^3 a^{6(3)}b^{2(3)}}$

$= -\dfrac{1}{8a^{18}b^6}$

39. $(5h^{-2}k^0)^3(5k^{-2})^{-4}$

$= (5^3)(h^{-2})^3(k^0)^3(5^{-4})(k^{-2})^{-4}$

$= (5^3)h^{-6}k^0(5^{-4})k^8$

$= 5^{3-4}h^{-6}(1)k^8$

$= 5^{-1}h^{-6}k^8$

$= \dfrac{k^8}{5h^6}$

Section 5.5 Practice Exercises

1. (a) A **polynomial** in one variable, x, is defined as a sum of terms of the form ax^n, where a is a real number and n is a nonnegative integer.

(b) For a polynomial with terms of the form ax^n, a is called the **coefficient.**

(c) For a polynomial with terms of the form ax^n, n is called the **degree of the term.**

(d) A **monomial** is a polynomial with exactly one term.

(e) A **binomial** is a polynomial with exactly two terms.

(f) A **trinomial** is a polynomial with exactly three terms.

(g) The **leading term** of a polynomial is the term with highest degree.

(h) The coefficient of the leading term of a polynomial is called the **leading coefficient.**

(i) The **degree of a polynomial** is the largest degree of all of its terms.

3. $(3x)^2(5x^{-4}) = 9 \cdot 5 \cdot x^2 \cdot x^{-4} = 45x^{-2} = \dfrac{45}{x^2}$

5. $\dfrac{8t^{-6}}{4t^{-2}} = 2t^{-6-(-2)} = 2t^{-4} = \dfrac{2}{t^4}$

7. $\dfrac{3^4 \cdot 3^{-8}}{3^{12} \cdot 3^{-4}} = \dfrac{3^{-4}}{3^8} = 3^{-4-8} = 3^{-12} = \dfrac{1}{3^{12}}$

9. $4.0 \cdot 10^{-2}$ is in scientific notation in which 10 is raised to the negative 2 power. 4^{-2} is not in scientific notation and 4 is being raised to the negative 2 power.

11. To write the polynomial in descending order, start with term with the highest power; $-7x^4 + 7x^2 + 9x + 6$

13. Binomial; leading coefficient 10; degree 2

15. Trinomial; leading coefficient 2.1; degree 3

17. Binomial; leading coefficient −1; degree 4

19. Trinomial; leading coefficient 12; degree 4

21. Monomial; leading coefficient 23; degree 0

23. Monomial; leading coefficient −32; degree 3

25. The exponents on the x-factors are different.

27. $23x^2y + 12x^2y = 35x^2y$

29. $3b^5d^2 + (5b^5d^2 - 9d) = 3b^5d^2 + 5b^5d^2 - 9d$
$= 8b^5d^2 - 9d$

31. $(7y^2 + 2y - 9) + (-3y^2 - y)$
$= 7y^2 - 3y^2 - y + 2y - 9$
$= 4y^2 + y - 9$

33. $(6.1y + 3.2x) + (4.8y - 3.2x)$
$= 6.1y + 4.8y + 3.2x - 3.2x$
$= 10.9y$

35.
$$6a + 2b - 5c$$
$$+ \quad \underline{-2a - 2b - 3c}$$
$$4a \qquad - 8c$$

37. $\left(\dfrac{2}{5}a + \dfrac{1}{4}b - \dfrac{5}{6}\right) + \left(\dfrac{3}{5}a - \dfrac{3}{4}b - \dfrac{7}{6}\right)$
$= \dfrac{2}{5}a + \dfrac{3}{5}a + \dfrac{1}{4}b - \dfrac{3}{4}b - \dfrac{5}{6} - \dfrac{7}{6}$
$= a - \dfrac{1}{2}b - 2$

39. $\left(z - \dfrac{8}{3}\right) + \left(\dfrac{4}{3}z^2 - z + 1\right) = \dfrac{4}{3}z^2 + z - z - \dfrac{8}{3} + 1$
$= \dfrac{4}{3}z^2 - \dfrac{5}{3}$

41.
$$7.9t^3 \qquad\qquad + 2.6t - 1.1$$
$$+ \quad \underline{\qquad - 3.4t^2 + 3.4t - 3.1}$$
$$7.9t^3 - 3.4t^2 + \ 6t - 4.2$$

43. $-(4h - 5) = -4h + 5$

45. $-(-2.3m^2 + 3.1m - 1.5)$
$= 2.3m^2 - 3.1m + 1.5$

47. $-(3v^3 + 5v^2 + 10v + 22)$
$= -3v^3 - 5v^2 - 10v - 22$

49. $4a^3b^2 - 12a^3b^2 = -8a^3b^2$

51. $-32x^3 - 21x^3 = -53x^3$

53. $(7a - 7) - (12a - 4) = 7a - 7 - 12a + 4$
$= -5a - 3$

55. $(4k + 3) - (-12k - 6) = 4k + 3 + 12k + 6$
$= 16k + 9$

57. $25m^4 - (23m^4 + 14m) = 25m^4 - 23m^4 - 14m$
$= 2m^4 - 14m$

59. $(5s^2 - 3st - 2t^2) - (2s^2 + st + t^2)$
$= 5s^2 - 2s^2 - 3st - st - 2t^2 - t^2$
$= 3s^2 - 4st - 3t^2$

61. To subtract the polynomials vertically, add the opposite of the second polynomial to the first.
$$10r - 6s + 2t$$
$$+ \quad \underline{-12r + 3s + \ t}$$
$$-2r - 3s + 3t$$

63. $\left(\dfrac{7}{8}x + \dfrac{2}{3}y - \dfrac{3}{10}\right) - \left(\dfrac{1}{8}x + \dfrac{1}{3}y\right)$
$= \dfrac{7}{8}x - \dfrac{1}{8}x + \dfrac{2}{3}y - \dfrac{1}{3}y - \dfrac{3}{10}$
$= \dfrac{3}{4}x + \dfrac{1}{3}y - \dfrac{3}{10}$

65. $\left(\dfrac{2}{3}h^2 - \dfrac{1}{5}h - \dfrac{3}{4}\right) - \left(\dfrac{4}{3}h^2 - \dfrac{4}{5}h + \dfrac{7}{4}\right)$
$= \dfrac{2}{3}h^2 - \dfrac{4}{3}h^2 - \dfrac{1}{5}h + \dfrac{4}{5}h - \dfrac{7}{4} - \dfrac{3}{4}$
$= -\dfrac{2}{3}h^2 + \dfrac{3}{5}h - \dfrac{5}{2}$

67. To subtract the polynomials vertically, add the opposite of the second polynomial to the first.
$$4.5x^4 - 3.1x^2 \qquad\qquad - 6.7$$
$$+ \quad \underline{-2.1x^4 \qquad\qquad - 4.4x \ - 1.2}$$
$$2.4x^4 - \ 3.1x^2 - 4.4x - 7.9$$

69. $(4b^3 + 6b - 7) - (-12b^2 + 11b + 5)$
$= 4b^3 + 12b^2 + 6b - 11b - 7 - 5$
$= 4b^3 + 12b^2 - 5b - 12$

71. $(-2x^2 - 11) - (\frac{3}{2}x^2 - 5x)$

$= -2x^2 - \frac{3}{2}x^2 + 5x - 11$

$= \frac{1}{2}x^2 + 5x - 11$

73. $(y^2 + 3) + (3y^3 - y^2 - 1) + (y^3 + 2y^2)$

$= 3y^3 + y^3 + y^2 - y^2 + 2y^2 + 3 - 1$

$= 4y^3 + 2y^2 + 2$

75. $P = 5a^2 - 2a + 1$

$\left(\begin{array}{c} \text{missing} \\ \text{side} \end{array}\right) + (a - 3) + (2a^2 - 1) = P$

$\left(\begin{array}{c} \text{missing} \\ \text{side} \end{array}\right) = 5a^2 - 2a + 1 - (a - 3) - (2a^2 - 1)$

$\left(\begin{array}{c} \text{missing} \\ \text{side} \end{array}\right) = 3a^2 - 3a + 5$

77. $(2ab^2 + 9a^2b) + (7ab^2 - 3ab + 7a^2b) = 2ab^2 + 7ab^2 + 9a^2b + 7a^2b - 3ab = 9ab^2 - 3ab + 16a^2b$

79. To subtract the polynomials vertically, add the opposite of the second polynomial to the first.

$$\begin{array}{l} \quad 4z^5 \qquad + z^3 - 3z + 13 \\ + \quad \underline{\quad z^4 + 8z^3 \qquad - 15} \\ \quad 4z^5 + z^4 + 9z^3 - 3z - 2 \end{array}$$

81. $(9x^4 + 2x^3 - x + 5) + (9x^3 - 3x^2 + 8x + 3) - (7x^4 - x + 12)$

$= 9x^4 - 7x^4 + 2x^3 + 9x^3 - 3x^2 - x + x + 8x + 5 + 3 - 12$

$= 2x^4 + 11x^3 - 3x^2 + 8x - 4$

83. $(0.2w^2 + 3w + 1.3) - (w^3 - 0.7w + 2)$

$= -w^3 + 0.2w^2 + 3w + 0.7w + 1.3 - 2$

$= -w^3 + 0.2w^2 + 3.7w + 0.7$

85. $(7p^2q - 3pq^2) - (8p^2q + pq) + (4pq - pq^2)$

$= 7p^2q - 3pq^2 - 8p^2q - pq + 4pq - pq^2$

$= -p^2q - 4pq^2 + 3pq$

87. $(5x - 2x^3) + (2x^3 - 5x) = 5x - 5x - 2x^3 + 2x^3 = 0$

89. To subtract the polynomials vertically, add the opposite of the second polynomial to the first.

$$\begin{array}{l} \quad 2a^2b - 4ab + ab^2 \\ + \quad \underline{-2a^2b - ab + 5ab^2} \\ \qquad - 5ab + 6ab^2 \end{array}$$

91. $[(3y^2 - 5y) - (2y^2 + y - 1)] + (10y^2 - 4y - 5) = (3y^2 - 2y^2 - 5y - y + 1) + (10y^2 - 4y - 5)$
$$= y^2 - 6y + 1 + 10y^2 - 4y - 5$$
$$= y^2 + 10y^2 - 6y - 4y + 1 - 5$$
$$= 11y^2 - 10y - 4$$

93. Answers will vary; $x^3 + 6$

95. Answers will vary; $8x^5$

97. Answers will vary; $-6x^2 + 2x + 5$

Section 5.6 Practice Exercises

1. **(a)** The sum and difference of the same two terms are called **conjugates.**

(b) The product of a pair of conjugates results in a **difference of squares:**
$$(a + b)(a - b) = a^2 - b^2$$

(c) The square of a sum or difference of terms is called a **perfect square trinomial:**
$$(a + b)^2 = a^2 + 2ab + b^2$$
$$(a - b)^2 = a^2 - 2ab + b^2$$

3. $2y^2 - 4y^2 = -2y^2$

5. $(2y^2)(-4y^2) = -8y^4$

7. $7uvw^2 + uvw^2 = 8uvw^2$

9. $(7uvw^2)(uvw^2) = 7u^2v^2w^4$

11. $-2(6y) = -12y$

13. $7(3p) = 21p$

15. $(a^{13}b^4)(12ab^4) = 12a^{13+1}b^{4+4} = 12a^{14}b^8$

17. $(2c^7 d)(-c^3 d^{11}) = -2c^{7+3}d^{1+11} = -2c^{10}d^{12}$

19. $8pq(2pq - 3p + 5q)$
$$= 8pq(2pq) - 8pq(3p) + 8pq(5q)$$
$$= 16p^2q^2 - 24p^2q + 40pq^2$$

21. $(k^2 - 13k - 6)(-4k)$
$$= k^2(-4k) - 13k(-4k) - 6(-4k)$$
$$= -4k^3 + 52k^2 + 24k$$

23. $-15pq(3p^2 + p^3q^2 - 2q)$
$$= -15pq(3p^2) - 15pq(p^3q^2) - 15pq(-2q)$$
$$= -45p^3q - 15p^4q^3 + 30pq^2$$

25. $(y - 10)(y + 9) = y^2 + 9y - 10y - 90$
$$= y^2 - y - 90$$

27. $(m - 12)(m - 2) = m^2 - 2m - 12m + 24$
$$= m^2 - 14m + 24$$

29. $(3p - 2)(4p + 1) = 3p^2 + 3p - 8p - 2$
$$= 3p^2 - 5p - 2$$

31. $(-4w + 8)(-3w + 2) = 12w^2 - 8w - 24w + 16$
$$= 12w^2 - 32w + 16$$

33. $(p - 3w)(p - 11w)$
$$= p^2 - 11pw - 3pw + 33w^2$$
$$= p^2 - 14pw + 33w^2$$

35. $(6x - 1)(2x + 5) = 6x(2x) + 5(6x) - 2x - 5$
$$= 12x^2 + 28x - 5$$

37. $(4a - 9)(1.5a - 2)$
$$= 4a(1.5a) - 8a - 13.5a + 18$$
$$= 6a^2 - 21.5a + 18$$

39. $(3t - 7)(3t + 1) = 3t(3t) + 3t - 21t - 7$
$$= 9t^2 - 18t - 7$$

41. $(3m+4n)(m+8n)$

$= 3m(m)+24mn+4mn+4n(8n)$

$= 3m^2+28mn+32n^2$

43. $(5s+3)(s^2+s-2)$

$= 5s(s^2)+5s(s)-5s(2)+3s^2+3s-6$

$= 5s^3+5s^2-10s+3s^2+3s-6$

$= 5s^3+8s^2-7s-6$

45. $(3w-2)(9w^2+6w+4)$

$= 3w(9w^2)+3w(6w)+12w-2(9w^2)-12w-8$

$= 27w^3+18w^2+12w-18w^2-12w-8$

$= 27w^3-8$

47. $(p^2+p-5)(p^2+4p-1)$

$= p^4+4p^3-p^2+p^3+4p^2$

$\quad -p-5p^2-20p+5$

$= p^4+5p^3-2p^2-21p+5$

49.
$$\begin{array}{r} 3a^2-4a+9 \\ \times \quad 2a-5 \\ \hline 6a^3-8a^2+18a \\ +\quad -15a^2+20a-45 \\ \hline 6a^3-23a^2+38a-45 \end{array}$$

51.
$$\begin{array}{r} 4x^2-12xy+9y^2 \\ \times \quad 2x-3y \\ \hline 8x^3-24x^2y+18xy^2 \\ +\quad -12x^2y+36xy^2-27y^3 \\ \hline 8x^3-36x^2y+54xy^2-27y^3 \end{array}$$

53.
$$\begin{array}{r} 6x+2y \\ \times \quad 0.2x+1.2y \\ \hline 1.2x^2+7.2xy \\ +\quad 0.4xy+2.4y^2 \\ \hline 1.2x^2+7.6xy+2.4y^2 \end{array}$$

55. $(y-6)(y+6)=(y)^2-(6)^2$

$\qquad = y^2-36$

57. $(3a-4b)(3a+4b)=(3a)^2-(4b)^2$

$\qquad = 9a^2-16b^2$

59. $(9k+6)(9k-6)=(9k)^2-6^2=81k^2-36$

61. $\left(\dfrac{2}{3}t-3\right)\left(\dfrac{2}{3}t-3\right)=\left(\dfrac{2}{3}t\right)^2-(3)^2=\dfrac{4}{9}t^2-9$

63. $(u^3+5v)(u^3-5v)=(u^3)^2-(5v)^2$

$\qquad = u^6-25v^2$

65. $\left(\dfrac{2}{3}-p\right)\left(\dfrac{2}{3}+p\right)=\left(\dfrac{2}{3}\right)^2-p^2=\dfrac{4}{9}-p^2$

67. $(a+5)^2=a^2+2a(5)+(5)^2=a^2+10a+25$

69. $(x-y)^2=x^2-2xy+y^2$

71. $(2c+5)^2=(2c)^2+2(2c)(5)+5^2$

$\qquad = 4c^2+20c+25$

73. $(3t^2-4s)^2=(3t^2)^2-2(3t^2)(4s)+(4s)^2$

$\qquad = 9t^4-24st^2+16s^2$

75. $(7-t)^2=7^2-2(7)(t)+t^2$

$\qquad = 49-14t+t^2$

$\qquad = t^2-14t+49$

77. $(3+4q)^2=3^2+2(3)(4q)+(4q)^2$

$\qquad = 9+24q+16q^2$

$\qquad = 16q^2+24q+9$

79. (a) $(2+4)^2=(6)^2=36$

(b) $2^2+4^2=4+16=20$

(c) $(a+b)^2 \neq a^2+b^2$ in general

81. $A = (2x+5)(2x-5) = (2x)^2 - 5^2 = 4x^2 - 25$

83. $A = (4p+5)^2$
$= (4p)^2 + 2(4p)(5) + 5^2$
$= 16p^2 + 40p + 25$

85. V
$= s^3$
$= (3p-5)^3$
$= (3p-5)(3p-5)^2$
$= (3p-5)(9p^2 - 30p + 25)$
$= 27p^3 - 90p^2 + 75p - 45p^2 + 150p - 125$
$= 27p^3 - 135p^2 + 225p - 125$

87. $A = \frac{1}{2}bh$
$= \frac{1}{2}(5a^3 - 2)(6a^2)$
$= \frac{1}{2}(30a^5 - 12a^2)$
$= 15a^5 - 6a^2$

89. $(7x+y)(7x-y) = (7x)^2 - y^2 = 49x^2 - y^2$

91. $(5s+3t)^2 = (5s)^2 + 2(5s)(3t) + (3t)^2$
$= 25s^2 + 30st + 9t^2$

93. $(7x-3y)(3x-8y)$
$= 7x(3x) - 7x(8y) - 3y(3x) + 3y(8y)$
$= 21x^2 - 65xy + 24y^2$

95. $\left(\frac{2}{3}t + 2\right)(3t + 4)$
$= \frac{2}{3}t(3t) + \frac{2}{3}t(4) + 2(3t) + 2(4)$
$= 2t^2 + \frac{8}{3}t + 6t + 8$
$= 2t^2 + \frac{26}{3}t + 8$

97. $(5z+3)(z^2 + 4z - 1)$
$= 5z(z^2) + 5z(4z) - 1(5z) + 3z^2 + 3(4z) - 3$
$= 5z^3 + 23z^2 + 7z - 3$

99. $(3a-2)(5a+1+2a^2)$
$= 15a^2 + 3a + 6a^3 - 10a - 2 - 4a^2$
$= 6a^3 + 11a^2 - 7a - 2$

101. $(y^2 + 2y + 4)(y - 5)$
$= y^3 - 5y^2 + 2y^2 - 10y + 4y - 20$
$= y^3 - 3y^2 - 6y - 20$

103. $\left(\frac{1}{3}m - n\right)^2 = \left(\frac{1}{3}m\right)^2 - 2\left(\frac{1}{3}m\right)(n) + n^2$
$= \frac{1}{9}m^2 - \frac{2}{3}mn + n^2$

105. $6w^2(7w - 14) = 6w^2(7w) - 6w^2(14)$
$= 42w^3 - 84w^2$

107. $(4y - 8.1)(4y + 8.1)$
$(4y)^2 - (8.1)^2 = 16y^2 - 65.61$

109. $(3c^2 + 4)(7c^2 - 8)$
$= 3c^2(7c^2) - (3c^2)(8) + 4(7c^2) - 4(8)$
$= 21c^4 + 4c^2 - 32$

111. $(3.1x + 4.5)^2$
$= (3.1x)^2 + 2(3.1x)(4.5) + (4.5)^2$
$= 9.61x^2 + 27.9x + 20.25$

113. $(k-4)^3 = (k-4)(k-4)^2$
$= (k-4)(k^2 - 8k + 16)$
$= k^3 - 8k^2 + 16k - 4k^2 + 32k - 64$
$= k^3 - 12k^2 + 48k - 64$

115. $(5x+3)^3$
$= (5x+3)^2(5x+3)$
$= (25x^2 + 30x + 9)(5x+3)$
$= 125x^3 + 75x^2 + 150x^2 + 90x + 45x + 27$
$= 125x^3 + 225x^2 + 135x + 27$

117. $(y^2 + 2y + 1)(2y^2 - y + 3)$

$= 2y^4 - y^3 + 3y^2 + 4y^3 - 2y^2 + 6y$

$\qquad + 2y^2 - y + 3$

$= 2y^4 + 3y^3 + 3y^2 + 5y + 3$

119. $2a(3a - 4)(a + 5) = 2a(3a^2 + 11a - 20)$

$\qquad\qquad\qquad = 6a^3 + 22a^2 - 40a$

121. $(x - 3)(2x + 1)(x - 4)$

$= (x - 3)(2x^2 - 7x - 4)$

$= 2x^3 - 7x^2 - 4x - 6x^2 + 21x + 12$

$= 2x^3 - 13x^2 + 17x + 12$

123. $(3x + 5)(a + b) = 6x^2 - 11x - 35$

$\quad 3ax = 6x^2 \quad$ and $\quad 5b = -35$

$\quad\quad a = 2x \quad$ and $\quad\quad b = -7$

So, $a = 2$, $b = -7$, and the binomial is

$y = 2x - 7$.

125. $x^2 + kx + 25 = x^2 + kx + 5^2$

$k = 2(5) = 10$

or

$x^2 + kx + 25 = x^2 + kx + (-5)^2$

$k = 2(-5) = -10$

127. $a^2 + ka + 16 = a^2 + ka + 4^2$

$k = 2(4) = 8$

or

$a^2 + ka + 16 = a^2 + ka + (-4)^2$

$k = 2(-4) = -8$

Section 5.7 Practice Exercises

1. $(6z^5 - 2z^3 + z - 6) - (10z^4 + 2z^3 + z^2 + z)$

$= 6z^5 - 2z^3 + z - 6 - 10z^4 - 2z^3 - z^2 - z$

$= 6z^5 - 10z^4 - 4z^3 - z^2 - 6$

3. $(10x + y)(x - 3y) = 10x^2 - 30xy + xy - 3y^2$

$\qquad\qquad\qquad = 10x^2 - 29xy - 3y^2$

5. $(10x + y) + (x - 3y) = 10x + y + x - 3y$

$\qquad\qquad\qquad = 11x - 2y$

7. $\left(\dfrac{4}{3}y^2 - \dfrac{1}{2}y + \dfrac{3}{8}\right) - \left(\dfrac{1}{3}y^2 + \dfrac{1}{4}y - \dfrac{1}{8}\right)$

$= \dfrac{4}{3}y^2 - \dfrac{1}{2}y + \dfrac{3}{8} - \dfrac{1}{3}y^2 - \dfrac{1}{4}y + \dfrac{1}{8}$

$= \dfrac{4}{3}y^2 - \dfrac{1}{3}y^2 - \dfrac{1}{2}y - \dfrac{1}{4}y + \dfrac{3}{8} + \dfrac{1}{8}$

$= y^2 - \dfrac{3}{4}y + \dfrac{1}{2}$

9. $(a + 3)(a^2 - 3a + 9)$

$= a^3 - 3a^2 + 9a + 3a^2 - 9a + 27$

$= a^3 + 27$

11. Use long division when the divisor is a polynomial with two or more terms.

13. (a) $\dfrac{15t^3 + 18t^2}{3t} = \dfrac{15t^3}{3t} + \dfrac{18t^2}{3t} = 5t^2 + 6t$

(b) $3t(5t^2 + 6t) = 15t^3 + 18t^2$

15. $(6a^2 + 4a - 14) \div 2 = \dfrac{6a^2}{2} + \dfrac{4a}{2} - \dfrac{14}{2}$

$\qquad\qquad\qquad\qquad = 3a^2 + 2a - 7$

17. $\dfrac{-5x^2 - 20x + 5}{-5} = \dfrac{-5x^2}{-5} - \dfrac{20x}{-5} + \dfrac{5}{-5}$

$\qquad\qquad\qquad\qquad = x^2 + 4x - 1$

19. $\dfrac{3p^3 - p^2}{p} = \dfrac{3p^3}{p} - \dfrac{p^2}{p} = 3p^2 - p$

21. $(4m^2 + 8m) \div 4m^2 = \dfrac{4m^2}{4m^2} + \dfrac{8m}{4m^2} = 1 + \dfrac{2}{m}$

23. $\dfrac{14y^4 - 7y^3 + 21y^2}{-7y^2} = \dfrac{14y^4}{-7y^2} - \dfrac{7y^3}{-7y^2} + \dfrac{21y^2}{-7y^2}$

$\qquad\qquad\qquad\qquad = -2y^2 + y - 3$

25. $(4x^3 - 24x^2 - x + 8) \div (4x)$

$= \dfrac{4x^3}{4x} - \dfrac{24x^2}{4x} - \dfrac{x}{4x} + \dfrac{8}{4x}$

$= x^2 - 6x - \dfrac{1}{4} + \dfrac{2}{x}$

27. $\dfrac{-a^3b^2 + a^2b^2 - ab^3}{-a^2b^2}$

$= \dfrac{-a^3b^2}{-a^2b^2} + \dfrac{a^2b^2}{-a^2b^2} - \dfrac{ab^3}{-a^2b^2}$

$= a - 1 + \dfrac{b}{a}$

29. $(6t^4 - 2t^3 + 3t^2 - t + 4) \div (2t^3)$

$= \dfrac{6t^4}{2t^3} - \dfrac{2t^3}{2t^3} + \dfrac{3t^2}{2t^3} - \dfrac{t}{2t^3} + \dfrac{4}{2t^3}$

$= 3t - 1 + \dfrac{3}{2t} - \dfrac{1}{2t^2} + \dfrac{2}{t^3}$

31. (a)
$$
\begin{array}{r}
z + 2 \\
z + 5 \overline{\smash{)}\; z^2 + 7z + 11} \\
\underline{-(z^2 + 5z)} \\
2z + 11 \\
\underline{-(2z + 10)} \\
1
\end{array}
$$

$z + 2 + \dfrac{1}{z + 5}$

(b) $(z + 5)(z + 2) + 1 = z^2 + 2z + 5z + 10 + 1$

$ = z^2 + 7z + 11$

33.
$$
\begin{array}{r}
t + 3 \\
t + 1 \overline{\smash{)}\; t^2 + 4t + 5} \\
\underline{-(t^2 + t)} \\
3t + 5 \\
\underline{-(3t + 3)} \\
2
\end{array}
$$

$t + 3 + \dfrac{2}{t + 1}$

35.
$$
\begin{array}{r}
7b + 4 \\
b - 1 \overline{\smash{)}\; 7b^2 - 3b - 4} \\
\underline{-(7b^2 - 7b)} \\
4b - 4 \\
\underline{-(4b - 4)} \\
7b + 4
\end{array}
$$

37.
$$
\begin{array}{r}
k - 6 \\
5k + 1 \overline{\smash{)}\; 5k^2 - 29k - 6} \\
\underline{-(5k^2 + k)} \\
-30k - 6 \\
\underline{-(-30k - 6)} \\
k - 6
\end{array}
$$

39.
$$
\begin{array}{r}
2p^2 + 3p - 4 \\
2p + 3 \overline{\smash{)}\; 4p^3 + 12p^2 + p - 12} \\
\underline{-(4p^3 + 6p^2)} \\
6p^2 + p \\
\underline{-(6p^2 + 9p)} \\
-8p - 12 \\
\underline{-(-8p - 12)} \\
2p^2 + 3p - 4
\end{array}
$$

41. Arrange both the dividend and divisor in descending order.
$$
\begin{array}{r}
k - 2 \\
k + 1 \overline{\smash{)}\; k^2 - k - 6} \\
\underline{-(k^2 + k)} \\
-2k - 6 \\
\underline{-(-2k - 2)} \\
-4
\end{array}
$$

$k - 2 + \dfrac{-4}{k + 1}$

43.
$$2x-3 \overline{\smash{\big)}\ 4x^3 -8x^2 +15x -16}$$
quotient: $2x^2 -x+6$
$$\underline{-(4x^3 -6x^2)}$$
$$-2x^2 +15x$$
$$\underline{-(-2x^2 + 3x)}$$
$$12x-16$$
$$\underline{-(12x-18)}$$
$$2$$

$$2x^2 -x+6+\dfrac{2}{2x-3}$$

45.
$$3y-1 \overline{\smash{\big)}\ 3y^3 +5y^2 + y+1}$$
quotient: $y^2 +2y+1$
$$\underline{-(3y^3 -y^2)}$$
$$6y^2 + y$$
$$\underline{-(6y^2 -2y)}$$
$$3y+1$$
$$\underline{-(3y-1)}$$
$$2$$

$$y^2 +2y+1+\dfrac{2}{3y-1}$$

47. Arrange the dividend in descending order. The term $0a$ is a placeholder for the missing term.

$$a+3 \overline{\smash{\big)}\ a^2 +0a+9}$$
quotient: $a-3$
$$\underline{-(a^2 +3a)}$$
$$-3a+9$$
$$\underline{-(-3a-9)}$$
$$18$$

$$a-3+\dfrac{18}{a+3}$$

49. The term $0x^2$ is a placeholder for the missing term in the dividend.

$$x-2 \overline{\smash{\big)}\ 4x^3 +0x^2 -3x-26}$$
quotient: $4x^2 +8x+13$
$$\underline{-(4x^3 -8x^2)}$$
$$8x^2 -3x$$
$$\underline{-(8x^2 -16x)}$$
$$13x-26$$
$$\underline{-(13x-26)}$$

$$4x^2 +8x+13$$

51. The term $0w$ is a placeholder for the missing term in the divisor.

$$w^2 +0w-3 \overline{\smash{\big)}\ w^4 +5w^3 -5w^2 -15w+7}$$
quotient: $w^2 +5w-2$
$$\underline{-(w^4 +0w^3 -3w^2)}$$
$$5w^3 -2w^2 -15w$$
$$\underline{-(5w^3 +0w^2 -15w)}$$
$$-2w^2 +0w+7$$
$$\underline{-(-2w^2 +0w+6)}$$
$$1$$

$$w^2 +5w-2+\dfrac{1}{w^2 -3}$$

53.
$$2n^2 +3n-2 \overline{\smash{\big)}\ 2n^4 +5n^3 -11n^2 -20n+12}$$
quotient: $n^2 +n-6$
$$\underline{-(2n^4 +3n^3 -2n^2)}$$
$$2n^3 -9n^2 -20n$$
$$\underline{-(2n^3 +3n^2 -2n)}$$
$$-12n^2 -18n+12$$
$$\underline{-(-12n^2 -18n+12)}$$

$$n^2 +n-6$$

55.
$$
\begin{array}{r}
x - 1 \\
5x^2 + 5x + 1 \overline{\smash{\big)}\ 5x^3 + 0x^2 - 4x - 9} \\
\underline{-(5x^3 + 5x^2\ \ \ + x)} \\
-5x^2 - 5x - 9 \\
\underline{-(-5x^2 - 5x - 1)} \\
-8
\end{array}
$$

$$x - 1 + \dfrac{-8}{5x^2 + 5x + 1}$$

57. To check, multiply the divisor $(x - 2)$ by the quotient $(x^2 + 4)$.

$(x - 2)(x^2 + 4) = x^3 - 2x^2 + 4x - 8$ which

does not equal $x^3 - 8$.

59. Monomial division;

$$\dfrac{9a^3}{3a} + \dfrac{12a^2}{3a} = 3a^2 + 4a$$

61. Long division;

$$
\begin{array}{r}
p + 2 \\
p^2 - p - 2 \overline{\smash{\big)}\ p^3 + p^2 - 4p - 4} \\
\underline{-(p^3 - p^2 - 2p)} \\
2p^2 - 2p - 4 \\
\underline{-(2p^2 - 2p - 4)} \\
\end{array}
$$

$p + 2$

63. Long division; the terms $0t^3$ and $0t$ are placeholders for the missing terms in the dividend.

$$
\begin{array}{r}
t^3 - 2t^2 + 5t - 10 \\
t + 2 \overline{\smash{\big)}\ t^4 + 0t^3\ + t^2 + 0t - 16} \\
\underline{-(t^4 + 2t^3)} \\
-2t^3\ + t^2 \\
\underline{-(-2t^3 - 4t^2)} \\
5t^2\ + 0t \\
\underline{-(5t^2 + 10t)} \\
-10t - 16 \\
\underline{-(-10t - 20)} \\
4
\end{array}
$$

$$t^3 - 2t^2 + 5t - 10 + \dfrac{4}{t + 2}$$

65. Long division; the terms $0w^3$ and $0w$ are placeholders for the missing terms in the dividend and $0w$ in the divisor.

$$
\begin{array}{r}
w^2 + 3 \\
w^2 + 0w - 2 \overline{\smash{\big)}\ w^4 + 0w^3\ + w^2 + 0w - 5} \\
\underline{-(w^4 + 0w^3 - 2w^2)} \\
3w^2 + 0w - 5 \\
\underline{-(3w^2 + 0w - 6)} \\
1
\end{array}
$$

$$w^2 + 3 + \dfrac{1}{w^2 - 2}$$

67. Long division; the terms $0n^2$ and $0n$ are placeholders for the missing terms in the dividend.

$$
\begin{array}{r}
n^2 + 4n + 16 \\
n - 4 \overline{\smash{\big)}\ n^3 + 0n^2\ + 0n - 64} \\
\underline{-(n^3 - 4n^2)} \\
4n^2\ + 0n \\
\underline{-(4n^2 - 16n)} \\
16n - 64 \\
\underline{-(16n - 64)} \\
\end{array}
$$

$n^2 + 4n + 16$

69. Monomial division;

$$\frac{9r^3}{-3r^2} + \frac{-12r^2}{-3r^2} + \frac{9}{-3r^2} = -3r + 4 - \frac{3}{r^2}$$

71. Insert placeholders for missing terms in the dividend.

$$\begin{array}{r} x+1 \\ x-1\overline{)\; x^2 + 0x - 1} \\ \underline{-(x^2 - x)} \\ x - 1 \\ \underline{-(x-1)} \\ \end{array}$$

$$\frac{x^2 - 1}{x - 1} = x + 1$$

73. Insert placeholders for missing terms in the dividend.

$$\begin{array}{r} x^3 + x^2 + x + 1 \\ x-1\overline{)\; x^4 + 0x^3 + 0x^2 + 0x - 1} \\ \underline{-(x^4 - x^3)} \\ x^3 + 0x^2 \\ \underline{-(x^3 - x^2)} \\ x^2 + 0x \\ \underline{-(x^2 - x)} \\ x - 1 \\ \underline{-(x-1)} \\ \end{array}$$

$$\frac{x^4 - 1}{x - 1} = x^3 + x^2 + x + 1$$

75. Insert placeholders for missing terms in the dividend.

$$\begin{array}{r} x+1 \\ x-1\overline{)\; x^2 + 0x + 0} \\ \underline{-(x^2 - x)} \\ x + 0 \\ \underline{-(x-1)} \\ 1 \\ \end{array}$$

$$\frac{x^2}{x - 1} = x + 1 + \frac{1}{x - 1}$$

77. Insert placeholders for missing terms in the dividend.

$$\begin{array}{r} x^3 + x^2 + x + 1 \\ x-1\overline{)\; x^4 + 0x^3 + 0x^2 + 0x + 0} \\ \underline{-(x^4 - x^3)} \\ x^3 + 0x^2 \\ \underline{-(x^3 - x^2)} \\ x^2 + 0x \\ \underline{-(x^2 - x)} \\ x + 0 \\ \underline{-(x-1)} \\ 1 \\ \end{array}$$

$$\frac{x^4}{x - 1} = x^3 + x^2 + x + 1 + \frac{1}{x - 1}$$

Problem Recognition Exercises

1. $(2x - 4)(x^2 - 2x + 3)$
$= 2x^3 - 4x^2 + 6x - 4x^2 + 8x - 12$
$= 2x^3 - 8x^2 + 14x - 12$

3. $(2x - 4) + (x^2 - 2x + 3)$
$= 2x - 4 + x^2 - 2x + 3$
$= x^2 - 1$

5. $(6y - 7)^2 = (6y)^2 - 2(6y)(7) + (7)^2$
$= 36y^2 - 84y + 49$

7. $(6y - 7)(6y + 7) = (6y)^2 - (7)^2 = 36y^2 - 49$

9. $(4x + y)^2 = (4x)^2 + 2(4x)y + y^2$
$= 16x^2 + 8xy + y^2$

11. $(4xy)^2 = 4^2 x^2 y^2 = 16x^2 y^2$

13. $(-2x^4 - 6x^3 + 8x^2) \div (2x^2)$

$= \dfrac{-2x^4}{2x^2} - \dfrac{6x^3}{2x^2} + \dfrac{8x^2}{2x^2}$

$= -x^2 - 3x + 4$

15. $(m^3 - 4m^2 - 6) - (3m^2 + 7m) + (-m^3 - 9m + 6)$

$= m^3 - 4m^2 - 6 - 3m^2 - 7m - m^3 - 9m + 6$

$= -7m^2 - 16m$

17. Insert a placeholder for the missing term in the dividend.

$$
\begin{array}{r}
8x^2 + 16x + 34 \\
x-2{\overline{\smash{\big)}\,8x^3 + 0x^2 + 2x + 6}} \\
\underline{-(8x^3 - 16x^2)} \\
16x^2 + 2x \\
\underline{-(16x^2 - 32x)} \\
34x + 6 \\
\underline{-(34x - 68)} \\
74
\end{array}
$$

$8x^2 + 16x + 34 + \dfrac{74}{x-2}$

19. $(2x - y)(3x^2 + 4xy - y^2)$

$= 6x^3 + 8x^2y - 2xy^2 - 3x^2y - 4xy^2 + y^3$

$= 6x^3 + 5x^2y - 6xy^2 + y^3$

21. $(x + y^2)(x^2 - xy^2 + y^4)$

$= x^3 - x^2y^2 + xy^4 + x^2y^2 - xy^4 + y^6$

$= x^3 + y^6$

23. $(a^2 + 2b) - (a^2 - 2b) = a^2 + 2b - a^2 + 2b$

$= 4b$

25. $(a^2 + 2b)(a^2 - 2b) = (a^2)^2 - (2b)^2$

$= a^4 - 4b^2$

27. $(8u + 3v)^2 = (8u)^2 + 2(8u)(3v) + (3v)^2$

$= 64u^2 + 48uv + 9v^4$

29.
$$
\begin{array}{r}
4p + 4 \\
2p-1{\overline{\smash{\big)}\,8p^2 + 4p - 6}} \\
\underline{-(8p^2 - 4p)} \\
8p - 6 \\
\underline{-(8p - 4)} \\
-2
\end{array}
$$

$4p + 4 + \dfrac{-2}{2p-1}$

31. $\dfrac{12x^3y^7}{3xy^5} = \dfrac{12}{3}x^{3-1}y^{7-5} = 4x^2y^2$

33. $(2a - 9)(5a - 6) = 10a^2 - 12a - 45a + 54$

$= 10a^2 - 57a + 54$

35. $\left(\dfrac{3}{7}x - \dfrac{1}{2}\right)\left(\dfrac{3}{7}x + \dfrac{1}{2}\right)$

$= \left(\dfrac{3}{7}x\right)^2 - \left(\dfrac{1}{2}\right)^2$

$= \dfrac{9}{49}x^2 - \dfrac{1}{4}$

37. $\left(\dfrac{1}{9}x^3 + \dfrac{2}{3}x^2 + \dfrac{1}{6}x - 3\right) -$

$\qquad \left(\dfrac{4}{3}x^3 + \dfrac{1}{9}x^2 + \dfrac{2}{3}x + 1\right)$

$= \dfrac{1}{9}x^3 + \dfrac{2}{3}x^2 + \dfrac{1}{6}x - 3$

$\qquad - \dfrac{4}{3}x^3 - \dfrac{1}{9}x^2 - \dfrac{2}{3}x - 1$

$= \dfrac{1}{9}x^3 - \dfrac{4}{3}x^3 + \dfrac{2}{3}x^2 - \dfrac{1}{9}x^2$

$\qquad + \dfrac{1}{6}x - \dfrac{2}{3}x - 3 - 1$

$= \dfrac{1}{9}x^3 - \dfrac{12}{9}x^3 + \dfrac{6}{9}x^2 - \dfrac{1}{9}x^2$

$\qquad + \dfrac{1}{6}x - \dfrac{4}{6}x - 3 - 1$

$= -\dfrac{11}{9}x^3 + \dfrac{5}{9}x^2 - \dfrac{3}{6}x - 4$

$= -\dfrac{11}{9}x^3 + \dfrac{5}{9}x^2 - \dfrac{1}{2}x - 4$

39. $(0.05x^2 - 0.16x - 0.75)$

$\qquad + (1.25x^2 - 0.14x + 0.25)$

$= 0.05x^2 + 1.25x^2 - 0.16x - 0.14x$

$\qquad - 0.75 + 0.25$

$= 1.3x^2 - 0.3x - 0.5$

Group Activity

1. $a = 5$
   $b = 12$
   $c = 13$

$\qquad a^2 + b^2 = c^2$

$\qquad (5)^2 + (12)^2 \overset{?}{=} (13)^2$

$\qquad 25 + 144 = 169$

3. $\qquad (a+b)^2 = c^2 + 4 \cdot (\tfrac{1}{2}ab)$

$\qquad a^2 + 2ab + b^2 = c^2 + 2ab$

$\qquad\qquad a^2 + b^2 = c^2$

Chapter 5 Review Exercises

Section 5.1

1. Base 5; exponent 3

3. Base (−2); exponent 0

5. **(a)** $6^2 = 6 \cdot 6 = 36$

   (b) $(-6)^2 = (-6)(-6) = 36$

   (c) $-6^2 = -(6 \cdot 6) = -36$

7. $5^3 \cdot 5^{10} = 5^{3+10} = 5^{13}$

9. $x \cdot x^6 \cdot x^2 = x^{1+6+2} = x^9$

11. $\dfrac{10^7}{10^4} = 10^{7-4} = 10^3$

13. $\dfrac{b^9}{b} = b^{9-1} = b^8$

15. $\dfrac{k^2 k^3}{k^4} = k^{5-4} = k^1 = k$

17. $\dfrac{2^8 \cdot 2^{10}}{2^3 \cdot 2^7} = \dfrac{2^{18}}{2^{10}} = 2^{18-10} = 2^8$

19. Exponents are added only when multiplying factors with the same base. In such a case, the base does not change.

21. Substitute $P = 6000$, $t = 3$, and $r = 0.06$ into the formula.

$\qquad A = P(1+r)^t = 6000(1+0.06)^3 = \$7146.10$

Section 5.2

23. $(7^3)^4 = 7^{3 \cdot 4} = 7^{12}$

25. $(p^4 p^2)^3 = (p^6)^3 = p^{6 \cdot 3} = p^{18}$

27. $\left(\dfrac{a}{b}\right)^2 = \dfrac{a^2}{b^2}$

29. $\left(\dfrac{5}{c^2 d^5}\right)^2 = \dfrac{5^2}{(c^2 d^5)^2} = \dfrac{5^2}{c^4 d^{10}}$

31. $(2ab^2)^4 = 2^4 a^4 (b^2)^4 = 2^4 a^4 b^8$

33. $\left(\dfrac{-3x^3}{5y^2 z}\right)^3 = \dfrac{(-3x^3)^3}{(5y^2 z)^3}$

$= \dfrac{-3^3 (x^3)^3}{5^3 (y^2)^3 z^3}$

$= -\dfrac{3^3 x^9}{5^3 y^6 z^3}$

35. $\dfrac{a^4 (a^2)^8}{(a^3)^3} = \dfrac{a^4 a^{16}}{a^9} = \dfrac{a^{20}}{a^9} = a^{11}$

37. $\dfrac{(4h^2 k)^2 (h^3 k)^4}{(2hk^3)^2} = \dfrac{4^2 h^4 k^2 h^{12} k^4}{2^2 h^2 k^6}$

$= \dfrac{16 h^{16} k^6}{4 h^2 k^6}$

$= 4h^{14}$

39. $\left(\dfrac{2x^4 y^3}{4xy^2}\right)^2 = \dfrac{(2x^4 y^3)^2}{(4xy^2)^2} = \dfrac{2^2 x^8 y^6}{4^2 x^2 y^4} = \dfrac{x^6 y^2}{4}$

Section 5.3

41. $8^0 = 1$

43. $-x^0 = -1$

45. $2y^0 = 2(1) = 2$

47. $z^{-5} = \dfrac{1}{z^5}$

49. $(6a)^{-2} = \dfrac{1}{(6a)^2} = \dfrac{1}{36a^2}$

51. $4^0 + 4^{-2} = 1 + \dfrac{1}{4^2} = \dfrac{16}{16} + \dfrac{1}{16} = \dfrac{17}{16}$

53. $t^{-6} t^{-2} = t^{-8} = \dfrac{1}{t^8}$

55. $\dfrac{12x^{-2} y^3}{6x^4 y^{-4}} = 2x^{-2-4} y^{3-(-4)} = 2x^{-6} y^7 = \dfrac{2y^7}{x^6}$

57. $(-2m^2 n^{-4})^{-4} = (-2)^{-4} m^{-8} n^{16}$

$= \dfrac{n^{16}}{2^4 m^8}$

$= \dfrac{n^{16}}{16m^8}$

59. $\dfrac{(k^{-6})^{-2} (k^3)}{5k^{-6} k^0} = \dfrac{k^{12} k^3}{5k^{-6}} = \dfrac{k^{15-(-6)}}{5} = \dfrac{k^{21}}{5}$

61. $2 \cdot 3^{-1} - 6^{-1} = 2 \cdot \dfrac{1}{3} - \dfrac{1}{6}$

$= \dfrac{2}{3} - \dfrac{1}{6}$

$= \dfrac{4}{6} - \dfrac{1}{6}$

$= \dfrac{3}{6}$

$= \dfrac{1}{2}$

Section 5.4

63. (a) 9.74×10^7

(b) 4.2×10^{-3} in.

65. $(4.1 \times 10^{-6})(2.3 \times 10^{11}) = (4.1)(2.3) \times 10^{-6+11}$

$= 9.43 \times 10^5$

67. $\dfrac{2000}{0.000008} = \dfrac{2.0 \times 10^3}{8.0 \times 10^{-6}}$

$= \dfrac{2.0}{8.0} \times 10^{3-(-6)}$

$= 0.25 \times 10^9$

$= 2.5 \times 10^{-1} \times 10^9$

$= 2.5 \times 10^8$

69. $5^{20} \approx 9.5367 \times 10^{13}$

This number has too many digits to fit on most calculator displays.

71. **(a)** $C = 2\pi r$

$= 2(3.14)(9.3 \times 10^7)$

$\approx 58.4 \times 10^7$

$= 5.84 \times 10^1 \times 10^7$

$= 5.84 \times 10^8$ miles

(b) $\dfrac{5.84 \times 10^8 \text{ miles}}{8.76 \times 10^3 \text{ hours}} \approx 0.667 \times 10^5$

$= 6.67 \times 10^{-1} \times 10^5$

$= 6.67 \times 10^4$ mph

Section 5.5

73. **(a)** Trinomial

(b) degree 4

(c) leading coefficient 7

75. $(4x + 2) + (3x - 5) = 7x - 3$

77. $(9a^2 - 6) - (-5a^2 + 2a)$

$= 9a^2 + 5a^2 - 2a - 6$

$= 14a^2 - 2a - 6$

79. $\begin{array}{r} 8w^4 \qquad\quad -6w + 3 \\ + \ \underline{2w^4 + 2w^3 - \ w + 1} \\ 10w^4 + 2w^3 - 7w + 4 \end{array}$

81. $(7x^2 - 5x) - (9x^2 + 4x + 6)$

$= 7x^2 - 5x - 9x^2 - 4x - 6$

$= -2x^2 - 9x - 6$

83. Answers will vary; $-5x^2 + 2x - 4$

85. $P = 2w + 2l$

$= 2(w) + 2(2w + 3)$

$= 2w + 4w + 6$

$= 6w + 6$

Section 5.6

87. $(9a^6)(2a^2 b^4) = 18a^{6+2} b^4 = 18a^8 b^4$

89. $(x^2 + 5x - 3)(-2x)$

$= x^2(-2x) + 5x(-2x) - 3(-2x)$

$= -2x^3 - 10x^2 + 6x$

91. $(4t - 1)(5t + 2) = 4t(5t) + 4t(2) - 1(5t) - 1(2)$

$= 20t^2 + 8t - 5t - 2$

$= 20t^2 + 3t - 2$

93. $(2a - 6)(a + 5) = 2a(a) + 2a(5) - 6a - 6(5)$

$= 2a^2 + 4a - 30$

95. $(b - 4)^2 = b^2 - 2(b)(4) + 4^2 = b^2 - 8b + 16$

97. $(2w - 1)(-w^2 - 3w - 4)$

$= -2w(w^2) - 2w(3w) - 2w(4) + w^2 + 3w + 4$

$= -2w^3 - 6w^2 - 8w + w^2 + 3w + 4$

$= -2w^3 - 5w^2 - 5w + 4$

99. $\begin{array}{r} 4a^2 + a - 5 \\ \times \ \underline{\qquad\qquad 3a + 2} \\ 12a^3 + 3a^2 - 15a \\ + \ \underline{\qquad 8a^2 + \ 2a - 10} \\ 12a^3 + 11a^2 - 13a - 10 \end{array}$

101. $\left(\dfrac{1}{3}r^4 - s^2\right)\left(\dfrac{1}{3}r^4 + s^2\right)$

$= \left(\dfrac{1}{3}r^4\right)^2 - (s^2)^2$

$= \dfrac{1}{9}r^8 - s^4$

103. $(2h+3)(h^4 - h^3 + h^2 - h + 1)$

$= 2h^5 - 2h^4 + 2h^3 - 2h^2 + 2h$
$\quad + 3h^4 - 3h^3 + 3h^2 - 3h + 3$
$= 2h^5 + h^4 - h^3 + h^2 - h + 3$

Section 5.7

105. $\dfrac{20y^3 - 10y^2}{5y} = \dfrac{20y^3}{5y} - \dfrac{10y^2}{5y}$

$\qquad\qquad = 4y^2 - 2y$

107. $(12x^4 - 8x^3 + 4x^2) \div (-4x^2)$

$= \dfrac{12x^4}{-4x^2} + \dfrac{-8x^3}{-4x^2} + \dfrac{4x^2}{-4x^2}$

$= -3x^2 + 2x - 1$

109.
$$
\begin{array}{r}
x+2 \\
x+5 \overline{\smash{\big)}\ x^2 + 7x + 10} \\
\underline{-(x^2 + 5x)} \\
2x + 10 \\
\underline{-(2x + 10)} \\
\end{array}
$$
$x + 2$

111.
$$
\begin{array}{r}
p-3 \\
2p+7 \overline{\smash{\big)}\ 2p^2 + p - 16} \\
\underline{-(2p^2 + 7p)} \\
-6p - 16 \\
\underline{-(-6p - 21)} \\
5 \\
\end{array}
$$
$p - 3 + \dfrac{5}{2p + 7}$

113.
$$
\begin{array}{r}
b^2 + 5b + 25 \\
b-5 \overline{\smash{\big)}\ b^3 + 0b^2 + 0b - 125} \\
\underline{-(b^3 - 5b^2)} \\
5b^2 + 0b \\
\underline{-(5b^2 - 25b)} \\
25b - 125 \\
\underline{-(25b - 125)} \\
\end{array}
$$
$b^2 + 5b + 25$

115.
$$
\begin{array}{r}
y^2 - 4y + 2 \\
y^2 + 0y + 3 \overline{\smash{\big)}\ y^4 - 4y^3 + 5y^2 - 3y + 2} \\
\underline{-(y^4 + 0y^3 + 3y^2)} \\
-4y^3 + 2y^2 - 3y \\
\underline{-(-4y^3 + 0y^2 - 12y)} \\
2y^2 + 9y + 2 \\
\underline{-(2y^2 + 0y + 6)} \\
9y - 4 \\
\end{array}
$$
$y^2 - 4y + 2 + \dfrac{9y - 4}{y^2 + 3}$

117.
$$
\begin{array}{r}
w^2 + w - 1 \\
2w^2 - w + 3 \overline{\smash{\big)}\ 2w^4 + w^3 + 0w^2 + 4w - 3} \\
\underline{-(2w^4 - w^3 + 3w^2)} \\
2w^3 - 3w^2 + 4w \\
\underline{-(2w^3 - w^2 + 3w)} \\
-2w^2 + w - 3 \\
\underline{-(-2w^2 + w - 3)} \\
\end{array}
$$
$w^2 + w - 1$

Chapter 5 Test

1. $\dfrac{3^4 \cdot 3^3}{3^6} = \dfrac{(3 \cdot 3 \cdot 3 \cdot 3)(3 \cdot 3 \cdot 3)}{3 \cdot 3 \cdot 3 \cdot 3 \cdot 3 \cdot 3} = 3$

3. $\dfrac{q^{10}}{q^2} = q^{10-2} = q^8$

5. $\left(\dfrac{2x}{y^3}\right)^4 = \dfrac{(2x)^4}{(y^3)^4} = \dfrac{2^4 x^4}{y^{12}} = \dfrac{16x^4}{y^{12}}$

7. $c^{-3} = \dfrac{1}{c^3}$

9. $\dfrac{(s^2 t)^3 (7s^4 t)^4}{(7s^2 t^3)^2} = \dfrac{s^6 t^3 7^4 s^{16} t^4}{7^2 s^4 t^6}$

$= \dfrac{7^4 s^{22} t^7}{7^2 s^4 t^6}$

$= 7^2 s^{18} t$

$= 49 s^{18} t$

11. $\left(\dfrac{6a^{-5}b}{8ab^{-2}}\right)^{-2} = \left(\dfrac{6a^{-5-1}b^{1-(-2)}}{8}\right)^{-2}$

$= \left(\dfrac{6a^{-6}b^3}{8}\right)^{-2}$

$= \left(\dfrac{3b^3}{4a^6}\right)^{-2}$

$= \left(\dfrac{4a^6}{3b^3}\right)^{2}$

$= \dfrac{16a^{12}}{9b^6}$

13. $4 \cdot 8^{-1} + 16^0 = {}^1\!4 \cdot \dfrac{1}{8_2} + 1$

$= \dfrac{1}{2} + 1 = \dfrac{1}{2} + \dfrac{2}{2} = \dfrac{3}{2}$

15. $\left(1.2 \times 10^6\right)\left(7.0 \times 10^{-15}\right)$

$= \left(1.2 \times 7.0\right)\left(10^{6+-15}\right)$

$= 8.4 \times 10^{-9}$

17. (a) 1440 minutes in one day;

$\quad 1.68 \times 10^5 \text{ m}^3/\text{min}(1440 \text{ min/day})$

$= 1.68 \times 10^5 \times 1.44 \times 10^3$

$= 2.4192 \times 10^8 \text{ m}^3 \text{ in one day}$

(b) $2.4192 \times 10^8 \text{ m}^3$ in one day

$\quad 2.4192 \times 10^8 \text{ m}^3/\text{day}(365 \text{ days/year})$

$= 2.4192 \times 10^8 \times 3.65 \times 10^2$

$= 8.83008 \times 10^{10} \text{ m}^3 \text{ in one year}$

19. $\left(5t^4 - 2t^2 - 17\right) + \left(12t^3 + 2t^2 + 7t - 2\right)$

$= 5t^4 + 12t^3 - 2t^2 + 2t^2 + 7t - 17 - 2$

$= 5t^4 + 12t^3 + 7t - 19$

21. $(10x^3 - 4x^2 + 1) - (3x^2 - 5x^3 + 2x)$

$= 10x^3 + 5x^3 - 4x^2 - 3x^2 - 2x + 1$

$= 15x^3 - 7x^2 - 2x + 1$

23. $(4a - 3)(2a - 1) = 8a^2 - 4a - 6a + 3$

$\qquad\qquad\qquad = 8a^2 - 10a + 3$

25. $(2 + 3b)(2 - 3b) = 2^2 - (3b)^2 = 4 - 9b^2$

27. $(5x + 3)(3x - 2) = 15x^2 - 10x + 9x - 6$

$\qquad\qquad\qquad = 15x^2 - x - 6$

29. $P = 2w + 2l$

$\quad = 2(x - 3) + 2(5x + 2)$

$\quad = 2x - 6 + 10x + 4$

$\quad = 12x - 2$

$A = lw = (5x + 2)(x - 3) = 5x^2 - 13x - 6$

31. $\dfrac{16a^3 b - 2a^2 b^2 + 8ab}{-4ab}$

$= \dfrac{16a^3 b}{-4ab} + \dfrac{-2a^2 b^2}{-4ab} + \dfrac{8ab}{-4ab}$

$= -4a^2 + \dfrac{1}{2}ab - 2$

33.

$$\begin{array}{r} w^2 - 4w + 5 \\ 2w+3\overline{\smash{\big)}\ 2w^3 - 5w^2 - 2w\ + 5} \\ \underline{-(2w^3 + 3w^2)} \\ -8w^2\ - 2w \\ \underline{-(-8w^2 - 12w)} \\ 10w\ + 5 \\ \underline{-(10w+15)} \\ -10 \end{array}$$

$$w^2 - 4w + 5 + \dfrac{-10}{2w+3}$$

Cumulative Review Exercises
Chapters 1–5

1. $\begin{aligned}[t] -5 - \dfrac{1}{2}[4 - 3(-7)] &= -5 - \dfrac{1}{2}[4+21] \\ &= -5 - \dfrac{1}{2}(25) \\ &= -5 - \dfrac{25}{2} \\ &= -\dfrac{35}{2} \end{aligned}$

3. $5^2 - \sqrt{4};\ 25 - 2 = 23$

5. $\begin{aligned} -2y - 3 &= -5(y-1) + 3y \\ -2y - 3 &= -5y + 5 + 3y \\ -2y - 3 &= -2y + 5 \\ -3 &= -5 \qquad \text{Contradiction} \end{aligned}$

No solution

7. y-axis

9. (a) Substitute $x = 4$ into the equation.

$$y = \dfrac{3}{2}(4) + 6 = 6 + 6 = 12 \text{ in.}$$

(b) Substitute $x = 9$ into the equation.

$$y = \dfrac{3}{2}(9) + 6 = \dfrac{27}{2} + 6 = 19.5 \text{ in.}$$

(c) Substitute $y = 14\dfrac{1}{4}$ into the equation and solve for x.

$$\begin{aligned} 14\dfrac{1}{4} &= \dfrac{3}{2}x + 6 \\ 4\left(\dfrac{57}{4}\right) &= 4\left(\dfrac{3}{2}x + 6\right) \\ 57 &= 6x + 24 \\ 6x &= 33 \\ x &= \dfrac{33}{6} = 5.5 \text{ hours} \end{aligned}$$

11. $\begin{aligned} 2 - 3(2x+4) &\le -2x - (x-5) \\ 2 - 6x - 12 &\le -2x - x + 5 \\ -6x - 10 &\le -3x + 5 \\ -3x &\le 15 \\ x &\ge -5 \end{aligned}$

$[-5, \infty)$

13. $\begin{aligned}[t] (2y + 3z)(-y - 5z) &= -2y^2 - 10yz - 3yz - 15z^2 \\ &= -2y^2 - 13yz - 15z^2 \end{aligned}$

15. $\begin{aligned}[t] \left(\dfrac{2}{5}a + \dfrac{1}{3}\right)\left(\dfrac{2}{5}a - \dfrac{1}{3}\right) &= \left(\dfrac{2}{5}a\right)^2 - \left(\dfrac{1}{3}\right)^2 \\ &= \dfrac{4}{25}a^2 - \dfrac{1}{9} \end{aligned}$

17.

$$\begin{array}{r} 4m^2 + 8m + 11 \\ m-2\overline{\smash{\big)}\ 4m^3 + 0m^2\ - 5m + 2} \\ \underline{-(4m^3 - 8m^2)} \\ 8m^2\ - 5m \\ \underline{-(8m^2 - 16m)} \\ 11m\ + 2 \\ \underline{-(11m - 22)} \\ 24 \end{array}$$

$$4m^2 + 8m + 11 + \dfrac{24}{m-2}$$

19. $\dfrac{10a^{-2}b^{-3}}{5a^0 b^{-6}} = 2a^{-2}b^3 = \dfrac{2b^3}{a^2}$

Chapter 6

Chapter 6 Opener

A. 1

B. 4

C. 1

D. 6

E. 5

F. 8

G. 2

H. 3

I. 2

J. 3

5	2	6	A 1	3	B 4
3	C 1	4	2	D 6	E 5
F 4	6	1	5	G 2	H 3
I 2	3	5	4	1	6
1	4	3	6	5	2
6	5	2	J 3	4	1

Section 6.1 Practice Exercises

1. Answers will vary.

3. 7

5. 6

7. y

9. $4w^2z$

11. $2xy^4z^2$

13. $(x-y)$

15. (a) $3(x-2y) = 3x - 3(2y) = 3x - 6y$

  (b) $3x - 6y = 3x - 3(2y) = 3(x-2y)$

17. $4p + 12 = 4p + 4 \cdot 3 = 4(p+3)$

19. $5c^2 - 10c + 15 = 5 \cdot c^2 - 5 \cdot 2c + 5 \cdot 3$
$$= 5(c^2 - 2c + 3)$$

21. $x^5 + x^3 = x^3x^2 + x^3 = x^3(x^2+1)$

23. $t^4 - 4t + 8t^2 = tt^3 - 4t + 8tt = t(t^3 - 4 + 8t)$

25. $2ab + 4a^3b = 2ab + 2ab(2a^2)$
$$= 2ab(1 + 2a^2)$$

27. $38x^2y - 19x^2y^4 = 19x^2y(2) - 19x^2y(y^3)$
$$= 19x^2y(2 - y^3)$$

29. $6x^3y^5 - 18xy^9z = 6xy^5(x^2 - 3y^4z)$

31. $5 + 7y^3$ is prime because it is not factorable.

33. $42p^3q^2 + 14pq^2 - 7p^4q^4$
$$= 7pq^2(6p^2 + 2 - p^3q^2)$$

35. $t^5 + 2rt^3 - 3t^4 + 4r^2t^2$
$$= t^2(t^3 + 2rt - 3t^2 + 4r^2)$$

37. (a) $-2x^3 - 4x^2 + 8x = -2x(x^2 + 2x - 4)$

  (b) $-2x^3 - 4x^2 + 8x = 2x(-x^2 - 2x + 4)$

39. $-8t^2 - 9t - 2 = -1(8t^2 + 9t + 2)$

41. $-15p^3 - 30p^2 = -15p^2(p+2)$

43. $-12p^3t + 2p^2t^3 + 6pt^2$
$$= -2pt(6p^2 - pt^2 - 3t)$$

45. $-7x - 6y - 2z = -1(7x + 6y + 2z)$

47. $13(a+6)-4b(a+6)=(a+6)(13-4b)$

49. $8v(w^2-2)+(w^2-2)$
$=8v(w^2-2)+1(w^2-2)$
$=(w^2-2)(8v+1)$

51. $21x(x+3)+7x^2(x+3)=7x(x+3)(3+x)$
$=7x(x+3)^2$

53. $8a^2-4ab+6ac-3bc$
$=4a(2a-b)+3c(2a-b)$
$=(2a-b)(4a+3c)$

55. $3q+3p+qr+pr=3(q+p)+r(q+p)$
$=(q+p)(3+r)$

57. $6x^2+3x+4x+2=3x(2x+1)+2(2x+1)$
$=(2x+1)(3x+2)$

59. $2t^2+6t-t-3=2t(t+3)+(-1)(t+3)$
$=(2t-1)(t+3)$

61. $6y^2-2y-9y+3=2y(3y-1)+(-3)(3y-1)$
$=(3y-1)(2y-3)$

63. $b^4+b^3-4b-4=b^3(b+1)+(-4)(b+1)$
$=(b+1)(b^3-4)$

65. $3j^2k+15k+j^2+5=3k(j^2+5)+1(j^2+5)$
$=(j^2+5)(3k+1)$

67. $14w^6x^6+7w^6-2x^6-1$
$=7w^6(2x^6+1)+(-1)(2x^6+1)$
$=(2x^6+1)(7w^6-1)$

69. $ay+bx+by+ax=ay+ax+by+bx$
$=a(y+x)+b(y+x)$
$=(a+b)(y+x)$

71. $vw^2-3+w-3wv=vw^2-3vw+w-3$
$=vw(w-3)+1(w-3)$
$=(vw+1)(w-3)$

73. $15x^4+15x^2y^2+10x^3y+10xy^3$
$=5x(3x^3+3xy^2+2x^2y+2y^3)$
$=5x(3x(x^2+y^2)+2y(x^2+y^2))$
$=5x(x^2+y^2)(3x+2y)$

75. $4abx-4b^2x-4ab+4b^2$
$=4b(ax-bx-a+b)$
$=4b(x(a-b)-1(a-b))$
$=4b(a-b)(x-1)$

77. $6st^2-18st-6t^4+18t^3$
$=6t(st-3s-t^3+3t^2)$
$=6t(s(t-3)-t^2(t-3))$
$=6t(t-3)(s-t^2)$

79. $P=2l+2w$
$P=2(l+w)$

81. $S=2\pi r^2+2\pi rh$
$S=2\pi r(r+h)$

83. $\frac{1}{7}x^2+\frac{3}{7}x-\frac{5}{7}=\frac{1}{7}(x^2+3x-5)$

85. $\frac{5}{4}w^2+\frac{3}{4}w+\frac{9}{4}=\frac{1}{4}(5w^2+3w+9)$

87. Answers may vary. For example: $6x^2+9x$

89. Answers may vary. For example:
$16p^4q^2+8p^3q-4p^2q$

Section 6.2 Practice Exercises

1. $4x^3y^7-12x^4y^5+8xy^8$
$=4xy^5(x^2y^2-3x^3+2y^3)$

3. $3t(t-5)-6(t-5)$
$=3(t-5)(t-2)$

5. $ax+2bx-5a-10b$
$=x(a+2b)-5(a+2b)$
$=(a+2b)(x-5)$

7. $x^2 + 10x + 16 = (x + 8)(x + 2)$

9. $z^2 - 11z + 18 = (z - 9)(z - 2)$

11. $z^2 - 3z - 18 = (z - 6)(z + 3)$

13. $p^2 - 3p - 40 = (p - 8)(p + 5)$

15. $t^2 + 6t - 40 = (t + 10)(t - 4)$

17. $x^2 - 3x + 20$ is prime

19. $n^2 + 8n + 16 = (n + 4)(n + 4) = (n + 4)^2$

21. a

23. c

25. They are both correct because multiplication of polynomials is a commutative operation..

27. The expressions are equal and both are correct

29. Descending order

31. $-13x + x^2 - 30 = x^2 - 13x - 30$
$= (x - 15)(x + 2)$

33. $-18w + 65 + w^2 = w^2 - 18w + 65$
$= (w - 13)(w - 5)$

35. $22t + t^2 + 72 = t^2 + 22t + 72$
$= (t + 18)(t + 4)$

37. $3x^2 - 30x - 72 = 3(x^2 - 10x - 24)$
$= 3(x - 12)(x + 2)$

39. $8p^3 - 40p^2 + 32p = 8p(p^2 - 5p + 4)$
$= 8p(p - 1)(p - 4)$

41. $y^4 z^2 - 12y^3 z^2 + 36y^2 z^2$
$= y^2 z^2 (y^2 - 12y + 36)$
$= y^2 z^2 (y - 6)(y - 6)$ or $y^2 z^2 (y - 6)^2$

43. $-x^2 + 10x - 24 = -(x^2 - 10x + 24)$
$= -(x - 4)(x - 6)$

45. $-5a^2 + 5ax + 30x^2 = -5(a^2 - ax - 6x^2)$
$= -5(a - 3x)(a + 2x)$

47. $-4 - 2c^2 - 6c = -2(c^2 + 3c + 2)$
$= -2(c + 2)(c + 1)$

49. $x^2 y^3 - 19x^2 y^3 + 60xy^3$
$= xy^3 (x^2 - 19x + 60)$
$= xy^3 (x - 15)(x - 4)$

51. $12p^2 - 96p + 84 = 12(p^2 - 8p + 7)$
$= 12(p - 7)(p - 1)$

53. $-2m^2 + 22m - 20 = -2(m^2 - 11m + 10)$
$= -2(m - 10)(m - 1)$

55. $c^2 + 6cd + 5d^2 = (c + 5d)(c + d)$

57. $a^2 - 9ab + 14b^2 = (a - 2b)(a - 7b)$

59. $a^2 + 4a + 18$ is Prime

61. $2q + q^2 - 63 = q^2 + 2q - 63$
$= (q - 7)(q + 9)$

63. $x^2 + 20x + 100 = (x + 10)(x + 10)$
$= (x + 10)^2$

65. $t^2 + 18t - 40 = (t + 20)(t - 2)$

67. The student forgot to factor out the GCF before factoring the trinomial further. The polynomial is not factored completely, because $(2x - 4)$ has a common factor of 2.

69. $(x-4)(x+13) = x^2 + 9x - 52$

71. $x^4 + 10x^2 + 9 = (x^2+1)(x^2+9)$

73. $w^4 + 2w^2 - 15 = (w^2+5)(w^2-3)$

75. $7, 5, -7, -5$

77. For example, $c = -16$

Section 6.3 Practice Exercises

1. $21a^2b^2 + 12ab^2 - 15a^2b$
$= 3ab(7ab + 4b - 5a)$

3. $mn - m - 2n + 2 = m(n-1) - 2(n-1)$
$= (n-1)(m-2)$

5. $6a^2 - 30a - 84 = 6(a^2 - 5a - 14)$
$= 6(a-7)(a+2)$

7. a

9. b

11. $2y^2 - 3y - 2 = (2y+1)(y-2)$

13. $3n^2 + 13n + 4 = (3n+1)(n+4)$

15. $5x^2 - 14x - 3 = (5x+1)(x-3)$

17. $12c^2 - 5c - 2 = (4c+1)(3c-2)$

19. $-12 + 10w^2 + 37w = 10w^2 + 37w - 12$
$= (10w-3)(w+4)$

21. $-5q - 6 + 6q^2 = 6q^2 - 5q - 6$
$= (3q+2)(2q-3)$

23. $6b - 23 + 4b^2 = 4b^2 + 6b - 23$ is prime

25. $-8 + 25m^2 - 10m = 25m^2 - 10m - 8$
$= (5m+2)(5m-4)$

27. $6y^2 + 19xy - 20x^2 = (6y-5x)(y+4x)$

29. $2m^2 - 12m - 80 = 2(m^2 - 6m - 40)$
$= 2(m-10)(m+4)$

31. $2y^5 + 13y^4 + 6y^3 = y^3(2y^2 + 13y + 6)$
$= y^3(2y+1)(y+6)$

33. $-a^2 - 15a + 34 = -(a^2 + 15a - 34)$
$= -(a+17)(a-2)$

35. $-80m^2 + 100mp + 30p^2$
$= -10(8m^2 - 10mp - 3p^2)$
$= -10(4m+p)(2m-3p)$

37. $x^4 + 10x^2 + 9 = (x^2+1)(x^2+9)$

39. $w^4 + 2w^2 - 15 = (w^2+5)(w^2-3)$

41. $2x^4 - 7x^2 - 15 = (2x^2+3)(x^2-5)$

43. $-2z^2 + 20z - 18 = -2(z^2 - 10z + 9)$
$= -2(z-9)(z-1)$

45. $q^2 - 13q + 42 = (q-6)(q-7)$

47. $6t^2 + 7t - 3 = (2t+3)(3t-1)$

49. $4m^2 - 20m + 25 = (2m-5)(2m-5)$
$= (2m-5)^2$

51. $5c^2 - c + 2$ is prime

53. $6x^2 - 19xy + 10y^2 = (2x-5y)(3x-2y)$

55. $12m^2 + 11mn - 5n^2 = (4m+5n)(3m-n)$

57. $30r^2 + 5r - 10 = 5(6r^2 + r - 2)$
$= 5(3r+2)(2r-1)$

59. $4s^2 - 8st + t^2$ is prime

61. $10t^2 - 23t - 5 = (2t-5)(5t+1)$

63. $14w^2 + 13w - 12 = (7w - 4)(2w + 3)$

65. $a^2 - 10a - 24 = (a - 12)(a + 2)$

67. $x^2 + 9xy + 20y^2 = (x + 5y)(x + 4y)$

69. $a^2 + 21ab + 20b^2 = (a + 20b)(a + b)$

71. $t^2 - 10t + 21 = (t - 7)(t - 3)$

73. $5d^6 + 3d^2 - 10d = d(5d^5 + 3d - 10)$

75. $4b^3 - 4b^2 - 80b = 4b(b^2 - b - 20)$
$ = 4b(b + 4)(b - 5)$

77. $x^2y^2 - 13xy^2 + 30y^2 = y^2(x^2 - 13x + 30)$
$ = y^2(x - 3)(x - 10)$

79. $-12u^3 - 22u^2 + 20u = -2u(6u^2 + 11u - 10)$
$ = -2u(3u - 2)(2u + 5)$

81. $8x^4 + 14x^2 + 3 = (2x^2 + 3)(4x^2 + 1)$

83. $10z^4 + 9z^2 - 9 = (5z^2 - 3)(2z^2 + 3)$

85. (a) $x^2 - 10x - 24 = (x - 12)(x + 2)$

    (b) $x^2 - 10x + 24 = (x - 6)(x - 4)$

87. (a) $x^2 - 5x - 6 = (x - 6)(x + 1)$

    (b) $x^2 - 5x + 6 = (x - 2)(x - 3)$

Section 6.4 Practice Exercises

1. $2pr + 12p - 6r - 36$
$= 2p(r + 6) - 6(r + 6)$
$= (r + 6)(2p - 6)$
$= 2(r + 6)(p - 3)$

3. $\quad 8(y + 5) + 9y(y + 5) = (y + 5)(8 + 9y)$

5. 12 and 1

7. −8 and −1

9. 5 and −4

11. 9 and −2

13. $3x^2 + 13x + 4 = 3x^2 + 12x + x + 4$
$ = 3x(x + 4) + 1(x + 4)$
$ = (x + 4)(3x + 1)$

15. $4w^2 - 9w + 2 = 4w^2 - 8w - w + 2$
$ = 4w(w - 2) - 1(w - 2)$
$ = (w - 2)(4w - 1)$

17. $x^2 + 7x - 18 = x^2 + 9x - 2x - 18$
$ = x(x + 9) - 2(x + 9)$
$ = (x + 9)(x - 2)$

19. $2m^2 + 5m - 3 = 2m^2 + 6m - m - 3$
$ = 2m(m + 3) - 1(m + 3)$
$ = (m + 3)(2m - 1)$

21. $8k^2 - 6k - 9 = 8k^2 - 12k + 6k - 9$
$ = 4k(2k - 3) + 3(2k - 3)$
$ = (2k - 3)(4k + 3)$

23. $4k^2 - 20k + 25 = 4k^2 - 10k - 10k + 25$
$ = 2k(2k - 5) - 5(2k - 5)$
$ = (2k - 5)(2k - 5)$
$ = (2k - 5)^2$

25. Prime

27. $9z^2 - 21z + 10 = 9z^2 - 15z - 6z + 10$
$ = 3z(3z - 5) - 2(3z - 5)$
$ = (3z - 5)(3z - 2)$

29. $\quad 12y^2 + 8yz - 15z^2$
$= 12y^2 + 18yz - 10yz - 15z^2$
$= 6y(2y + 3z) - 5z(2y + 3z)$
$= (2y + 3z)(6y - 5z)$

31. $14y^2 + 50y + 24 = 2(7y^2 + 25y + 12)$
$= 2(7y^2 + 21y + 4y + 12)$
$= 2(7y(y+3) + 4(y+3))$
$= 2(y+3)(7y+4)$

33. $-15w^2 + 22w + 5 = -(15w^2 - 22w - 5)$
$= -(3w-5)(5w+1)$

35. $-12x^2 + 20xy - 8y^2 = -4(3x^2 - 5xy + 2y^2)$
$= -4(3x-2y)(x-y)$

37. $18y^3 + 60y^2 + 42y = 6y(3y^2 + 10y + 7)$
$= 6y(3y+7)(y+1)$

39. $a^4 + 5a^2 + 6 = (a^2+3)(a^2+2)$

41. $6x^4 - x^2 - 15 = (3x^2-5)(2x^2+3)$

43. $8p^4 + 37p^2 - 15 = (8p^2-3)(p^2+5)$

45. $20p^2 - 19p + 3 = 20p^2 - 15p - 4p + 3$
$= 5p(4p-3) - 1(4p-3)$
$= (4p-3)(5p-1)$

47. $6u^2 - 19uv + 10v^2$
$= 6u^2 - 15uv - 4uv + 10v^2$
$= 3u(2u-5v) - 2v(2u-5v)$
$= (2u-5v)(3u-2v)$

49. $12a^2 + 11ab - 5b^2$
$= 12a^2 + 15ab - 4ab - 5b^2$
$= 3a(4a+5b) - b(4a+5b)$
$= (4a+5b)(3a-b)$

51. $3h^2 + 19hk - 14k^2$
$= 3h^2 + 21hk - 2hk - 14k^2$
$= 3h(h+7k) - 2k(h+7k)$
$= (h+7k)(3h-2k)$

53. Prime.

55. $16z^2 - 14z + 3 = 16z^2 - 8z - 6z + 3$
$= 8z(2z-1) - 3(2z-1)$
$= (2z-1)(8z-3)$

57. $b^2 - 8b + 16 = b^2 - 4b - 4b + 16$
$= b(b-4) - 4(b-4)$
$= (b-4)(b-4)$
$= (b-4)^2$

59. $-5x^2 + 25x - 30 = -5(x^2 - 5x + 6)$
$= -5(x^2 - 3x - 2x + 6)$
$= -5(x(x-3) - 2(x-3))$
$= -5(x-3)(x-2)$

61. $t^2 - t - 6 = t^2 - 3t + 2t - 6$
$= t(t-3) + 2(t-3)$
$= (t-3)(t+2)$

63. $v^2 + 2v + 15$
prime

65. $72x^2 + 18x - 2 = 2(36x^2 + 9x - 1)$
$= 2(36x^2 + 12x - 3x - 1)$
$= 2(12x(3x+1) - 1(3x+1))$
$= 2(3x+1)(12x-1)$

67. $p^3 - 6p^2 - 27p = p(p^2 - 6p - 27)$
$= p(p^2 - 9p + 3p - 27)$
$= p(p(p-9) + 3(p-9))$
$= p(p-9)(p+3)$

69. $3x^3 + 10x^2 + 7x = x(3x^2 + 10x + 7)$
$= x(3x^2 + 3x + 7x + 7)$
$= x(3x(x+1) + 7(x+1))$
$= x(3x+7)(x+1)$

71. $2p^3 - 38p^2 + 120p$
$= 2p(p^2 - 19p + 60)$
$= 2p(p^2 - 4p - 15p + 60)$
$= 2p(p(p-4) - 15(p-4))$
$= 2p(p-4)(p-15)$

73. $x^2y^2 + 14x^2y + 33x^2$
$= x^2(y^2 + 14y + 33)$
$= x^2(y^2 + 11y + 3y + 33)$
$= x^2(y(y + 11) + 3(y + 11))$
$= x^2(y + 11)(y + 3)$

75. $-k^2 - 7k - 10 = -1(k^2 + 7k + 10)$
$= -1(k^2 + 5k + 2k + 10)$
$= -1(k(k + 5) + 2(k + 5))$
$= -1(k + 5)(k + 2)$

77. $-3n^2 - 3n + 90 = -3(n^2 + n - 30)$
$= -3(n^2 + 6n - 5n - 30)$
$= -3(n(n + 6) - 5(n + 6))$
$= -3(n + 6)(n - 5)$

79. $x^4 - 7x^2 + 10 = (x^2 - 5)(x^2 - 2)$

81. No. $(2x + 4)$ contains a common factor of 2.

Section 6.5 Practice Exercises

1. (a) The product of two conjugates results in a **difference of squares.**

(b) The **sum of squares** is a prime polynomial.

(c) The square of a binomial results in a **perfect square trinomial.**

3. $6x^2 - 17x + 5 = (3x - 1)(2x - 5)$

5. $15x^2y^2 - 10xy^6$
$= 5xy^2(3x - 2y^4)$

7. $ax + ab - 6x - 6b = a(x + b) - 6(x + b)$
$= (x + b)(a - 6)$

9. $6y - 10 + y^2 = y^2 + 6y - 40 = (y + 10)(y - 4)$

11. $x^2 - 5^2 = x^2 - 25$

13. $(2p - 3q)(2p + 3q) = 4p^2 - 9q^2$

15. $x^2 - 36 = (x + 6)(x - 6)$

17. $3w^2 - 300 = 3(w^2 - 100) = 3(w + 10)(w - 10)$

19. $4a^2 - 121b^2 = (2a)^2 - (11b)^2$
$= (2a + 11b)(2a - 11b)$

21. $49m^2 - 16n^2 = (7m)^2 - (4n)^2$
$= (7m + 4n)(7m - 4n)$

23. $9q^2 + 16$ is prime

25. $y^2 - 4z^2 = (y + 2z)(y - 2z)$

27. $a^2 - b^4 = (a + b^2)(a - b^2)$

29. $25p^2q^2 - 1 = (5pq - 1)(5pq + 1)$

31. $c^2 - \dfrac{1}{25} = (c)^2 - \left(\dfrac{1}{5}\right)^2 = \left(c + \dfrac{1}{5}\right)\left(c - \dfrac{1}{5}\right)$

33. $50 - 32t^2 = 2(25 - 16t^2)$
$= 2\left[5^2 - (4t)^2\right]$
$= 2(5 + 4t)(5 - 4t)$

35. $z^4 - 16 = (z^2 + 4)(z^2 - 4)$
$= (z^2 + 4)(z + 2)(z - 2)$

37. $81 - a^4 = \left(9 - a^2\right)\left(9 + a^2\right)$
$= (3 - a)(3 + a)\left(9 + a^2\right)$

39. $x^3 + 5x^2 - 9x - 45 = x^2(x + 5) - 9(x + 5)$
$= (x + 5)(x^2 - 9)$
$= (x + 5)(x + 3)(x - 3)$

41. $c^3 - c^2 - 25c + 25 = c^2(c - 1) - 25(c - 1)$
$= (c - 1)(c^2 - 25)$
$= (c - 1)(c + 5)(c - 5)$

43. $2x^2 - 18 + x^2y - 9y = 2(x^2 - 9) + y(x^2 - 9)$
$$= (2 + y)(x^2 - 9)$$
$$= (2 + y)(x + 3)(x - 3)$$

45. $x^2y^2 - 9x^2 - 4y^2 + 36$
$$= x^2(y^2 - 9) - 4(y^2 - 9)$$
$$= (x^2 - 4)(y^2 - 9)$$
$$= (x + 2)(x - 2)(y + 3)(y - 3)$$

47. $(3x + 5)^2 = 9x^2 + 30x + 25$

49. (a) $x^2 + 4x + 4$ is a perfect square trinomial

(b) $x^2 + 4x + 4 = (x + 2)^2$;
$$x^2 + 5x + 4 = (x + 1)(x + 4)$$

51. $x^2 + 18x + 81 = x^2 + 2(9)(x) + 9^2 = (x + 9)^2$

53. $25z^2 - 20z + 4 = (5z)^2 - 2(5z)(2) + 2^2$
$$= (5z - 2)^2$$

55. $49a^2 + 42ab + 9b^2$
$$= (7a)^2 + 2(7a)(3b) + (3b)^2$$
$$= (7a + 3b)^2$$

57. $-2y + y^2 + 1 = y^2 - 2y + 1 = (y - 1)^2$

59. $80z^2 + 120zw + 45w^2$
$$= 5(16z^2 + 24zw + 9w^2)$$
$$= 5((4z)^2 + 2(4z)(3w) + (3w)^2)$$
$$= 5(4z + 3w)^2$$

61. $9y^2 + 78y + 25 = (3y + 25)(3y + 1)$

63. $2a^2 - 20a + 50 = 2(a^2 - 10a + 25)$
$$= 2(a - 5)^2$$

65. $4x^2 + x + 9$ is prime

67. $4x^2 + 4xy + y^2 = (2x)^2 + 2(2x)y + y^2$
$$= (2x + y)^2$$

69. $(y - 3)^2 - 9 = ((y - 3) + 3)((y - 3) - 3)$
$$= y(y - 6)$$

71. $(2p + 1)^2 - 36 = ((2p + 1) + 6)((2p + 1) - 6)$
$$= (2p + 7)(2p - 5)$$

73. $16 - (t + 2)^2$
$$= (4 + (t + 2))(4 - (t + 2))$$
$$= (4 + t + 2)(4 - t - 2)$$
$$= (t + 6)(-t + 2) \text{ or } -(t + 6)(t - 2)$$

75. $100 - (2b - 5)^2$
$$= (10 + (2b - 5))(10 - (2b - 5))$$
$$= (10 + 2b - 5)(10 - 2b + 5)$$
$$= (2b + 5)(-2b + 15) \text{ or } -(2b + 5)(2b - 15)$$

77. (a) a^2 (area of outer square)
b^2 (area of inner square)
Total area $= a^2 - b^2$

(b) $a^2 - b^2 = (a + b)(a - b)$

Section 6.6 Practice Exercises

1. **(a)** A binomial $a^3 + b^3$ is a **sum of cubes** and can be factored as $(a + b)(a^2 - ab + b^2)$.

(b) A binomial $a^3 - b^3$ is a **difference of cubes** and can be factored as $(a - b)(a^2 + ab + b^2)$.

3. $20 - 5t^2 = 5(4 - t^2) = 5(2 - t)(2 + t)$

5. $2t + 2u + st + su = 2(t + u) + s(t + u)$
$$= (t + u)(2 + s)$$

7. $3v^2 + 5v - 12 = (3v - 4)(v + 3)$

9. $-c^2 - 10c - 25 = -(c^2 + 10c + 25) = -(c + 5)^2$

11. $x^3, 8, y^6, 27q^3, w^{12}, r^3s^6$

13. $a^3 + b^3 = (a+b)(a^2 - ab + b^2)$

15. $y^3 - 8 = y^3 - 2^3 = (y-2)(y^2 + 2y + 4)$

17. $1 - p^3 = (1-p)(1+p+p^2)$

19. $w^3 + 64 = w^3 + 4^3 = (w+4)(w^2 - 4w + 16)$

21. $x^3 - 1000 = x^3 - 10^3$
$$= (x-10)(x^2 + 10x + 100)$$

23. $64t^3 + 1 = (4t)^3 + 1^3 = (4t+1)(16t^2 - 4t + 1)$

25. $1000a^3 + 27 = (10a)^3 + 3^3$
$$= (10a+3)(100a^2 - 30a + 9)$$

27. $n^3 - \dfrac{1}{8} = n^3 - \left(\dfrac{1}{2}\right)^3 = \left(n-\dfrac{1}{2}\right)\left(n^2 + \dfrac{1}{2}n + \dfrac{1}{4}\right)$

29. $125m^3 + 8 = (5m)^3 + 2^3$
$$= (5m+2)(25m^2 - 10m + 4)$$

31. $x^4 - 4 = (x^2)^2 - 2^2 = (x^2 + 2)(x^2 - 2)$

33. $a^2 + 9$ is prime.

35. $t^3 + 64 = t^3 + 4^3 = (t+4)(t^2 - 4t + 16)$

37. $g^3 - 4$ is prime.

39. $4b^3 + 108 = 4(b^3 + 27)$
$$= 4(b+3)(b^2 - 3b + 9)$$

41. $5p^2 - 125 = 5(p^2 - 25) = 5(p+5)(p-5)$

43. $\dfrac{1}{64} - 8h^3 = \left(\dfrac{1}{4}\right)^3 - (2h)^3$
$$= \left(\dfrac{1}{4} - 2h\right)\left(\dfrac{1}{16} + \dfrac{1}{2}h + 4h^2\right)$$

45. $x^4 - 16 = (x^2)^2 - 4^2$
$$= (x^2 + 4)(x^2 - 4)$$
$$= (x^2 + 4)(x+2)(x-2)$$

47. $q^6 - 64$
$$= (q^3)^2 - 8^2$$
$$= (q^3 + 8)(q^3 - 8)$$
$$= (q+2)(q^2 - 2q + 4)(q-2)(q^2 + 2q + 4)$$

49. $\dfrac{4}{9}x^2 - w^2 = \left(\dfrac{2x}{3}\right)^2 - w^2$
$$= \left(\dfrac{2x}{3} - w\right)\left(\dfrac{2x}{3} + w\right)$$

51. $x^9 + 64y^3 = \left(x^3\right)^3 + (4y)^3$
$$= \left(x^3 + 4y\right)\left(x^6 - 4x^3 y + 16y^2\right)$$

53. $2x^3 + 3x^2 - 2x - 3 = x^2(2x+3) - 1(2x+3)$
$$= (2x+3)(x^2 - 1)$$
$$= (2x+3)(x+1)(x-1)$$

55. $16x^4 - y^4 = (4x^2 + y^2)(4x^2 - y^2)$
$$= (4x^2 + y^2)(2x+y)(2x-y)$$

57. $81y^4 - 16 = (9y^2 + 4)(9y^2 - 4)$
$$= (9y^2 + 4)(3y+2)(3y-2)$$

59. $a^3 + b^6 = a^3 + (b^2)^3$
$$= (a+b^2)(a^2 - ab^2 + b^4)$$

61. $x^4 - y^4 = (x^2 + y^2)(x^2 - y^2)$
$$= (x^2 + y^2)(x+y)(x-y)$$

63. $k^3 + 4k^2 - 9k - 36 = k^2(k+4) - 9(k+4)$
$$= (k+4)(k^2 - 9)$$
$$= (k+4)(k+3)(k-3)$$

65. $2t^3 - 10t^2 - 2t + 10 = 2t^2(t-5) - 2(t-5)$
$$= 2(t-5)(t^2 - 1)$$
$$= 2(t-5)(t+1)(t-1)$$

67. $\dfrac{64}{125}p^3 - \dfrac{1}{8}q^3$

$= \left(\dfrac{4}{5}p\right)^3 - \left(\dfrac{1}{2}q\right)^3$

$= \left(\dfrac{4}{5}p - \dfrac{1}{2}q\right)\left(\dfrac{16}{25}p^2 + \dfrac{2}{5}pq + \dfrac{1}{4}q^2\right)$

69. $a^{12} + b^{12} = (a^4)^3 + (b^4)^3$

$\qquad\qquad = (a^4 + b^4)(a^8 - a^4b^4 + b^8)$

71. (a)
$$
\begin{array}{r}
x^2 + 2x + 4 \\
x-2 \enclose{longdiv}{x^3 + 0x^2 + 0x - 8} \\
\underline{-(x^3 - 2x^2)} \\
2x^2 + 0x \\
\underline{-(2x^2 - 4x)} \\
4x - 8 \\
\underline{-(4x - 8)}
\end{array}
$$

(b) $x^3 - 8 = (x-2)(x^2 + 2x + 4)$

73. $x^2 + 2x + 4$

75. $2x + 1$

Problem Recognition Exercises

1. A prime factor cannot be factored further.

3. Look for the difference of squares: $a^2 - b^2$, a difference of cubes: $a^3 - b^3$, or a sum of cubes: $a^3 + b^3$

5. (a) Difference of squares

(b) $2a^2 - 162 = 2(a^2 - 81) = 2(a+9)(a-9)$

7. (a) None of these

(b) $6w^2 - 6w = 6w(w-1)$

9. (a) Non-perfect square trinomial

(b) $3t^2 + 13t + 4 = (3t+1)(t+4)$

11. (a) Four terms-grouping

(b) $\quad 3ac + ad - 3bc - bd$
$\quad = a(3c+d) - b(3c+d)$
$\quad = (3c+d)(a-b)$

13. (a) Sum of cubes

(b) $y^3 + 8 = (y+2)(y^2 - 2y + 4)$

15. (a) Non-perfect square trinomial

(b) $3q^2 - 9q - 12 = 3(q^2 - 3q - 4)$
$\qquad\qquad\qquad = 3(q-4)(q+1)$

17. (a) None of these

(b) $18a^2 + 12a = 6a(3a+2)$

19. (a) Difference of squares

(b) $4t^2 - 100 = 4(t^2 - 25) = 4(t+5)(t-5)$

21. (a) Non-perfect square trinomial

(b) $10c^2 + 10c + 10 = 10(c^2 + c + 1)$

23. (a) Sum of cubes

(b) $x^3 + 0.001 = (x+0.1)(x^2 - 0.1x + 0.01)$

25. (a) Perfect square trinomial

(b) $64 + 16k + k^2 = 8^2 + 2(8)(k) + k^2$
$\qquad\qquad\qquad = (8+k)^2$

27. (a) Four terms-grouping

(b) $\quad 2x^2 + 2x - xy - y$
$\quad = 2x(x+1) - y(x+1)$
$\quad = (x+1)(2x-y)$

29. (a) Difference of cubes

(b) $a^3 - c^3 = (a-c)(a^2 + ac + c^2)$

31. (a) Non-perfect square trinomial

(b) $c^2 + 8c + 9$ is Prime

33. (a) Perfect square trinomial

(b) $b^2 + 10b + 25 = (b+5)^2$

35. (a) Non-perfect square trinomial

(b) $-p^3 - 5p^2 - 4p = -p(p^2 + 5p + 4)$
$= -p(p+1)(p+4)$

37. (a) Non-perfect square trinomial

(b) $6x^2 - 21x - 45 = 3(2x^2 - 7x - 15)$
$= 3(2x+3)(x-5)$

39. (a) None of these

(b) $5a^2bc^3 - 7abc^2 = abc^2(5ac - 7)$

41. (a) Non-perfect square trinomial

(b) $t^2 + 2t - 63 = (t-7)(t+9)$

43. (a) Four terms-grouping

(b) $ab + ay - b^2 - by$
$= a(b+y) - b(b+y)$
$= (b+y)(a-b)$

45. (a) Non-perfect square trinomial

(b) $14u^2 - 11uv + 2v^2 = (7u - 2v)(2u - v)$

47. (a) Non-perfect square trinomial

(b) $4q^2 - 8q - 6 = 2(2q^2 - 4q - 3)$

49. (a) Sum of squares

(b) $9m^2 + 16n^2$ is prime

51. (a) Non-perfect square trinomial

(b) $6r^2 + 11r + 3 = (3r+1)(2r+3)$

53. (a) Difference of squares

(b) $16a^4 - 1 = (4a^2 + 1)(4a^2 - 1)$
$= (4a^2 + 1)(2a+1)(2a-1)$

55. (a) Perfect square trinomial

(b) $81u^2 - 90uv + 25v^2$
$= (9u)^2 - 2(9u)(5v) + (5v)^2$
$= (9u - 5v)^2$

57. (a) Non-perfect square trinomial

(b) $x^2 - 5x - 6 = (x-6)(x+1)$

59. (a) Four terms-grouping

(b) $2ax - 6ay + 4bx - 12by$
$= 2a(x-y) + 4b(x-y)$
$= 2(x-y)(a+2b)$

61. (a) Non-perfect square trinomial

(b) $21x^4y + 41x^3y + 10x^2y$
$= x^2y(21x^2 + 41x + 10)$
$= x^2y(7x+2)(3x+5)$
$= (p+c)(p+3)(p-3)$

63. (a) Four terms-grouping

(b) $8uv - 6u + 12v - 9$
$= 2u(4v-3) + 3(4v-3)$
$= (4v-3)(2u+3)$

65. (a) Perfect square trinomial

(b) $12x^2 - 12x + 3 = 3(4x^2 - 4x + 1)$
$= 3([2x]^2 - 2(2x)(1) + 1^2)$
$= 3(2x-1)^2$

67. **(a)** Non-perfect square trinomial

(b) $6n^3 + 5n^2 - 4n$
$= n(6n^2 + 5n - 4)$
$= n(6n^2 - 3n + 8n - 4)$
$= n[3n(2n-1) + 4(2n-1)]$
$= n[(2n-1)(3n+4)]$
$= n(2n-1)(3n+4)$

69. **(a)** Difference of squares

(b) $64 - y^2 = 8^2 - y^2 = (8-y)(8+y)$

71. **(a)** Non-perfect square trinomial

(b) $b^2 - 4b + 10$ is prime.

73. **(a)** Non-perfect square trinomial

(b) $c^4 - 12c^2 + 20 = (c^2 - 10)(c^2 - 2)$

Section 6.7 Practice Exercises

1. **(a)** A **quadratic equation** is a second-degree polynomial equation in one variable.

(b) The **zero product rule** states that if the product of two factors is zero, then one or both of its factors is zero.

3. $4b^2 - 44b + 120 = 4(b^2 - 11b + 30)$
$= 4(b-6)(b-5)$

5. $3x^2 + 10x - 8 = (3x-2)(x+4)$

7. $4x^2 + 16y^2 = 4(x^2 + 4y^2)$

9. Neither

11. Quadratic

13. Linear

15. $(x+3)(x-1) = 0$
$x + 3 = 0$ or $x - 1 = 0$
$x = -3$ $x = 1$

17. $(2x-7)(2x+7) = 0$
$2x - 7 = 0$ or $2x + 7 = 0$
$2x = 7$ $2x = -7$
$x = \dfrac{7}{2}$ $x = -\dfrac{7}{2}$

19. $3(x+5)(x+5) = 0$
$x + 5 = 0$
$x = -5$

21. $x(5x-1) = 0$
$x = 0$ or $5x - 1 = 0$
$x = 0$ or $5x = 1$
$x = 0$ or $x = \dfrac{1}{5}$

23. The polynomial must be factored completely before applying the zero product rule.

25. $p^2 - 2p - 15 = 0$
$(p+3)(p-5) = 0$
$p + 3 = 0$ or $p - 5 = 0$
$p = -3$ $p = 5$

27. $z^2 + 10z - 24 = 0$
$(z+12)(z-2) = 0$
$z + 12 = 0$ or $z - 2 = 0$
$z = -12$ $z = 2$

29. $2q^2 - 7q - 4 = 0$
$(2q+1)(q-4) = 0$
$2q + 1 = 0$ or $q - 4 = 0$
$q = -\dfrac{1}{2}$ $q = 4$

31. $0 = 9x^2 - 4$
$0 = (3x+2)(3x-2)$
$3x + 2 = 0$ or $3x - 2 = 0$
$x = -\dfrac{2}{3}$ $x = \dfrac{2}{3}$

33. $2k^2 - 28k + 96 = 0$

$2(k^2 - 14k + 48) = 0$

$2(k - 6)(k - 8) = 0$

$k - 6 = 0 \quad \text{or} \quad k - 8 = 0$

$\quad k = 6 \qquad\qquad k = 8$

35. $0 = 2m^3 - 5m^2 - 12m$

$m(2m^2 - 5m - 12) = 0$

$m(2m + 3)(m - 4) = 0$

$m = 0 \quad \text{or} \quad 2m + 3 = 0 \quad \text{or} \quad m - 4 = 0$

$m = 0 \qquad\qquad m = -\dfrac{3}{2} \qquad\qquad m = 4$

37. $(3p + 1)(p - 3)(p + 6) = 0$

$3p + 1 = 0 \quad \text{or} \quad p - 3 = 0 \quad \text{or} \quad p + 6 = 0$

$p = -\dfrac{1}{3} \quad \text{or} \quad p = 3 \quad \text{or} \quad p = -6$

39. $x(x - 4)(2x + 3) = 0$

$x = 0 \quad \text{or} \quad x - 4 = 0 \quad \text{or} \quad 2x + 3 = 0$

$x = 0 \quad \text{or} \qquad x = 4 \quad \text{or} \qquad 2x = -3$

$\qquad\qquad\qquad\qquad\qquad\qquad\qquad x = -\dfrac{3}{2}$

$x = 0 \quad \text{or} \qquad x = 4 \quad \text{or}$

41. $-5x(2x + 9)(x - 11) = 0$

$-5x = 0 \quad \text{or} \quad 2x + 9 = 0 \quad \text{or} \quad x - 11 = 0$

$x = \dfrac{0}{-5} \quad \text{or} \qquad 2x = -9 \quad \text{or} \qquad x = 11$

$\qquad\qquad\qquad\qquad x = -\dfrac{9}{2} \quad \text{or}$

$x = 0 \quad \text{or} \qquad\qquad\qquad\quad \text{or} \qquad x = 11$

43. $x^3 - 16x = 0$

$x(x^2 - 16) = 0$

$x(x + 4)(x - 4) = 0$

$x = 0 \quad \text{or} \quad x + 4 = 0 \quad \text{or} \quad x - 4 = 0$

$x = 0 \quad \text{or} \qquad x = -4 \quad \text{or} \qquad x = 4$

45. $3x^2 + 18x = 0$

$3x(x + 6) = 0$

$3x = 0 \quad \text{or} \quad x + 6 = 0$

$x = 0 \quad \text{or} \qquad x = -6$

47. $16m^2 = 9$

$16m^2 - 9 = 0$

$(4m + 3)(4m - 3) = 0$

$4m + 3 = 0 \quad \text{or} \quad 4m - 3 = 0$

$m = -\dfrac{3}{4} \quad \text{or} \qquad m = \dfrac{3}{4}$

49. $2y^3 + 14y^2 = -20y$

$2y^3 + 14y^2 + 20y = 0$

$2y(y^2 + 7y + 10) = 0$

$2y(y + 5)(y + 2) = 0$

$2y = 0 \quad \text{or} \quad y + 5 = 0 \quad \text{or} \quad y + 2 = 0$

$y = 0 \quad \text{or} \qquad y = -5 \quad \text{or} \qquad y = -2$

51. $5t - 2(t - 7) = 0$

$5t - 2t + 14 = 0$

$3t + 14 = 0$

$t = -\dfrac{14}{3}$

53. $2c(c - 8) = -30$

$2c^2 - 16c + 30 = 0$

$2(c^2 - 8c + 15) = 0$

$2(c - 5)(c - 3) = 0$

$c - 5 = 0 \quad \text{or} \quad c - 3 = 0$

$c = 5 \quad \text{or} \qquad c = 3$

55. $b^3 = -4b^2 - 4b$

$b^3 + 4b^2 + 4b = 0$

$b(b^2 + 4b + 4) = 0$

$b(b + 2)(b + 2) = 0$

$b = 0 \quad \text{or} \quad b + 2 = 0 \quad \text{or} \quad b + 2 = 0$

$b = 0 \quad \text{or} \qquad b = -2 \quad \text{or} \qquad b = -2$

57. $3(a^2 + 2a) = 2a^2 - 9$

$3a^2 + 6a = 2a^2 - 9$

$a^2 + 6a + 9 = 0$

$(a + 3)(a + 3) = 0$

$a + 3 = 0$

$a = -3$

59. $2n(n+2)=6$

$2n^2+4n-6=0$

$2(n^2+2n-3)=0$

$2(n+3)(n-1)=0$

$n+3=0$ or $n-1=0$

$n=-3$ $\qquad$ $n=1$

61. $x(2x+5)-1=2x^2+3x+2$

$2x^2+5x-1=2x^2+3x+2$

$2x-3=0$

$x=\dfrac{3}{2}$

63. $27q^2=9q$

$27q^2-9q=0$

$9q(3q-1)=0$

$9q=0$ or $3q-1=0$

$q=0$ $\qquad$ $q=\dfrac{1}{3}$

65. $3(c^2-2c)=0$

$3c(c-2)=0$

$3c=0$ or $c-2=0$

$c=0$ $\qquad$ $c=2$

67. $y^3-3y^2-4y+12=0$

$y^2(y-3)-4(y-3)=0$

$(y-3)(y+2)(y-2)=0$

$y-3=0$ or $y+2=0$ or $y-2=0$

$y=3$ $\qquad$ $y=-2$ $\qquad$ $y=2$

69. $(x-1)(x+2)=18$

$x^2+x-2-18=0$

$x^2+x-20=0$

$(x+5)(x-4)=0$

$x+5=0$ or $x-4=0$

$x=-5$ $\qquad$ $x=4$

71. $(p+2)(p+3)=1-p$

$p^2+5p+6=1-p$

$p^2+6p+5=0$

$(p+5)(p+1)=0$

$p+5=0$ or $p+1=0$

$p=-5$ $\qquad$ $p=-1$

Problem Recognition Exercises

1. (a) $x^2+6x-7=(x+7)(x-1)$

(b) $(x+7)(x-1)=0$

$x+7=0$ or $x-1=0$

$x=-7$ $\qquad$ $x=1$

3. (a) $2y^2+7y+3=(2y+1)(y+3)$

(b) $(2y+1)(y+3)=0$

$2y+1=0$ or $y+3=0$

$y=-\dfrac{1}{2}$ $\qquad$ $y=-3$

5. (a) $5q^2+q-4=(5q-4)(q+1)=0$

$5q-4=0$ or $q+1=0$

$q=\dfrac{4}{5}$ $\qquad$ $q=-1$

(b) $5q^2+q-4=(5q-4)(q+1)$

7. (a) $a^2-64=(a+8)(a-8)=0$

$a+8=0$ or $a-8=0$

$a=-8$ $\qquad$ $a=8$

(b) $a^2-64=(a+8)(a-8)$

9. (a) $4b^2-81=(2b+9)(2b-9)$

(b) $(2b+9)(2b-9)=0$

$2b+9=0$ or $2b-9=0$

$b=-\dfrac{9}{2}$ $\qquad$ $b=\dfrac{9}{2}$

11. (a)
$$8x^2 + 16x + 6 = 0$$
$$2(4x^2 + 8x + 3) = 0$$
$$2(2x + 3)(2x + 1) = 0$$
$$2x + 3 = 0 \quad \text{or} \quad 2x + 1 = 0$$
$$x = -\frac{3}{2} \qquad x = -\frac{1}{2}$$

(b) $8x^2 + 16x + 6 = 2(2x + 3)(2x + 1)$

13. (a) $x^3 - 8x^2 - 20x = x(x^2 - 8x - 20)$
$$= x(x - 10)(x + 2)$$

(b) $x(x - 10)(x + 8) = 0$
$$x = 0 \quad \text{or} \quad x - 10 = 0 \quad \text{or} \quad x + 2 = 0$$
$$x = 0 \qquad x = 10 \qquad x = -2$$

15. (a)
$$b^3 + b^2 - 9b - 9 = 0$$
$$b^2(b + 1) - 9(b + 1) = 0$$
$$(b + 1)(b^2 - 9) = 0$$
$$(b + 1)(b + 3)(b - 3) = 0$$
$$b + 1 = 0 \quad \text{or} \quad b + 3 = 0 \quad \text{or} \quad b - 3 = 0$$
$$b = -1 \qquad b = -3 \qquad b = 3$$

(b) $b^3 + b^2 - 9b - 9 = (b + 1)(b - 3)(b + 3)$

17. $2s^2 - 6s + rs - 3r = 2s(s - 3) + r(s - 3)$
$$= (s - 3)(2s + r)$$

19. $8x^3 - 2x = 2x(4x^2 - 1)$
$$= 2x(2x - 1)(2x + 1) = 0$$
$$2x = 0 \quad \text{or} \quad 2x - 1 = 0 \quad \text{or} \quad 2x + 1 = 0$$
$$x = 0 \qquad x = \frac{1}{2} \qquad x = -\frac{1}{2}$$

21. $2x^3 - 4x^2 + 2x = 2x(x^2 - 2x + 1)$
$$= 2x(x - 1)^2 = 0$$
$$2x = 0 \quad \text{or} \quad x - 1 = 0 \quad \text{or} \quad x - 1 = 0$$
$$x = 0 \qquad x = 1 \qquad x = 1$$

23. $7c^2 - 2c + 3 = 7(c^2 + c)$
$$7c^2 - 2c + 3 = 7c^2 + 7c$$
$$3 = 9c$$
$$c = \frac{3}{9}$$
$$c = \frac{1}{3}$$

25. $8w^3 + 27 = (2w)^3 + (3)^3$
$$= (2w + 3)(4w^2 - 6w + 9)$$

27.
$$5z^2 + 2z = 7$$
$$5z^2 + 2z - 7 = 0$$
$$(5z + 7)(z - 1) = 0$$
$$5z + 7 = 0 \quad \text{or} \quad z - 1 = 0$$
$$z = -\frac{7}{5} \qquad z = 1$$

29.
$$3b(b + 6) = b - 10$$
$$3b^2 + 18b = b - 10$$
$$3b^2 + 17b + 10 = 0$$
$$(3b + 2)(b + 5) = 0$$
$$3b + 2 = 0 \quad \text{or} \quad b + 5 = 0$$
$$b = -\frac{2}{3} \qquad b = -5$$

31. $5(2x - 3) - 2(3x + 1) = 4 - 3x$
$$10x - 15 - 6x - 2 = 4 - 3x$$
$$4x - 17 = 4 - 3x$$
$$7x = 21$$
$$x = 3$$

33.
$$4s^2 = 64$$
$$4s^2 - 64 = 0$$
$$4(s^2 - 16) = 0$$
$$4(s + 4)(s - 4) = 0$$
$$s + 4 = 0 \quad \text{or} \quad s - 4 = 0$$
$$s = -4 \qquad s = 4$$

35. $(x-3)(x-4) = 6$

$x^2 - 7x + 12 = 6$

$x^2 - 7x + 6 = 0$

$(x-6)(x-1) = 0$

$x-6 = 0$ or $x-1 = 0$

$x = 6$ $\quad\quad x = 1$

Section 6.8 Practice Exercises

1. The **Pythagorean theorem** states that $a^2 + b^2 = c^2$, where a and b are the lengths of the legs of a right triangle and c is the length of its hypotenuse.

3. $9x(3x + 2) = 0$

$9x = 0$ or $3x + 2 = 0$

$x = 0$ $\quad\quad x = -\dfrac{2}{3}$

5. $x^2 - 5x = 6$

$x^2 - 5x - 6 = 0$

$(x-6)(x+1) = 0$

$x-6 = 0$ or $x+1 = 0$

$x = 6$ $\quad\quad x = -1$

7. $6x^2 - 7x - 10 = 0$

$(6x + 5)(x - 2) = 0$

$6x + 5 = 0$ or $x - 2 = 0$

$x = -\dfrac{5}{6}$ $\quad\quad x = 2$

9. Let x = the number. Then,

$x^2 + 11 = 60$

$x^2 - 49 = 0$

$(x+7)(x-7) = 0$

$x+7 = 0$ or $x-7 = 0$

$x = -7$ $\quad\quad x = 7$

The numbers are 7 and −7.

11. Let x = a number. Then,

$12 + 6x = x^2 - 28$

$x^2 - 6x - 40 = 0$

$(x+4)(x-10) = 0$

$x+4 = 0$ or $x-10 = 0$

$x = -4$ $\quad\quad x = 10$

The numbers are −4 and 10.

13. Let x = first integer. Then the next consecutive odd integer is $(x + 2)$.

$x(x+2) = 63$

$x^2 + 2x - 63 = 0$

$(x+9)(x-7) = 0$

$x+9 = 0$ or $x-7 = 0$

$x = -9$ $\quad\quad x = 7$

The numbers are −9 and −7, or 7 and 9.

15. Let x = first integer. Then the next consecutive integer is $(x + 1)$.

$x^2 + (x+1)^2 = 61$

$x^2 + x^2 + 2x + 1 = 61$

$2x^2 + 2x - 60 = 0$

$2(x+6)(x-5) = 0$

$x+6 = 0$ or $x-5 = 0$

$x = -6$ $\quad\quad x = 5$

The numbers are −6 and -5, or 5 and 6.

17. Let x = width of the painting and $x + 2$ is the length of the painting. Then,

$A = (\text{length})(\text{width})$

$99 = x(x+2)$

$99 = x^2 + 2x$

$x^2 + 2x - 99 = 0$

$(x+11)(x-2) = 0$

$x = -11$ or $x = 9$

The height of the painting is 11 ft and the width is 9 ft.

19. Let x = length and $x - 3$ be the width.

(a)
$$A = lw$$
$$28 = x(x - 3)$$
$$x^2 - 3x - 28 = 0$$
$$(x + 4)(x - 7) = 0$$
$$x = -4 \text{ or } x = 7$$
The dimensions are 7 m by 4 m.

(b) $P = 2w + 2l$
$$P = 2(4) + 2(7)$$
$$P = 8 + 14 = 22 \text{ m}$$

21. Let x = height and $x + 3$ = the base.
$$A = \frac{1}{2}bh$$
$$14 = \frac{1}{2}(x)(x + 3)$$
$$28 = x^2 + 3x$$
$$x^2 + 3x - 28 = 0$$
$$(x + 7)(x - 4) = 0$$
$$x + 7 = 0 \quad \text{or} \quad x - 4 = 0$$
$$x = \cancel{-7} \qquad x = 4$$
The height is 4 ft and the base is 7 ft.

23. If you let $h = 0$, then,
$$0 = -16t^2 + 144$$
$$0 = -16(t^2 - 9)$$
$$-16(t + 3)(t - 3) = 0$$
$$t + 3 = 0 \quad \text{or} \quad t - 3 = 0$$
$$t = -3 \qquad t = 3$$
It will take 3 seconds to hit the ground.

25. Ground level is when $h = 0$. Then,
$$0 = -16t^2 + 24t$$
$$0 = -8t(2t - 3)$$
$$-8t = 0 \quad \text{or} \quad 2t - 3 = 0$$
$$t = 0 \qquad t = \frac{3}{2} = 1.5$$
The times are 0 seconds and 1.5 seconds.

27. Pictures may vary.

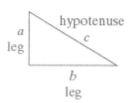

29.
$$c^2 = a^2 + b^2$$
$$c^2 = 24^2 + 7^2$$
$$c^2 = 625$$
$$c^2 - 625 = 0$$
$$(c + 25)(c - 25) = 0$$
$$c = \cancel{-25} \text{ or } c = 25$$
$$c = 25 \text{ cm}$$

31. $c^2 = a^2 + b^2$
$$17^2 = a^2 + 8^2$$
$$289 = a^2 + 64$$
$$a^2 - 225 = 0$$
$$(a + 15)(a - 15) = 0$$
$$a = \cancel{-15} \text{ or } a = 15$$
$$a = 15 \text{ in.}$$

33. Let $x = c$.
$$c^2 = a^2 + b^2$$
$$x^2 = 16^2 + 12^2$$
$$x^2 = 400$$
$$x^2 - 400 = 0$$
$$(x + 20)(x - 20) = 0$$
$$x = \cancel{-20} \text{ or } x = 20$$
The brace is 20 in. long.

35. Let h = height of the kite. Then, $a = h - 1$.
$$c^2 = a^2 + b^2$$
$$30^2 = (h - 1)^2 + 24^2$$
$$900 = h^2 - 2h + 1 + 576$$
$$h^2 - 2h - 323 = 0$$
$$(h + 17)(h - 19) = 0$$
$$h = \cancel{-17} \text{ or } h = 19$$
The kit is 19 yd high.

37. Let x = distance between the base of the ladder and the bottom of the house. Then, the distance between the top of the ladder and the ground is $x + 7$ ft.

$$c^2 = a^2 + b^2$$
$$17^2 = x^2 + (x+7)^2$$
$$289 = x^2 + x^2 + 14x + 49$$
$$2x^2 + 14x - 240 = 0$$
$$2(x+15)(x-8) = 0$$
$$x = \cancel{-15} \text{ or } x = 8$$

The bottom of the ladder is 8 ft from the house. The distance from the top of the ladder to the ground is 15 ft.

39. Let x = hypotenuse. Then, one leg is $x - 4$ m and the other leg is $x - 2$ m.

$$x^2 = (x-4)^2 + (x-2)^2$$
$$x^2 = x^2 - 8x + 16 + x^2 - 4x + 4$$
$$x^2 = 2x^2 - 12x + 20$$
$$x^2 - 12x + 20 = 0$$
$$(x-10)(x-2) = 0$$
$$x = 10 \text{ or } x = \cancel{2}$$

The hypotenuse is 10 m.

Group Activity

1. Answers will vary. For example:
$$2x^3 - 10x^2 + 2x = 2x(x^2 - 5x + 1)$$

3. Answers will vary. For example:
$$x^2 - 5x - 14 = (x+2)(x-7)$$

5. Answers will vary. For example:
$$7x^3 - 14x^2 - 21x = 7x(x-3)(x+1)$$

7. Answers will vary. For example:
$$216 - 125b^3 = (6-5b)(36+30b+25b^2)$$

9. Answers will vary. For example:
$$(x-4)(x+7) = 0$$
$$x^2 + 3x - 28 = 0$$

Chapter 6 Review Exercises

Section 6.1

1. GCF: $3a^2b$

3. GCF: $2c(3c-5)$

5. $6x^2 + 2x^4 - 8x = 2x(3x + x^3 - 4)$

7. $-t^2 + 5t = -t(t-5) \text{ or } t(-t+5)$

9. $3b(b+2) - 7(b+2) = (b+2)(3b-7)$

11. $7w^2 + 14w + wb + 2b = 7w(w+2) + b(w+2)$
$$= (w+2)(7w+b)$$

13. $60y^2 - 45y - 12y + 9$
$$= 3(20y^2 - 15y - 4y + 3)$$
$$= 3(5y(4y-3) - 1(4y-3))$$
$$= 3(4y-3)(5y-1)$$

Section 6.2

15. $x^2 - 10x + 21 = x^2 - 7x - 3x + 21$
$$= x(x-7) - 3(x-7)$$
$$= (x-3)(x-7)$$

17. $-6z + z^2 - 72 = z^2 - 6z - 72$
$$= z^2 + 6z - 12z - 72$$
$$= z(z+6) - 12(z+6)$$
$$= (z-12)(z+6)$$

19. $3p^2w + 36pw + 60w$
$$= 3w(p^2 + 12p + 20)$$
$$= 3w(p^2 + 2p + 10p + 20)$$
$$= 3w(p(p+2) + 10(p+2))$$
$$= 3w(p+10)(p+2)$$

21. $-t^2 + 10t - 16 = -(t^2 - 10t + 16)$
$$= -(t^2 - 2t - 8t + 16)$$
$$= -(t(t-2) - 8(t-2))$$
$$= -(t-8)(t-2)$$

22. $-w^2 - w + 20 = -(w^2 + w - 20)$
$$= -(w^2 + 5w - 4w - 20)$$
$$= -(w(w + 5) - 4(w + 5))$$
$$= -(w - 4)(w + 5)$$

24. $c^2 - 3cd - 18d^2 = c^2 + 3cd - 6cd - 18d^2$
$$= c(c + 3d) - 6d(c + 3d)$$
$$= (c - 6d)(c + 3d)$$

Section 6.3

25. Different

27. Both positive

29. $2y^2 - 5y - 12 = 2y^2 - 8y + 3y - 12$
$$= 2y(y - 4) + 3(y - 4)$$
$$= (2y + 3)(y - 4)$$

31. $10z^2 + 29z + 10 = 10z^2 + 4z + 25z + 10$
$$= 2z(5z + 2) + 5(5z + 2)$$
$$= (2z + 5)(5z + 2)$$

33. $2p^2 - 5p + 1$ is prime.

35. $10w^2 - 60w - 270 = 10(w^2 - 6w - 27)$
$$= 10(w^2 - 9w + 3w - 27)$$
$$= 10(w(w - 9) + 3(w - 9))$$
$$= 10(w + 3)(w - 9)$$

37. $9c^2 - 30cd + 25d^2$
$$= 9c^2 - 15cd - 15cd + 25d^2$$
$$= 3c(3c - 5d) - 5d(3c - 5d)$$
$$= (3c - 5d)(3c - 5d)$$
$$= (3c - 5d)^2$$

39. $6g^2 + 7gh + 2h^2 = (3g + 2h)(2g + h)$

41. $v^4 - 2v^2 - 3 = (v^2)^2 - 2v^2 - 3$
$$= (v^2)^2 + v^2 - 3v^2 - 3$$
$$= v^2(v^2 + 1) - 3(v^2 + 1)$$
$$= (v^2 - 3)(v^2 + 1)$$

Section 6.4

43. $5, -1$

45. $3c^2 - 5c - 2 = 3c^2 - 6c + c - 2$
$$= 3c(c - 2) + 1(c - 2)$$
$$= (c - 2)(3c + 1)$$

47. $t^2 + 13tw + 12w^2 = t^2 + 12tw + tw + 12w^2$
$$= t(t + 12w) + 1(t + 12w)$$
$$= (t + 1w)(t + 12w)$$

49. $w^4 + 7w^2 + 10 = w^4 + 5w^2 + 2w^2 + 10)$
$$= w^2(w^2 + 5) + 2(w^2 + 5))$$
$$= (w^2 + 5)(w^2 + 2)$$

51. $40v^2 + 22v - 6 = 2(20v^2 + 11v - 3)$
$$= 2(20v^2 + 15v - 4v - 3)$$
$$= 2(5v(4v + 3) - 1(4v + 3))$$
$$= 2(4v + 3)(5v - 1)$$

53. $a^3b - 10a^2b^2 + 24ab^3$
$$= ab(a^2 - 10ab + 24b^2)$$
$$= ab(a^2 - 6ab - 4ab + 24b^2)$$
$$= ab(a(a - 6b) - 4b(a - 6b))$$
$$= ab(a - 6b)(a - 4b)$$

55. $m + 9m^2 - 2$
prime

57. $49x^2 + 140x + 100$
$$= (7x)^2 + 2(7x)(10) + 10^2$$
$$= (7x + 10)^2$$

Section 6.5

59. $a^2 - b^2 = (a - b)(a + b)$

61. $a^2 - 49 = a^2 - 7^2 = (a + 7)(a - 7)$

63. $100 - 81t^2 = 10^2 - (9t)^2 = (10 + 9t)(10 - 9t)$

65. $x^2 + 16$; this is a sum of squares, not a difference.

67. $y^2 + 12y + 36 = (y+6)^2$

69. $9a^2 - 12a + 4 = (3a-2)^2$

71. $-3v^2 - 12v - 12 = -3(v^2 + 4v + 4)$
$$= -3(v+2)^2$$

73. $2c^4 - 18 = 2(c^4 - 9) = 2(c^2 + 3)(c^2 - 3)$

75. $p^3 + 3p^2 - 16p - 48$
$= p^3 + 3p^2 - 16(p+3)$
$= p^2(p+3) - 16(p+3)$
$= (p^2 - 16)(p+3)$
$= (p-4)(p+4)(p+3)$

Section 6.6

77. $a^3 + b^3 = (a+b)(a^2 - ab + b^2)$

79. $64 + a^3 = 4^3 + a^3$
$$= (4+a)(4^2 - 4a + a^2)$$
$$= (4+a)(16 - 4a + a^2)$$

81. $p^6 + 8 = (p^2)^3 + 2^3$
$$= (p^2 + 2)((p^2)^2 - p^2 2 + 2^2)$$
$$= (p^2 + 2)(p^4 - 2p^2 + 4)$$

83. $6x^3 - 48 = 6(x^3 - 8)$
$$= 6(x^3 - 2^3)$$
$$= 6(x-2)(x^2 + 2x + 4)$$

85. $x^3 - 36x = x(x^2 - 36) = x(x+6)(x-6)$

87. $8h^2 + 20 = 4(2h^2 + 5)$

89. $x^3 + 4x^2 - x - 4 = x^2(x+4) - 1(x+4)$
$$= (x+4)(x^2 - 1)$$
$$= (x+4)(x+1)(x-1)$$

91. $8n + n^4 = n(8 + n^3) = n(2+n)(4 - 2n + n^2)$

Section 6.7

93. The equation $(x-3)(2x+1) = 0$ can be solved directly by the zero product rule because it is a product of factors set equal to zero.

95. $(a-9)(2a-1) = 0$
$a - 9 = 0$ or $2a - 1 = 0$
$a = 9 \qquad\qquad a = \dfrac{1}{2}$

97. $6u(u-7)(4u-9) = 0$
$6u = 0$ or $u - 7 = 0$ or $4u - 9 = 0$
$u = 0 \qquad\quad u = 7 \qquad\quad u = \dfrac{9}{4}$

99. $4h^2 - 23h - 6 = 0$
$(4h+1)(h-6) = 0$
$4h + 1 = 0$ or $h - 6 = 0$
$h = -\dfrac{1}{4} \qquad\qquad h = 6$

101. $r^2 = 25$
$r^2 - 25 = 0$
$(r+5)(r-5) = 0$
$r + 5 = 0$ or $r - 5 = 0$
$r = -5 \qquad\qquad r = 5$

103. $x(x-6) = -8$
$x^2 - 6x + 8 = 0$
$(x-4)(x-2) = 0$
$x - 4 = 0$ or $x - 2 = 0$
$x = 4 \qquad\qquad x = 2$

105. $9s^2 + 12s = -4$
$9s^2 + 12s + 4 = 0$
$(3s+2)(3s+2) = 0$
$3s + 2 = 0$
$s = -\dfrac{2}{3}$

107.
$$2(p^2 - 66) = -13p$$
$$2p^2 + 13p - 132 = 0$$
$$(2p - 11)(p + 12) = 0$$
$$2p - 11 = 0 \quad \text{or} \quad p + 12 = 0$$
$$p = \frac{11}{2} \qquad\qquad p = -12$$

109.
$$x^3 - 4x = 0$$
$$x(x^2 - 4) = 0$$
$$x(x + 2)(x - 2) = 0$$
$$x = 0 \quad \text{or} \quad x + 2 = 0 \quad \text{or} \quad x - 2 = 0$$
$$x = 0 \quad \text{or} \qquad x = -2 \quad \text{or} \qquad x = 2$$

Section 6.8

111. At $h = 0$, the ball is ground level.
$$0 = -16x^2 + 16x$$
$$0 = -16x(x - 1)$$
$$x = 0 \text{ or } x = 1$$
The ball is at ground level at 0 and 1 second.

113. Let x = shorter leg. Then, the other leg is $x + 2$ and the hypotenuse is $2x - 2$.
$$x^2 + (x + 2)^2 = (2x - 2)^2$$
$$x^2 + x^2 + 4x + 4 = 4x^2 - 8x + 4$$
$$2x^2 - 12x = 0$$
$$2x(x - 6) = 0$$
$$x = 0 \text{ or } x = 6$$
The legs are 6 ft and 8 ft; the hypotenuse is 10 ft.

115. x = first integer and $x + 1$ is the next integer.
$$x(x + 1) = 14(x + x + 1) + 44$$
$$x^2 + x = 28x + 14 + 44$$
$$x^2 - 27x - 58 = 0$$
$$(x + 2)(x - 29) = 0$$
$$x = -2 \text{ and } x = 29$$
The numbers are −2 and −1 or 29 and 30.

Chapter 6 Test

1. $15x^4 - 3x + 6x^3 = 3x(5x^3 - 1 + 2x^2)$

3. $6w^2 - 43w + 7 = (6w - 1)(w - 7)$

5. $q^2 - 16q + 64 = (q - 8)^2$

7. $a^2 + 12a + 32 = (a + 4)(a + 8)$

9. $2y^2 - 17y + 8 = (2y - 1)(y - 8)$

11. $9t^2 - 100 = (3t + 10)(3t - 10)$

13. $3a^2 + 27ab + 54b^2 = 3(a^2 + 9ab + 18b^2)$
$$= 3(a + 6b)(a + 3b)$$

15. $xy - 7x + 3y - 21 = x(y - 7) + 3(y - 7)$
$$= (y - 7)(x + 3)$$

17. $-10u^2 + 30u - 20 = -10(u^2 - 3u + 2)$
$$= -10(u - 2)(u - 1)$$

19. $5y^2 - 50y + 125 = 5(y^2 - 10y + 25)$
$$= 5(y - 5)(y - 5)$$
$$= 5(y - 5)^2$$

21. $2x^3 + x^2 - 8x - 4 = x^2(2x + 1) - 4(2x + 1)$
$$= (2x + 1)(x^2 - 4)$$
$$= (2x + 1)(x + 2)(x - 2)$$

23. $m^2n^2 - 81 = (mn + 9)(mn - 9)$

25. $64x^3 - 27y^6$
$$= (4x - 3y^2)(16x^2 + 12xy^2 + 9y^4)$$

27. $(2x - 3)(x + 5) = 0$
$$2x - 3 = 0 \quad \text{or} \quad x + 5 = 0$$
$$x = \frac{3}{2} \qquad\qquad x = -5$$

29.
$$x^2 - 6x = 16$$
$$x^2 - 6x - 16 = 0$$
$$(x+2)(x-8) = 0$$
$$x+2 = 0 \quad \text{or} \quad x-8 = 0$$
$$x = -2 \qquad\qquad x = 8$$

31.
$$y^3 + 10y^2 - 9y - 90 = 0$$
$$y^2(y+10) - 9(y+10) = 0$$
$$(y^2 - 9)(y+10) = 0$$
$$(y+3)(y-3)(y+10) = 0$$
$$y+3 = 0 \quad \text{or} \quad y-3 = 0 \quad \text{or} \quad y+10 = 0$$
$$y = -3 \quad \text{or} \qquad y = 3 \quad \text{or} \qquad y = -10$$

33. Let x represent the first odd integer. Then $x + 2$ represents the second odd integer.
$$x(x+2) = 35$$
$$x^2 + 2x = 35$$
$$x^2 + 2x - 35 = 0$$
$$(x+7)(x-5) = 0$$
$$x+7 = 0 \quad \text{or} \quad x-5 = 0$$
$$x = -7 \quad \text{or} \qquad x = 5$$
$$x+2 = -5 \quad \text{or} \quad x+2 = 7$$

The two integers are −5 and −7 or 5 and 7.

35. Let x = shorter leg, $3x - 3$ the longer leg, and $3x - 2$ the length of the hypotenuse.
$$(x)^2 + (3x-3)^2 = (3x-2)^2$$
$$x^2 + 9x^2 - 18x + 9 = 9x^2 - 12x + 4$$
$$x^2 - 6x + 5 = 0$$
$$(x-1)(x-5) = 0$$
$x = 1$ or $x = 5$
The shorter leg is 5 ft.

Cumulative Review Exercises
Chapters 1–6

1.
$$\frac{|4 - 25 \div (-5) \cdot 2|}{\sqrt{8^2 + 6^2}} = \frac{|4 - (-5) \cdot 2|}{\sqrt{64 + 36}}$$
$$= \frac{|4 - (-10)|}{\sqrt{100}}$$
$$= \frac{|14|}{10}$$
$$= \frac{7}{5}$$

3.
$$3x - 2y = 8$$
$$-2y = 8 - 3x$$
$$\frac{-2y}{-2} = \frac{8 - 3x}{-2}$$
$$y = \frac{3x - 8}{2} \text{ or } y = \frac{8 - 3x}{-2}$$

5.
$$-\frac{5}{12}x \le \frac{5}{3}$$
$$-\frac{12}{5} \cdot \left(-\frac{5}{12}x\right) \le -\frac{12}{5} \cdot \frac{5}{3}$$
$$x \ge -4$$
$[-4, \infty)$

7. **(a)** Vertical line

(b) Undefined

(c) $(5, 0)$

(d) Does not exist

9. $2x - 3y = 4$

$5x - 6y = 13$

Multiply the first equation by -2 to obtain opposite coefficients on y. Then add the equations and solve the resulting equation for x.

$$-4x + 6y = -8$$
$$\underline{5x - 6y = 13}$$
$$x \quad\ = 5$$

$$2(5) - 3y = 4$$
$$10 - 3y = 4$$
$$-3y = -6$$
$$y = 2$$

Solution: $(5, 2)$

11. $(4p^2 - 5p - 1)(2p - 3)$

$= 8p^3 - 10p^2 - 2p - 12p^2 + 15p + 3$

$= 8p^3 - 22p^2 + 13p + 3$

13.

$$
\begin{array}{r}
r^3 + 5r^2 + 15r + 40 \\
r - 3 \overline{\smash{)}\; r^4 + 2r^3 + 0r^2 - 5r + 1} \\
\underline{-(r^4 - 3r^3)} \\
5r^3 + 0r^2 \\
\underline{-(5r^3 - 15r^2)} \\
15r^2 - 5r \\
\underline{-(15r^2 - 45r)} \\
40r + 1 \\
\underline{-(40r - 120)} \\
121
\end{array}
$$

$$r^3 + 5r^2 + 15r + 40 + \frac{121}{r - 3}$$

15. $\dfrac{6a^2 b^{-4}}{2a^4 b^{-5}} = 3a^{2-4} b^{-4-5} = 3a^{-2} b^{-9} = \dfrac{3}{a^2 b^9}$

17. $w^4 - 16 = (w^2)^2 - 4^2$

$= (w^2 + 4)(w^2 - 4)$

$= (w^2 + 4)(w + 2)(w - 2)$

19. $4x^2 - 8x - 5 = (2x + 1)(2x - 5)$

Chapter 7

Chapter 7 opener

1. $\dfrac{7}{4}+\dfrac{5}{3}+\dfrac{1}{2}=\dfrac{7}{4}\cdot\dfrac{3}{3}+\dfrac{5}{3}\cdot\dfrac{4}{4}+\dfrac{1}{2}\cdot\dfrac{6}{6}$

$\qquad\qquad\quad=\dfrac{21}{12}+\dfrac{20}{12}+\dfrac{6}{12}$

$\qquad\qquad\quad=\dfrac{47}{12}$

2. $\dfrac{5}{3}\cdot\dfrac{11}{4}=\dfrac{55}{12}$

3. t.

4. p.

5. a.

$\underset{4\;12}{\underline{p\;\;o}}\;\underset{15}{\underline{c\;r\;a}}\;\underset{3}{\underline{s\;t}}\;\underset{5\,3}{\underline{i\;n\;a}}\;\underset{2}{\underline{t\;i\;o\;n}}$.

Section 7.1 Practice Exercises

1. Answers will vary.

3. **(a)** A number $\dfrac{p}{q}$ where p and q are integers and $q \neq 0$

(b) An expression $\dfrac{p}{q}$ where p and q are polynomials and $q \neq 0$

5. $x=-2;\ \dfrac{1}{-2-6}=\dfrac{1}{-8}=-\dfrac{1}{8}$

7. $w=0;\ \dfrac{0-4}{2(0)+8}=\dfrac{-4}{8}=-\dfrac{1}{2}$

9. $a=2;$

$\dfrac{(2-7)(2+1)}{(2-2)(2+5)}=\dfrac{(-5)(3)}{(0)(7)}=\dfrac{-15}{0}$ is undefined

11. **(a)** Let $x=12;\ t=\dfrac{24}{x}+\dfrac{24}{x+8}$

$\qquad\qquad\ =\dfrac{24}{12}+\dfrac{24}{12+8}$

$\qquad\qquad\ =2+\dfrac{24}{20}$

$\qquad\qquad\ =2+\dfrac{6}{5}$

$\qquad\qquad\ =3\dfrac{1}{5}$ hr or 3.2 hr

(b) Let $x=24;\ t=\dfrac{24}{x}+\dfrac{24}{x+8}$

$\qquad\qquad\ =\dfrac{24}{24}+\dfrac{24}{24+8}$

$\qquad\qquad\ =1+\dfrac{24}{32}$

$\qquad\qquad\ =1+\dfrac{3}{4}$

$\qquad\qquad\ =1\dfrac{3}{4}$ hr or 1.75 hr

13. k= -2

15. $x=\dfrac{5}{2}$, x= -8

17. m= -2, m= -3

19. There are no restricted values.

21. There are no restricted values.

23. t = 0

25. Answers may vary; $\dfrac{1}{x-2}$

27. Answers may vary; $\dfrac{1}{(x+3)(x-7)}$

29. (a) $\dfrac{3(-1)^2 - 2(-1) - 1}{6(-1)^2 - 7(-1) - 3} = \dfrac{3(1) - 2(-1) - 1}{6(1) - 7(-1) - 3}$

$= \dfrac{3 + 2 - 1}{6 + 7 - 3}$

$= \dfrac{4}{10}$

$= \dfrac{2}{5}$

(b) $\dfrac{-1-1}{2(-1)-3} = \dfrac{-2}{-2-3} = \dfrac{-2}{-5} = \dfrac{2}{5}$

31. (a) $\dfrac{5(1)+5}{(1)^2 - 1} = \dfrac{10}{1-1} = \dfrac{10}{0}$ is undefined

(b) $\dfrac{5}{1-1} = \dfrac{5}{0}$ is undefined

33. (a) $y = -2$

(b) $\dfrac{3y+6}{6y+12} = \dfrac{3(y+2)}{6(y+2)} = \dfrac{3}{6} = \dfrac{1}{2}$

35. (a) $t = -1$

(b) $\dfrac{t^2 - 1}{t+1} = \dfrac{(t+1)(t-1)}{(t+1)} = t - 1$

37. (a) $w = 0, w = \dfrac{5}{3}$

(b) $\dfrac{7w}{21w^2 - 35w} = \dfrac{7w}{7w(3w-5)} = \dfrac{1}{3w-5}$

39. (a) $x = -\dfrac{2}{3}$

(b) $\dfrac{9x^2 - 4}{6x+4} = \dfrac{(3x+2)(3x-2)}{2(3x+2)} = \dfrac{3x-2}{2}$

41. (a) $a = -3, a = 2$

(b) $\dfrac{a^2 + 3a - 10}{a^2 + a - 6} = \dfrac{(a+5)(a-2)}{(a+3)(a-2)} = \dfrac{a+5}{a+3}$

43. $\dfrac{7b^2}{21b} = \dfrac{7 \cdot b \cdot b}{3 \cdot 7 \cdot b} = \dfrac{b}{3}$

45. $\dfrac{18st^5}{12st^3} = \dfrac{6 \cdot 3 \cdot s \cdot t^3 \cdot t^2}{6 \cdot 2 \cdot s \cdot t^3} = \dfrac{3t^2}{2}$

47. $\dfrac{-24x^2 y^5 z}{8xy^4 z^3} = \dfrac{-3 \cdot 8 \cdot x \cdot x \cdot y^4 \cdot y \cdot z}{8 \cdot x \cdot y^4 \cdot z \cdot z^2} = -\dfrac{3xy}{z^2}$

49. $\dfrac{3(y+2)}{6(y+2)} = \dfrac{3}{6} = \dfrac{1}{2}$

51. $\dfrac{(p-3)(p+5)}{(p+5)(p+4)} = \dfrac{p-3}{p+4}$

53. $\dfrac{(m+11)}{4(m+11)(m-11)} = \dfrac{1}{4(m-11)}$

55. $\dfrac{x(2x+1)^2}{4x^3(2x+1)} = \dfrac{2x+1}{4x^2}$

57. $\dfrac{5}{20a-25} = \dfrac{5}{5(4a-5)} = \dfrac{1}{4a-5}$

59. $\dfrac{4w-8}{w^2-4} = \dfrac{4(w-2)}{(w+2)(w-2)} = \dfrac{4}{w+2}$

61. $\dfrac{3x^2 - 6x}{9xy+18x} = \dfrac{3x(x-2)}{9x(y+2)} = \dfrac{x-2}{3(y+2)}$

63. $\dfrac{2x+4}{x^2-3x-10} = \dfrac{2(x+2)}{(x-5)(x+2)} = \dfrac{2}{x-5}$

65. $\dfrac{a^2-49}{a-7} = \dfrac{(a+7)(a-7)}{a-7} = a+7$

67. $\dfrac{q^2+25}{q+5}$ cannot be simplified.

69. $\dfrac{y^2+6y+9}{2y^2+y-15}=\dfrac{(y+3)(y+3)}{(2y-5)(y+3)}=\dfrac{y+3}{2y-5}$

71. $\dfrac{3x^2+7x-6}{x^2+7x+12}=\dfrac{(3x-2)(x+3)}{(x+3)(x+4)}=\dfrac{3x-2}{x+4}$

73. $\dfrac{5q^2+5}{q^4-1}=\dfrac{5(q^2+1)}{(q+1)(q-1)(q^2+1)}$

$=\dfrac{5}{(q+1)(q-1)}$

75. $\dfrac{ac-ad+2bc-2bd}{2ac+ad+4bc+2bd}=\dfrac{(c-d)(a+2b)}{(2c+d)(a+2b)}$

$=\dfrac{c-d}{2c+d}$

77. $\dfrac{2t^2-3t}{2t^4-13t^3+15t^2}=\dfrac{t(2t-3)}{t^2(2t^2-13t+15)}$

$=\dfrac{t(2t-3)}{t^2(2t-3)(t-5)}$

$=\dfrac{1}{t(t-5)}$

79. $\dfrac{49p^2-28pq+4q^2}{14p-4q}=\dfrac{(7p-2q)^2}{2(7p-2q)}$

$=\dfrac{7p-2q}{2}$

81. $\dfrac{5x^3+4x^2-45x-36}{x^2-9}$

$=\dfrac{x^2(5x+4)-9(5x+4)}{x^2-9}$

$=\dfrac{(x^2-9)(5x+4)}{x^2-9}$

$=5x+4$

83. $\dfrac{2x^2-xy-3y^2}{2x^2-11xy+12y^2}=\dfrac{(2x-3y)(x+y)}{(2x-3y)(x-4y)}$

$=\dfrac{x+y}{x-4y}$

85. They are opposites.

87. $\dfrac{x-5}{5-x}=\dfrac{(-1)(5-x)}{5-x}=-1$

89. $\dfrac{-4-y}{4+y}=\dfrac{(-1)(4+y)}{4+y}=-1$

91. $\dfrac{3y-6}{12-6y}=\dfrac{3(y-2)}{-6(y-2)}=\dfrac{3}{-6}=-\dfrac{1}{2}$

93. $\dfrac{k+5}{5-k}$ cannot be simplified.

95. $\dfrac{10x-12}{10x+12}=\dfrac{2(5x-6)}{2(5x+6)}=\dfrac{5x-6}{5x+6}$

97. $\dfrac{x^2-x-12}{16-x^2}=\dfrac{(x-4)(x+3)}{(-1)(x+4)(x-4)}=-\dfrac{x+3}{x+4}$

99. $\dfrac{w^3-8}{w^2+2w+4}=\dfrac{(w-2)(w^2+2w+4)}{w^2+2w+4}=w-2$

101. $\dfrac{z^2-16}{z^3-64}=\dfrac{(z+4)(z-4)}{(z-4)(z^2+4z+16)}$

$=\dfrac{z+4}{z^2+4z+16}$

Section 7.2 Practice Exercises

1. $\dfrac{3}{5}\cdot\dfrac{1}{2}=\dfrac{3}{10}$

3. $\dfrac{3}{4}\div\dfrac{3}{8}=\dfrac{3}{4}\cdot\dfrac{8}{3}=\dfrac{24}{12}=2$

5. $6\cdot\dfrac{5}{12}=\dfrac{6}{1}\cdot\dfrac{5}{12}=\dfrac{30}{12}=\dfrac{5}{2}$

7. $\dfrac{\frac{21}{4}}{\frac{7}{5}} = \dfrac{21}{4} \cdot \dfrac{5}{7} = \dfrac{105}{28} = \dfrac{15}{4}$

9. $\dfrac{2xy}{5x^2} \cdot \dfrac{15}{4y} = \dfrac{2 \cdot x \cdot \cancel{y}}{\cancel{5} \cdot \cancel{x} \cdot x} \cdot \dfrac{3 \cdot \cancel{5}}{\cancel{2} \cdot 2 \cdot \cancel{y}} = \dfrac{3}{2x}$

11. $\dfrac{6x^3}{9x^6 y^2} \cdot \dfrac{18x^4 y^7}{4y}$

$= \dfrac{2 \cdot \cancel{3} \cdot x^3}{\cancel{3} \cdot 3 \cdot x^6 y^2} \cdot \dfrac{2 \cdot \cancel{3} \cdot 3 \cdot x^4 y^7}{\cancel{4}\,y}$

$= 3xy^4$

13. $\dfrac{4x-24}{20x} \cdot \dfrac{5x}{8} = \dfrac{4(x-6)}{20x} \cdot \dfrac{5x}{8} = \dfrac{x-6}{8}$

15. $\dfrac{3y+18}{y^2} \cdot \dfrac{4y}{6y+36} = \dfrac{3(y+6)}{y^2} \cdot \dfrac{4y}{6(y+6)} = \dfrac{2}{y}$

17. $\dfrac{10}{2-a} \cdot \dfrac{a-2}{16} = \dfrac{10}{-(a-2)} \cdot \dfrac{a-2}{16} = -\dfrac{5}{8}$

19. $\dfrac{b^2-a^2}{a-b} \cdot \dfrac{a}{a^2-ab} = \dfrac{-(a+b)(a-b)}{a-b} \cdot \dfrac{a}{a(a-b)}$

$\qquad\qquad = -\dfrac{a+b}{a-b}$

21. $\dfrac{y^2+2y+1}{5y-10} \cdot \dfrac{y^2-3y+2}{y^2-1}$

$= \dfrac{(y+1)^2}{5(y-2)} \cdot \dfrac{(y-1)(y-2)}{(y-1)(y+1)}$

$= \dfrac{y+1}{5}$

23. $\dfrac{10x}{2x^2+3x+1} \cdot \dfrac{x^2+7x+6}{5x}$

$= \dfrac{10x}{(2x+1)(x+1)} \cdot \dfrac{(x+1)(x+6)}{5x}$

$= \dfrac{\cancel{10}_2 \cancel{x}}{(2x+1)\cancel{(x+1)}} \cdot \dfrac{\cancel{(x+1)}(x+6)}{\cancel{5}\cancel{x}}$

$= \dfrac{2(x+6)}{2x+1}$

25. $\dfrac{4x}{7y} \div \dfrac{2x^2}{21xy} = \dfrac{4x}{7y} \cdot \dfrac{21xy}{2x^2}$

$\qquad = \dfrac{\cancel{2} \cdot 2 \cdot x}{\cancel{7} \cdot y} \cdot \dfrac{3 \cdot \cancel{7} \cdot x \cdot y}{\cancel{2} \cdot x^2}$

$\qquad = 6$

27. $\dfrac{8m^4 n^5}{5n^6} \div \dfrac{24mn}{15m^3}$

$= \dfrac{8m^4 n^5}{5n^6} \cdot \dfrac{15m^3}{24mn}$

$= \dfrac{\cancel{2} \cdot \cancel{2} \cdot \cancel{2} \cdot m^4 \cdot n^5}{\cancel{5} \cdot n^6} \cdot \dfrac{\cancel{3} \cdot \cancel{5} \cdot m^3}{\cancel{2} \cdot \cancel{2} \cdot \cancel{2} \cdot \cancel{3} \cdot m \cdot n}$

$= \dfrac{m^6}{n^2}$

29. $\dfrac{4a+12}{6a-18} \div \dfrac{3a+9}{5a-15} = \dfrac{4(a+3)}{6(a-3)} \cdot \dfrac{5(a-3)}{3(a+3)} = \dfrac{10}{9}$

31. $\dfrac{3x-21}{6x^2-42x} \div \dfrac{7}{12x} = \dfrac{3(x-7)}{6x(x-7)} \cdot \dfrac{12x}{7} = \dfrac{6}{7}$

33. $\dfrac{m^2-n^2}{9} \div \dfrac{3n-3m}{27m}$

$= \dfrac{(m+n)(m-n)}{9} \cdot \dfrac{27m}{-3(m-n)}$

$= -m(m+n)$

35. $\dfrac{3p+4q}{p^2+4pq+4q^2} \div \dfrac{4}{p+2q}$

$= \dfrac{3p+4q}{(p+2q)(p+2q)} \cdot \dfrac{p+2q}{4}$

$= \dfrac{3p+4q}{4(p+2q)}$

37. $\dfrac{p^2-2p-3}{p^2-p-6} \div \dfrac{p^2-1}{p^2+2p}$

$= \dfrac{p^2-2p-3}{p^2-p-6} \cdot \dfrac{p^2+2p}{p^2-1}$

$= \dfrac{(p+1)\,(p-3)}{(p+2)\,(p-3)} \cdot \dfrac{p\,(p+2)}{(p-1)(p+1)}$

$= \dfrac{p}{(p-1)}$

39. $(w+3) \cdot \dfrac{w}{2w^2+5w-3}$

$= \dfrac{(w+3)}{1} \cdot \dfrac{w}{(2w-1)(w+3)}$

$= \dfrac{w}{2w-1}$

41. $(r-5) \cdot \dfrac{4r}{2r^2-7r-15}$

$= \dfrac{(r-5)}{1} \cdot \dfrac{4r}{(2r+3)(r-5)}$

$= \dfrac{4r}{2r+3}$

43. $\dfrac{\frac{5t-10}{12}}{\frac{4t-8}{8}} = \dfrac{5(t-2)}{12} \cdot \dfrac{8}{4(t-2)} = \dfrac{5}{6}$

45. $\dfrac{2a^2+13a-24}{8a-12} \div (a+8)$

$= \dfrac{(2a-3)(a+8)}{4(2a-3)} \cdot \dfrac{1}{(a+8)}$

$= \dfrac{1}{4}$

47. $\dfrac{y^2+5y-36}{y^2-2y-8} \cdot \dfrac{y+2}{y-6} = \dfrac{(y+9)(y-4)}{(y-4)(y+2)} \cdot \dfrac{y+2}{y-6}$

$= \dfrac{y+9}{y-6}$

49. $\dfrac{t^2+4t-5}{t^2+7t+10} \cdot \dfrac{t+4}{t-1} = \dfrac{(t+5)(t-1)}{(t+5)(t+2)} \cdot \dfrac{t+4}{t-1}$

$= \dfrac{t+4}{t+2}$

51. $(5t-1) \div \dfrac{5t^2+9t-2}{3t+8}$

$= \dfrac{(5t-1)}{1} \cdot \dfrac{3t+8}{(5t-1)(t+2)}$

$= \dfrac{3t+8}{t+2}$

53. $\dfrac{x^2+2x-3}{x^2-3x+2} \cdot \dfrac{x^2+2x-8}{x^2+4x+3}$

$= \dfrac{(x+3)(x-1)}{(x-2)(x-1)} \cdot \dfrac{(x+4)(x-2)}{(x+3)(x+1)}$

$= \dfrac{x+4}{x+1}$

55. $\dfrac{\frac{w^2-6w+9}{8}}{\frac{9-w^2}{4w+12}} = \dfrac{(w-3)(w-3)}{8} \cdot \dfrac{4(w+3)}{-(w+3)(w-3)}$

$= -\dfrac{w-3}{2}$

57. $\dfrac{5k^2+7k+2}{k^2+5k+4} \div \dfrac{5k^2+17k+6}{k^2+10k+24}$

$= \dfrac{(k+1)(5k+2)}{(k+4)(k+1)} \cdot \dfrac{(k+6)(k+4)}{(5k+2)(k+3)}$

$= \dfrac{k+6}{k+3}$

59. $\dfrac{ax+a+bx+b}{2x^2+4x+2} \cdot \dfrac{4x+4}{a^2+ab}$

$= \dfrac{a(x+1)+b(x+1)}{2(x^2+2x+1)} \cdot \dfrac{4(x+1)}{a(a+b)}$

$= \dfrac{(a+b)\,(x+1)}{2(x+1)\,(x+1)} \cdot \dfrac{4\,(x+1)}{a\,(a+b)}$

$= \dfrac{2}{a}$

61. $\dfrac{y^4-1}{2y^2-3y+1} \div \dfrac{2y^2+2}{8y^2-4y}$

$= \dfrac{(y^2-1)(y^2+1)}{(2y-1)(y-1)} \cdot \dfrac{4y(2y-1)}{2(y^2+1)}$

$= \dfrac{(y-1)(y+1)(y^2+1)}{(2y-1)(y-1)} \cdot \dfrac{4y(2y-1)}{2(y^2+1)}$

$= 2y(y+1)$

63. $\dfrac{x^2-xy-2y^2}{x+2y} \div \dfrac{x^2-4xy+4y^2}{x^2-4y^2} = \dfrac{(x-2y)(x+y)}{x+2y} \cdot \dfrac{(x-2y)(x+2y)}{(x-2y)(x-2y)}$

$= x+y$

65. $\dfrac{y^3-3y^2+4y-12}{y^4-16} \cdot \dfrac{3y^2+5y-2}{3y^2-10y+3} \div \dfrac{3}{6y-12} = \dfrac{(y^2+4)(y-3)}{(y+2)(y-2)(y^2+4)} \cdot \dfrac{(3y-1)(y+2)}{(3y-1)(y-3)} \cdot \dfrac{6(y-2)}{3} = \dfrac{6}{3} = 2$

67. $\dfrac{a^2-5a}{a^2+7a+12} \div \dfrac{a^3-7a^2+10a}{a^2+9a+18} \div \dfrac{a+6}{a+4} = \dfrac{a(a-5)}{(a+3)(a+4)} \cdot \dfrac{(a+6)(a+3)}{a(a-5)(a-2)} \cdot \dfrac{a+4}{a+6} = \dfrac{1}{a-2}$

69. $\dfrac{p^3-q^3}{p-q} \cdot \dfrac{p+q}{2p^2+2pq+2q^2} = \dfrac{(p-q)(p^2+pq+q^2)}{p-q} \cdot \dfrac{p+q}{2(p^2+pq+q^2)}$

$= \dfrac{p+q}{2}$

Section 7.3 Practice Exercises

1. The **least common denominator** (LCD) of two or more rational expressions is the least common multiple of the denominators.

3. x = 1, x = -1

$\dfrac{3x+3}{5x^2-5} = \dfrac{3(x+1)}{5(x+1)(x-1)} = \dfrac{3}{5(x-1)}$

5. $\dfrac{a+3}{a+7} \cdot \dfrac{a^2+3a-10}{a^2+a-6} = \dfrac{a+3}{a+7} \cdot \dfrac{(a+5)(a-2)}{(a+3)(a-2)}$

$= \dfrac{a+5}{a+7}$

7. $\dfrac{16y^2}{9y+36} \div \dfrac{8y^3}{3y+12} = \dfrac{16y^2}{9(y+4)} \cdot \dfrac{3(y+4)}{8y^3} = \dfrac{2}{3y}$

9. a, b, c, d

11. Because x^5 is the greatest power of x that appears in any denominator.

13. $3^2 \cdot 5 = 45$

15. $2^4 \cdot 3 = 48$

17. $7 \cdot 9 = 63$

19. $3^2 \cdot x^2 y^3 = 9x^2 y^3$

21. $w^2 y$

23. $(p + 3)(p - 1)(p + 2)$

25. $9t(t + 1)^2$

27. $(y - 2)(y + 2)(y + 3)$

29. $3 - x$ or $x - 3$

31. Because $(b - 1)$ and $(1 - b)$ are opposites; they differ by a factor of -1.

33. LCD: $5x^2$; $\dfrac{6}{5x^2}, \dfrac{5x}{5x^2}$

35. LCD: $5 \cdot 6x^3 = 30x^3$; $\dfrac{24x}{30x^3}, \dfrac{5y}{30x^3}$

37. LCD: $12a^2b$; $\dfrac{10}{12a^2b}, \dfrac{a^3}{12a^2b}$

39. LCD: $(m + 4)(m - 1)$;

$\dfrac{6(m-1)}{(m+4)(m-1)} = \dfrac{6m-6}{(m+4)(m-1)},$

$\dfrac{3}{m-1} = \dfrac{3(m+4)}{(m+4)(m-1)} = \dfrac{3m+12}{(m+4)(m-1)}$

41. LCD: $(2x - 5)(x + 3)$

$\dfrac{6(x+3)}{(2x-5)(x+3)} = \dfrac{6x+18}{(2x-5)(x+3)},$

$\dfrac{1(2x-5)}{(x+3)(2x-5)} = \dfrac{2x-5}{(2x-5)(x+3)}$

43. LCD: $(w + 3)(w - 8)(w - 1)$;

$\dfrac{6(w+1)}{(w+3)(w-8)(w-1)} = \dfrac{6w+6}{(w+3)(w-8)(w-1)},$

$\dfrac{w(w+3)}{(w+3)(w-8)(w-1)} = \dfrac{w^2+3w}{(w+3)(w-8)(w-1)}$

45. LCD:

$(p - 2)(p + 2)(p + 2) = (p - 2)(p + 2)^2$

$\dfrac{6p(p+2)}{(p-2)(p+2)^2} = \dfrac{6p^2+12p}{(p-2)(p+2)^2},$

$\dfrac{3(p-2)}{(p-2)(p+2)^2} = \dfrac{3p-6}{(p-2)(p+2)^2}$

47. LCD: $a - 4$ or $4 - a$;

$\dfrac{1}{a-4}, \dfrac{(-1)a}{(-1)(4-a)} = -\dfrac{a}{a-4}$ or

$\dfrac{(-1)(1)}{(-1)(a-4)} = -\dfrac{1}{4-a}, \dfrac{a}{4-a}$

49. LCD: $2(x - 7)$ or $2(7 - x)$;

$\dfrac{8}{2(x-7)}, \dfrac{-1(y)}{(2)(x-7)} = -\dfrac{y}{2(x-7)}$ or

$\dfrac{-1(8)}{2(7-x)} = -\dfrac{8}{2(7-x)}, \dfrac{y}{2(7-x)}$

51. LCD: $a + b$;

$\dfrac{1}{a+b}, \dfrac{6}{-1(a+b)} = -\dfrac{6}{a+b}$

53. $24y + 8 = 8(3y + 1)$
$18y + 6 = 6(3y + 1)$
LCD: $24(3y + 1)$

$\dfrac{-3}{24y+8} = \dfrac{-3(3)}{8(3y+1)(3)} = \dfrac{-9}{24(3y+1)},$

$\dfrac{5}{18y+6} = \dfrac{5(4)}{6(3y+1)(4)} = \dfrac{20}{24(3y+1)}$

55. LCD: $5z(z + 4)$

$\dfrac{3(z+4)}{5z(z+4)} = \dfrac{3z+12}{5z(z+4)}$

$\dfrac{1(5z)}{(z+4)(5z)} = \dfrac{5z}{5z(z+4)}$

57. LCD: $(z + 2)(z + 3)(z + 7)$;

$\dfrac{z(z+3)}{(z+2)(z+3)(z+7)} = \dfrac{z^2+3z}{(z+2)(z+3)(z+7)},$

$\dfrac{-3z(z+2)}{(z+2)(z+3)(z+7)} = \dfrac{-3z^2-6z}{(z+2)(z+3)(z+7)},$

$\dfrac{5(z+7)}{(z+2)(z+3)(z+7)} = \dfrac{5z+35}{(z+2)(z+3)(z+7)}$

59. LCD: $(p-2)(p+2)(p^2+2p+4)$;

$$\frac{\dfrac{3(p+2)}{(p^2-4)(p^2+2p+4)}}{}$$

$$=\frac{3p+6}{(p^2-4)(p^2+2p+4)},$$

$$\frac{p(p^2+2p+4)}{(p^2-4)(p^2+2p+4)}$$

$$=\frac{p^3+2p^2+4p}{(p^2-4)(p^2+2p+4)}$$

$$\frac{5p(p+2)(p-2)}{(p^2-4)(p^2+2p+4)}$$

$$=\frac{5p^3-20p}{(p^2-4)(p^2+2p+4)}$$

Section 7.4 Practice Exercises

1. (a) $x=0$; $\dfrac{-5}{10}=-\dfrac{1}{2}$

$x=1$; $\dfrac{1^2-4(1)-5}{1^2-7(1)+10}=-2$

$x=-1$; $\dfrac{(-1)^2-4(-1)-5}{(-1)^2-7(-1)+10}=\dfrac{0}{18}=0$

$x=2$;

$\dfrac{(2)^2-4(2)-5}{(2)^2-7(2)-10}=\dfrac{-9}{0}$ is undefined

$x=5$; $\dfrac{5^2-4(5)-5}{5^2-7(5)+10}=\dfrac{0}{0}$ is undefined

(b) $x=5$, $x=2$

(c) $\dfrac{(x-5)(x+1)}{(x-5)(x-2)}=\dfrac{x+1}{x-2}$

3. $\dfrac{2x^2-x-3}{2x^2-3x-9}\div\dfrac{x^2-1}{4x+6}$

$=\dfrac{(2x-3)\cancel{(x+1)}}{\cancel{(2x+3)}(x-3)}\cdot\dfrac{2\cancel{(2x+3)}}{\cancel{(x+1)}(x-1)}$

$=\dfrac{2(2x-3)}{(x-3)(x-1)}$

5. $\dfrac{7}{8}+\dfrac{3}{8}=\dfrac{10}{8}=\dfrac{5}{4}$

7. $\dfrac{9}{16}-\dfrac{3}{16}=\dfrac{6}{16}=\dfrac{3}{8}$

9. $\dfrac{5a}{a+2}-\dfrac{3a-4}{a+2}=\dfrac{5a-(3a-4)}{a+2}$

$=\dfrac{2a+4}{a+2}$

$=\dfrac{2(a+2)}{a+2}$

$=2$

11. $\dfrac{5c}{c+6}+\dfrac{30}{c+6}=\dfrac{5c+30}{c+6}=\dfrac{5(c+6)}{c+6}=5$

13. $\dfrac{5}{t-8}-\dfrac{2t+1}{t-8}=\dfrac{5-2t-1}{t-8}=\dfrac{4-2t}{t-8}=\dfrac{-2(t-2)}{t-8}$

15. $\dfrac{9x^2}{3x-7}-\dfrac{49}{3x-7}=\dfrac{9x^2-49}{3x-7}$

$=\dfrac{\cancel{(3x-7)}(3x+7)}{\cancel{3x-7}}$

$=3x+7$

17. $\dfrac{m^2}{m+5}+\dfrac{10m+25}{m+5}=\dfrac{m^2+10m+25}{m+5}$

$=\dfrac{(m+5)^2}{m+5}$

$=m+5$

19. $\dfrac{2a}{a+2}+\dfrac{4}{a+2}=\dfrac{2a+4}{a+2}=\dfrac{2(a+2)}{a+2}=2$

21. $\dfrac{x^2}{x+5} - \dfrac{25}{x+5} = \dfrac{x^2-25}{x+5}$

$\quad = \dfrac{(x+5)(x-5)}{x+5}$

$\quad = x-5$

23. $\dfrac{r}{r^2+3r+2} + \dfrac{2}{r^2+3r+2} = \dfrac{r+2}{r^2+3r+2}$

$\quad = \dfrac{\cancel{r+2}}{\cancel{(r+2)}(r+1)}$

$\quad = \dfrac{1}{r+1}$

25. $\dfrac{1}{3y^2+22y+7} - \dfrac{-3y}{3y^2+22y+7}$

$= \dfrac{1+3y}{3y^2+22y+7}$

$= \dfrac{\cancel{3y+1}}{\cancel{(3y+1)}(y+7)}$

$= \dfrac{1}{y+7}$

27. $P = \dfrac{2x}{y} + \dfrac{6x}{y} + \dfrac{7x}{y} = \dfrac{15x}{y}$

29. $\dfrac{5}{4} + \dfrac{3}{2a} = \dfrac{5a}{4a} + \dfrac{3(2)}{2a(2)} = \dfrac{5a+6}{4a}$

31. $\dfrac{4}{5xy^3} + \dfrac{2x}{15y^2} = \dfrac{4(3)}{5xy^3(3)} + \dfrac{2x(xy)}{15y^2(xy)}$

$\quad = \dfrac{12+2x^2y}{15xy^3}$

$\quad = \dfrac{2(6+x^2y)}{15xy^3}$

33. $\dfrac{2}{s^3t^3} - \dfrac{3}{s^4t} = \dfrac{2s}{s^3t^3 \cdot s} - \dfrac{3t^2}{s^4t \cdot t^2} = \dfrac{2s-3t^2}{s^4t^3}$

35. $\dfrac{z}{3z-9} - \dfrac{z-2}{z-3} = \dfrac{z}{3(z-3)} - \dfrac{3(z-2)}{3(z-3)}$

$= \dfrac{z-3z+6}{3(z-3)}$

$= \dfrac{-2z+6}{3(z-3)}$

$= \dfrac{-2(z-3)}{3(z-3)}$

$= -\dfrac{2}{3}$

37. $\dfrac{5}{a+1} + \dfrac{4}{3a+3} = \dfrac{5(3)}{3(a+1)} + \dfrac{4}{3(a+1)}$

$= \dfrac{15+4}{3(a+1)}$

$= \dfrac{19}{3(a+1)}$

39. $\dfrac{k}{k^2-9} - \dfrac{4}{k-3}$

$= \dfrac{k}{(k+3)(k-3)} - \dfrac{4(k+3)}{(k+3)(k-3)}$

$= \dfrac{k-4k-12}{(k+3)(k-3)}$

$= \dfrac{-3(k+4)}{(k+3)(k-3)}$

41. $\dfrac{3a-7}{6a+10} - \dfrac{10}{3a^2+5a}$

$= \dfrac{a(3a-7)}{2a(3a+5)} - \dfrac{10(2)}{2a(3a+5)}$

$= \dfrac{3a^2-7a-20}{2a(3a+5)}$

$= \dfrac{(3a+5)(a-4)}{2a(3a+5)}$

$= \dfrac{a-4}{2a}$

43. $\dfrac{x}{x-4}+\dfrac{3}{x+1}=\dfrac{x(x+1)}{(x-4)(x+1)}+\dfrac{3(x-4)}{(x+1)(x-4)}$

$=\dfrac{x^2+x+3x-12}{(x-4)(x+1)}$

$=\dfrac{x^2+4x-12}{(x-4)(x+1)}$

$=\dfrac{(x+6)(x-2)}{(x-4)(x+1)}$

45. $\dfrac{6a}{a^2-b^2}+\dfrac{2a}{a^2+ab}$

$=\dfrac{6a}{(a+b)(a-b)}+\dfrac{2a}{a(a+b)}$

$=\dfrac{6a^2}{a(a+b)(a-b)}+\dfrac{2a(a-b)}{a(a+b)(a-b)}$

$=\dfrac{6a^2+2a^2-2ab}{a(a+b)(a-b)}$

$=\dfrac{8a^2-2ab}{a(a+b)(a-b)}$

$=\dfrac{2a(4a-b)}{a(a+b)(a-b)}$

$=\dfrac{2(4a-b)}{(a+b)(a-b)}$

47. $\dfrac{p}{3}-\dfrac{4p-1}{-3}=\dfrac{p}{3}-\dfrac{-(4p-1)}{3}$

$=\dfrac{p+4p-1}{3}$

$=\dfrac{5p-1}{3}$ or $\dfrac{-5p+1}{-3}$

49. $\dfrac{4n}{n-8}-\dfrac{2n-1}{8-n}=\dfrac{4n}{n-8}-\dfrac{2n-1}{-1(n-8)}$

$=\dfrac{4n}{n-8}+\dfrac{2n-1}{n-8}$

$=\dfrac{4n+2n-1}{n-8}$

$=\dfrac{6n-1}{n-8}$ or $\dfrac{-6n+1}{8-n}$

51. $\dfrac{5}{x}+\dfrac{3}{x+2}=\dfrac{5(x+2)}{x(x+2)}+\dfrac{3x}{x(x+2)}$

$=\dfrac{5x+10+3x}{x(x+2)}$

$=\dfrac{8x+10}{x(x+2)}$

$=\dfrac{2(4x+5)}{x(x+2)}$

53. $\dfrac{5}{p-3}-\dfrac{2}{p-1}$

$=\dfrac{5(p-1)}{(p-3)(p-1)}-\dfrac{2(p-3)}{(p-3)(p-1)}$

$=\dfrac{5p-5-2p+6}{(p-3)(p-1)}$

$=\dfrac{3p+1}{(p-3)(p-1)}$

55. $\dfrac{y}{4y+2}+\dfrac{3y}{6y+3}$

$=\dfrac{y\cdot 3}{2(2y+1)(3)}+\dfrac{3y\cdot 2}{3(2y+1)(2)}$

$=\dfrac{3y+6y}{3\cdot 2(2y+1)}$

$=\dfrac{9y}{3\cdot 2(2y+1)}$

$=\dfrac{3y}{2(2y+1)}$

57. $\dfrac{4w}{w^2+2w-3}+\dfrac{2}{1-w}$

$=\dfrac{4w}{(w+3)(w-1)}+\dfrac{-2}{w-1}$

$=\dfrac{4w}{(w+3)(w-1)}-\dfrac{2(w+3)}{(w+3)(w-1)}$

$=\dfrac{4w-2w-6}{(w+3)(w-1)}$

$=\dfrac{2w-6}{(w+3)(w-1)}$

$=\dfrac{2(w-3)}{(w+3)(w-1)}$

59. $\dfrac{3a-8}{a^2-5a+6}+\dfrac{a+2}{a^2-6a+8}=\dfrac{3a-8}{(a-2)(a-3)}+\dfrac{a+2}{(a-2)(a-4)}$

$\qquad\qquad\qquad\qquad = \dfrac{(3a-8)(a-4)}{(a-2)(a-3)(a-4)}+\dfrac{(a+2)(a-3)}{(a-2)(a-3)(a-4)}$

$\qquad\qquad\qquad\qquad = \dfrac{3a^2-20a+32+a^2-a-6}{(a-2)(a-3)(a-4)}$

$\qquad\qquad\qquad\qquad = \dfrac{4a^2-21a+26}{(a-2)(a-3)(a-4)}$

$\qquad\qquad\qquad\qquad = \dfrac{(4a-13)(a-2)}{(a-2)(a-3)(a-4)}$

$\qquad\qquad\qquad\qquad = \dfrac{4a-13}{(a-3)(a-4)}$

61. $\dfrac{3x}{x^2+x-6}+\dfrac{x}{x^2+5x+6}=\dfrac{3x}{(x+3)(x-2)}+\dfrac{x}{(x+3)(x+2)}$

$\qquad\qquad\qquad\qquad = \dfrac{3x(x+2)}{(x+3)(x-2)(x+2)}+\dfrac{x(x-2)}{(x+3)(x-2)(x+2)}$

$\qquad\qquad\qquad\qquad = \dfrac{3x^2+6x+x^2-2x}{(x+3)(x-2)(x+2)}$

$\qquad\qquad\qquad\qquad = \dfrac{4x^2+4x}{(x+3)(x-2)(x+2)}$

$\qquad\qquad\qquad\qquad = \dfrac{4x(x+1)}{(x+3)(x-2)(x+2)}$

63. $\dfrac{3y}{2y^2-y-1}-\dfrac{4y}{2y^2-7y-4}=\dfrac{3y}{(2y+1)(y-1)}-\dfrac{4y}{(2y+1)(y-4)}$

$\qquad\qquad\qquad\qquad = \dfrac{3y(y-4)}{(2y+1)(y-1)(y-4)}-\dfrac{4y(y-1)}{(2y+1)(y-1)(y-4)}$

$\qquad\qquad\qquad\qquad = \dfrac{3y^2-12y-4y^2+4y}{(2y+1)(y-1)(y-4)}$

$\qquad\qquad\qquad\qquad = \dfrac{-y^2-8y}{(2y+1)(y-1)(y-4)}$

$\qquad\qquad\qquad\qquad = \dfrac{-y(y+8)}{(2y+1)(y-1)(y-4)}$

65. $\dfrac{3}{2p-1} - \dfrac{4p+4}{4p^2-1} = \dfrac{3}{2p-1} - \dfrac{4p+4}{(2p+1)(2p-1)}$

$\qquad = \dfrac{3(2p+1)}{(2p+1)(2p-1)} - \dfrac{4p+4}{(2p+1)(2p-1)}$

$\qquad = \dfrac{6p+3-4p-4}{(2p+1)(2p-1)}$

$\qquad = \dfrac{2p-1}{(2p+1)(2p-1)}$

$\qquad = \dfrac{1}{2p+1}$

67. $\dfrac{m}{m+n} - \dfrac{m}{m-n} + \dfrac{1}{m^2-n^2} = \dfrac{m(m-n)}{(m+n)(m-n)} - \dfrac{m(m+n)}{(m-n)(m+n)} + \dfrac{1}{(m+n)(m-n)}$

$\qquad = \dfrac{m^2-mn-m^2-mn+1}{(m+n)(m-n)}$

$\qquad = \dfrac{-2mn+1}{(m+n)(m-n)}$

69. $\dfrac{2}{a+b} + \dfrac{2}{a-b} - \dfrac{4a}{a^2-b^2} = \dfrac{2(a-b)}{(a+b)(a-b)} + \dfrac{2(a+b)}{(a+b)(a-b)} - \dfrac{4a}{(a+b)(a-b)}$

$\qquad = \dfrac{2a-2b+2a+2b-4a}{(a+b)(a-b)}$

$\qquad = 0$

71. $P = 2w + 2l$

$\qquad = 2\left(\dfrac{2}{x+3}\right) + 2\left(\dfrac{1}{x+2}\right)$

$\qquad = \dfrac{4}{x+3} + \dfrac{2}{x+2}$

$\qquad = \dfrac{4(x+2)}{(x+3)(x+2)} + \dfrac{2(x+3)}{(x+3)(x+2)}$

$\qquad = \dfrac{4x+8+2x+6}{(x+3)(x+2)}$

$\qquad = \dfrac{6x+14}{(x+3)(x+2)}$

$\qquad = \dfrac{2(3x+7)}{(x+3)(x+2)}$

73. $\dfrac{1}{n}$

75. Let n = number; $\dfrac{5}{n+2}$

77. Let n = the number, then $n + \left(7 \cdot \dfrac{1}{n}\right)$; $n + \dfrac{7}{n} = \dfrac{n^2}{n} + \dfrac{7}{n} = \dfrac{n^2+7}{n}$

79. $\dfrac{1}{n} - \dfrac{2}{n}$; $\dfrac{1}{n} - \dfrac{2}{n} = -\dfrac{1}{n}$

81. $\dfrac{-3}{w^3+27} - \dfrac{1}{w^2-9} = \dfrac{-3}{(w+3)(w^2-3w+9)} - \dfrac{1}{(w+3)(w-3)}$

$$= \dfrac{-3(w-3)}{(w-3)(w+3)(w^2-3w+9)} - \dfrac{w^2-3w+9}{(w-3)(w+3)(w^2-3w+9)}$$

$$= \dfrac{-3w+9-w^2+3w-9}{(w-3)(w+3)(w^2-3+9)}$$

$$= \dfrac{-w^2}{(w-3)(w+3)(w^2-3w+9)}$$

83. $\dfrac{2p}{p^2+5p+6} - \dfrac{p+1}{p^2+2p-3} + \dfrac{3}{p^2+p-2}$

$$= \dfrac{2p}{(p+2)(p+3)} - \dfrac{p+1}{(p-1)(p+3)} + \dfrac{3}{(p+2)(p-1)}$$

$$= \dfrac{2p(p-1)}{(p-1)(p+2)(p+3)} - \dfrac{(p+1)(p+2)}{(p-1)(p+2)(p+3)} + \dfrac{3(p+3)}{(p-1)(p+2)(p+3)}$$

$$= \dfrac{2p^2-2p-p^2-3p-2+3p+9}{(p-1)(p+2)(p+3)}$$

$$= \dfrac{p^2-2p+7}{(p-1)(p+2)(p+3)}$$

85. $\dfrac{3m}{m^2+3m-10} + \dfrac{5}{4-2m} - \dfrac{1}{m+5} = \dfrac{3m}{(m+5)(m-2)} + \dfrac{5}{-2(m-2)} - \dfrac{1}{m+5}$

$$= \dfrac{6m}{2(m+5)(m-2)} - \dfrac{5(m+5)}{2(m+5)(m-2)} - \dfrac{2(m-2)}{2(m+5)(m-2)}$$

$$= \dfrac{6m-5m-25-2m+4}{2(m+5)(m-2)}$$

$$= \dfrac{-m-21}{2(m+5)(m-2)} \text{ or } \dfrac{m+21}{2(m+5)(2-m)}$$

87. $\left(\dfrac{2}{k+1} + 3\right)\left(\dfrac{k+1}{4k+7}\right) = \left(\dfrac{2}{k+1} + \dfrac{3(k+1)}{k+1}\right)\left(\dfrac{k+1}{4k+7}\right) = \left(\dfrac{3k+5}{k+1}\right)\left(\dfrac{k+1}{4k+7}\right) = \dfrac{3k+5}{4k+7}$

89. $\left(\dfrac{1}{10a} - \dfrac{b}{10a^2}\right) \div \left(\dfrac{1}{10} - \dfrac{b}{10a}\right)$

$= \left(\dfrac{a}{10a^2} - \dfrac{b}{10a^2}\right) \div \left(\dfrac{a}{10a} - \dfrac{b}{10a}\right)$

$= \left(\dfrac{a-b}{10a^2}\right) \cdot \left(\dfrac{10a}{a-b}\right)$

$= \dfrac{1}{a}$

Problem Recognition Exercises

1. $\dfrac{5}{3x+1} - \dfrac{2x-4}{3x+1} = \dfrac{5-2x+4}{3x+1}$

$= \dfrac{-2x+9}{3x+1}$

3. $\dfrac{3}{y} \cdot \dfrac{y^2-5y}{6y-9} = \dfrac{\cancel{3}}{\cancel{y}} \cdot \dfrac{\cancel{y}(y-5)}{\cancel{3}(2y-3)}$

$= \dfrac{y-5}{2y-3}$

5. $\dfrac{x-9}{9x-x^2} = \dfrac{x-9}{x(9-x)}$

$= \dfrac{\cancel{x-9}}{-x(\cancel{x-9})}$

$= \dfrac{-1}{x}$

7. $\dfrac{c^2+5c+6}{c^2+c-2} \div \dfrac{c}{c-1} = \dfrac{c^2+5c+6}{c^2+c-2} \cdot \dfrac{c-1}{c}$

$= \dfrac{(c+2)(c+3)}{(c-1)(c+2)} \cdot \dfrac{c-1}{c}$

$= \dfrac{c+3}{c}$

9. $\dfrac{6a^2b^3}{72ab^7c} = \dfrac{6aab^3}{6\cdot12ab^3b^4c} = \dfrac{a}{12b^4c}$

11. $\dfrac{p^2+10pq+25q^2}{p^2+6pq+5q^2} \div \dfrac{10p+50q}{2p^2-2q^2}$

$= \dfrac{(p+5q)(p+5q)}{(p+5q)(p+q)} \cdot \dfrac{2(p+q)(p-q)}{10(p+5q)}$

$= \dfrac{p-q}{5}$

13. $\dfrac{20x^2+10x}{4x^3+4x^2+x} = \dfrac{10x(2x+1)}{x(2x+1)(2x+1)} = \dfrac{10}{2x+1}$

15. $\dfrac{8x^2-18x-5}{4x^2-25} \div \dfrac{4x^2-11x-3}{3x-9}$

$= \dfrac{8x^2-18x-5}{4x^2-25} \cdot \dfrac{3x-9}{4x^2-11x-3}$

$= \dfrac{(4x+1)(2x-5)}{(2x-5)(2x+5)} \cdot \dfrac{3(x-3)}{(4x+1)(x-3)}$

$= \dfrac{3}{2x+5}$

17. $\dfrac{a}{a^2-9} - \dfrac{3}{6a-18}$

$= \dfrac{a}{(a+3)(a-3)} - \dfrac{3}{6(a-3)}$

$= \dfrac{2a}{2(a+3)(a-3)} - \dfrac{(a+3)}{2(a+3)(a-3)}$

$= \dfrac{2a-a-3}{2(a+3)(a-3)}$

$= \dfrac{a-3}{2(a+3)(a-3)}$

$= \dfrac{1}{2(a+3)}$

19. $(t^2+5t-24)\left(\dfrac{t+8}{t-3}\right) = \dfrac{(t+8)(t-3)}{1}\left(\dfrac{t+8}{t-3}\right)$

$= (t+8)^2$

Section 7.5 Practice Exercises

1. A **complex fraction** is a fraction whose numerator or denominator contains one or more rational expressions.

3. $\dfrac{a+5}{2a^2+7a-15}=\dfrac{a+5}{(2a-3)(a+5)}=\dfrac{1}{2a-3}$

5. $\dfrac{6}{5}-\dfrac{3}{5k-10}=\dfrac{6(k-2)}{5(k-2)}-\dfrac{3}{5(k-2)}$

$\qquad =\dfrac{6k-15}{5(k-2)}$

$\qquad =\dfrac{3(2k-5)}{5(k-2)}$

7. $\dfrac{\frac{7}{18y}}{\frac{2}{9}}=\dfrac{(18y)\,\frac{7}{18y}}{(18y)\,\frac{2}{9}}=\dfrac{7}{4y}$

9. $\dfrac{\frac{3x+2y}{2y}}{\frac{6x+4y}{2}}=\dfrac{\cancel{3x+2y}}{2y}\cdot\dfrac{2}{2\,\cancel{(3x+2y)}}=\dfrac{1}{2y}$

11. $\dfrac{\frac{8a^4b^3}{3c}}{\frac{a^7b^2}{9c}}=\dfrac{8a^4b^3}{3c}\cdot\dfrac{9c}{a^7b^2}=\dfrac{24b}{a^3}$

13. $\dfrac{\frac{4r^3s}{t^5}}{\frac{2s^7}{r^2t^9}}=\dfrac{4r^3s}{t^5}\cdot\dfrac{r^2t^9}{2s^7}=\dfrac{2r^5t^4}{s^6}$

15. $\dfrac{\frac{1}{8}+\frac{4}{3}}{\frac{1}{2}-\frac{5}{12}}=\dfrac{\frac{3}{24}+\frac{32}{24}}{\frac{6}{12}-\frac{5}{12}}=\dfrac{\frac{35}{24}}{\frac{1}{12}}=\dfrac{35}{24}\cdot\dfrac{12}{1}=\dfrac{35}{2}$

17. $\dfrac{\frac{1}{h}+\frac{1}{k}}{\frac{1}{hk}}=\dfrac{\frac{k}{hk}+\frac{h}{hk}}{\frac{1}{hk}}=\dfrac{\frac{k+h}{hk}}{\frac{1}{hk}}=\dfrac{k+h}{hk}\cdot\dfrac{hk}{1}=k+h$

19. $\dfrac{\frac{n+1}{n^2-9}}{\frac{2}{n+3}}=\dfrac{n+1}{(n+3)(n-3)}\cdot\dfrac{n+3}{2}=\dfrac{n+1}{2(n-3)}$

21. $\dfrac{2+\frac{1}{x}}{4+\frac{1}{x}}=\dfrac{\frac{2x}{x}+\frac{1}{x}}{\frac{4x}{x}+\frac{1}{x}}$

$\qquad =\dfrac{\frac{2x+1}{x}}{\frac{4x+1}{x}}$

$\qquad =\dfrac{2x+1}{x}\cdot\dfrac{x}{4x+1}$

$\qquad =\dfrac{2x+1}{4x+1}$

23. $\dfrac{\frac{m}{7}-\frac{7}{m}}{\frac{1}{7}+\frac{1}{m}}=\dfrac{(7m)\,\frac{m}{7}-\frac{7}{m}}{(7m)\,\frac{1}{7}+\frac{1}{m}}$

$\qquad =\dfrac{m^2-49}{m+7}$

$\qquad =\dfrac{(m+7)(m-7)}{m+7}$

$\qquad =m-7$

25. $\dfrac{\frac{1}{5}-\frac{1}{y}}{\frac{7}{10}+\frac{1}{y^2}}=\dfrac{10y^2\,\frac{1}{5}-\frac{1}{y}}{10y^2\left(\frac{7}{10}+\frac{1}{y^2}\right)}$

$\qquad =\dfrac{2y^2-10y}{7y^2+10}$

$\qquad =\dfrac{2y(y-5)}{7y^2+10}$

27. $\dfrac{\frac{8}{a+4}+2}{\frac{12}{a+4}-2}=\dfrac{(a+4)\,\frac{8}{a+4}+2}{(a+4)\,\frac{12}{a+4}-2}$

$\qquad =\dfrac{8+2a+8}{12-2a-8}$

$\qquad =\dfrac{2a+16}{4-2a}$

$\qquad =\dfrac{2(a+8)}{2(2-a)}$

$\qquad =\dfrac{a+8}{2-a}$ or $-\dfrac{a+8}{a-2}$

29.
$$\frac{1-\frac{4}{t^2}}{1-\frac{2}{t}-\frac{8}{t^2}} = \frac{t^2\left(1-\frac{4}{t^2}\right)}{t^2\left(1-\frac{2}{t}-\frac{8}{t^2}\right)}$$
$$= \frac{t^2-4}{t^2-2t-8}$$
$$= \frac{(t+2)(t-2)}{(t-4)(t+2)}$$
$$= \frac{t-2}{t-4}$$

31.
$$\frac{t+4+\frac{3}{t}}{t-4-\frac{5}{t}} = \frac{\frac{t^2+4t+3}{t}}{\frac{t^2-4t-5}{t}}$$
$$= \frac{t^2+4t+3}{t^2-4t-5}$$
$$= \frac{(t+1)(t+3)}{(t-5)(t+1)}$$
$$= \frac{t+3}{t-5}$$

33.
$$\frac{\frac{1}{k-6}-1}{\frac{2}{k-6}-2} = \frac{\frac{1}{k-6}-1}{2\left(\frac{1}{k-6}-1\right)}$$
$$= \frac{1}{2}$$

35. $\dfrac{\frac{1}{2}+\frac{2}{3}}{5}$; $\dfrac{\frac{1}{2}+\frac{2}{3}}{5} = \dfrac{\frac{3}{6}+\frac{4}{6}}{5} = \dfrac{\frac{7}{6}}{5} = \dfrac{7}{6}\cdot\dfrac{1}{5} = \dfrac{7}{30}$

37. $\dfrac{3}{\frac{2}{3}+\frac{3}{4}}$; $\dfrac{3}{\frac{8}{12}+\frac{9}{12}} = \dfrac{3}{\frac{17}{12}} = 3\cdot\dfrac{12}{17} = \dfrac{36}{17}$

39. (a) $R = \dfrac{1}{\frac{1}{2}+\frac{1}{3}} = \dfrac{1}{\frac{5}{6}} = \dfrac{6}{5}\ \Omega$

(b) $R = \dfrac{1}{\frac{1}{10}+\frac{1}{15}} = \dfrac{1}{\frac{5}{30}} = \dfrac{30}{5} = 6\ \Omega$

41.
$$\frac{2x^{-1}+8y^{-1}}{4x^{-1}} = \frac{\frac{2}{x}+\frac{8}{y}}{\frac{4}{x}}$$
$$= \frac{\frac{2y+8x}{xy}}{\frac{4}{x}}$$
$$= \frac{2y+8x}{xy}\cdot\frac{x}{4}$$
$$= \frac{y+4x}{2y}$$

43.
$$\frac{(mn)^{-2}}{m^{-2}+n^{-2}} = \frac{\frac{1}{m^2n^2}}{\frac{1}{m^2}+\frac{1}{n^2}}$$
$$= \frac{\frac{1}{m^2n^2}}{\frac{n^2+m^2}{m^2n^2}}$$
$$= \frac{1}{m^2n^2}\cdot\frac{m^2n^2}{n^2+m^2}$$
$$= \frac{1}{n^2+m^2}$$

45.
$$\frac{\frac{1}{z^2-9}+\frac{2}{z+3}}{\frac{3}{z-3}} = \frac{(z+3)(z-3)\left[\frac{1}{(z+3)(z-3)}+\frac{2}{z+3}\right]}{(z+3)(z-3)\frac{3}{z-3}}$$
$$= \frac{1+2z-6}{3z+9}$$
$$= \frac{2z-5}{3(z+3)}$$

47.
$$\frac{\frac{2}{x-1}+2}{\frac{2}{x+1}-2} = \frac{(x-1)(x+1)\left[\frac{2}{x-1}+2\right]}{(x-1)(x+1)\left[\frac{2}{x+1}-2\right]}$$
$$= \frac{2(x+1)+2(x+1)(x-1)}{2(x-1)-2(x+1)(x-1)}$$
$$= \frac{2x^2+2x}{2x-2x^2}$$
$$= \frac{2x(x+1)}{2x(1-x)}$$
$$= \frac{x+1}{1-x}\ \text{or}\ -\frac{x+1}{x-1}$$

49. $1+\dfrac{1}{1+1} = 1+\dfrac{1}{2} = \dfrac{3}{2}$

Section 7.6 Practice Exercises

1. (a) A **linear equation** is an equation of the form $ax + b = 0$, $a \neq 0$.

(b) A **quadratic equation** is an equation of the form $ax^2 + bx + c = 0$, $a \neq 0$.

(c) A **rational equation** is an equation with one or more rational expressions.

3.
$$\frac{2x-6}{4x^2+9x-2} \div \frac{x^2-5x+6}{x^2-4}$$
$$= \frac{2(x-3)}{(4x-1)(x+2)} \cdot \frac{(x+2)(x-2)}{(x-2)(x-3)}$$
$$= \frac{2}{4x-1}$$

5.
$$\frac{h-\frac{1}{h}}{\frac{1}{5}-\frac{1}{5h}} = \frac{5h \; h-\frac{1}{h}}{5h \; \frac{1}{5}-\frac{1}{5h}}$$
$$= \frac{5h^2-5}{h-1}$$
$$= \frac{5(h+1)(h-1)}{(h-1)}$$
$$= 5(h+1)$$

7.
$$1+\frac{1}{x}-\frac{12}{x^2} = \frac{x^2+x+12}{x^2}$$
$$= \frac{(x+4)(x-3)}{x^2}$$

9.
$$\frac{5}{2}+\frac{1}{2}b = 5-\frac{1}{3}b$$
$$6\left(\frac{5}{2}+\frac{1}{2}b\right) = 6\left(5-\frac{1}{3}b\right)$$
$$15+3b = 30-2b$$
$$5b = 15$$
$$b = 3$$

11.
$$\frac{5}{3}-\frac{1}{6}k = \frac{3k+5}{4}$$
$$12\left(\frac{5}{3}-\frac{1}{6}k\right) = 12\left(\frac{3k+5}{4}\right)$$
$$20-2k = 9k+15$$
$$-11k = -5$$
$$k = \frac{5}{11}$$

13.
$$\frac{4y+2}{3}-\frac{7}{6} = -\frac{y}{6}$$
$$6\left(\frac{4y+2}{3}-\frac{7}{6}\right) = 6\left(-\frac{y}{6}\right)$$
$$8y+4-7 = -y$$
$$9y = 3$$
$$y = \frac{1}{3}$$

15. (a) $z = 0$

(b) LCD: $5z$

(c)
$$\frac{3}{z}-\frac{4}{5} = -\frac{1}{5}$$
$$5z\left(\frac{3}{z}-\frac{4}{5}\right) = 5z\left(-\frac{1}{5}\right)$$
$$15-4z = -z$$
$$3z = 15$$
$$z = 5$$

17.
$$\frac{1}{8} = \frac{3}{5}+\frac{5}{y}$$
$$40y\left(\frac{1}{8}\right) = 40y\left(\frac{3}{5}+\frac{5}{y}\right)$$
$$5y = 24y+200$$
$$-19y = 200$$
$$y = -\frac{200}{19}$$

19.
$$\frac{4}{t} = \frac{3}{t}+\frac{1}{8}$$
$$8t\left(\frac{4}{t}\right) = 8t\left(\frac{3}{t}+\frac{1}{8}\right)$$
$$32 = 24+t$$
$$t = 8$$

21. $\dfrac{5}{6x} + \dfrac{7}{x} = 1$

$6x\left(\dfrac{5}{6x} + \dfrac{7}{x}\right) = 6x(1)$

$5 + 42 = 6x$

$6x = 47$

$x = \dfrac{47}{6}$

23. $1 - \dfrac{2}{y} = \dfrac{3}{y^2}$

$y^2\left(1 - \dfrac{2}{y}\right) = y^2\left(\dfrac{3}{y^2}\right)$

$y^2 - 2y = 3$

$y^2 - 2y - 3 = 0$

$(y - 3)(y + 1) = 0$

$y - 3 = 0 \quad \text{or} \quad y + 1 = 0$

$y = 3 \qquad\qquad y = -1$

25. $\dfrac{a+1}{a} = 1 + \dfrac{a-2}{2a}$

$2a\left(\dfrac{a+1}{a}\right) = 2a\left(1 + \dfrac{a-2}{2a}\right)$

$2a + 2 = 2a + a - 2$

$-a = -4$

$a = 4$

27. $\dfrac{w}{5} - \dfrac{w+3}{w} = -\dfrac{3}{w}$

$5w\left(\dfrac{w}{5} - \dfrac{w+3}{w}\right) = 5w\left(-\dfrac{3}{w}\right)$

$w^2 - 5w - 15 = -15$

$w^2 - 5w = 0$

$w(w - 5) = 0$

$w = 0 \text{ or } w = 5$

$w = 0$ is extraneous, $w = 5$ is the solution.

29. $\dfrac{2}{m+3} = \dfrac{5}{4m+12} - \dfrac{3}{8}$

$\dfrac{2}{m+3} = \dfrac{5}{4(m+3)} - \dfrac{3}{8}$

$8(m+3) \cdot \dfrac{2}{m+3} = 8(m+3)\left(\dfrac{5}{4(m+3)} - \dfrac{3}{8}\right)$

$16 = 8(m+3)\left(\dfrac{5}{4(m+3)}\right) - 8(m+3) \cdot \dfrac{3}{8}$

$16 = 10 - 3m - 9$

$15 = -3m$

$m = -5$

31. $\dfrac{p}{p-4} - 5 = \dfrac{4}{p-4}$

$(p-4)\left(\dfrac{p}{p-4} - 5\right) = (p-4) \cdot \dfrac{4}{p-4}$

$(p-4) \cdot \dfrac{p}{p-4} - 5(p-4) = 4$

$p - 5p + 20 = 4$

$-4p = -16$

$p = 4$

No solution; $p = 4$ is extraneous.

33. $\dfrac{2t}{t+2} - 2 = \dfrac{t-8}{t+2}$

$(t+2)\left(\dfrac{2t}{t+2} - 2\right) = (t+2) \cdot \dfrac{t-8}{t+2}$

$(t+2)\dfrac{2t}{t+2} - 2(t+2) = t - 8$

$2t - 2t - 4 = t - 8$

$-4 = t - 8$

$t = 4$

35. $\dfrac{x^2 - x}{x-2} = \dfrac{12}{x-2}$

$(x-2) \cdot \dfrac{x^2 - x}{x-2} = (x-2) \cdot \dfrac{12}{x-2}$

$x^2 - x = 12$

$x^2 - x - 12 = 0$

$(x-4)(x+3) = 0$

$x = 4 \text{ or } x = -3$

37.
$$\frac{x^2 + 3x}{x - 1} = \frac{4}{x - 1}$$
$$(x - 1) \cdot \frac{x^2 + 3x}{x - 1} = (x - 1) \cdot \frac{4}{x - 1}$$
$$x^2 + 3x = 4$$
$$x^2 + 3x - 4 = 0$$
$$(x + 4)(x - 1) = 0$$
$$x + 4 = 0 \text{ or } x - 1 = 0$$
$$x = -4 \text{ is the solution } (x = 1 \text{ is extraneous}).$$

39.
$$\frac{2x}{x + 4} - \frac{8}{x - 4} = \frac{2x^2 + 32}{x^2 - 16}$$
$$\frac{2x}{x + 4} - \frac{8}{x - 4} = \frac{2x^2 + 32}{(x + 4)(x - 4)}$$
Multiply both sides by LCD: $(x + 4)(x - 4)$
$$2x(x - 4) - 8(x + 4) = 2x^2 + 32$$
$$2x^2 - 8x - 8x - 32 = 2x^2 + 32$$
$$-16x = 64$$
$$x = -4$$
No solution ($x = -4$ is extraneous).

41.
$$\frac{x}{x + 6} = \frac{72}{x^2 - 36} + 4$$
$$\frac{x}{x + 6} = \frac{72}{(x + 6)(x - 6)} + 4$$
Multiply both sides by LCD: $(x + 6)(x - 6)$
$$x(x - 6) = 72 + 4(x + 6)(x - 6)$$
$$x^2 - 6x = 72 + 4x^2 - 144$$
$$-3x^2 - 6x + 72 = 0$$
$$-3(x^2 + 2x - 24) = 0$$
$$(x + 6)(x - 4) = 0$$
$$x + 6 = 0 \text{ or } x - 4 = 0$$
$$x = 4 \text{ is the solution } (x = -6 \text{ is extraneous})..$$

43.
$$\frac{5}{3x - 3} - \frac{2}{x - 2} = \frac{7}{x^2 - 3x + 2}$$
$$\frac{5}{3(x - 1)} - \frac{2}{x - 2} = \frac{7}{(x - 2)(x - 1)}$$
Multiply both sides by LCD: $3(x - 1)(x - 2)$
$$5(x - 2) - 2(3)(x - 1) = 7(3)$$
$$5x - 10 - 6x + 6 = 21$$
$$-x - 4 = 21$$
$$-x = 25$$
$$x = -25$$

45.
$$\frac{y - 2}{y - 3} = \frac{11}{y^2 - 7y + 12} + \frac{y}{y - 4}$$
$$\frac{y - 2}{y - 3} = \frac{11}{(y - 3)(y - 4)} + \frac{y}{y - 4}$$
Multiply both sides by LCD: $(y - 3)(y - 4)$
$$(y - 2)(y - 4) = 11 + y(y - 3)$$
$$y^2 - 6y + 8 = 11 + y^2 - 3y$$
$$-3y = 3$$
$$y = -1$$

47. Let x = a number. Then,
$$3 + \frac{1}{x} = \frac{25}{x}$$
$$x\left(3 + \frac{1}{x}\right) = x \cdot \frac{25}{x}$$
$$3x + 1 = 25$$
$$3x = 24$$
$$x = 8$$
The number is 8.

49. Let x = a number. Then,
$$\frac{x + 5}{x - 2} = \frac{3}{4}$$
$$4(x - 2) \cdot \frac{x + 5}{x - 2} = 4(x - 2) \cdot \frac{3}{4}$$
$$4x + 20 = 3x - 6$$
$$x = -26$$
The number is -26.

51.
$$K = \frac{ma}{F}$$
$$FK = ma$$
$$m = \frac{FK}{a}$$

53. $K = \dfrac{IR}{E}$

$EK = IR$

$E = \dfrac{IR}{K}$

55. $I = \dfrac{E}{R+r}$

$I(R+r) = E$

$IR + Ir = E$

$IR = E - Ir$

$R = \dfrac{E-Ir}{I}$ or $R = \dfrac{E}{I} - r$

57. $h = \dfrac{2A}{B+b}$

$h(B+b) = 2A$

$Bh + bh = 2A$

$Bh = 2A - bh$

$B = \dfrac{2A-bh}{h}$ or $B = \dfrac{2A}{h} - b$

59. $\dfrac{V}{\pi h} = r^2$

$V = r^2 \pi h$

$h = \dfrac{V}{r^2 \pi}$

61. $x = \dfrac{at+b}{t}$

$xt = at + b$

$xt - at = b$

$(x-a)t = b$

$t = \dfrac{b}{x-a}$ or $t = \dfrac{-b}{a-x}$

63. $\dfrac{x-y}{xy} = z$

$x - y = xyz$

$x - xyz = y$

$x(1-yz) = y$

$x = \dfrac{y}{1-yz}$ or $x = \dfrac{-y}{yz-1}$

65. $a + b = \dfrac{2A}{h}$

$h(a+b) = 2A$

$h = \dfrac{2A}{a+b}$

67. $\dfrac{1}{R} = \dfrac{1}{R_1} + \dfrac{1}{R_2}$

$RR_1R_2 \cdot \dfrac{1}{R} = RR_1R_2 \left(\dfrac{1}{R_1} + \dfrac{1}{R_2} \right)$

$R_1R_2 = RR_2 + RR_1$

$R_1R_2 = R(R_2 + R_1)$

$R = \dfrac{R_1R_2}{R_1 + R_2}$

Problem Recognition Exercises

1. $\dfrac{y}{2y+4} - \dfrac{2}{y^2+2y} = \dfrac{y}{2(y+2)} - \dfrac{2}{y(y+2)}$

$= \dfrac{y^2-4}{2y(y+2)}$

$= \dfrac{(y-2)(y+2)}{2y(y+2)}$

$= \dfrac{y-2}{2y}$

3.

$\dfrac{5t}{2} - \dfrac{t-2}{3} = 5$

$\dfrac{5t \cdot 3}{2 \cdot 3} - \dfrac{2(t-2)}{2 \cdot 3} = 5$

$\dfrac{15t - 2t + 4}{2 \cdot 3} = 5$

$\dfrac{13t+4}{6} = 5$

$13t + 4 = 5 \cdot 6 = 30$

$13t = 26$

$t = 2$

5. $\dfrac{7}{6p^2} + \dfrac{2}{9p} + \dfrac{1}{3p^2}$

$= \dfrac{3 \cdot 7}{3 \cdot 6p^2} + \dfrac{2 \cdot 2p}{2 \cdot 9p^2} + \dfrac{6}{3 \cdot 6p^2}$

$= \dfrac{21 + 4p + 6}{18p^2}$

$= \dfrac{27 + 4p}{18p^2}$

7. $4 + \dfrac{2}{h-3} = 5$

$\dfrac{2}{h-3} = 1$

$h - 3 = 2$

$h = 5$

9.

$\dfrac{1}{x-6} - \dfrac{3}{x^2 - 6x} = \dfrac{4}{x}$

$\dfrac{1}{x-6} - \dfrac{3}{x(x-6)} = \dfrac{4}{x}$

$\dfrac{x}{x(x-6)} - \dfrac{3}{x(x-6)} = \dfrac{4(x-6)}{x(x-6)}$

$\dfrac{x-3}{x(x-6)} = \dfrac{4x-24}{x(x-6)}$

$\dfrac{21}{x(x-6)} = \dfrac{3x}{x(x-6)}$

$x = 7$

11. $\dfrac{7}{2x+2} + \dfrac{3x}{4x+4} = \dfrac{7}{2(x+1)} + \dfrac{3x}{4(x+1)}$

$= \dfrac{7 \cdot 2 + 3x}{4(x+1)}$

$= \dfrac{14 + 3x}{4(x+1)}$

13. $\dfrac{3}{5x} + \dfrac{7}{2x} = 1$

$\dfrac{6}{10x} + \dfrac{35}{10x} = 1$

$\dfrac{41}{10x} = 1$

$41 = 10x$

$\dfrac{41}{10} = x$

15. $\dfrac{5}{2a-1} + 4 = \dfrac{5}{2a-1} + \dfrac{4(2a-1)}{2a-1}$

$= \dfrac{5 + 8a - 4}{2a-1} = \dfrac{8a-1}{2a-1}$

17.

$\dfrac{3}{u} + \dfrac{12}{u^2 - 3u} = \dfrac{u+1}{u-3}$

$\dfrac{3}{u} + \dfrac{12}{u(u-3)} = \dfrac{u+1}{u-3}$

$\dfrac{3(u-3)}{u(u-3)} + \dfrac{12}{u(u-3)} = \dfrac{u}{u} \dfrac{u+1}{u-3}$

$3u - 9 + 12 = u^2 + u$

$3u + 3 = u^2 + u$

$0 = u^2 + u - 3u - 3$

$0 = u^2 - 2u - 3$

$0 = (u-3)(u+1)$

$u - 3 = 0 \quad \text{or} \quad u + 1 = 0$

$u = 3 \qquad\qquad u = -1$

The solution is -1, The value of 3 does not check.

19. $\dfrac{-2h}{h^2-9}+\dfrac{3}{h-3}=\dfrac{-2h}{h-3 \;\; h+3}+\dfrac{3}{h-3}$

$=\dfrac{-2h}{h-3 \;\; h+3}+\dfrac{3 \;\; h+3}{h-3 \;\; h+3}$

$=\dfrac{-2h+3h+9}{h-3 \;\; h+3}=\dfrac{h+9}{h-3 \;\; h+3}$

Section 7.7 Practice Exercises

1. (a) A **proportion** is an equation that equates two ratios or rates.

   (b) Two triangles are said to be **similar triangles** if their angles have equal measure.

3. Expression;

$\dfrac{m}{m-1}-\dfrac{2}{m+3}$

$=\dfrac{m(m+3)}{(m-1)(m+3)}-\dfrac{2(m-1)}{(m-1)(m+3)}$

$=\dfrac{m^2+3m-2m+2}{(m-1)(m+3)}$

$=\dfrac{m^2+m+2}{(m-1)(m+3)}$

5. Expression;

$\dfrac{3y+6}{20}\div\dfrac{4y+8}{8}=\dfrac{3(y+2)}{20}\cdot\dfrac{8}{4(y+2)}=\dfrac{3}{10}$

7. Equation; $\dfrac{3}{p+3}=\dfrac{12p+19}{p^2+7p+12}-\dfrac{5}{p+4}$

$\dfrac{3}{p+3}=\dfrac{12p+19}{(p+3)(p+4)}-\dfrac{5}{p+4}$

Multiply both sides by the LCD $(p+3)(p+4)$

$3(p+4)=12p+19-5(p+3)$

$3p+12=12p+19-5p-15$

$3p+12=7p+4$

$-4p=-8$

$p=2$

9. $\dfrac{8}{5}=\dfrac{152}{p}$

$5p\left(\dfrac{8}{5}\right)=5p\left(\dfrac{152}{p}\right)$

$8p=760$

$p=95$

11. $\dfrac{19}{76}=\dfrac{z}{4}$

$76\left(\dfrac{19}{76}\right)=76\left(\dfrac{z}{4}\right)$

$19=19z$

$1=z$

13. $\dfrac{5}{3}=\dfrac{a}{8}$

$24\cdot\dfrac{5}{3}=24\cdot\dfrac{a}{8}$

$40=3a$

$a=\dfrac{40}{3}$

15. $\dfrac{2}{1.9}=\dfrac{x}{38}$

$1.9x=76$

$x=\dfrac{76}{1.9}=40$

17. $\dfrac{y+1}{2y}=\dfrac{2}{3}$

$6y\left(\dfrac{y+1}{2y}\right)=6y\left(\dfrac{2}{3}\right)$

$3(y+1)=4y$

$3y+3=4y$

$3=y$

19. $\dfrac{9}{2z-1}=\dfrac{3}{z}$

$z(2z-1)\left(\dfrac{9}{2z-1}\right)=z(2z-1)\left(\dfrac{3}{z}\right)$

$9z=3(2z-1)$

$9z=6z-3$

$3z=-3$

$z=-1$

21. $\dfrac{8}{9a-1} = \dfrac{5}{3a+2}$

$8(3a+2) = 5(9a-1)$

$24a+16 = 45a-5$

$-21a = -21$

$a = 1$

23. (a) $\dfrac{V_i}{V_f} = \dfrac{T_i}{T_f}$

$V_iT_f = T_iV_f$

$V_f = \dfrac{V_iT_f}{T_i}$

(b) $\dfrac{V_i}{V_f} = \dfrac{T_i}{T_f}$

$V_iT_f = T_iV_f$

$T_f = \dfrac{T_iV_f}{V_i}$

25. Let x represent the number of miles Toni can drive on 9 gallons of gas.

$\dfrac{132 \text{ mi}}{4 \text{ gal}} = \dfrac{x \text{ mi}}{9 \text{ gal}}$

$132(9) = 4x$

$1188 = 4x$

$297 = x$

Toni can drive 297 mi on 9 gallons of gas.

27. Let x represent the number of pounds of garbage produced by 48 people in one week.

$\dfrac{4 \text{ people}}{128 \text{ lb}} = \dfrac{48 \text{ people}}{x \text{ lb}}$

$4x = 128(48)$

$4x = 6144$

$x = 1536$

48 people would produce 1536 lb.

29. Let x represent the carbohydrate.

$\dfrac{8 \text{ oz}}{19.2 \text{ g}} = \dfrac{5 \text{ oz}}{x \text{ g}}$

$x = \dfrac{5(19.2)}{8} = 12$

The 5 oz pineapple contains 12 g carbohydrate.

31. Let x = length required. Then,

$\dfrac{1}{12} = \dfrac{1\frac{2}{3}}{x}$

$1x = (12)(1\frac{2}{3})$

$x = 20$

The minimum length of the ramp is 20 ft.

33. $\dfrac{15}{3} = \dfrac{20}{x}$ $\qquad$ $\dfrac{15}{3} = \dfrac{25}{y}$

$15x = 60$ $\qquad\qquad$ $15y = 75$

$x = 4 \text{ cm}$ $\qquad\quad$ $y = 5 \text{ cm}$

35. $\dfrac{x}{15} = \dfrac{3}{12}$ $\qquad$ $\dfrac{y}{18} = \dfrac{3}{12}$

$12x = 45$ $\qquad\qquad$ $12y = 54$

$x = 3.75 \text{ cm}$ $\qquad$ $y = 4.5 \text{ cm}$

37. $\dfrac{x}{16.8} = \dfrac{1}{2.4}$

$2.4x = 16.8$

$x = 7$

The height of the pole is 7 m.

39. Let x = the height of the post. Then,

$\dfrac{x}{54+18} = \dfrac{6}{18}$

$\dfrac{x}{72} = \dfrac{6}{18}$

$18x = 432$

$x = 24$

The post is 24 ft. high.

43. Let x = speed of plane.

	Distance	Rate	Time
With the wind	700	$35 + x$	$\frac{700}{35+x}$
Against the wind	500	x-35	$\frac{500}{x-35}$

$$\frac{700}{35+x} = \frac{500}{x-35}$$
$$700(x-35) = 500(35+x)$$
$$7(x-35) = 5(35+x)$$
$$7x - 245 = 175 + 5x$$
$$2x = 420$$
$$x = 210$$
The plane speed is 210 mph

45. Let x = running speed. 2x=biking speed

	Distance	Speed	Time
Biking	20	$2x$	$\frac{20}{2x}$
Running	10	x	$\frac{10}{x}$

$$\frac{20}{2x} + \frac{10}{x} = 2.5$$
$$\frac{10}{x} + \frac{10}{x} = 2.5$$
$$\frac{20}{x} = 2.5$$
$$x = \frac{20}{2.5}$$
$$x = 8, \ 2x = 16$$
He runs at 8 mph and bikes at 16 mph.

47. Let x = Floyd's speed. x-2 = Rachel's speed

	Distance	Speed	Time
Floyd	12	x	$\frac{12}{x}$
Rachel	12	x-2	$\frac{12}{x-2}$

$$\frac{12}{x} + 3 = \frac{12}{x-2}$$
$$\frac{12}{x} + \frac{3x}{x} = \frac{12}{x-2}$$
$$\frac{12 + 3x}{x} = \frac{12}{x-2}$$
$$(12 + 3x)(x-2) = 12x$$
$$12x - 24 + 3x^2 - 6x = 12x$$
$$3x^2 - 6x - 24 = 0$$
$$(3x - 12)(x + 2) = 0$$
$$x = 4 \text{ or } \cancel{x = -2}$$
$$x - 2 = 2$$
Floyd's speed is 4 mph and Rachelle's speed is 2 mph

49. Let x represent the riding rate. Then $x - 9$ represents the walking rate.

	Distance	Rate	Time
Bike ride	4	x	$\frac{4}{x}$
Walk	4	$x - 9$	$\frac{4}{x-9}$

$$\left(\begin{array}{c}\text{Time to}\\\text{ride bike}\end{array}\right) + (1 \text{ hour}) = \left(\begin{array}{c}\text{Time to}\\\text{Walk}\end{array}\right)$$
$$\frac{4}{x} + 1 = \frac{4}{x-9}$$
$$x(x-9)\left(\frac{4}{x} + 1\right) = x(x-9)\left(\frac{4}{x-9}\right)$$
$$4(x-9) + x(x-9) = 4x$$
$$4x - 36 + x^2 - 9x = 4x$$
$$x^2 - 9x - 36 = 0$$
$$(x-12)(x+3) = 0$$
$$x = 12 \text{ or } \cancel{x = -3}$$
Sergio rode 12 mph and walked 3 mph.

51. In one minute, the cold water can fill $\dfrac{1}{10}$ of the sink; the hot water can fill $\dfrac{1}{12}$ of the sink. If $x =$ how long it would take both faucets to fill the sink together, then both faucets can fill $\dfrac{1}{x}$ of the sink.

$$\frac{1}{10} + \frac{1}{12} = \frac{1}{x}$$

$$60x\left(\frac{1}{10} + \frac{1}{12}\right) = 60x\left(\frac{1}{x}\right)$$

$$60x\left(\frac{1}{10}\right) + 60x\left(\frac{1}{12}\right) = 60x\left(\frac{1}{x}\right)$$

$$6x + 5x = 60$$

$$11x = 60$$

$$x = \frac{60}{11} = 5\frac{5}{11}$$

Both faucets can fill the sink in $5\dfrac{5}{11}$ or $5.\overline{45}$ minutes.

53. In one minute, one printer can do $\dfrac{1}{50}$ of the job; the other printer can do $\dfrac{1}{40}$ of the job. If $x =$ how long it takes both printers to do the job together, then $\dfrac{1}{x}$ of the job can be completed in 1 minute.

$$\frac{1}{50} + \frac{1}{40} = \frac{1}{x}$$

$$200x\left(\frac{1}{50} + \frac{1}{40}\right) = 200x\left(\frac{1}{x}\right)$$

$$4x + 5x = 200$$

$$9x = 200$$

$$x = \frac{200}{9} = 22\frac{2}{9}$$

Together they can do the job in $22\dfrac{2}{9}$ or $22.\overline{2}$ minutes.

55. Let $x =$ how long it takes both pipes to fill the reservoir. In one hour, the first pipe can fill $\dfrac{1}{16}$ of the reservoir; the second pipe can empty $\dfrac{1}{24}$ of the reservoir. Together in 1 hour they can fill $\dfrac{1}{x}$ of the reservoir.

$$\frac{1}{16} - \frac{1}{24} = \frac{1}{x}$$

$$\frac{3}{16 \cdot 3} - \frac{2}{24 \cdot 2} = \frac{1}{x}$$

$$\frac{3 - 2}{48} = \frac{1}{x}$$

$$\frac{1}{48} = \frac{1}{x}$$

$$x = 48$$

The reservoir would be filled in 48 hours.

57. Let $x =$ how long it will take Al. Then, in 1 day, Al can complete $\dfrac{1}{x}$, Tim can complete $\dfrac{1}{5}$, and together they can complete $\dfrac{1}{2}$ of the job.

$$\frac{1}{x} + \frac{1}{5} = \frac{1}{2}$$

$$10x\left(\frac{1}{x} + \frac{1}{5}\right) = 10x\left(\frac{1}{2}\right)$$

$$10 + 2x = 5x$$

$$3x = 10$$

$$x = \frac{10}{3} = 3\frac{1}{3}$$

It would take Al $3\dfrac{1}{3}$ or $3.\overline{3}$ days.

59. Let x represent the number of smokers. Then $x + 100$ represents the number of nonsmokers.

$$\frac{2}{7} = \frac{x}{x+100}$$
$$7x = 2(x+100)$$
$$7x = 2x + 200$$
$$5x = 200$$
$$x = 40$$

There are 40 smokers and 140 nonsmokers.

61. Let x represent the number of men. Then $440 - x$ represents the number of women.

$$\frac{6}{5} = \frac{x}{440-x}$$
$$6(440-x) = 5x$$
$$2640 - 6x = 5x$$
$$2640 = 11x$$
$$240 = x$$

There are 240 men and 200 women.

Section 7.8 Practice Exercises

1. (a) A **direct variation** shows one quantity directly proportional to another, as in $y = kx$.

(b) An **inverse variation** shows one quantity inversely proportional to another, as in $y = \dfrac{k}{x}$.

(c) A **joint variation** shows one quantity jointly proportional to at least two other quantities, as in $y = kwz$.

3.
$$\frac{2y}{3} - \frac{3y-1}{5} = 1$$
$$15\left(\frac{2y}{3} - \frac{3y-1}{5}\right) = 15(1)$$
$$5(2y) - 3(3y-1) = 15$$
$$10y - 9y + 3 = 15$$
$$y + 3 = 15$$
$$y = 12$$

5.
$$\frac{a}{4} + \frac{3}{a} = 2$$
$$4a\left(\frac{a}{4} + \frac{3}{a}\right) = 4a(2)$$
$$a^2 + 12 = 8a$$
$$a^2 - 8a + 12 = 0$$
$$(a-6)(a-2) = 0$$
$$a-6 = 0 \quad \text{or} \quad a-2 = 0$$
$$a = 6 \qquad\qquad a = 2$$

7.
$$\frac{a + \dfrac{a}{b}}{\dfrac{a}{b} - a} = \frac{\dfrac{ab}{b} + \dfrac{a}{b}}{\dfrac{a}{b} - \dfrac{ab}{b}}$$
$$= \frac{\dfrac{ab+a}{b}}{\dfrac{a-ab}{b}}$$
$$= \frac{ab+a}{b} \cdot \frac{b}{a-ab}$$
$$= \frac{ab+a}{a-ab}$$
$$= \frac{a(b+1)}{a(1-b)} = \frac{b+1}{1-b}$$

9. Inversely

11. $T = kq$

13. $b = \dfrac{k}{c}$

15. $Q = \dfrac{kx}{y}$

17. $c = kst$

19. $L = kw\sqrt{v}$

21. $x = \dfrac{ky^2}{z}$

23. $y = kx$

$18 = k(4)$

$\dfrac{18}{4} = k$

$\dfrac{9}{2} = k$

25. $p = \dfrac{k}{q}$

$32 = \dfrac{k}{16}$

$512 = k$

27. $y = kwv$

$8.75 = k(50)(0.1)$

$8.75 = k(5)$

$\dfrac{8.75}{5} = k$

$1.75 = k$

29. $x = kp$

$50 = k(10)$

$\dfrac{50}{10} = k$

$5 = k$

$x = 5p = 5(14)$

$\quad = 70$

31. $b = \dfrac{k}{c}$

$4 = \dfrac{k}{3}$

$12 = k$

$b = \dfrac{12}{c} = \dfrac{12}{2}$

$\quad = 6$

33. $Z = kw^2$

$14 = k(4)^2$

$14 = k(16)$

$\dfrac{14}{16} = k$

$\dfrac{7}{8} = k$

$Z = \dfrac{7}{8}(8)^2$

$Z = \dfrac{7}{8}(64)$

$Z = 56$

35. $Q = \dfrac{k}{p^2}$

$4 = \dfrac{k}{3^2}$

$4 = \dfrac{k}{9}$

$36 = k$

$Q = \dfrac{36}{2^2}$

$Q = \dfrac{36}{4}$

$Q = 9$

37. $L = ka\sqrt{b}$

$72 = k(8)\sqrt{9}$

$72 = k8(3)$

$72 = k(24)$

$3 = k$

$L = 3\left(\dfrac{1}{2}\right)\sqrt{36}$

$L = 3\left(\dfrac{1}{2}\right)(6)$

$L = 9$

39.
$$B = k \cdot \frac{m}{n}$$
$$20 = k \cdot \frac{10}{3}$$
$$\frac{3}{10} \cdot 20 = k$$
$$6 = k$$
$$B = (6) \cdot \frac{15}{12}$$
$$B = \frac{15}{2}$$

41.
$$h = k \cdot w$$
$$0.75 = k \cdot (150)$$
$$\frac{0.75}{150} = k$$
$$\frac{1}{200} = k$$
$$h = \frac{1}{200} w$$

a. $h = \dfrac{1}{200}(184)$
$$h = .92$$

b. Answers will vary

43.
$$m = k \cdot w$$
$$3 = k \cdot (150)$$
$$\frac{3}{150} = k$$
$$\frac{1}{50} = k$$
$$m = \frac{1}{50} w$$

a. $m = \dfrac{1}{50} w = \dfrac{1}{50}(180)$
$$= 3.6 \text{ g}$$

b. $m = \dfrac{1}{50} w = \dfrac{1}{50}(225)$
$$= 4.5 \text{ g}$$

c. $m = \dfrac{1}{50} w = \dfrac{1}{50}(120)$
$$= 2.4 \text{ g}$$

45.
$$c = \frac{k}{n}$$
$$0.48 = \frac{k}{5000}$$
$$0.48 \cdot 5000 = k$$
$$2400 = k$$
$$c = \frac{2400}{n}$$

a. $c = \dfrac{2400}{n} = \dfrac{2400}{6000}$
$$= 0.4$$
$$= \$0.40$$

b. $c = \dfrac{2400}{n} = \dfrac{2400}{8000}$
$$= 0.3$$
$$= \$0.30$$

c. $c = \dfrac{2400}{n} = \dfrac{2400}{2400}$
$$= 1.00$$
$$= \$1.00$$

47.
$$A = k \cdot n$$
$$56,800 = k \cdot (80,000)$$
$$\frac{56,800}{80,000} = k$$
$$\frac{71}{100} = k$$

$$A = \frac{71}{100} \cdot (500,000)$$
$$A = 355,000 \text{ tons}$$

49.
$$d = ks^2$$
$$109 = k(40)^2$$
$$109 = k(1600)$$
$$\frac{109}{1600} = k$$
$$d = \frac{109}{1600}(25)^2$$
$$d = \frac{109}{1600}(625)$$
$$d = 42.6 \text{ feet}$$

51. $P = kcr^2$

$144 = k(4)(6)^2$

$144 = k(4)(36)$

$144 = k(144)$

$1 = k$

$P = (3)(10)^2$

$P = (3)(100)$

$P = 300$ watts

53. $C = k \cdot \dfrac{v}{r}$

$9 = k \cdot \dfrac{90}{10}$

$\dfrac{10}{90} \cdot 9 = k$

$1 = k$

$C = (1) \cdot \dfrac{185}{10}$

$C = 18.5$ amps

55. $W = kr^3$

$4.32 = k(3)^3$

$4.32 = k(27)$

$\dfrac{4.32}{27} = k$

$0.16 = k$

$W = 0.16(5)^3$

$W = 0.16(125)$

$W = 20$ pounds

57. $i = kpt$

$500 = k(2500)(4)$

$500 = k10000$

$\dfrac{500}{10000} = k$

$0.05 = k$

$i = 0.05pt$

$i = 0.05(7000)(10)$

$= 3500 = \$3500$

Group Activity

1. Amount down payment $= \$200{,}000 \times 20\% = \$40{,}000$

3. $p = \dfrac{\dfrac{Ar}{12}}{1 - \dfrac{1}{\left(1 + \dfrac{r}{12}\right)^{12t}}}$

$p = \dfrac{\dfrac{(160000)(0.075)}{12}}{1 - \dfrac{1}{\left(1 + \dfrac{0.075}{12}\right)^{12 \cdot 30}}}) = \dfrac{1000}{1 - \dfrac{1}{9.421}}$

$= \dfrac{1000}{1 - 0.10614} = \dfrac{1000}{0.89386}$

$p = 1118.74$

$= \$1118.74$

5. $\$402{,}746.40 - \$160{,}000 = \$242{,}746.40$

Chapter 7 Review Exercises

1. (a) $\dfrac{0-2}{0+9} = -\dfrac{2}{9}; \dfrac{1-2}{1+9} = -\dfrac{1}{10}; \dfrac{2-2}{2+9} = 0;$

$\dfrac{-3-2}{-3+9} = -\dfrac{5}{6}; \dfrac{-9-2}{-9+9} = \dfrac{-11}{0}$ is undefined

(b) $x = -9$

3. (a) $\dfrac{2-1}{1-2} = -1$

(b) $\dfrac{-1-5}{-1+5} = \dfrac{-6}{4} = -\dfrac{3}{2}$

(c) $\dfrac{-x-7}{x+7} = \dfrac{-(-1)-7}{-1+7} = -1$

(d) $\dfrac{(-1)^2 - 4}{4 - (-1)^2} = -1$

a, c, d are the expressions equal to -1.

5. $h = -\dfrac{1}{3}, h = -7$

$$\dfrac{h+7}{(3h+1)(h+7)} = \dfrac{1}{3h+1}$$

7. $w = 4, w = -4$

$$\dfrac{2w^2+11w+12}{w^2-16} = \dfrac{(2w+3)(w+4)}{(w+4)(w-4)} = \dfrac{2w+3}{w-4}$$

9. $k = 0, k = 5$

$$\dfrac{15-3k}{2k^2-10k} = \dfrac{-3(k-5)}{2k(k-5)} = -\dfrac{3}{2k}$$

11. $m = -1$

$$\dfrac{3m^2-12m-15}{9m+9} = \dfrac{3(m+1)(m-5)}{9(m+1)} = \dfrac{m-5}{3}$$

13. $p = -7$

$$\dfrac{p+7}{p^2+14p+49} = \dfrac{p+7}{(p+7)^2} = \dfrac{1}{p+7}$$

15. $\dfrac{2u+10}{u} \cdot \dfrac{u^3}{4u+20} = \dfrac{2(u+5)}{u} \cdot \dfrac{u^3}{4(u+5)} = \dfrac{u^2}{2}$

17. $\dfrac{8}{x^2-25} \cdot \dfrac{3x+15}{16} = \dfrac{8}{(x+5)(x-5)} \cdot \dfrac{3(x+5)}{16}$

$$= \dfrac{3}{2(x-5)}$$

19. $\dfrac{q^2-5q+6}{2q+4} \div \dfrac{2q-6}{q+2}$

$$= \dfrac{(q-3)(q-2)}{2(q+2)} \cdot \dfrac{q+2}{2(q-3)}$$

$$= \dfrac{q-2}{4}$$

21. $(s^2-6s+8)\left(\dfrac{4s}{s-2}\right) = \dfrac{(s-4)(s-2)}{1} \cdot \dfrac{4s}{s-2}$

$$= 4s(s-4)$$

23. $\dfrac{\frac{n^2+n+1}{n^2-4}}{\frac{n^2+n+1}{n+2}} = \dfrac{n^2+n+1}{(n+2)(n-2)} \cdot \dfrac{n+2}{n^2+n+1} = \dfrac{1}{n-2}$

25. $\dfrac{3m-3}{6m^2+18m+12} \cdot \dfrac{2m^2-8}{m^2-3m+2} \div \dfrac{m+3}{m+1}$

$$= \dfrac{3(m-1)}{6(m+2)(m+1)} \cdot \dfrac{2(m+2)(m-2)}{(m-2)(m-1)} \cdot \dfrac{m+1}{m+3}$$

$$= \dfrac{1}{m+3}$$

27. $\dfrac{4y^2-1}{1+2y} \div \dfrac{y^2-4y-5}{5-y}$

$$= \dfrac{(2y+1)(2y-1)}{2y+1} \cdot \dfrac{-1(y-5)}{(y-5)(y+1)}$$

$$= -\dfrac{2y-1}{y+1}$$

29. $\dfrac{7}{4x}; \dfrac{11}{6y}$

$\text{LCD} = 12xy;$

$$\dfrac{7}{4x} = \dfrac{7(3y)}{4x(3y)} = \dfrac{21y}{12xy}$$

$$\dfrac{11}{6y} = \dfrac{11(2x)}{6y(2x)} = \dfrac{22x}{12xy}$$

31. $\dfrac{5}{ab^3}; \dfrac{3}{ac^2}$

$\text{LCD} = ab^3c^2;$

$$\dfrac{5}{ab^3} = \dfrac{5(c^2)}{ab^3(c^2)} = \dfrac{5c^2}{ab^3c^2}$$

$$\dfrac{3}{ac^2} = \dfrac{3(b^3)}{ac^2(b^3)} = \dfrac{3b^3}{ab^3c^2}$$

33. $\dfrac{6}{q}; \dfrac{1}{q+8}$

$\text{LCD} = q(q+8)$

$$\dfrac{6}{q} = \dfrac{6(q+8)}{q(q+8)} = \dfrac{6q+48}{q(q+8)}$$

$$\dfrac{1}{q+8} = \dfrac{1(q)}{q(q+8)} = \dfrac{q}{q(q+8)}$$

35. $\text{LCD}: (m-4)(m+4)(m+3)$

37. $\text{LCD}: 3-x \text{ or } x-3$

39. $\dfrac{b-6}{b-2}+\dfrac{b+2}{b-2}=\dfrac{b-6+b+2}{b-2}$

$\qquad\qquad\qquad=\dfrac{2b-4}{b-2}$

$\qquad\qquad\qquad=\dfrac{2(b-2)}{b-2}$

$\qquad\qquad\qquad=2$

41. $\dfrac{x^2}{x+7}-\dfrac{49}{x+7}=\dfrac{x^2-49}{x+7}$

$\qquad\qquad\qquad=\dfrac{(x+7)(x-7)}{x+7}$

$\qquad\qquad\qquad=x-7$

43. $\dfrac{3}{4-t^2}+\dfrac{t}{2-t}=\dfrac{3}{(2+t)(2-t)}+\dfrac{t(2+t)}{(2+t)(2-t)}$

$\qquad\qquad\qquad=\dfrac{3+2t+t^2}{(2+t)(2-t)}$

$\qquad\qquad\qquad=\dfrac{t^2+2t+3}{(2+t)(2-t)}$

45. $\dfrac{5}{2r+12}-\dfrac{1}{r}=\dfrac{5}{2(r+6)}-\dfrac{1}{r}$

$\qquad\qquad\qquad=\dfrac{5r}{2r(r+6)}-\dfrac{2(r+6)}{2r(r+6)}$

$\qquad\qquad\qquad=\dfrac{5r-2r-12}{2r(r+6)}$

$\qquad\qquad\qquad=\dfrac{3r-12}{2r(r+6)}$

$\qquad\qquad\qquad=\dfrac{3(r-4)}{2r(r+6)}$

47. $\dfrac{3q}{q^2+7q+10}-\dfrac{2q}{q^2+6q+8}$

$\qquad=\dfrac{3q}{(q+5)(q+2)}-\dfrac{2q}{(q+4)(q+2)}$

$\qquad=\dfrac{3q(q+4)}{(q+5)(q+4)(q+2)}-\dfrac{2q(q+5)}{(q+5)(q+4)(q+2)}$

$\qquad=\dfrac{3q^2+12q-2q^2-10q}{(q+5)(q+4)(q+2)}$

$\qquad=\dfrac{q^2+2q}{(q+5)(q+4)(q+2)}$

$\qquad=\dfrac{q(q+2)}{(q+5)(q+4)(q+2)}$

$\qquad=\dfrac{q}{(q+5)(q+4)}$

49. $\dfrac{x}{3x+9}-\dfrac{3}{x^2+3x}+\dfrac{1}{x}$

$\qquad=\dfrac{x}{3(x+3)}-\dfrac{3}{x(x+3)}+\dfrac{1}{x}$

$\qquad=\dfrac{x^2}{3x(x+3)}-\dfrac{9}{3x(x+3)}+\dfrac{3(x+3)}{3x(x+3)}$

$\qquad=\dfrac{x^2-9+3x+9}{3x(x+3)}$

$\qquad=\dfrac{x^2+3x}{3x(x+3)}$

$\qquad=\dfrac{x(x+3)}{3x(x+3)}$

$\qquad=\dfrac{1}{3}$

51. $\dfrac{\frac{z+5}{z}}{\frac{z-5}{3}}=\dfrac{z+5}{z}\cdot\dfrac{3}{z-5}=\dfrac{3(z+5)}{z(z-5)}$

53.
$$\frac{\frac{2}{y}+6}{\frac{3y+1}{4}} = \frac{4y\,\frac{2}{y}+6}{4y\,\frac{3y+1}{4}}$$
$$= \frac{8+24y}{3y^2+y}$$
$$= \frac{8(1+3y)}{y(3y+1)}$$
$$= \frac{8}{y}$$

55.
$$\frac{\frac{b}{a}-\frac{a}{b}}{\frac{1}{b}-\frac{1}{a}} = \frac{ab\,\frac{b}{a}-\frac{a}{b}}{ab\,\frac{1}{b}-\frac{1}{a}}$$
$$= \frac{b^2-a^2}{a-b}$$
$$= \frac{(b+a)(b-a)}{-(b-a)}$$
$$= -(b+a)$$

57.
$$\frac{\frac{25}{k+5}+5}{\frac{5}{k+5}-5} = \frac{(k+5)\,\frac{25}{k+5}+5}{(k+5)\,\frac{5}{k+5}-5}$$
$$= \frac{25+5(k+5)}{5-5(k+5)}$$
$$= \frac{5k+50}{-5k-20}$$
$$= \frac{5(k+10)}{-5(k+4)}$$
$$= -\frac{k+10}{k+4}$$

59.
$$\frac{1}{y}+\frac{3}{4}=\frac{1}{4}$$
$$4y\left(\frac{1}{y}+\frac{3}{4}\right)=4y\cdot\frac{1}{4}$$
$$4+3y=y$$
$$4=-2y$$
$$-2=y$$

61.
$$\frac{w}{w-1}=\frac{3}{w+1}+1$$
Multiply both sides by LCD: $(w+1)(w-1)$
$$w(w+1)=3(w-1)+(w+1)(w-1)$$
$$w^2+w=3w-3+w^2-1$$
$$w=3w-4$$
$$-2w=-4$$
$$w=2$$

63.
$$\frac{w+1}{w-3}-\frac{3}{w}=\frac{12}{w^2-3w}$$
$$\frac{w+1}{w-3}-\frac{3}{w}=\frac{12}{w(w-3)}$$
Multiply both sides by LCD: $w(w-3)$
$$w(w+1)-3(w-3)=12$$
$$w^2+w-3w+9=12$$
$$w^2-2w-3=0$$
$$(w-3)(w+1)=0$$

$$w-3=0 \quad \text{or} \quad w+1=0$$
$$w=3 \quad \text{or} \quad w=-1$$

$$w=-1 \text{ (The value 3 does not check)}$$

65.
$$\frac{y+1}{y+3}=\frac{y^2-11y}{y^2+y-6}-\frac{y-3}{y-2}$$
$$\frac{y+1}{y+3}=\frac{y^2-11y}{(y+3)(y-2)}-\frac{y-3}{y-2}$$
Multiply both sides by LCD: $(y+3)(y-2)$
$$(y-2)(y+1)=y^2-11y-(y+3)(y-3)$$
$$y^2-y-2=y^2-11y-y^2+9$$
$$y^2-y-2=-11y+9$$
$$y^2+10y-11=0$$
$$(y-1)(y+11)=0$$
$$y-1=0 \quad \text{or} \quad y+11=0$$
$$y=1 \quad \text{or} \quad y=-11$$

67.
$$\frac{V}{h} = \frac{\pi r^2}{3}$$
$$3h\left(\frac{V}{h}\right) = 3h\left(\frac{\pi r^2}{3}\right)$$
$$3V = h\pi r^2$$
$$h = \frac{3V}{\pi r^2}$$

69.
$$\frac{m+2}{8} = \frac{m}{3}$$
$$3(m+2) = 8m$$
$$3m+6 = 8m$$
$$6 = 5m$$
$$m = \frac{6}{5}$$

71. Let x represent the number of grams of fat in a 5-oz bag.
$$\frac{4 \text{ g}}{2 \text{ oz}} = \frac{x \text{ g}}{5 \text{ oz}}$$
$$4(5) = 2x$$
$$20 = 2x$$
$$10 = x$$
There are 10 g of fat.

73. Let x = time to fill pool if both pumps are working together. Then in 1 minute the first pump can fill $\frac{1}{24}$ of the pool, the second pump can fill $\frac{1}{56}$ of the pool, and together they can fill $\frac{1}{x}$ of the pool.
$$\frac{1}{24} + \frac{1}{56} = \frac{1}{x}$$
$$168x\left(\frac{1}{24} + \frac{1}{56}\right) = 168x\left(\frac{1}{x}\right)$$
$$7x + 3x = 168$$
$$10x = 168$$
$$x = 16.8$$
Together both pumps can fill the pool in 16.8 minutes.

75. (a) $F = kd$

(b) $6 = k \cdot 2$
$3 = k$

(c)
$$F = 3d$$
$$F = 3(4.2)$$
$$F = 12.6$$
The force required to stretch 4.2 ft is 12.6 lb.

77. $y = kx\sqrt{z}$
$$3 = k \cdot 3\sqrt{4}$$
$$3 = k \cdot 3(2)$$
$$\frac{1}{2} = k$$

The variation model is: $y = \frac{1}{2}x\sqrt{z}$

$$y = \frac{1}{2}(8)\sqrt{9} = \frac{1}{2}(8)(3) = 12$$

Chapter 7 Test

1. (a) x= 2

(b) $\dfrac{5(x-2)(x+1)}{30(2-x)} = \dfrac{5(x-2)(x+1)}{-30(x-2)} = -\dfrac{x+1}{6}$

3. (a) $\dfrac{-1+4}{-1-4} = \dfrac{3}{-5} = -\dfrac{3}{5}$

(b) $\dfrac{7-2(-1)}{2(-1)-7} = \dfrac{9}{-9} = -1$

(c) $\dfrac{9(-1)^2+16}{-9(-1)^2-16} = \dfrac{25}{-25} = -1$

(d) $-\dfrac{-1+5}{-1+5} = -\dfrac{4}{4} = -1$

b, c and d are the expressions equal to -1.

5. $\dfrac{2}{y^2+4y+3}+\dfrac{1}{3y+9}$

$=\dfrac{2}{(y+3)(y+1)}+\dfrac{1}{3(y+3)}$

$=\dfrac{6}{3(y+3)(y+1)}+\dfrac{y+1}{3(y+3)(y+1)}$

$=\dfrac{6+y+1}{3(y+3)(y+1)}$

$=\dfrac{y+7}{3(y+3)(y+1)}$

7. $\dfrac{w^2-4w}{w^2-8w+16}\cdot\dfrac{w-4}{w^2+w}$

$=\dfrac{w(w-4)}{(w-4)(w-4)}\cdot\dfrac{w-4}{w(w+1)}$

$=\dfrac{1}{w+1}$

9. $\dfrac{1}{x+4}+\dfrac{2}{x^2+2x-8}+\dfrac{x}{x-2}$

$=\dfrac{1(x-2)}{(x+4)(x-2)}+\dfrac{2}{(x+4)(x-2)}+\dfrac{x(x+4)}{(x+4)(x-2)}$

$=\dfrac{x-2+2+x^2+4x}{(x+4)(x-2)}$

$=\dfrac{x^2+5x}{(x+4)(x-2)}$

$=\dfrac{x(x+5)}{(x+4)(x-2)}$

11. $\dfrac{3}{a}+\dfrac{5}{2}=\dfrac{7}{a}$

$2a\left(\dfrac{3}{a}+\dfrac{5}{2}\right)=2a\cdot\dfrac{7}{a}$

$2(3)+a(5)=2(7)$

$6+5a=14$

$5a=8$

$a=\dfrac{8}{5}$

13. $\dfrac{3}{c-2}-\dfrac{1}{c+1}=\dfrac{7}{c^2-c-2}$

$\dfrac{3}{c-2}-\dfrac{1}{c+1}=\dfrac{7}{(c-2)(c+1)}$

Multiply both sides by LCD: $(c-2)(c+1)$

$3(c+1)-(c-2)=7$

$3c+3-c+2=7$

$2c+5=7$

$2c=2$

$c=1$

15.

$\dfrac{y^2+7y}{y-2}-\dfrac{36}{2y-4}=4$

$\dfrac{y\ \ y+7}{y-2}-\dfrac{36}{2(y-2)}=4$

$2y(y-7)-36=4(2)(y-2)$

$2y^2+14y-36=8(y-2)$

$2y^2+14y-36=8y-16$

$2y^2+6y-20=0$

$2(y^2+3y-10)=0$

$2(y+5)(y-2)=0$

$2\neq0 \quad y+5=0 \quad y-2=0$

$\qquad\quad y=-5 \qquad y=2$

(The solution is -5, the value 2 does not check)

17. $\dfrac{y+7}{-4}=\dfrac{1}{4}$

$4(y+7)=-4(1)$

$4y+28=-4$

$4y=-32$

$y=-8$

19. Let x = speed of current. Then the speed downstream is $x + 23$ and the speed upstream is $23 - x$. If time $= \dfrac{\text{distance}}{\text{rate}}$ then,

$$\dfrac{\dfrac{\text{distance}}{\text{downstream}}}{\text{speed}} = \dfrac{\dfrac{\text{distance}}{\text{upstream}}}{\text{speed}}$$

$$\dfrac{28}{x+23} = \dfrac{18}{23-x}$$
$$28(23-x) = 18(x+23)$$
$$644 - 28x = 18x + 414$$
$$-46x = -230$$
$$x = 5$$

The speed of the current is 5 mph.

21.
$$\dfrac{a}{7} = \dfrac{9.6}{12} \qquad\qquad \dfrac{b}{15} = \dfrac{9.6}{12}$$
$$12a = 67.2 \qquad\qquad 12b = 144$$
$$a = 5.6 \qquad\qquad b = 12$$

23.
$$n = \dfrac{k}{p}$$
$$400 = \dfrac{k}{1.25}$$
$$400 \cdot 1.25 = k$$
$$500 = k$$
$$n = \dfrac{500}{p}$$
$$n = \dfrac{500}{(2.50)}$$
$$= 200 \text{ drinks sold}$$

Cumulative Review Exercises
Chapters 1–7

1. $\left(\dfrac{1}{2}\right)^{-4} + 2^4 = 2^4 + 2^4 = 16 + 16 = 32$

3.
$$\dfrac{1}{2} - \dfrac{3}{4}(y-1) = \dfrac{5}{12}$$
$$12\left(\dfrac{1}{2} - \dfrac{3}{4}(y-1)\right) = 12 \cdot \dfrac{5}{12}$$
$$6 - 9(y-1) = 5$$
$$6 - 9y + 9 = 5$$
$$-9y = -10$$
$$y = \dfrac{10}{9}$$

5. Let x = width of the pool. Then, $(2x + 1)$ is the length.
$$P = 2w + 2l$$
$$104 = 2x + 2(2x+1)$$
$$104 = 2x + 4x + 2$$
$$102 = 6x$$
$$x = 17$$
The width is 17 m and the length is 35 m.

7.
$$\left(\dfrac{4x^{-1}y^{-2}}{z^4}\right)^{-2}(2y^{-1}z^3)^3$$
$$= \left(\dfrac{z^4}{4x^{-1}y^{-2}}\right)^2\left(\dfrac{2z^3}{y}\right)^3$$
$$= \left(\dfrac{z^8}{16x^{-2}y^{-4}}\right)\left(\dfrac{8z^9}{y^3}\right)$$
$$= \left(\dfrac{z^8x^2y^4}{16}\right)\left(\dfrac{8z^9}{y^3}\right)$$
$$= \dfrac{x^2yz^{17}}{2}$$

9. $25x^2 - 30x + 9 = (5x-3)(5x-3) = (5x-3)^2$

11. $x - 5, x = -\dfrac{1}{2}$

13.
$$\dfrac{2x-6}{x^2-16} \div \dfrac{10x^2-90}{x^2-x-12}$$
$$= \dfrac{2(x-3)}{(x+4)(x-4)} \cdot \dfrac{(x+3)(x-4)}{10(x+3)(x-3)}$$
$$= \dfrac{1}{5(x+4)}$$

15.
$$\frac{7}{y^2-4} = \frac{3}{y-2} + \frac{2}{y+2}$$

$$\frac{7}{(y-2)(y+2)} = \frac{3(y+2)}{(y-2)(y+2)} + \frac{2(y-2)}{(y-2)(y+2)}$$

$$\frac{7}{(y-2)(y+2)} = \frac{3y+6}{(y-2)(y+2)} + \frac{2y-4}{(y-2)(y+2)}$$

$$7 = 3y+6+2y-4$$
$$5 = 5y$$
$$1 = y$$

17. (a) $-2x+4y=8$

x-intercept: $-2x+4(0)=8$
$$-2x=8$$
$$x=-4$$
$$(-4, 0)$$

y-intercept: $-2(0)+4y=8$
$$4y=8$$
$$y=2$$
$$(0, 2)$$

(b) $y=5x$

x-intercept: $0=5x$
$$0=x$$
$$(0, 0)$$

y-intercept: $y=5(0)$
$$y=0$$
$$(0, 0)$$

19. $y-y_1 = m(x-x_1)$
$$y-2=5(x-1)$$
$$y-2=5x-5$$
$$y=5x-3$$

Chapter 8

Chapter 8 opener

1. ANT

2. HAG

3. REM

4. ORE

5. PYT

6. HEO

P	Y	T	H	A	G	O	R	E	A	N	T	H	E	O	R	E	M
5		2		4		1			6			3					

9. $\sqrt[3]{7} \approx 1.913$

$$\sqrt[3]{(7)}$$
$$1.912931183$$

11. $\sqrt[3]{65} \approx 4.021$

$$\sqrt[3]{(65)}$$
$$4.020725759$$

Calculator Exercises

1. $\sqrt{5} \approx 2.236$

$$\sqrt{(5)}$$
$$2.236067977$$

3. $\sqrt{50} \approx 7.071$

$$\sqrt{(50)}$$
$$7.071067812$$

5. $\sqrt{33} \approx 5.745$

$$\sqrt{(33)}$$
$$5.744562647$$

7. $\sqrt{80} \approx 8.944$

$$\sqrt{(80)}$$
$$8.94427191$$

Section 8.1 Practice Exercises

1. (a) b is a **square root** of a if $b^2 = a$.

   (b) $\sqrt{a}$ is the **positive square root** of a.

   (c) The **principal square root** is another name for the positive square root.

   (d) $-\sqrt{a}$ is the **negative square root** of a.

   (e) **Perfect squares** are numbers whose square roots are rational numbers.

   (f) b is an **nth-root** of a if $b^n = a$.

   (g) In the expression $\sqrt[n]{a}$, n is called the **index** of the radical.

   (h) In the expression $\sqrt[n]{a}$, a is called the **radicand**.

   (i) A radical with an index of three is called a **cube root**.

   (j) The **Pythagorean theorem** relates the lengths of the three sides of a right triangle: $a^2 + b^2 = c^2$.

3. 12 is a square root of 144 because $(12)^2 = 144$. -12 is a square root of 144 because $(-12)^2 = 144$.

5. There are no real-valued square roots of -49.

7. 0 is a square root of 0 because $(0)^2 = 0$.

9. $\dfrac{1}{5}$ is a square root of $\dfrac{1}{25}$ because $\left(\dfrac{1}{5}\right)^2 = \dfrac{1}{25}$. $-\dfrac{1}{5}$ is a square root of $\dfrac{1}{25}$ because $\left(-\dfrac{1}{5}\right)^2 = \dfrac{1}{25}$.

11. (a) 13

(b) -13

13. 0

15. 9, 16, 25, 36, 64, 121, and 169

17. $\sqrt{4} = 2$

19. $\sqrt{49} = 7$

21. $\sqrt{0.16} = 0.4$

23. $\sqrt{0.09} = 0.3$

25. $\sqrt{\dfrac{25}{16}} = \dfrac{5}{4}$

27. $\sqrt{\dfrac{1}{144}} = \dfrac{1}{12}$

29. $\sqrt{16+9} = \sqrt{25} = 5$

31. $\sqrt{225-144} = \sqrt{81} = 9$

33. There is no real value of b for which $b^2 = -16$.

35. $-\sqrt{4} = -1 \cdot \sqrt{4} = -1 \cdot 2 = -2$

37. $\sqrt{-4}$ is not a real number.

39. $\sqrt{-\dfrac{4}{49}}$ is not a real number.

41. $-\sqrt{-\dfrac{1}{36}}$ is not a real number.

43. $-\sqrt{400} = -1 \cdot \sqrt{400} = -1 \cdot 20 = -20$

45. $\sqrt{-900}$ is not a real number.

47. 0, 1, 27, 125

49. Yes, -3

51. $\sqrt[3]{27} = 3$

53. $\sqrt[3]{64} = 4$

55. $-\sqrt[4]{16} = -2$

57. $\sqrt[4]{-1}$ is not a real number.

59. $\sqrt[4]{-256}$ is not a real number.

61. $\sqrt[5]{-\dfrac{1}{32}} = -\dfrac{1}{2}$

63. $-\sqrt[6]{1} = -1$

65. $\sqrt[6]{0} = 0$

67. $\sqrt{(4)^2} = |4| = 4$

69. $\sqrt{(-4)^2} = |-4| = 4$

71. $\sqrt[3]{(5)^3} = 5$

73. $\sqrt[3]{(-5)^3} = -5$

75. $\sqrt[4]{(2)^4} = |2| = 2$

77. $\sqrt[4]{(-2)^4} = |-2| = 2$

79. $\sqrt{a^2} = |a|$

81. $\sqrt[3]{y^3} = y$

83. $\sqrt[4]{w^4} = |w|$

85. $\sqrt[5]{x^5} = x$

87. $x^2, y^4, (ab)^6, w^8 x^8, m^{10}$

The expression is a perfect square if the exponent is even.

89. $p^4, t^8, (cd)^{12}$

The expression is a perfect fourth power if the exponent is a multiple of 4.

91. $\sqrt{y^{12}} = y^6$

93. $\sqrt{a^8 b^{30}} = a^4 b^{15}$

95. $\sqrt[3]{q^{24}} = q^8$

97. $\sqrt[3]{8w^6} = 2w^2$

99. $\sqrt{(5x)^2} = 5x$

101. $-\sqrt{25x^2} = -5x$

103. $\sqrt[3]{(5p^2)^3} = 5p^2$

105. $\sqrt[3]{125p^6} = 5p^2$

107. $\sqrt{q} + p^2$

109. $\dfrac{6}{\sqrt[4]{x}}$

111. Let x represent the length of the missing leg.
$$x^2 + 12^2 = 15^2$$
$$x^2 + 144 = 225$$
$$x^2 = 81$$
$$x = \sqrt{81}$$
$$x = 9 \qquad \text{9 cm}$$

113. Let x represent the length of the missing leg.
$$x^2 + 12^2 = 13^2$$
$$x^2 + 144 = 169$$
$$x^2 = 25$$
$$x = \sqrt{25}$$
$$x = 5 \qquad \text{5 ft}$$

115. Let x represent the length of the hypotenuse.
$$x^2 = (2.4)^2 + (6.5)^2$$
$$x^2 = 5.76 + 42.25$$
$$x^2 = 48.01$$
$$x = \sqrt{48.01}$$
$$x \approx 6.9 \qquad \text{6.9 cm}$$

117. Let x represent the length of the diagonal.
$$x^2 = 12^2 + 12^2$$
$$x^2 = 144 + 144$$
$$x^2 = 288$$
$$x = \sqrt{288}$$
$$x \approx 17.0 \qquad \text{17.0 in.}$$

119. Let x represent the width of the screen.
$$x^2 + 28^2 = 42^2$$
$$x^2 + 784 = 1764$$
$$x^2 = 980$$
$$x = \sqrt{980}$$
$$x \approx 31.3 \qquad \text{31.3 in.}$$

121. Let x represent the distance between Greensboro to Asheville.

$$x^2 + 134^2 = 300^2$$
$$x^2 + 17,956 = 90,000$$
$$x^2 = 72,044$$
$$x = \sqrt{72,044}$$
$$x \approx 268 \qquad 268 \text{ km}$$

123. For all $x \geq 0$

Calculator Exercises

1.

```
√(125)
       11.18033989
5*√(5)
       11.18033989
```

3.

```
³√(54)
       3.77976315
3*³√(2)
       3.77976315
```

Section 8.2 Practice Exercises

1. (a) The **simplified form of a radical** includes all of the following:
   i. The radicand has no factor raised to a power greater than or equal to the index.
   ii. There are no radicals in the denominator of a fraction.
   iii. The radicand does not contain a fraction.

(b) The **multiplication property of radicals** indicates that a product within a radicand can be written as a product of radicals provided the roots are real numbers.

3. $8, 27, y^3, y^9, y^{12},$ and y^{27}

5. $-\sqrt{25} = -5$. $\sqrt{-25}$ is not a real number.

7. $-\sqrt[3]{27} = -3$

9. $\sqrt[4]{a^8} = a^2$

11. $\sqrt{4x^2y^4} = 2xy^2$

13. Let x represent the distance between Portland and Spokane.

$$x^2 = 236^2 + 378^2$$
$$x^2 = 55,696 + 142,884$$
$$x^2 = 198,580$$
$$x = \sqrt{198,580}$$
$$x \approx 446 \qquad\qquad 446 \text{ km}$$

15. $\sqrt{18} = \sqrt{9 \cdot 2} = \sqrt{3^2} \cdot \sqrt{2} = 3\sqrt{2}$

17. $\sqrt{28} = \sqrt{4 \cdot 7} = \sqrt{2^2} \cdot \sqrt{7} = 2\sqrt{7}$

19. $6\sqrt{20} = 6\sqrt{2^2 \cdot 5}$
$$= 6\sqrt{2^2} \cdot \sqrt{5}$$
$$= 6 \cdot 2\sqrt{5}$$
$$= 12\sqrt{5}$$

21. $-2\sqrt{50} = -2\sqrt{5^2 \cdot 2}$
$$= -2\sqrt{5^2} \cdot \sqrt{2}$$
$$= -2 \cdot 5\sqrt{2}$$
$$= -10\sqrt{2}$$

23. $\sqrt{a^5} = \sqrt{a^4 \cdot a} = \sqrt{a^4} \cdot \sqrt{a} = a^2\sqrt{a}$

25. $\sqrt{w^{22}} = w^{11}$

27. $\sqrt{m^4n^5} = \sqrt{m^4n^4 \cdot n}$
$$= \sqrt{m^4n^4} \cdot \sqrt{n}$$
$$= m^2n^2\sqrt{n}$$

29. $x\sqrt{x^{13}y^{10}} = x\sqrt{x^{12}y^{10} \cdot x}$
$= x\sqrt{x^{12}y^{10}} \cdot \sqrt{x}$
$= x^7 y^5 \sqrt{x}$

31. $3\sqrt{t^{10}} = 3t^5$

33. $\sqrt{8x^3} = \sqrt{2^3 x^3}$
$= \sqrt{2^2 x^2 \cdot 2x}$
$= \sqrt{2^2 x^2} \cdot \sqrt{2x}$
$= 2x\sqrt{2x}$

35. $\sqrt{16z^3} = \sqrt{4^2 z^3}$
$= \sqrt{4^2 z^2 \cdot z}$
$= \sqrt{4^2 z^2} \cdot \sqrt{z}$
$= 4z\sqrt{z}$

37. $-\sqrt{45w^6} = -\sqrt{3^2 \cdot 5w^6}$
$= -\sqrt{3^2 w^6} \cdot \sqrt{5}$
$= -3w^3\sqrt{5}$

39. $\sqrt{z^{25}} = \sqrt{z^{24} \cdot z} = \sqrt{z^{24}} \cdot \sqrt{z} = z^{12}\sqrt{z}$

41. $-\sqrt{15z^{11}} = -\sqrt{z^{10} \cdot 15z}$
$= -\sqrt{z^{10}} \cdot \sqrt{15z}$
$= -z^5\sqrt{15z}$

43. $5\sqrt{104a^2 b^7} = 5\sqrt{2^3 \cdot 13a^2 b^7}$
$= 5\sqrt{2^2 a^2 b^6 \cdot 2 \cdot 13b}$
$= 5\sqrt{2^2 a^2 b^6} \cdot \sqrt{26b}$
$= 10ab^3\sqrt{26b}$

45. $\sqrt{26pq} = \sqrt{26pq}$
This radical is simplified.

47. $m\sqrt{m^{10}n^{16}} = m\sqrt{m^{10} \cdot n^{16}}$
$= m\sqrt{m^{10}} \cdot \sqrt{n^{16}}$
$= m \cdot m^5 \cdot n^8$
$= m^6 n^8$

49. $\sqrt{48a^3 b^5 c^4} = \sqrt{4^2 \cdot 3 \cdot a^2 \cdot a \cdot b^4 \cdot b \cdot c^4}$
$= \sqrt{4^2} \cdot \sqrt{a^2} \cdot \sqrt{b^4} \cdot \sqrt{c^4} \cdot \sqrt{3ab}$
$= 4 \cdot a \cdot b^2 \cdot c^2 \sqrt{3ab}$
$= 4ab^2 c^2 \sqrt{3ab}$

51. $\sqrt{\dfrac{a^9}{a}} = \sqrt{a^8} = a^4$

53. $\sqrt{\dfrac{y^{15}}{y^5}} = \sqrt{y^{10}} = y^5$

55. $\sqrt{\dfrac{5}{20}} = \sqrt{\dfrac{5}{4 \cdot 5}} = \sqrt{\dfrac{1}{4}}$
$= \sqrt{\dfrac{1}{2^2}} = \dfrac{1}{2}$

57. $\sqrt{\dfrac{40}{10}} = \sqrt{4} = 2$

59. $\sqrt{\dfrac{32x^3}{8x}} = \sqrt{\dfrac{4x^3}{x}} = \sqrt{4x^2} = 2x$

61. $\sqrt{\dfrac{50p^7}{2p}} = \sqrt{\dfrac{25p^7}{p}} = \sqrt{25p^6} = 5p^3$

63. $\dfrac{3\sqrt{20}}{2} = \dfrac{3\sqrt{2^2 \cdot 5}}{2}$
$= \dfrac{3\sqrt{2^2} \cdot \sqrt{5}}{2}$
$= \dfrac{3 \cdot 2\sqrt{5}}{2}$
$= 3\sqrt{5}$

65. $\dfrac{5\sqrt{24}}{10} = \dfrac{\sqrt{2^3 \cdot 3}}{2}$

$= \dfrac{\sqrt{2^2} \cdot \sqrt{2} \cdot \sqrt{3}}{2}$

$= \dfrac{2\sqrt{2} \cdot \sqrt{3}}{2}$

$= \sqrt{2} \cdot \sqrt{3} = \sqrt{6}$

67. $\dfrac{10 + \sqrt{4}}{3} = \dfrac{10 + 2}{3}$

$= \dfrac{12}{3}$

$= 4$

69. $\dfrac{20 - \sqrt{36}}{2} = \dfrac{20 - 6}{2}$

$= \dfrac{14}{2} = 7$

71. Let x represent the length of the missing side.

$x^2 = 11^2 + 11^2$

$x^2 = 121 + 121$

$x^2 = 242$

$x = \sqrt{242} = \sqrt{2 \cdot 11^2}$

$x = \sqrt{11^2} \cdot \sqrt{2} = 11\sqrt{2}$ $11\sqrt{2}$ ft

73. Let x represent the length of the missing side.

$x^2 + 5^2 = 17^2$

$x^2 + 25 = 289$

$x^2 = 264$

$x = \sqrt{264}$

$x = \sqrt{2^3 \cdot 3 \cdot 11}$

$x = \sqrt{2^2 \cdot 2 \cdot 3 \cdot 11}$

$x = \sqrt{2^2} \cdot \sqrt{66}$

$x = 2\sqrt{66}$ $2\sqrt{66}$ cm

75. $\sqrt[3]{a^8} = \sqrt[3]{a^6 \cdot a^2} = \sqrt[3]{a^6} \cdot \sqrt[3]{a^2} = a^2 \sqrt[3]{a^2}$

76. $\sqrt[3]{8v^3} = \sqrt[3]{2^3 v^3} = 2v$

77. $7\sqrt[3]{16z^3} = 7\sqrt[3]{2^4 z^3}$

$= 7\sqrt[3]{2^3 z^3 \cdot 2}$

$= 7\sqrt[3]{2^3 z^3} \cdot \sqrt[3]{2}$

$= 14z\sqrt[3]{2}$

79. $\sqrt[3]{16a^5 b^6} = \sqrt[3]{2^3 \cdot 2 \cdot a^3 \cdot a^2 \cdot b^6}$

$= \sqrt[3]{2^3} \cdot \sqrt[3]{a^3} \cdot \sqrt[3]{b^6} \cdot \sqrt[3]{2a^2}$

$= 2ab^2 \sqrt[3]{2a^2}$

81. $\dfrac{\sqrt[3]{z^4}}{\sqrt[3]{z}} = \sqrt[3]{\dfrac{z^4}{z}} = \sqrt[3]{z^3} = z$

83. $\sqrt[3]{-\dfrac{32}{4}} = \sqrt[3]{-8}$

$= \sqrt[3]{-1 \cdot 2^3}$

$= \sqrt[3]{-1} \cdot \sqrt[3]{2^3}$

$= -1 \cdot 2$

$= -2$

85. $\sqrt[3]{40} = \sqrt[3]{8 \cdot 5}$

$= \sqrt[3]{2^3} \cdot \sqrt[3]{5}$

$= 2\sqrt[3]{5}$

87. $\dfrac{\sqrt{3}}{\sqrt{27}} = \sqrt{\dfrac{3}{27}} = \sqrt{\dfrac{1}{9}} = \dfrac{\sqrt{1}}{\sqrt{9}} = \dfrac{1}{3}$

89. $\sqrt{16a^3} = \sqrt{2^4 a^3}$

$= \sqrt{2^4 a^2 \cdot a}$

$= \sqrt{2^4 a^2} \cdot \sqrt{a}$

$= 2^2 a\sqrt{a}$

$= 4a\sqrt{a}$

91. $\sqrt{\dfrac{4x^3}{x}} = \sqrt{4x^2}$

$= \sqrt{2^2} \cdot \sqrt{x^2}$

$= 2x$

93. $\sqrt{8p^2q} = \sqrt{2^2 \cdot 2 \cdot p^2 \cdot q}$
$= \sqrt{2^2} \cdot \sqrt{p^2} \cdot \sqrt{2q}$
$= 2p\sqrt{2q}$

95. $\sqrt{32} = \sqrt{4^2 \cdot 2} = \sqrt{4^2} \cdot \sqrt{2} = 4\sqrt{2}$

97. $\sqrt{52u^4v^7} = \sqrt{2^2 \cdot 13u^4v^7}$
$= \sqrt{2^2 u^4 v^6 \cdot 13v}$
$= \sqrt{2^2 u^4 v^6} \cdot \sqrt{13v}$
$= 2u^2v^3\sqrt{13v}$

99. $\sqrt{216} = \sqrt{6^3} = \sqrt{6^2 \cdot 6} = \sqrt{6^2} \cdot \sqrt{6} = 6\sqrt{6}$

101. $\sqrt[3]{216} = \sqrt[3]{2^3 \cdot 3^3} = 2 \cdot 3 = 6$

103. $\sqrt[3]{16a^3} = \sqrt[3]{2^3 \cdot 2 \cdot a^3}$
$= \sqrt[3]{2^3} \cdot \sqrt[3]{2} \cdot \sqrt[3]{a^3}$
$= 2a\sqrt[3]{2}$

105. $\sqrt[3]{\dfrac{x^5}{x^2}} = \sqrt[3]{x^3} = x$

107. $\dfrac{-6\sqrt{20}}{12} = \dfrac{-\sqrt{20}}{2} = \dfrac{-\sqrt{2^2 \cdot 5}}{2}$
$= \dfrac{-\sqrt{2^2}\sqrt{5}}{2} = \dfrac{-2\sqrt{5}}{2} = -\sqrt{5}$

109. $\dfrac{-4-\sqrt{25}}{18} = \dfrac{-4-5}{18} = \dfrac{-9}{18} = -\dfrac{1}{2}$

111. $\sqrt{(-2-5)^2 + (-4+3)^2} = \sqrt{(-7)^2 + (-1)^2}$
$= \sqrt{49+1}$
$= \sqrt{50}$
$= \sqrt{5^2 \cdot 2}$
$= 5\sqrt{2}$

113. $\sqrt{x^2 + 10x + 25} = \sqrt{(x+5)^2} = x+5$

Section 8.3 Practice Exercises

1. Two radical terms are said to be *like radicals* if they have the same index and the same radicand.

3. $\sqrt[3]{8y^3} = 2y$

5. $\sqrt{36x^3} = \sqrt{36x^2 \cdot x} = \sqrt{36x^2} \cdot \sqrt{x} = 6x\sqrt{x}$

7. $\dfrac{\sqrt{25c^6}}{16} = \dfrac{\sqrt{5^2 \cdot c^6}}{16} = \dfrac{5 \cdot \sqrt{c^6}}{16} = \dfrac{5c^3}{16}$

9. $\sqrt{-25}$ Not a real number.

11. For example: $2\sqrt{3}, 6\sqrt[3]{3}$

13. c

15. $3\sqrt{2} + 5\sqrt{2} = (3+5)\sqrt{2} = 8\sqrt{2}$

17. $5\sqrt{7} - 3\sqrt{7} + 2\sqrt{7} = (5-3+2)\sqrt{7} = 4\sqrt{7}$

19. $\sqrt{10} + \sqrt{10} = 1\sqrt{10} + 1\sqrt{10}$
$= (1+1)\sqrt{10}$
$= 2\sqrt{10}$

21. $15\sqrt{y} - 4\sqrt{y} = (15-4)\sqrt{y} = 11\sqrt{y}$

23. $5\sqrt{c} - 6\sqrt{c} + \sqrt{c} = 5\sqrt{c} - 6\sqrt{c} + 1\sqrt{c}$
$$= (5 - 6 + 1)\sqrt{c}$$
$$= 0$$

25. $8y\sqrt{15} - 3y\sqrt{15} = (8y - 3y)\sqrt{15} = 5y\sqrt{15}$

27. $x\sqrt{y} - y\sqrt{x} = x\sqrt{y} - y\sqrt{x}$

Cannot be simplified—the radicals are not *like* radicals.

29. $2\sqrt{12} + \sqrt{48} = 2\sqrt{2^2 \cdot 3} + \sqrt{2^4 \cdot 3}$
$$= 2 \cdot 2\sqrt{3} + 2^2 \cdot \sqrt{3}$$
$$= 4\sqrt{3} + 4\sqrt{3}$$
$$= (4 + 4)\sqrt{3}$$
$$= 8\sqrt{3}$$

31. $4\sqrt{45} - 6\sqrt{20} = 4\sqrt{3^2 \cdot 5} - 6\sqrt{2^2 \cdot 5}$
$$= 4 \cdot 3\sqrt{5} - 6 \cdot 2\sqrt{5}$$
$$= 12\sqrt{5} - 12\sqrt{5}$$
$$= 0$$

33. $\dfrac{1}{2}\sqrt{8} + \dfrac{1}{3}\sqrt{18} = \dfrac{1}{2}\sqrt{2^3} + \dfrac{1}{3}\sqrt{2 \cdot 3^2}$
$$= \dfrac{1}{2}\sqrt{2^2 \cdot 2} + \dfrac{1}{3}\sqrt{2 \cdot 3^2}$$
$$= \dfrac{1}{2} \cdot 2\sqrt{2} + \dfrac{1}{3} \cdot 3\sqrt{2}$$
$$= 1\sqrt{2} + 1\sqrt{2}$$
$$= (1 + 1)\sqrt{2}$$
$$= 2\sqrt{2}$$

35. $6p\sqrt{20p^2} + p^2\sqrt{80}$
$$= 6p\sqrt{2^2 p^2 \cdot 5} + p^2\sqrt{2^4 \cdot 5}$$
$$= 6p \cdot 2p\sqrt{5} + p^2 \cdot 2^2\sqrt{5}$$
$$= 12p^2\sqrt{5} + 4p^2\sqrt{5}$$
$$= (12p^2 + 4p^2)\sqrt{5}$$
$$= 16p^2\sqrt{5}$$

37. $-2\sqrt{2k} + 6\sqrt{8k} = -2\sqrt{2k} + 6\sqrt{2^2 \cdot 2k}$
$$= -2\sqrt{2k} + 6 \cdot 2\sqrt{2k}$$
$$= -2\sqrt{2k} + 12\sqrt{2k}$$
$$= (-2 + 12)\sqrt{2k}$$
$$= 10\sqrt{2k}$$

39. $11\sqrt{a^4 b} - a^2\sqrt{b} - 9a\sqrt{a^2 b}$
$$= 11 \cdot a^2\sqrt{b} - a^2\sqrt{b} - 9a \cdot a\sqrt{b}$$
$$= 11a^2\sqrt{b} - 1a^2\sqrt{b} - 9a^2\sqrt{b}$$
$$= (11a^2 - 1a^2 - 9a^2)\sqrt{b}$$
$$= a^2\sqrt{b}$$

41. $4\sqrt{5} - \sqrt{5} = 4\sqrt{5} - 1\sqrt{5} = (4 - 1)\sqrt{5} = 3\sqrt{5}$

43. $\dfrac{5}{6}z\sqrt{6} + \dfrac{7}{9}z\sqrt{6} = \dfrac{15}{18}z\sqrt{6} + \dfrac{14}{18}z\sqrt{6}$
$$= \left(\dfrac{15}{18}z + \dfrac{14}{18}z\right)\sqrt{6}$$
$$= \dfrac{29}{18}z\sqrt{6}$$

45. $1.1\sqrt{10} - 5.6\sqrt{10} + 2.8\sqrt{10}$
$$= (1.1 - 5.6 + 2.8)\sqrt{10}$$
$$= -1.7\sqrt{10}$$

47. $4\sqrt{x^3} - 2x\sqrt{x} = 4\sqrt{x^2 \cdot x} - 2x\sqrt{x}$
$$= 4 \cdot x\sqrt{x} - 2x\sqrt{x}$$
$$= 4x\sqrt{x} - 2x\sqrt{x}$$
$$= (4x - 2x)\sqrt{x}$$
$$= 2x\sqrt{x}$$

49. $4\sqrt{7} + \sqrt{63} - 2\sqrt{28}$
$$= 4\sqrt{7} + \sqrt{3^2 \cdot 7} - 2\sqrt{2^2 \cdot 7}$$
$$= 4\sqrt{7} + 3\sqrt{7} - 2 \cdot 2\sqrt{7}$$
$$= 4\sqrt{7} + 3\sqrt{7} - 4\sqrt{7}$$
$$= (4 + 3 - 4)\sqrt{7}$$
$$= 3\sqrt{7}$$

51. $\sqrt{16w} + \sqrt{24w} + \sqrt{40w}$

$\qquad = \sqrt{4^2 \cdot w} + \sqrt{2^2 \cdot 6w} + \sqrt{2^2 \cdot 10w}$

$\qquad = 4\sqrt{w} + 2\sqrt{6w} + 2\sqrt{10w}$

53. $\sqrt{x^6 y} + 5x^2 \sqrt{x^2 y} = \sqrt{x^6 \cdot y} + 5x^2 \sqrt{x^2 \cdot y}$

$\qquad\qquad = x^3 \sqrt{y} + 5x^2 \cdot x\sqrt{y}$

$\qquad\qquad = x^3 \sqrt{y} + 5x^3 \sqrt{y}$

$\qquad\qquad = (x^3 + 5x^3)\sqrt{y}$

$\qquad\qquad = 6x^3 \sqrt{y}$

55. $4\sqrt{6} + 2\sqrt{3} - 8\sqrt{6} = (4-8)\sqrt{6} + 2\sqrt{3}$

$\qquad\qquad\qquad\qquad = -4\sqrt{6} + 2\sqrt{3}$

57. $x\sqrt{8} - 2\sqrt{18x^2} + \sqrt{2x}$

$\qquad = x\sqrt{2^2 \cdot 2} - 2\sqrt{3^2 \cdot 2 \cdot x^2} + \sqrt{2x}$

$\qquad = 2x\sqrt{2} - 6x\sqrt{2} + \sqrt{2x}$

$\qquad = (2x - 6x)\sqrt{2} + \sqrt{2x}$

$\qquad = -4x\sqrt{2} + \sqrt{2x}$

59. The perimeter is the sum of the lengths of the sides.

$\sqrt{18} + \sqrt{8} + \sqrt{32} = \sqrt{3^2 \cdot 2} + \sqrt{2^2 \cdot 2} + \sqrt{2^4 \cdot 2}$

$\qquad\qquad\qquad\quad = 3\sqrt{2} + 2\sqrt{2} + 2^2\sqrt{2}$

$\qquad\qquad\qquad\quad = (3 + 2 + 4)\sqrt{2}$

$\qquad\qquad\qquad\quad = 9\sqrt{2} \text{ m}$

61. The perimeter is the sum of the lengths of the four sides of the rectangle. Remember that opposite sides are the same.

$2\sqrt{3} + 2\sqrt{3} + 3\sqrt{12} + 3\sqrt{12}$

$= 2\sqrt{3} + 2\sqrt{3} + 3\sqrt{2^2 \cdot 3} + 3\sqrt{2^2 \cdot 3}$

$= 2\sqrt{3} + 2\sqrt{3} + 3 \cdot 2\sqrt{3} + 3 \cdot 2\sqrt{3}$

$= 2\sqrt{3} + 2\sqrt{3} + 6\sqrt{3} + 6\sqrt{3}$

$= (2 + 2 + 6 + 6)\sqrt{3}$

$= 16\sqrt{3} \text{ in.}$

63. Radicands are not the same.

65. One term has a radical. One does not.

67. The indices are different.

69. $m = \dfrac{2\sqrt{3} - \sqrt{3}}{4 - 1} = \dfrac{\sqrt{3}}{3}$

71. $x = 23\sqrt{3}t$

  (a) $x = 23\sqrt{3}(2)$

  $\qquad x \approx 80 \text{ m}$

  (b) $x = 23\sqrt{3}(4)$

  $\qquad x \approx 159 \text{ m}$

Section 8.4 Practice Exercises

1. The answer varies.

$\quad x^3 \sqrt{y}$

$\quad x\sqrt[3]{y}$

3. $\sqrt{100} - \sqrt{4} + \sqrt{9} = 10 - 2 + 3 = 11$

5. $10\sqrt{zw^4} - w^2\sqrt{49z} = 10w^2\sqrt{z} - w^2 \cdot 7\sqrt{z}$

$\qquad\qquad\qquad\qquad = 10w^2\sqrt{z} - 7w^2\sqrt{z}$

$\qquad\qquad\qquad\qquad = 3w^2\sqrt{z}$

7. $\sqrt{5} \cdot \sqrt{3} = \sqrt{5 \cdot 3} = \sqrt{15}$

9. $\sqrt{47} \cdot \sqrt{47} = \sqrt{47 \cdot 47} = 47$

11. $\sqrt{b} \cdot \sqrt{b} = \sqrt{b \cdot b} = \sqrt{b^2} = b$

13. $2\sqrt{15} \cdot 3\sqrt{p} = 6\sqrt{15p}$

15. $\sqrt{10} \cdot \sqrt{5} = \sqrt{10 \cdot 5} = \sqrt{50} = \sqrt{25 \cdot 2} = 5\sqrt{2}$

17. $(-\sqrt{7})(-2\sqrt{14}) = 2\sqrt{7 \cdot 14} = 2\sqrt{98}$

$\qquad\qquad\qquad\qquad = 2\sqrt{49 \cdot 2} = 2 \cdot 7\sqrt{2}$

$\qquad\qquad\qquad\qquad = 14\sqrt{2}$

19. $3x\sqrt{2} \cdot \sqrt{14} = 3x\sqrt{2} \cdot \sqrt{2 \cdot 7} = 3x\sqrt{2} \cdot \sqrt{2} \cdot \sqrt{7}$

$\qquad\qquad\qquad = 3x \cdot 2\sqrt{7} = 6x\sqrt{7}$

21. $\left(\dfrac{1}{6}x\sqrt{xy}\right)24x\sqrt{x} = 4x^2\sqrt{xy}\cdot\sqrt{x}$

$$= 4x^2\sqrt{x}\cdot\sqrt{y}\cdot\sqrt{x}$$
$$= 4x^2 x\cdot\sqrt{y}$$
$$= 4x^3\sqrt{y}$$

23. $6w\sqrt{5}\cdot w\sqrt{8} = 6w^2\sqrt{5}\cdot\sqrt{8}$

$$= 6w^2\sqrt{5}\cdot\sqrt{2^2\cdot 2}$$
$$= 6w^2\sqrt{5}\cdot\sqrt{2^2}\cdot\sqrt{2}$$
$$= 6w^2\sqrt{5}\cdot 2\cdot\sqrt{2}$$
$$= 12w^2\sqrt{5}\cdot\sqrt{2} = 12w^2\sqrt{10}$$

25. $-2\sqrt{3}\cdot 4\sqrt{5} = -8\sqrt{15}$

27. Perimeter: $P = 2l + 2w$

$$P = 2\sqrt{20} + 2\sqrt{5}$$
$$P = 2\sqrt{4\cdot 5} + 2\sqrt{5}$$
$$P = 2\cdot 2\sqrt{5} + 2\sqrt{5}$$
$$P = 4\sqrt{5} + 2\sqrt{5}$$
$$P = 6\sqrt{5}\ \text{ft}$$

Area: $A = lw$

$$A = \sqrt{20}\cdot\sqrt{5}$$
$$A = \sqrt{20\cdot 5}$$
$$A = \sqrt{100}$$
$$A = 10\ \text{ft}^2$$

29. Area: $A = \dfrac{1}{2}bh$

$$A = \dfrac{1}{2}\cdot\sqrt{3}\cdot\sqrt{12}$$
$$A = \dfrac{1}{2}\cdot\sqrt{3\cdot 12}$$
$$A = \dfrac{1}{2}\cdot\sqrt{36}$$
$$A = \dfrac{1}{2}\cdot 6$$
$$A = 3\ \text{cm}^2$$

31. $\sqrt{3w}\cdot\sqrt{3w} = \sqrt{3w\cdot 3w} = \sqrt{9w^2} = 3w$

33. $8\sqrt{5y}\ -2\sqrt{2} = (8\cdot(-2))\sqrt{5y}\cdot\sqrt{2}$

$$= -16\sqrt{5y\cdot 2}$$
$$= -16\sqrt{10y}$$

35. $\sqrt{2}\ \sqrt{6} - \sqrt{3} = \sqrt{2}\cdot\sqrt{6} - \sqrt{2}\cdot\sqrt{3}$

$$= \sqrt{12} - \sqrt{6}$$
$$= \sqrt{4\cdot 3} - \sqrt{6}$$
$$= 2\sqrt{3} - \sqrt{6}$$

37. $4\sqrt{x}\ \sqrt{x} + 5 = 4\sqrt{x}\cdot\sqrt{x} + 4\sqrt{x}\cdot 5$

$$= 4x + 20\sqrt{x}$$

39. $\sqrt{3} + 2\sqrt{10}\ 4\sqrt{3} - \sqrt{10} = \sqrt{3}\cdot 4\sqrt{3} - \sqrt{3}\cdot\sqrt{10} + 2\sqrt{10}\cdot 4\sqrt{3} - 2\sqrt{10}\cdot\sqrt{10}$

$$= 4\sqrt{9} - \sqrt{30} + 8\sqrt{30} - 2\sqrt{100}$$
$$= 4\cdot 3 - 1\sqrt{30} + 8\sqrt{30} - 2\cdot 10$$
$$= 12 + 7\sqrt{30} - 20$$
$$= -8 + 7\sqrt{30}$$

41. $\sqrt{a} - 3b\ 9\sqrt{a} - b = \sqrt{a}\cdot 9\sqrt{a} - \sqrt{a}\cdot b - 3b\cdot 9\sqrt{a} + 3b\cdot b$

$$= 9\sqrt{a}^{\,2} - 28b\sqrt{a} + 3b^2$$
$$= 9a - 28b\sqrt{a} + 3b^2$$

43. $\left(p+2\sqrt{p}\right)\left(8p+3\sqrt{p}-4\right) = p\cdot 8p + p\cdot 3\sqrt{p} - p\cdot 4 + 2\sqrt{p}\cdot 8p + 2\sqrt{p}\cdot 3\sqrt{p} - 2\sqrt{p}\cdot 4$

$$= 8p^2 + 3p\sqrt{p} - 4p + 16p\sqrt{p} + 6\left(\sqrt{p}\right)^2 - 8\sqrt{p}$$
$$= 8p^2 + 3p\sqrt{p} - 4p + 16p\sqrt{p} + 6p - 8\sqrt{p}$$
$$= 8p^2 + 19p\sqrt{p} + 2p - 8\sqrt{p}$$

45. $\left(\sqrt{10}\right)^2 = 10$

47. $\left(\sqrt[3]{4}\right)^3 = 4$

49. $\left(\sqrt[4]{t}\right)^4 = t$

51. $\left(4\sqrt{c}\right)^2 = 4^2 \cdot \left(\sqrt{c}\right)^2 = 16c$

53. $\left(\sqrt{13}+4\right)^2 = \left(\sqrt{13}\right)^2 + 2\left(\sqrt{13}\right)(4) + 4^2$
$$= 13 + 8\sqrt{13} + 16$$
$$= 29 + 8\sqrt{13}$$

55. $\left(\sqrt{a}-2\right)^2 = \left(\sqrt{a}\right)^2 - 2\left(\sqrt{a}\right)(2) + 2^2$
$$= a - 4\sqrt{a} + 4$$

57. $\left(2\sqrt{a}-3\right)^2 = \left(2\sqrt{a}\right)^2 - 2\left(2\sqrt{a}\right)(3) + 3^2$
$$= 4a - 12\sqrt{a} + 9$$

59. $\left(\sqrt{10}-\sqrt{11}\right)^2$
$$= \left(\sqrt{10}\right)^2 - 2\left(\sqrt{10}\right)\left(\sqrt{11}\right) + \left(\sqrt{11}\right)^2$$
$$= 10 - 2\sqrt{110} + 11$$
$$= 21 - 2\sqrt{110}$$

61. $\left(\sqrt{5}+2\right)\left(\sqrt{5}-2\right) = \left(\sqrt{5}\right)^2 - 2^2 = 5 - 4 = 1$

63. $\left(\sqrt{x}+\sqrt{y}\right)\left(\sqrt{x}-\sqrt{y}\right) = \left(\sqrt{x}\right)^2 - \left(\sqrt{y}\right)^2$
$$= x - y$$

65. $\left(\sqrt{10}-\sqrt{11}\right)\left(\sqrt{10}+\sqrt{11}\right) = \left(\sqrt{10}\right)^2 - \left(\sqrt{11}\right)^2$
$$= 10 - 11$$
$$= -1$$

67. $\left(6\sqrt{m}+5\sqrt{n}\right)\left(6\sqrt{m}-5\sqrt{n}\right)$
$$= \left(6\sqrt{m}\right)^2 - \left(5\sqrt{n}\right)^2$$
$$= 36m - 25n$$

69. $\left(8\sqrt{x}-2\sqrt{y}\right)\left(8\sqrt{x}+2\sqrt{y}\right)$
$$= 8^2\left(\sqrt{x}\right)^2 - 2^2\left(\sqrt{y}\right)^2$$
$$= 64x - 4y$$

71. $\left(5\sqrt{3}-\sqrt{2}\right)\left(5\sqrt{3}+\sqrt{2}\right) = \left(5\sqrt{3}\right)^2 - \left(\sqrt{2}\right)^2$
$$= 25\cdot 3 - 2$$
$$= 75 - 2$$
$$= 73$$

73. **(a)** $3(x+2) = 3\cdot x + 3\cdot 2 = 3x + 6$

  (b) $\sqrt{3}\left(\sqrt{x}+\sqrt{2}\right) = \sqrt{3}\cdot\sqrt{x} + \sqrt{3}\cdot\sqrt{2}$
$$= \sqrt{3x} + \sqrt{6}$$

75. **(a)** $(2a+3)^2 = (2a)^2 + 2(2a)(3) + 3^2$
$$= 4a^2 + 12a + 9$$

  (b) $\left(2\sqrt{a}+3\right)^2$
$$= \left(2\sqrt{a}\right)^2 + 2\left(2\sqrt{a}\right)(3) + 3^2$$
$$= 2^2\cdot\left(\sqrt{a}\right)^2 + 2\cdot 2\cdot 3\sqrt{a} + 9$$
$$= 4a + 12\sqrt{a} + 9$$

77. (a) $(b-5)(b+5) = b^2 - 5^2 = b^2 - 25$

(b) $\left(\sqrt{b}-5\right)\left(\sqrt{b}+5\right) = \sqrt{b}^2 - 5^2 = b - 25$

79. (a) $(x-2y)^2 = (x)^2 - 2(x)(2y) + (-2y)^2$
$= x^2 - 4xy + 4y^2$

(b) $\left(\sqrt{x}-2\sqrt{y}\right)^2$
$= \sqrt{x}^2 - 2\left(\sqrt{x}\right)\left(2\sqrt{y}\right) + \left(-2\sqrt{y}\right)^2$
$= x - 4\sqrt{x}\sqrt{y} + 4y$
$= x - 4\sqrt{xy} + 4y$

81. (a) $(p-q)(p+q)$
$= (p)^2 + (p)(q) - (p)(q) - (q)^2$
$= p^2 - q^2$

(b) $\left(\sqrt{p}-\sqrt{q}\right)\left(\sqrt{p}+\sqrt{q}\right)$
$= \sqrt{p}^2 + \sqrt{p}\sqrt{q}$
$\quad - \sqrt{p}\sqrt{q} - \sqrt{q}^2$
$= p - q$

83. (a) $(y-3)^2$
$= (y)^2 + 2(y)(-3) + (-3)^2$
$= y^2 - 6y + 9$

(b) $\left(\sqrt{x-2}-3\right)^2$
$= \sqrt{x-2}^2 - 2\left(\sqrt{x-2}\right)(3) + 3^2$
$= x - 2 - 6\sqrt{x-2} + 9$
$= x - 6\sqrt{x-2} + 7$

Section 8.5 Practice Exercises

1. **Rationalizing the denominator** is the process of removing a radical from the denominator.

3. $\left(2\sqrt{y}+3\right)\left(3\sqrt{y}+7\right)$
$= 2\sqrt{y}\cdot 3\sqrt{y} + 2\sqrt{y}\cdot 7 + 3\cdot 3\sqrt{y} + 3\cdot 7$
$= 6\sqrt{y}^2 + 14\sqrt{y} + 9\sqrt{y} + 21$
$= 6y + 23\sqrt{y} + 21$

5. $4\sqrt{3} + \sqrt{5}\cdot\sqrt{15} = 4\sqrt{3} + \sqrt{5\cdot 15}$
$= 4\sqrt{3} + \sqrt{75}$
$= 4\sqrt{3} + \sqrt{25\cdot 3}$
$= 4\sqrt{3} + 5\sqrt{3}$
$= 9\sqrt{3}$

7. $\left(5-\sqrt{a}\right)^2 = 5^2 - 2(5)\sqrt{a} + \sqrt{a}^2$
$= 25 - 10\sqrt{a} + a$

9. $\left(\sqrt{2}+\sqrt{7}\right)\left(\sqrt{2}-\sqrt{7}\right) = \sqrt{2}^2 - \sqrt{7}^2$
$= 2 - 7$
$= -5$

11. $\sqrt{\dfrac{3}{16}} = \dfrac{\sqrt{3}}{\sqrt{4\cdot 4}} = \dfrac{\sqrt{3}}{\sqrt{4^2}} = \dfrac{\sqrt{3}}{4}$

13. $\sqrt{\dfrac{a^4}{b^4}} = \dfrac{\sqrt{a^2\cdot a^2}}{\sqrt{b^2\cdot b^2}} = \dfrac{a^2}{b^2}$

15. $\sqrt{\dfrac{c^3}{4}} = \dfrac{\sqrt{c^2\cdot c}}{\sqrt{2\cdot 2}} = \dfrac{c\sqrt{c}}{2}$

17. $\sqrt[3]{\dfrac{x^2}{27}} = \sqrt[3]{\dfrac{x^2}{3^3}} = \dfrac{\sqrt[3]{x^2}}{3}$

19. $\sqrt[3]{\dfrac{y^5}{27y^3}} = \sqrt[3]{\dfrac{y^2}{27}} = \sqrt[3]{\dfrac{y^2}{3^3}} = \dfrac{\sqrt[3]{y^2}}{3}$

21. $\sqrt{\dfrac{200}{81}} = \sqrt{\dfrac{2 \cdot 100}{9^2}} = \sqrt{\dfrac{2 \cdot 10^2}{9^2}} = \dfrac{10\sqrt{2}}{9}$

23. $\dfrac{\sqrt{8}}{\sqrt{50}} = \sqrt{\dfrac{8}{50}} = \sqrt{\dfrac{4}{25}} = \sqrt{\dfrac{2^2}{5^2}} = \dfrac{2}{5}$

25. $\dfrac{\sqrt{p}}{\sqrt{4p^3}} = \sqrt{\dfrac{p}{4p^3}} = \sqrt{\dfrac{1}{4p^2}} = \sqrt{\dfrac{1}{2^2 p^2}} = \dfrac{1}{2p}$

27. $\dfrac{\sqrt[3]{z^5}}{\sqrt[3]{z^2}} = \sqrt[3]{\dfrac{z^5}{z^2}} = \sqrt[3]{z^3} = z$

29. $\dfrac{\sqrt[3]{24x^5}}{\sqrt[3]{3x^4}} = \sqrt[3]{\dfrac{24x^5}{3x^4}} = \sqrt[3]{8x} = \sqrt[3]{2^3 x} = 2\sqrt[3]{x}$

31. $\dfrac{1}{\sqrt{6}} = \dfrac{1}{\sqrt{6}} \cdot \dfrac{\sqrt{6}}{\sqrt{6}} = \dfrac{\sqrt{6}}{\sqrt{6 \cdot 6}} = \dfrac{\sqrt{6}}{\sqrt{6^2}} = \dfrac{\sqrt{6}}{6}$

33. $\dfrac{15}{\sqrt{5}} = \dfrac{15}{\sqrt{5}} \cdot \dfrac{\sqrt{5}}{\sqrt{5}}$
$= \dfrac{15\sqrt{5}}{\sqrt{5 \cdot 5}}$
$= \dfrac{15\sqrt{5}}{\sqrt{5^2}}$
$= \dfrac{15\sqrt{5}}{5}$
$= 3\sqrt{5}$

35. $\dfrac{6}{\sqrt{x+1}} = \dfrac{6}{\sqrt{x+1}} \cdot \dfrac{\sqrt{x+1}}{\sqrt{x+1}}$
$= \dfrac{6\sqrt{x+1}}{\sqrt{(x+1)^2}}$
$= \dfrac{6\sqrt{x+1}}{x+1}$

37. $\sqrt{\dfrac{6}{x}} = \dfrac{\sqrt{6}}{\sqrt{x}} = \dfrac{\sqrt{6}}{\sqrt{x}} \cdot \dfrac{\sqrt{x}}{\sqrt{x}} = \dfrac{\sqrt{6x}}{\sqrt{x^2}} = \dfrac{\sqrt{6x}}{x}$

39. $\sqrt{\dfrac{3}{7}} = \dfrac{\sqrt{3}}{\sqrt{7}} \cdot \dfrac{\sqrt{7}}{\sqrt{7}} = \dfrac{\sqrt{21}}{\sqrt{7^2}} = \dfrac{\sqrt{21}}{7}$

41. $\dfrac{10}{\sqrt{6y}} = \dfrac{10}{\sqrt{6y}} \cdot \dfrac{\sqrt{6y}}{\sqrt{6y}}$
$= \dfrac{10\sqrt{6y}}{\sqrt{6y \cdot 6y}}$
$= \dfrac{10\sqrt{6y}}{\sqrt{6^2 y^2}}$
$= \dfrac{10\sqrt{6y}}{6y}$
$= \dfrac{5\sqrt{6y}}{3y}$

43. $\dfrac{9}{2\sqrt{6}} \cdot \dfrac{\sqrt{6}}{\sqrt{6}} = \dfrac{9\sqrt{6}}{2\sqrt{6^2}} = \dfrac{9\sqrt{6}}{2 \cdot 6} = \dfrac{9\sqrt{6}}{12} = \dfrac{3\sqrt{6}}{4}$

45. $\sqrt{\dfrac{p}{27}} = \dfrac{\sqrt{p}}{\sqrt{27}}$
$= \dfrac{\sqrt{p}}{\sqrt{3^2 \cdot 3}}$
$= \dfrac{\sqrt{p}}{3\sqrt{3}} \cdot \dfrac{\sqrt{3}}{\sqrt{3}}$
$= \dfrac{\sqrt{3p}}{3\sqrt{3^2}}$
$= \dfrac{\sqrt{3p}}{9}$

47. $\dfrac{5}{\sqrt{20}} = \dfrac{5}{\sqrt{2^2 \cdot 5}}$
$= \dfrac{5}{2\sqrt{5}} \cdot \dfrac{\sqrt{5}}{\sqrt{5}}$
$= \dfrac{5\sqrt{5}}{2\sqrt{5^2}}$
$= \dfrac{5\sqrt{5}}{2 \cdot 5}$
$= \dfrac{\sqrt{5}}{2}$

49. $\sqrt{\dfrac{x^2}{y^3}} = \dfrac{\sqrt{x^2}}{\sqrt{y^3}}$

$= \dfrac{x}{\sqrt{y^2 \cdot y}}$

$= \dfrac{x}{y\sqrt{y}} \cdot \dfrac{\sqrt{y}}{\sqrt{y}}$

$= \dfrac{x\sqrt{y}}{y\sqrt{y^2}}$

$= \dfrac{x\sqrt{y}}{y^2}$

51. $\left(\sqrt{2}+3\right)\left(\sqrt{2}-3\right) = \sqrt{2}^2 - 3^2 = 2 - 9 = -7$

53. The conjugate is $\sqrt{5}+\sqrt{3}$.

$\left(\sqrt{5}-\sqrt{3}\right)\left(\sqrt{5}+\sqrt{3}\right) = \sqrt{5}^2 - \sqrt{3}^2$

$= 5 - 3$

$= 2$

55. The conjugate is $\sqrt{x}-10$.

$\left(\sqrt{x}+10\right)\left(\sqrt{x}-10\right) = \sqrt{x}^2 - 10^2 = x - 100$

57. $\dfrac{4}{\sqrt{2}+3} = \dfrac{4}{\sqrt{2}+3} \cdot \dfrac{\sqrt{2}-3}{\sqrt{2}-3}$

$= \dfrac{4\left(\sqrt{2}-3\right)}{\sqrt{2}^2 - 3^2}$

$= \dfrac{4\sqrt{2}-12}{2-9}$

$= \dfrac{4\sqrt{2}-12}{-7}$ or $\dfrac{12-4\sqrt{2}}{7}$

59. $\dfrac{1}{\sqrt{5}-\sqrt{2}} = \dfrac{1}{\sqrt{5}-\sqrt{2}} \cdot \dfrac{\sqrt{5}+\sqrt{2}}{\sqrt{5}+\sqrt{2}}$

$= \dfrac{\sqrt{5}+\sqrt{2}}{\sqrt{5}^2 - \sqrt{2}^2}$

$= \dfrac{\sqrt{5}+\sqrt{2}}{5-2}$

$= \dfrac{\sqrt{5}+\sqrt{2}}{3}$

61. $\dfrac{\sqrt{8}}{\sqrt{3}+1} = \dfrac{\sqrt{8}}{\sqrt{3}+1} \cdot \dfrac{\sqrt{3}-1}{\sqrt{3}-1}$

$= \dfrac{\sqrt{8}\left(\sqrt{3}-1\right)}{\sqrt{3}^2 - 1^2}$

$= \dfrac{\sqrt{24}-\sqrt{8}}{3-1}$

$= \dfrac{\sqrt{4\cdot 6}-\sqrt{4\cdot 2}}{2}$

$= \dfrac{2\sqrt{6}-2\sqrt{2}}{2}$

$= \dfrac{2\left(\sqrt{6}-\sqrt{2}\right)}{2}$

$= \sqrt{6}-\sqrt{2}$

63. $\dfrac{1}{\sqrt{x}-\sqrt{3}} = \dfrac{1}{\sqrt{x}-\sqrt{3}} \cdot \dfrac{\sqrt{x}+\sqrt{3}}{\sqrt{x}+\sqrt{3}}$

$= \dfrac{\sqrt{x}+\sqrt{3}}{\sqrt{x}^2 - \sqrt{3}^2}$

$= \dfrac{\sqrt{x}+\sqrt{3}}{x-3}$

65. $\dfrac{2-\sqrt{3}}{2+\sqrt{3}} \cdot \dfrac{2-\sqrt{3}}{2-\sqrt{3}} = \dfrac{4-4\sqrt{3}+3}{4-3}$

$= \dfrac{7-4\sqrt{3}}{1}$

$= 7 - 4\sqrt{3}$

67.

$$\frac{\sqrt{5}+4}{2-\sqrt{5}} = \frac{\sqrt{5}+4}{2-\sqrt{5}} \cdot \frac{2+\sqrt{5}}{2+\sqrt{5}}$$

$$= \frac{\left(\sqrt{5}+4\right)\left(2+\sqrt{5}\right)}{2^2-\left(\sqrt{5}\right)^2}$$

$$= \frac{\sqrt{5}\cdot 2 + \sqrt{5}\cdot\sqrt{5} + 4\cdot 2 + 4\cdot\sqrt{5}}{4-5}$$

$$= \frac{2\sqrt{5} + \sqrt{5}^2 + 8 + 4\sqrt{5}}{-1}$$

$$= \frac{2\sqrt{5} + 5 + 8 + 4\sqrt{5}}{-1}$$

$$= \frac{13 + 6\sqrt{5}}{-1}$$

$$= -13 - 6\sqrt{5}$$

69.

$$\frac{10-\sqrt{50}}{5} = \frac{10-\sqrt{5^2\cdot 2}}{5}$$

$$= \frac{10-5\sqrt{2}}{5}$$

$$= \frac{5\left(2-\sqrt{2}\right)}{5}$$

$$= 2 - \sqrt{2}$$

71.

$$\frac{21+\sqrt{98}}{14} = \frac{21+\sqrt{7^2\cdot 2}}{14}$$

$$= \frac{21+7\sqrt{2}}{14}$$

$$= \frac{7\left(3+\sqrt{2}\right)}{7\cdot 2}$$

$$= \frac{3+\sqrt{2}}{2}$$

73.

$$\frac{2-\sqrt{28}}{2} = \frac{2-\sqrt{2^2\cdot 7}}{2}$$

$$= \frac{2-2\sqrt{7}}{2}$$

$$= \frac{2\left(1-\sqrt{7}\right)}{2}$$

$$= 1 - \sqrt{7}$$

75.

$$\frac{14+\sqrt{72}}{6} = \frac{14+\sqrt{6^2\cdot 2}}{6}$$

$$= \frac{14+6\sqrt{2}}{6}$$

$$= \frac{2\left(7+3\sqrt{2}\right)}{2\cdot 3}$$

$$= \frac{7+3\sqrt{2}}{3}$$

77. (a) Condition 1 fails;

$$\sqrt{8x^9} = \sqrt{2^3\cdot x^9} = \sqrt{2\cdot 2^2\cdot x\cdot x^8}$$
$$= 2x^4\sqrt{2x}$$

(b) Condition 2 fails;

$$\frac{5}{\sqrt{5x}} = \frac{5}{\sqrt{5x}}\cdot\frac{\sqrt{5x}}{\sqrt{5x}} = \frac{5\sqrt{5x}}{5x} = \frac{\sqrt{5x}}{x}$$

(c) Condition 3 fails; $\sqrt{\dfrac{1}{3}} = \dfrac{1}{\sqrt{3}}\cdot\dfrac{\sqrt{3}}{\sqrt{3}} = \dfrac{\sqrt{3}}{3}$

79. (a) Condition 2 fails;

$$\frac{3}{\sqrt{x}+1} = \frac{3}{\sqrt{x}+1}\cdot\frac{\sqrt{x}-1}{\sqrt{x}-1} = \frac{3\sqrt{x}-3}{x-1}$$

(b) Condition 1 and 3 fail;

$$\sqrt{\frac{9w^2}{t}} = \sqrt{\frac{3^2 w^2}{t}\cdot\frac{t}{t}} = 3w\frac{\sqrt{t}}{t}$$

(c) Condition 1 fails;

$$\sqrt{24a^5b^9} = \sqrt{6\cdot 2^2 a^5 b^9}$$
$$= \sqrt{6\cdot 2^2\cdot a\cdot a^4\cdot b\cdot b^8}$$
$$= 2a^2 b^4\sqrt{6\cdot a\cdot b}$$
$$= 2a^2 b^4\sqrt{6ab}$$

81. $\sqrt{45} = \sqrt{3^2\cdot 5} = 3\sqrt{5}$

83. $-\sqrt{\dfrac{18w^2}{25}} = -\dfrac{\sqrt{3^2 w^2\cdot 2}}{\sqrt{5^2}} = -\dfrac{3w\sqrt{2}}{5}$

85. $\sqrt{-36}$ is not a real number.

87. $\sqrt{\dfrac{s^2}{t}} = \dfrac{\sqrt{s^2}}{\sqrt{t}} = \dfrac{s}{\sqrt{t}} \cdot \dfrac{\sqrt{t}}{\sqrt{t}} = \dfrac{s\sqrt{t}}{\sqrt{t^2}} = \dfrac{s\sqrt{t}}{t}$

89. $\dfrac{\sqrt{2m^5}}{\sqrt{8m}} = \sqrt{\dfrac{2m^5}{8m}} = \sqrt{\dfrac{m^4}{4}} = \dfrac{\sqrt{m^4}}{\sqrt{4}} = \dfrac{m^2}{2}$

91. $\sqrt{\dfrac{81}{t^3}} = \dfrac{\sqrt{3^4}}{\sqrt{t^2 \cdot t}}$

$= \dfrac{3^2}{t\sqrt{t}}$

$= \dfrac{9}{t\sqrt{t}} \cdot \dfrac{\sqrt{t}}{\sqrt{t}}$

$= \dfrac{9\sqrt{t}}{t\sqrt{t^2}}$

$= \dfrac{9\sqrt{t}}{t \cdot t}$

$= \dfrac{9\sqrt{t}}{t^2}$

93. $\dfrac{3}{\sqrt{11}+\sqrt{5}} = \dfrac{3}{\sqrt{11}+\sqrt{5}} \dfrac{\sqrt{11}-\sqrt{5}}{\sqrt{11}-\sqrt{5}}$

$= \dfrac{3\sqrt{11}-3\sqrt{5}}{11-5} = \dfrac{3\sqrt{11}-3\sqrt{5}}{6}$

$= \dfrac{\sqrt{11}-\sqrt{5}}{2}$

95. $\dfrac{\sqrt{a}+\sqrt{b}}{\sqrt{a}-\sqrt{b}} = \dfrac{\sqrt{a}+\sqrt{b}}{\sqrt{a}-\sqrt{b}} \cdot \dfrac{\sqrt{a}+\sqrt{b}}{\sqrt{a}+\sqrt{b}}$

$= \dfrac{a+2\sqrt{a}\sqrt{b}+b}{a-b} = \dfrac{a+2\sqrt{ab}+b}{a-b}$

97. $m = \dfrac{6-3}{\sqrt{2}-5\sqrt{2}}$

$= \dfrac{3}{-4\sqrt{2}}$

$= -\dfrac{3}{4\sqrt{2}} \cdot \dfrac{\sqrt{2}}{\sqrt{2}}$

$= -\dfrac{3\sqrt{2}}{4\sqrt{2^2}}$

$= -\dfrac{3\sqrt{2}}{4 \cdot 2}$

$= -\dfrac{3\sqrt{2}}{8}$

99. $m = \dfrac{0-(-1)}{4\sqrt{3}-\sqrt{3}}$

$= \dfrac{1}{3\sqrt{3}}$

$= \dfrac{1}{3\sqrt{3}} \cdot \dfrac{\sqrt{3}}{\sqrt{3}}$

$= \dfrac{\sqrt{3}}{3\sqrt{3^2}}$

$= \dfrac{\sqrt{3}}{3 \cdot 3}$

$= \dfrac{\sqrt{3}}{9}$

Problem Recognition Exercises

1. $\sqrt{3} \ \sqrt{6} = \sqrt{3 \cdot 6} = \sqrt{3 \cdot 3 \cdot 2} = 3\sqrt{2}$

3. $\sqrt{3}+\sqrt{6}$ Cannot be simplified further

5. $\dfrac{\sqrt{6}}{\sqrt{3}} = \sqrt{\dfrac{6}{3}} = \sqrt{2}$

7. $3+\sqrt{z} \ \ 3-\sqrt{z} = 3^2 - \sqrt{z}^{\,2} = 9-z$

9. $\left(2\sqrt{5}+1\right)\left(\sqrt{5}-2\right)$

$= 2\sqrt{5}\cdot\sqrt{5}-2\sqrt{5}\cdot 2+\sqrt{5}-2$

$= 2\cdot 5-3\sqrt{5}-2$

$= 8-3\sqrt{5}$

11. $2\sqrt{x^2 y}-3x\sqrt{y}=2x\sqrt{y}-3x\sqrt{y}$

$\qquad\qquad\qquad = -x\sqrt{y}$

13. $-3\sqrt{2}\left(4\sqrt{2}+2\sqrt{3}+1\right)$

$= -3\sqrt{2}\cdot 4\sqrt{2}-3\sqrt{2}\cdot 2\sqrt{3}-3\sqrt{2}$

$= -3\cdot 2\cdot 4-6\sqrt{2}\cdot\sqrt{3}-3\sqrt{2}$

$= -24-6\sqrt{2}\cdot\sqrt{3}-3\sqrt{2}$

$= -24-6\sqrt{6}-3\sqrt{2}$

15. $\dfrac{2}{\sqrt{x}-7}=\dfrac{2}{\sqrt{x}-7}\cdot\dfrac{\sqrt{x}+7}{\sqrt{x}+7}$

$\qquad = \dfrac{2\sqrt{x}+2\cdot 7}{x-49}=\dfrac{2\sqrt{x}+14}{x-49}$

17. $\dfrac{9}{\sqrt{3}}=\dfrac{9}{\sqrt{3}}\cdot\dfrac{\sqrt{3}}{\sqrt{3}}$

$\qquad = \dfrac{9\sqrt{3}}{3}=3\sqrt{3}$

19. $\sqrt{\dfrac{7}{x}}=\sqrt{\dfrac{7}{x}}\cdot\dfrac{\sqrt{x}}{\sqrt{x}}$

$\qquad = \dfrac{\sqrt{7x}}{x}$

21. $\sqrt{y^4 z^{11}}=\sqrt{y^4 z^{10}z}$

$\qquad = y^2 z^5\sqrt{z}$

23. $\sqrt[3]{27p^8}=\sqrt[3]{3^3 p^6 p^2}$

$\qquad = 3p^2\sqrt[3]{p^2}$

25. $\dfrac{\sqrt{10x^3}}{\sqrt{x}}=\sqrt{\dfrac{10x^3}{x}}$

$\qquad = \sqrt{10x^2}=x\sqrt{10}$

27. $6\sqrt{75}-5\sqrt{12}$

$= 6\sqrt{3\cdot 5^2}-5\sqrt{2^2\cdot 3}=6\cdot 5\sqrt{3}-5\cdot 2\sqrt{3}$

$= 30\sqrt{3}-10\sqrt{3}=20\sqrt{3}$

29. $\left(\sqrt{2}+7\right)^2=\left(\sqrt{2}\right)^2+2\left(\sqrt{2}\right)\left(7\right)+7^2$

$\qquad\qquad = 2+14\sqrt{2}+49$

$\qquad\qquad = 51+14\sqrt{2}$

31. $\dfrac{x-5}{\sqrt{x}+\sqrt{5}}$

$= \dfrac{x-5}{\sqrt{x}+\sqrt{5}}\cdot\dfrac{\sqrt{x}-\sqrt{5}}{\sqrt{x}-\sqrt{5}}$

$= \dfrac{x-5}{x-5}\cdot\left(\sqrt{x}-\sqrt{5}\right)$

$= \sqrt{x}-\sqrt{5}$

33. $\left(4\sqrt{x}+\sqrt{y}\right)\cdot\left(\sqrt{x}-3\sqrt{y}\right)$

$= 4\sqrt{x}\left(\sqrt{x}-3\sqrt{y}\right)+\sqrt{y}\left(\sqrt{x}-3\sqrt{y}\right)$

$= 4x-12\sqrt{xy}+\sqrt{xy}-3y$

$= 4x-11\sqrt{xy}-3y$

35. $\sqrt[3]{\dfrac{125}{27}}=\sqrt[3]{\dfrac{5^3}{3^3}}=\dfrac{5}{3}$

37. $\left(\sqrt{x}-6\right)^2=\left(\sqrt{x}\right)^2-2\sqrt{x}\left(6\right)+\left(6\right)^2$

$\qquad\qquad = x-12\sqrt{x}+36$

39. $5\sqrt{a}+7\sqrt{a}-\sqrt{a}=11\sqrt{a}$

41. $\left(\sqrt{u}-3\sqrt{v}\right)\left(\sqrt{u}+3\sqrt{v}\right)$

$= \left(\sqrt{u}\right)^2-\left(3\sqrt{v}\right)^2$

$= u-9v$

43. $4\sqrt{75}-20\sqrt{3}=4\sqrt{5^2\cdot 3}-20\sqrt{3}$

$\qquad\qquad\qquad = 4\cdot 5\sqrt{3}-20\sqrt{3}$

$\qquad\qquad\qquad = 0$

45. $\sqrt{a}\left(\sqrt{a}+2\right)=a+2\cdot\sqrt{a}=a+2\sqrt{a}$

Section 8.6 Practice Exercises

1. **(a)** An equation with one or more radicals containing a variable is called a **radical equation.**

   (b) An **extraneous solution** is a solution to an equation, produced by raising each side of a radical equation to a power, that is not a solution to the original radical equation.

3. $\dfrac{1}{\sqrt{2}+\sqrt{10}} = \dfrac{1}{\sqrt{2}+\sqrt{10}} \cdot \dfrac{\sqrt{2}-\sqrt{10}}{\sqrt{2}-\sqrt{10}}$

   $= \dfrac{\sqrt{2}-\sqrt{10}}{\sqrt{2}^2 - \sqrt{10}^2}$

   $= \dfrac{\sqrt{2}-\sqrt{10}}{2-10}$

   $= \dfrac{\sqrt{2}-\sqrt{10}}{-8}$ or $\dfrac{\sqrt{10}-\sqrt{2}}{8}$

5. $\dfrac{2\sqrt{2}}{\sqrt{3}} = \dfrac{2\sqrt{2}}{\sqrt{3}} \cdot \dfrac{\sqrt{3}}{\sqrt{3}} = \dfrac{2\sqrt{6}}{\sqrt{3^2}} = \dfrac{2\sqrt{6}}{3}$

7. $(x+4)^2 = x^2 + 2(x)(4) + 4^2 = x^2 + 8x + 16$

9. $\sqrt{x}+4^2 = x + 2\sqrt{x}\cdot 4 + 4^2$

   $= x + 8\sqrt{x} + 16$

11. $\sqrt{2x-3}^2 = 2x - 3$

   In this problem the binomial is the radicand. Raising a radicand to a power equivalent to the index gives the value of the radicand..

13. $t+1^2 = t^2 + 2\cdot t + 1$

   $= t^2 + 2t + 1$

15. $\sqrt{t} = 6$

   $\sqrt{t}^2 = 6^2$

   $t = 36$

17. $\sqrt{x+1} = 4$

   $\sqrt{x+1}^2 = 4^2$

   $x + 1 = 16$

   $x = 15$

   Check: $\sqrt{15+1} = \sqrt{16} = 4$ ✓

19. $\sqrt{y-4} = -5$

   The principal square root of a value is never negative. No solution.

21. $\sqrt{5-t} = 0$

   $\sqrt{5-t}^2 = 0^2$

   $5 - t = 0$

   $-t = -5$

   $t = 5$

   Check: $\sqrt{5-5} = \sqrt{0} = 0$ ✓

23. $\sqrt{2n+10} = 3$

   $\sqrt{2n+10}^2 = (3)^2$

   $2n + 10 = 9$

   $2n = -1$

   $n = -\dfrac{1}{2}$

   Check: $\sqrt{2\left(-\dfrac{1}{2}\right)+10} \overset{?}{=} 3$

   $\sqrt{-1+10} \overset{?}{=} 3$

   $\sqrt{9} \overset{?}{=} 3$

   $3 = 3$ ✓

25. $\sqrt{6w} - 8 = -2$

$\sqrt{6w} = 6$

$\sqrt{6w}^2 = (6)^2$

$6w = 36$

$w = 6$

Check: $\sqrt{6 \cdot 6} - 8 \overset{?}{=} -2$

$\sqrt{36} - 8 \overset{?}{=} -2$

$6 - 8 \overset{?}{=} -2$

$-2 = -2 \checkmark$

27. $\sqrt{5a - 4} - 2 = 4$

$\sqrt{5a - 4} = 6$

$\sqrt{5a - 4}^2 = 6^2$

$5a - 4 = 36$

$5a = 40$

$a = 8$

Check: $\sqrt{5(8) - 4} - 2 \overset{?}{=} 4$

$\sqrt{40 - 4} - 2 \overset{?}{=} 4$

$\sqrt{36} - 2 \overset{?}{=} 4$

$6 - 2 \overset{?}{=} 4$

$4 = 4 \checkmark$

29. $\sqrt{2x - 3} + 7 = 3$

$\sqrt{2x - 3} = -4$

$\sqrt{2x - 3}^2 = (-4)^2$

$2x - 3 = 16$

$2x = 19$

$x = \dfrac{19}{2}$

Check: $\sqrt{2\left(\dfrac{19}{2}\right) - 3} + 7 \overset{?}{=} 3$

$\sqrt{19 - 3} + 7 \overset{?}{=} 3$

$\sqrt{16} + 7 \overset{?}{=} 3$

$4 + 7 \overset{?}{=} 3$

$11 \neq 3$

The solution does not check. There is no solution.

31. $5\sqrt{c} = \sqrt{10c + 15}$

$5\sqrt{c}^2 = \sqrt{10c + 15}^2$

$25c = 10c + 15$

$15c = 15$

$c = 1$

Check: $5\sqrt{1} \overset{?}{=} \sqrt{10(1) + 15}$

$5(1) \overset{?}{=} \sqrt{10 + 15}$

$5 \overset{?}{=} \sqrt{25}$

$5 = 5 \checkmark$

33. $\sqrt{x^2 - x} = \sqrt{12}$

$\left(\sqrt{x^2 - x}\right)^2 = \sqrt{12}^2$

$x^2 - x = 12$

$x^2 - x - 12 = 0$

$(x - 4)(x + 3) = 0$

$x - 4 = 0 \quad$ or $\quad x + 3 = 0$

$x = 4 \qquad\qquad x = -3$

Check: $\sqrt{(4)^2 - 4} \overset{?}{=} \sqrt{12}$

$\sqrt{16 - 4} \overset{?}{=} \sqrt{12}$

$\sqrt{12} = \sqrt{12} \checkmark$

$\sqrt{(-3)^2 - (-3)} \overset{?}{=} \sqrt{12}$

$\sqrt{9 + 3} \overset{?}{=} \sqrt{12}$

$\sqrt{12} = \sqrt{12} \checkmark$

35. $\sqrt{9y^2 - 8y + 1} = 3y + 1$

$\left(\sqrt{9y^2 - 8y + 1}\right)^2 = (3y + 1)^2$

$9y^2 - 8y + 1 = 9y^2 + 6y + 1$

$-8y = 6y$

$-14y = 0$

$y = 0$

Check: $\sqrt{9(0)^2 - 8(0) + 1} \overset{?}{=} 3(0) + 1$

$\sqrt{1} \overset{?}{=} 1$

$1 = 1 \checkmark$

37. $\sqrt{x^2 + 4x + 16} = x$

$\sqrt{x^2 + 4x + 16}^2 = x^2$

$x^2 + 4x + 16 = x^2$

$4x + 16 = 0$

$4(x + 4) = 0$

$x = -4$

Check: $\sqrt{(-4)^2 + 4(-4) + 16} \overset{?}{=} -4$

$\sqrt{16 - 16 + 16} \overset{?}{=} -4$

$\sqrt{16} \overset{?}{=} -4$

$4 \neq -4$

The solution does not check. There is no solution

39. $\sqrt{2k^2 - 3k - 4} = k$

$\left(\sqrt{2k^2 - 3k - 4}\right)^2 = (k)^2$

$2k^2 - 3k - 4 = k^2$

$k^2 - 3k - 4 = 0$

$(k - 4)(k + 1) = 0$

$k - 4 = 0 \quad \text{or} \quad k + 1 = 0$

$k = 4 \qquad\qquad k = -1$

Check: $\sqrt{2(4)^2 - 3(4) - 4} \overset{?}{=} 4$

$\sqrt{2(16) - 3(4) - 4} \overset{?}{=} 4$

$\sqrt{32 - 12 - 4} \overset{?}{=} 4$

$\sqrt{16} \overset{?}{=} 4$

$4 = 4 \checkmark$

$\sqrt{2(-1)^2 - 3(-1) - 4} \overset{?}{=} -1$

$\sqrt{2(1) - 3(-1) - 4} \overset{?}{=} -1$

$\sqrt{2 + 3 - 4} \overset{?}{=} -1$

$\sqrt{1} \overset{?}{=} -1$

$1 \neq -1$

The solution $k = -1$ does not check.

41. $\sqrt{y + 1} = y + 1$

$\sqrt{y + 1}^2 = (y + 1)^2$

$y + 1 = y^2 + 2y + 1$

$0 = y^2 + y$

$0 = y(y + 1)$

$y = 0 \quad \text{or} \quad y + 1 = 0$

$y = -1$

Check: $\sqrt{0 + 1} \overset{?}{=} 0 + 1$

$\sqrt{1} \overset{?}{=} 1$

$1 = 1 \checkmark$

$\sqrt{-1 + 1} \overset{?}{=} -1 + 1$

$\sqrt{0} \overset{?}{=} 0$

$0 = 0 \checkmark$

43. $\sqrt{2m+1}+7=m$

$\sqrt{2m+1}=m-7$

$\sqrt{2m+1}^{\,2}=(m-7)^2$

$2m+1=m^2-14m+49$

$0=m^2-16m+48$

$0=(m-4)(m-12)$

$m-4=0 \quad\text{or}\quad m-12=0$

$m=4 \qquad\qquad m=12$

Check: $\sqrt{2(4)+1}+7\overset{?}{=}4$

$\sqrt{8+1}+7\overset{?}{=}4$

$\sqrt{9}+7\overset{?}{=}4$

$3+7\overset{?}{=}4$

$10\neq 4$

$m=4$ does not check.

$\sqrt{2(12)+1}+7\overset{?}{=}12$

$\sqrt{24+1}+7\overset{?}{=}12$

$\sqrt{25}+7\overset{?}{=}12$

$5+7\overset{?}{=}12$

$12=12\checkmark$

45. $\sqrt[3]{p-5}-\sqrt[3]{2p+1}=0$

$\sqrt[3]{p-5}=\sqrt[3]{2p+1}$

$\sqrt[3]{p-5}^{\,3}=\sqrt[3]{2p+1}^{\,3}$

$p-5=2p+1$

$-p-5=1$

$-p=6$

$p=-6$

Check: $\sqrt[3]{-6-5}\overset{?}{=}\sqrt[3]{2(-6)+1}$

$\sqrt[3]{-11}\overset{?}{=}\sqrt[3]{-12+1}$

$\sqrt[3]{-11}=\sqrt[3]{-11}\checkmark$

47. $\sqrt[3]{a-3}=\sqrt[3]{5a+1}$

$\sqrt[3]{a-3}^{\,3}=\sqrt[3]{5a+1}^{\,3}$

$a-3=5a+1$

$-4a=4$

$a=-1$

Check: $\sqrt[3]{-1-3}\overset{?}{=}\sqrt[3]{5(-1)+1}$

$\sqrt[3]{-4}\overset{?}{=}\sqrt[3]{-5+1}$

$\sqrt[3]{-4}=\sqrt[3]{-4}\checkmark$

49. $\sqrt{x+10}=1$

$\sqrt{x+10}^{\,2}=(1)^2$

$x+10=1$

$x=-9$

Check: $\sqrt{-9+10}\overset{?}{=}1$

$\sqrt{1}\overset{?}{=}1$

$1=1\checkmark$

51.
$$\sqrt{2x} = x - 4$$
$$\sqrt{2x}^{\,2} = (x-4)^2$$
$$2x = x^2 - 8x + 16$$
$$x^2 - 10x + 16 = 0$$
$$(x-8)(x-2) = 0$$
$$x - 8 = 0 \quad \text{or} \quad x - 2 = 0$$
$$x = 8 \qquad\qquad x = 2$$

Check: $\sqrt{2(8)} \overset{?}{=} 8 - 4$

$\sqrt{16} \overset{?}{=} 4$

$4 = 4 \checkmark$

$\sqrt{2(2)} \overset{?}{=} 2 - 4$

$\sqrt{4} \overset{?}{=} -2$

$2 \neq -2$

The solution $x = 2$ does not check.

53.
$$\sqrt[3]{x+1} = 2$$
$$\sqrt[3]{x+1}^{\,3} = (2)^3$$
$$x + 1 = 8$$
$$x = 7$$

Check: $\sqrt[3]{7+1} \overset{?}{=} 2$

$\sqrt[3]{8} \overset{?}{=} 2$

$2 = 2 \checkmark$

55. $v = 8\sqrt{x}$

(a) $v = 8\sqrt{100}$
$v = 8(10)$
$v = 80$
The velocity of an object that has fallen 100 ft is 80 ft/s.

(b)
$$136 = 8\sqrt{x}$$
$$17 = \sqrt{x}$$
$$(17)^2 = \sqrt{x}^{\,2}$$
$$289 = x$$
An object with a velocity of 136 ft/s has fallen 289 ft.

57. $y = 8\sqrt{t};\ 0 \leq t \leq 40$

(a) $y = 8\sqrt{4}$
$y = 8(2)$
$y = 16$
The height of the plant after 4 weeks is 16 in.

(b)
$$40 = 8\sqrt{t}$$
$$5 = \sqrt{t}$$
$$(5)^2 = \sqrt{t}^{\,2}$$
$$25 = t$$
It will take about 25 weeks for the plant to reach a height of 40 inches.

59.
$$\sqrt{5x-9} = \sqrt{5x} - 3$$
$$\sqrt{5x-9}^{\,2} = (\sqrt{5x} - 3)^2$$
$$5x - 9 = 5x + 9 - 6\sqrt{5x}$$
$$-18 = -6\sqrt{5x}$$
$$3 = \sqrt{5x}$$
$$9 = 5x \quad \text{or } x = \frac{9}{5}$$

Check: $\sqrt{5\left(\dfrac{9}{5}\right) - 9} \overset{?}{=} \sqrt{5\left(\dfrac{9}{5}\right)} - 3$

$\sqrt{9-9} \overset{?}{=} \sqrt{9} - 3$

$0 \overset{?}{=} 3 - 3$

$0 = 0 \checkmark$

61.
$$\sqrt{2m+6} = 1 + \sqrt{7-2m}$$
$$\sqrt{2m+6}^{\,2} = (1+\sqrt{7-2m})^2$$
$$2m+6 = 1 + 2\sqrt{7-2m} + 7 - 2m$$
$$4m = 2 + 2\sqrt{7-2m}$$
$$4m-2 = 2\sqrt{7-2m}$$
$$\overline{2m-1}^{\,2} = \sqrt{7-2m}^{\,2}$$
$$4m^2 - 4m + 1 = 7 - 2m$$
$$4m^2 - 2m - 6 = 0$$
$$0 = (4m-6)(m+1)$$
$$m = -1 \ \text{ or } \ m = \frac{3}{2}$$

Check:
$$\sqrt{2(-1)+6} \overset{?}{=} 1 + \sqrt{7-2(-1)}$$
$$\sqrt{-2+6} \overset{?}{=} 1 + \sqrt{7-2(-1)}$$
$$\sqrt{4} \overset{?}{=} 1 + \sqrt{7+2}$$
$$2 \overset{?}{=} 1 + 3$$
$$2 \neq 4$$

The solution $m = -1$ does not check
$$\sqrt{2\left(\frac{3}{2}\right)+6} \overset{?}{=} 1 + \sqrt{7-2\left(\frac{3}{2}\right)}$$
$$\sqrt{9} \overset{?}{=} 1 + \sqrt{7-3}$$
$$3 \overset{?}{=} 1 + 2$$
$$3 = 3 ✓$$

Section 8.7 Practice Exercises

1. $\sqrt[3]{125}$

   (a) 3

   (b) 125

3. $\sqrt[4]{81}^{\,3} = 3^3 = 27$

5. $\sqrt[3]{(a+1)^3} = a+1$

7. $81^{1/2} = \sqrt{81} = 9$

9. $125^{1/3} = \sqrt[3]{125} = 5$

11. $81^{1/4} = \sqrt[4]{81} = 3$

13. $(-8)^{1/3} = \sqrt[3]{-8} = -2$

15. $-8^{1/3} = -\sqrt[3]{8} = -2$

17. $36^{-1/2} = \dfrac{1}{36^{1/2}} = \dfrac{1}{\sqrt{36}} = \dfrac{1}{6}$

19. $x^{1/3} = \sqrt[3]{x}$

21. $(4a)^{1/2} = \sqrt{4a} = 2\sqrt{a}$

23. $(yz)^{1/5} = \sqrt[5]{yz}$

25. $(u^2)^{1/3} = \sqrt[3]{u^2}$

27. $5q^{1/2} = 5\sqrt{q}$

29. $\left(\dfrac{x}{9}\right)^{1/2} = \sqrt{\dfrac{x}{9}} = \dfrac{\sqrt{x}}{\sqrt{9}} = \dfrac{\sqrt{x}}{3}$

31. $a^{m/n} = \sqrt[n]{a^m}$ or $\sqrt[n]{a}^{\,m}$ provided the root exists.

33. $16^{3/4} = \sqrt[4]{16}^{\,3} = 2^3 = 8$

35. $27^{-2/3} = \dfrac{1}{27^{2/3}} = \dfrac{1}{\sqrt[3]{27}^{\,2}} = \dfrac{1}{3^2} = \dfrac{1}{9}$

37. $(-8)^{5/3} = \sqrt[3]{-8}^{\,5} = (-2)^5 = -32$

39. $\left(\dfrac{1}{4}\right)^{-1/2} = 4^{1/2} = \sqrt{4} = 2$

41. $y^{9/2} = \sqrt{y}^{\,9}$

43. $(c^5 d)^{1/3} = \sqrt[3]{c^5 d}$

45. $(qr)^{-1/5} = \dfrac{1}{(qr)^{1/5}} = \dfrac{1}{\sqrt[5]{qr}}$

47. $6y^{2/3} = 6 \sqrt[3]{y}^{\,2}$

49. $\sqrt[3]{y^2} = y^{2/3}$

51. $5\sqrt{x} = 5x^{1/2}$

53. $\sqrt[3]{xy} = (xy)^{1/3}$

55. $\sqrt[4]{m^3 n} = (m^3 n)^{1/4}$

57. $x^{1/4} x^{3/4} = x^{\frac{1}{4}+\frac{3}{4}} = x^{4/4} = x$

59. $(y^{1/5})^{10} = y^{\frac{1}{5}(10)} = y^{10/5} = y^2$

61. $6^{-1/5} 6^{6/5} = 6^{-\frac{1}{5}+\frac{6}{5}} = 6^{5/5} = 6$

63. $(a^{1/3} a^{1/4})^{12} = a^{12/3} a^{12/4} = a^4 a^3 = a^7$

65. $\dfrac{y^{5/3}}{y^{1/3}} = y^{\frac{5}{3}-\frac{1}{3}} = y^{4/3}$

67. $\dfrac{2^{4/3}}{2^{1/3}} = 2^{\frac{4}{3}-\frac{1}{3}} = 2^{3/3} = 2$

69. $x^{-2} y^{1/3} \, ^{1/2} = x^{-1} y^{1/6} = \dfrac{y^{1/6}}{x}$

71. $\left(\dfrac{w^{-2}}{z^{-4}}\right)^{-3/2} = \dfrac{w^3}{z^6}$

73. $(5a^2 c^{-1/2} d^{1/2})^2 = 5^2 a^4 c^{-2/2} d^{2/2}$
$$= 25a^4 c^{-1} d$$
$$= \dfrac{25a^4 d}{c}$$

75. $\left(\dfrac{x^{-2/3}}{y^{-3/4}}\right)^{12} = \dfrac{x^{-24/3}}{y^{-36/4}} = \dfrac{x^{-8}}{y^{-9}} = \dfrac{y^9}{x^8}$

77. $\left(\dfrac{16w^{-2}z}{2wz^{-8}}\right)^{1/3} = (8w^{-3}z^9)^{1/3}$
$$= 8^{1/3} w^{-3/3} z^{9/3}$$
$$= \sqrt[3]{8} w^{-1} z^3$$
$$= \dfrac{2z^3}{w}$$

79. $(25x^2 y^4 z^3)^{1/2} = 25^{1/2} x^{2/2} y^{4/2} z^{3/2}$
$$= \sqrt{25} x^1 y^2 z^{3/2}$$
$$= 5xy^2 z^{3/2}$$

81. $s = A^{1/2}$

 (a) $s = 100^{1/2}$
  $s = 10$
  The length of the sides of a square with an area of 100 in.^{2} is 10 in.

 (b) $s = 72^{1/2}$
  $s \approx 8.49$
  The length of the sides of a square with an area of 72 in.^{2} is about 8.49 in.

83. $r = \left(\dfrac{A}{P}\right)^{1/t} - 1$

 (a) $r = \left(\dfrac{16,802}{10,000}\right)^{1/5} - 1$
  $r \approx 0.109$
  The rate needed to grow \$10,000 to \$16,802 in 5 years is 10.9%.

 (b) $r = \left(\dfrac{18,000}{10,000}\right)^{1/7} - 1$
  $r \approx 0.088$
  The rate needed to grow \$10,000 to \$18,000 in 7 years is 8.8%.

 (c) The account in part a

85. They are *not* the same. For example:

$$(64+36)^{1/2} = 100^{1/2} = 10$$

but

$$64^{1/2} + 36^{1/2} = 8 + 6 = 14$$

As you can see, the resulting answers are not equal.

87.
$$\left(\frac{1}{8}\right)^{-2/3} + \left(\frac{1}{4}\right)^{-1/2} = 8^{2/3} + 4^{1/2}$$
$$= \sqrt[3]{8}^{\,2} + \sqrt{4}$$
$$= 2^2 + 2$$
$$= 4 + 2$$
$$= 6$$

89.
$$\left(\frac{1}{16}\right)^{1/4} - \left(\frac{1}{49}\right)^{1/2} = \sqrt[4]{\frac{1}{16}} - \sqrt{\frac{1}{49}}$$
$$= \frac{1}{2} - \frac{1}{7}$$
$$= \frac{7}{14} - \frac{2}{14}$$
$$= \frac{5}{14}$$

91.
$$\left(\frac{a^2 b^{1/2} c^{-2}}{a^{-3/4} b^0 c^{1/8}}\right)^8 = \frac{a^{16} b^{8/2} c^{-16}}{a^{-24/4} b^0 c^{8/8}}$$
$$= \frac{a^{16} b^4 c^{-16}}{a^{-6}(1)c^1}$$
$$= a^{16-(-6)} b^4 c^{-16-1}$$
$$= a^{22} b^4 c^{-17}$$
$$= \frac{a^{22} b^4}{c^{17}}$$

Group Activity

1. $\sqrt{28} \approx 5.2915$

```
              5
1/2(Ans+28/Ans)
            5.3
1/2(Ans+28/Ans)
      5.291509434
1/2(Ans+28/Ans)
      5.291502622
```

Chapter 8 Review Exercises

Section 8.1

1. Principal square root: 14
Negative square root: −14

3. Principal square root: 0.8
Negative square root: −0.8

5. There is no real number b such that $b^2 = -64$.

7. $-\sqrt{144} = -12$

9. $\sqrt{-144}$ is not a real number.

11. $\sqrt{y^2} = |y|$

13. $\sqrt[4]{y^4} = |y|$

15. $-\sqrt[4]{625} = -5$

17. $\sqrt[4]{\dfrac{81}{t^8}} = \dfrac{\sqrt[4]{81}}{\sqrt[4]{t^8}} = \dfrac{3}{t^2}$

19. $r = \sqrt{\dfrac{A}{\pi}}$

    (a) $r = \sqrt{\dfrac{160}{\pi}}$

    $r \approx 7.1$

    The radius of the garden is about 7.1 m.

    (b) $r = \sqrt{\dfrac{1600}{\pi}}$

    $r \approx 22.6$

    The radius of the fountain is about 22.6 ft.

21. $b^2 + \sqrt{5}$

23. The quotient of 2 and the principal square root of p

25. Let x represent the distance up the house the ladder is placed.

$$5^2 + x^2 = 13^2$$
$$25 + x^2 = 169$$
$$x^2 = 144$$
$$x = 12$$

The ladder is placed 12 ft up the side of the house.

Section 8.2

27. $\sqrt{x^{17}} = \sqrt{x^{16} \cdot x} = x^8 \sqrt{x}$

29. $\sqrt{28} = \sqrt{4 \cdot 7} = 2\sqrt{7}$

31. $\sqrt[3]{27 y^{10}} = \sqrt[3]{27 y^9 \cdot y} = 3 y^3 \sqrt[3]{y}$

33. $\sqrt{\dfrac{c^5}{c^3}} = \sqrt{c^2} = c$

35. $\sqrt{\dfrac{200 y^5}{2y}} = \sqrt{100 y^4} = 10 y^2$

37. $\sqrt[3]{\dfrac{48 x^4}{6x}} = \sqrt[3]{8 x^3} = \sqrt[3]{2^3 x^3} = 2x$

39. $\dfrac{5\sqrt{12}}{2} = \dfrac{5\sqrt{2^2 \cdot 3}}{2} = \dfrac{5 \cdot 2\sqrt{3}}{2} = 5\sqrt{3}$

41. $\dfrac{12 - \sqrt{49}}{5} = \dfrac{12 - \sqrt{7^2}}{5} = \dfrac{12 - 7}{5} = \dfrac{5}{5} = 1$

Section 8.3

43. $8\sqrt{6} - \sqrt{6} = 7\sqrt{6}$

45. $x\sqrt{20} - 2\sqrt{45 x^2} = x\sqrt{4 \cdot 5} - 2\sqrt{9 x^2 \cdot 5}$
$$= 2x\sqrt{5} - 2 \cdot 3 x\sqrt{5}$$
$$= 2x\sqrt{5} - 6x\sqrt{5}$$
$$= -4x\sqrt{5}$$

47. $3\sqrt{75} - 4\sqrt{28} + \sqrt{7}$
$$= 3\sqrt{5^2 \cdot 3} - 4\sqrt{2^2 \cdot 7} + \sqrt{7}$$
$$= 3 \cdot 5\sqrt{3} - 4 \cdot 2\sqrt{7} + \sqrt{7}$$
$$= 15\sqrt{3} - 8\sqrt{7} + \sqrt{7}$$
$$= 15\sqrt{3} - 7\sqrt{7}$$

49. $7\sqrt{3 x^9} - 3 x^4 \sqrt{75x}$
$$= 7\sqrt{3x \cdot x^8} - 3 x^4 \sqrt{3x \cdot 25}$$
$$= 7 \cdot x^4 \sqrt{3x} - 3 x^4 \cdot 5\sqrt{3x}$$
$$= 7 x^4 \sqrt{3x} - 15 x^4 \sqrt{3x}$$
$$= -8 x^4 \sqrt{3x}$$

51. $\sqrt{2} + \sqrt{98} + \sqrt{32} = \sqrt{2} + \sqrt{49 \cdot 2} + \sqrt{16 \cdot 2}$
$$= \sqrt{2} + 7\sqrt{2} + 4\sqrt{2}$$
$$= 12\sqrt{2} \text{ ft}$$

Section 8.4

53. $\sqrt{5} \cdot \sqrt{125} = \sqrt{5 \cdot 125} = \sqrt{625} = 25$

55. $5\sqrt{6} \ \ 7\sqrt{2x} = (5 \cdot 7) \ \sqrt{6} \cdot \sqrt{2x}$
$$= 35\sqrt{6 \cdot 2x}$$
$$= 35\sqrt{12x}$$
$$= 35\sqrt{4 \cdot 3x}$$
$$= 35 \cdot 2\sqrt{3x}$$
$$= 70\sqrt{3x}$$

57. $8\sqrt{m} \ \sqrt{m} + 3 = 8\sqrt{m} \cdot \sqrt{m} + 8\sqrt{m} \cdot 3$
$$= 8\sqrt{m^2} + 24\sqrt{m}$$
$$= 8m + 24\sqrt{m}$$

59. $5\sqrt{2} + \sqrt{13} \ \ -\sqrt{2} - 3\sqrt{13} = -5\sqrt{2} \cdot \sqrt{2} - 5\sqrt{2} \cdot 3\sqrt{13} - \sqrt{13} \cdot \sqrt{2} - \sqrt{13} \cdot 3\sqrt{13}$
$$= -5\sqrt{2 \cdot 2} - (5 \cdot 3)\sqrt{2 \cdot 13} - \sqrt{13 \cdot 2} - 3\sqrt{13 \cdot 13}$$
$$= -5\sqrt{4} - 15\sqrt{26} - \sqrt{26} - 3\sqrt{169}$$
$$= -5 \cdot 2 - 15\sqrt{26} - \sqrt{26} - 3 \cdot 13$$
$$= -10 - 16\sqrt{26} - 39$$
$$= -49 - 16\sqrt{26}$$

61. $\quad 8\sqrt{w} - \sqrt{z} \ \ 8\sqrt{w} + \sqrt{z}$
$$= \ 8\sqrt{w}^{\ 2} - \ \sqrt{z}^{\ 2}$$
$$= 64w - z$$

63. $V = \sqrt{10} \cdot \sqrt{5} \cdot \sqrt{6}$
$\quad V = \sqrt{300}$
$\quad V = \sqrt{100 \cdot 3}$
$\quad V = 10\sqrt{3} \ \text{m}^3$

Section 8.5

65. $\dfrac{\sqrt{a^{11}}}{\sqrt{a}} = \sqrt{\dfrac{a^{11}}{a}} = \sqrt{a^{10}} = a^5$

67. $\dfrac{\sqrt{96y^3}}{\sqrt{6y^2}} = \sqrt{\dfrac{96y^3}{6y^2}} = \sqrt{16y} = \sqrt{4^2 y} = 4\sqrt{y}$

69. Multiply both the numerator and denominator by the quantity in b
$$\dfrac{w}{\sqrt{w} - 4} = \dfrac{w}{\sqrt{w} - 4} \cdot \dfrac{\sqrt{w} + 4}{\sqrt{w} + 4}$$
$$= \dfrac{w\sqrt{w} + 4w}{w - 16}$$

71. $\sqrt{\dfrac{18}{y}} = \dfrac{\sqrt{18}}{\sqrt{y}}$
$$= \dfrac{\sqrt{18}}{\sqrt{y}} \cdot \dfrac{\sqrt{y}}{\sqrt{y}}$$
$$= \dfrac{\sqrt{18y}}{\sqrt{y^2}}$$
$$= \dfrac{\sqrt{9 \cdot 2y}}{y}$$
$$= \dfrac{3\sqrt{2y}}{y}$$

73. $\dfrac{10}{\sqrt{7}-\sqrt{2}} = \dfrac{10}{\sqrt{7}-\sqrt{2}} \cdot \dfrac{\sqrt{7}+\sqrt{2}}{\sqrt{7}+\sqrt{2}}$

$= \dfrac{10\ \sqrt{7}+\sqrt{2}}{\sqrt{7}^{\,2} - \sqrt{2}^{\,2}}$

$= \dfrac{10\ \sqrt{7}+\sqrt{2}}{7-2}$

$= \dfrac{10\ \sqrt{7}+\sqrt{2}}{5}$

$= 2\ \sqrt{7}+\sqrt{2}$

$= 2\sqrt{7}+2\sqrt{2}$

75. $\dfrac{\sqrt{7}+3}{\sqrt{7}-3} = \dfrac{\sqrt{7}+3}{\sqrt{7}-3} \cdot \dfrac{\sqrt{7}+3}{\sqrt{7}+3}$

$= \dfrac{\sqrt{7}+3^{\,2}}{\sqrt{7}^{\,2}-3^2}$

$= \dfrac{\sqrt{7}^{\,2}+2\ \sqrt{7}\ (3)+3^2}{7-9}$

$= \dfrac{7+6\sqrt{7}+9}{-2}$

$= \dfrac{16+6\sqrt{7}}{-2}$

$= \dfrac{2\ 8+3\sqrt{7}}{-2}$

$= -8-3\sqrt{7}$

Section 8.6

77. $\sqrt{p+6} = 12$

$\sqrt{p+6}^{\,2} = 12^2$

$p+6 = 144$

$p = 138$

Check: $\sqrt{138+6} \overset{?}{=} 12$

$\sqrt{144} \overset{?}{=} 12$

$12 = 12\ \checkmark$

79. $\sqrt{3x-17} - 10 = 0$

$\sqrt{3x-17} = 10$

$\sqrt{3x-17}^{\,2} = 10^2$

$3x-17 = 100$

$3x = 117$

$x = 39$

Check: $\sqrt{3(39)-17} - 10 \overset{?}{=} 0$

$\sqrt{117-17} - 10 \overset{?}{=} 0$

$\sqrt{100} - 10 \overset{?}{=} 0$

$10 - 10 \overset{?}{=} 0$

$0 = 0\ \checkmark$

81. $\sqrt{2z+2} = \sqrt{3z-5}$

$\sqrt{2z+2}^{\,2} = \sqrt{3z-5}^{\,2}$

$2z+2 = 3z-5$

$-z+2 = -5$

$-z = -7$

$z = 7$

Check: $\sqrt{2(7)+2} \overset{?}{=} \sqrt{3(7)-5}$

$\sqrt{14+2} \overset{?}{=} \sqrt{21-5}$

$\sqrt{16} \overset{?}{=} \sqrt{16}$

$4 = 4\ \checkmark$

83. $\sqrt{2m+5} = m+1$

$\sqrt{2m+5}^{\,2} = (m+1)^2$

$2m+5 = m^2 + 2m + 1$

$0 = m^2 - 4$

$0 = (m-2)(m+2)$

$m-2 = 0 \quad \text{or} \quad m+2 = 0$

$m = 2 \qquad\qquad m = -2$

Check: $\sqrt{2(2)+5} \overset{?}{=} 2+1$

$\sqrt{4+5} \overset{?}{=} 3$

$\sqrt{9} \overset{?}{=} 3$

$3 = 3 \checkmark$

$\sqrt{2(-2)+5} \overset{?}{=} -2+1$

$\sqrt{-4+5} \overset{?}{=} -1$

$\sqrt{1} \neq -1$

The principal square root of 1 is not -1, therefore $m = -2$ is not a solution of the equation.

85. $\sqrt[3]{2y+13} = -5$

$\sqrt[3]{2y+13}^{\,3} = (-5)^3$

$2y+13 = -125$

$2y = -138$

$y = -69$

Check: $\sqrt[3]{2(-69)+13} \overset{?}{=} -5$

$\sqrt[3]{-138+13} \overset{?}{=} -5$

$\sqrt[3]{-125} \overset{?}{=} -5$

$-5 = -5 \checkmark$

Section 8.7

87. $(-27)^{1/3} = \sqrt[3]{-27} = -3$

89. $-16^{1/4} = -\sqrt[4]{16} = -2$

91. $4^{-3/2} = \dfrac{1}{4^{3/2}} = \dfrac{1}{\sqrt{4}^{\,3}} = \dfrac{1}{2^3} = \dfrac{1}{8}$

93. $z^{1/5} = \sqrt[5]{z}$

95. $(w^3)^{1/4} = \sqrt[4]{w^3}$

97. $\sqrt[5]{a^2} = a^{2/5}$

99. $\sqrt[5]{a^2 b^4} = (a^2 b^4)^{1/5}$

101. $y^{2/3} y^{4/3} = y^{\frac{2}{3}+\frac{4}{3}} = y^{6/3} = y^2$

103. $\dfrac{6^{4/5}}{6^{1/5}} = 6^{\frac{4}{5}-\frac{1}{5}} = 6^{3/5}$

105. $(64a^3 b^6)^{1/3} = 64^{1/3} a^{3/3} b^{6/3} = 4ab^2$

107. $r = \left(\dfrac{V}{\pi h}\right)^{1/2}$

$r = \left(\dfrac{150.8}{12\pi}\right)^{1/2}$

$r \approx 2.0$

The radius is about 2.0 cm.

Chapter 8 Test

1. 1. The radicand has no factor raised to a power greater than or equal to the index.

2. There are no radicals in the denominator of a fraction.

3. The radicand does not contain a fraction.

3. $\sqrt[3]{48y^4} = \sqrt[3]{8y^3 \cdot 6y} = 2y\sqrt[3]{6y}$

5. $\sqrt{\dfrac{5a^6}{81}} = \dfrac{\sqrt{5a^6}}{\sqrt{81}} = \dfrac{a^3\sqrt{5}}{9}$

7. $\dfrac{2}{\sqrt{5}+6} = \dfrac{2}{\sqrt{5}+6} \cdot \dfrac{\sqrt{5}-6}{\sqrt{5}-6}$

$= \dfrac{2\left(\sqrt{5}-6\right)}{\sqrt{5}^2-6^2}$

$= \dfrac{2\sqrt{5}-12}{5-36}$

$= \dfrac{2\sqrt{5}-12}{-31}$ or $\dfrac{12-2\sqrt{5}}{31}$

9. $x = 56t\sqrt{3}$

   (a) $x = 56\sqrt{3}(1)$

      $x \approx 97$

     Its horizontal distance is about 97 ft.

11. $\sqrt{3}\left(4\sqrt{2}-5\sqrt{3}\right) = \sqrt{3}\cdot 4\sqrt{2} - \sqrt{3}\cdot 5\sqrt{3}$

$= 4\sqrt{2\cdot 3} - 5\sqrt{3\cdot 3}$

$= 4\sqrt{6} - 5\sqrt{3^2}$

$= 4\sqrt{6} - 5\cdot 3$

$= 4\sqrt{6} - 15$

13. $\sqrt{360} + \sqrt{250} - \sqrt{40}$

$= \sqrt{36\cdot 10} + \sqrt{25\cdot 10} - \sqrt{4\cdot 10}$

$= 6\sqrt{10} + 5\sqrt{10} - 2\sqrt{10}$

$= 9\sqrt{10}$

15. $\left(6\sqrt{2}-\sqrt{5}\right)\left(\sqrt{2}+4\sqrt{5}\right)$

$= 6\sqrt{2}\cdot\sqrt{2} + 6\sqrt{2}\cdot 4\sqrt{5} - \sqrt{5}\cdot\sqrt{2} - \sqrt{5}\cdot 4\sqrt{5}$

$= 6\sqrt{2\cdot 2} + (6\cdot 4)\sqrt{2\cdot 5} - \sqrt{5\cdot 2} - 4\sqrt{5\cdot 5}$

$= 6\sqrt{2^2} + 24\sqrt{10} - \sqrt{10} - 4\sqrt{5^2}$

$= 6\cdot 2 + 23\sqrt{10} - 4\cdot 5$

$= 12 + 23\sqrt{10} - 20$

$= -8 + 23\sqrt{10}$

17. $\left(4-3\sqrt{x}\right)\left(4+3\sqrt{x}\right) = (4)^2 - \left(3\sqrt{x}\right)^2$

$= 16 - 9x$

19. $\dfrac{6}{\sqrt{7}-\sqrt{3}} \cdot \dfrac{\sqrt{7}+\sqrt{3}}{\sqrt{7}+\sqrt{3}} = \dfrac{6\left(\sqrt{7}+\sqrt{3}\right)}{7-3}$

$= \dfrac{6\left(\sqrt{7}+\sqrt{3}\right)}{4}$

$= \dfrac{3\left(\sqrt{7}+\sqrt{3}\right)}{2}$

$= \dfrac{3\sqrt{7}+3\sqrt{3}}{2}$

21. $\sqrt{2x+7}+6 = 2$

     $\sqrt{2x+7} = -4$

The principal square root of a value is never negative, therefore this equation has no solution.

23. $\sqrt[3]{x+6} = \sqrt[3]{2x-8}$

    $\left(\sqrt[3]{x+6}\right)^3 = \left(\sqrt[3]{2x-8}\right)^3$

      $x+6 = 2x-8$

     $-x+6 = -8$

       $-x = -14$

        $x = 14$

   Check: $\sqrt[3]{14+6} \overset{?}{=} \sqrt[3]{2(14)-8}$

             $\sqrt[3]{20} = \sqrt[3]{20}$ ✓

25. $10{,}000^{3/4} = \left(\sqrt[4]{10{,}000}\right)^3 = 10^3 = 1000$

27. $x^{3/5} = \sqrt[5]{x^3}$ or $\left(\sqrt[5]{x}\right)^3$

29. $\sqrt[4]{ab^3} = \left(ab^3\right)^{1/4}$

31. $\dfrac{5^{4/5}}{5^{1/5}} = 5^{\frac{4}{5}-\frac{1}{5}} = 5^{3/5}$

Cumulative Review Exercises
Chapters 1–8

1. $\dfrac{|-3-12 \div 6+2|}{\sqrt{5^2-4^2}} = \dfrac{|-3-2+2|}{\sqrt{25-16}}$

$= \dfrac{|-3|}{\sqrt{9}}$

$= \dfrac{3}{3}$

$= 1$

3. $\left(\dfrac{1}{3}\right)^0 - \left(\dfrac{1}{4}\right)^{-2} = 1 - 4^2 = 1-16 = -15$

5. $\dfrac{14x^3y - 7x^2y^2 + 28xy^2}{7x^2y^2}$

$= \dfrac{14x^3y}{7x^2y^2} - \dfrac{7x^2y^2}{7x^2y^2} + \dfrac{28xy^2}{7x^2y^2}$

$= \dfrac{2x}{y} - 1 + \dfrac{4}{x}$

9.
$$\dfrac{1}{5} + \dfrac{z}{z-5} = \dfrac{5}{z-5}$$

$$5(z-5)\left(\dfrac{1}{5}\right) + 5(z-5)\left(\dfrac{z}{z-5}\right) = 5(z-5)\left(\dfrac{5}{z-5}\right)$$

$$(z-5) + 5z = 5(5)$$

$$z - 5 + 5z = 25$$

$$6z - 5 = 25$$

$$6z = 30$$

$$z = 5$$

$z = 5$ is not in the domain, so there is no solution.

7.
$$10x^2 = x+2$$

$$10x^2 - x - 2 = 0$$

$$10x^2 + 4x - 5x - 2 = 0$$

$$2x(5x+2) - 1(5x+2) = 0$$

$$(5x+2)(2x-1) = 0$$

$$5x+2 = 0 \quad \text{or} \quad 2x-1 = 0$$

$$5x = -2 \qquad\qquad 2x = 1$$

$$x = -\dfrac{2}{5} \qquad\qquad x = \dfrac{1}{2}$$

11. $3y = 6$

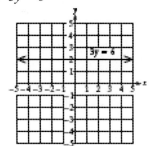

(b) $2770 = 210x + 250$
$$2520 = 210x$$
$$12 = x$$
The cost of renting office space for 12 months is $2770.

(c) $m = 210$
The increase in cost is 210 per month.

(d) y-intercept: $y = 210(0) + 250$
$$y = 250 \qquad (0, 250)$$
The down payment of renting the office space is $250.

13. First, use the slope formula to determine the slope of the line passing through the points.
$$m = \frac{4-(-1)}{-3-2} = \frac{5}{-5} = -1$$
Second, use the value found for the slope, one of the given points, and the point-slope formula to determine the equation of the line.
$$y - (-1) = -1(x - 2)$$
$$y + 1 = -x + 2$$
$$y = -x + 1$$

$$12x - 20y = 92$$
$$\underline{10x + 20y = -70}$$
$$22x \qquad = 22$$
$$x = 1$$

Substitute the value found for x into one of the given equations to find a value for y.
$$3(1) - 5y = 23$$
$$3 - 5y = 23$$
$$-5y = 20$$
$$y = -4 \qquad \text{Solution: } (1, -4)$$

15. $-2x - y > 3$
First, graph the associated equation with a dashed line. Using $(0, 0)$ as a test point results in a false statement. Using $(-4, 0)$ as a test point results in a true statement. Shade the region on the side of the dashed line containing the point $(-4, 0)$.

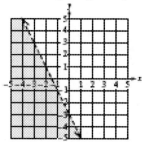

17. $\sqrt{99} = \sqrt{9 \cdot 11} = 3\sqrt{11}$

19. $\dfrac{\sqrt{x}}{\sqrt{x} - \sqrt{y}} = \dfrac{\sqrt{x}}{\sqrt{x} - \sqrt{y}} \cdot \dfrac{\sqrt{x} + \sqrt{y}}{\sqrt{x} + \sqrt{y}}$

$$= \frac{\sqrt{x}\ \sqrt{x} + \sqrt{y}}{\sqrt{x}^2 - \sqrt{y}^2}$$

$$= \frac{\sqrt{x \cdot x} + \sqrt{x \cdot y}}{x - y}$$

$$= \frac{x + \sqrt{xy}}{x - y}$$

Chapter 9

Chapter 9

Are you prepared?

1. **T**

2. **W**

3. **O**

Section 9.1 Practice Exercises

1. The **square root property** states that for any real number, k, if $x^2 = k$, then $x = \sqrt{k}$ or $x = -\sqrt{k}$.

3. **(a)** Linear

   (b) Quadratic

   (c) Linear

5. $(t + 5)(2t - 1) = 0$

   $t + 5 = 0$ or $2t - 1 = 0$

   $t = -5$ or $t = \dfrac{1}{2}$

7. $y^2 - 2y - 35 = 0$

   $(y - 7)(y + 5) = 0$

   $y - 7 = 0$ or $y + 5 = 0$

   $y = 7$ or $y = -5$

9. $6p^2 = -13p - 2$

   $6p^2 + 13p + 2 = 0$

   $(6p + 1)(p + 2) = 0$

   $6p + 1 = 0$ or $p + 2 = 0$

   $p = -\dfrac{1}{6}$ or $p = -2$

11. $2x^2 + 10x = -7(x + 3)$

    $2x^2 + 10x = -7x - 21$

    $2x^2 + 17x + 21 = 0$

    $(2x + 3)(x + 7) = 0$

    $2x + 3 = 0$ or $x + 7 = 0$

    $x = -\dfrac{3}{2}$ or $x = -7$

13. $c^2 = 144$

    $c^2 - 144 = 0$

    $(c - 12)(c + 12) = 0$

    $c - 12 = 0$ or $c + 12 = 0$

    $c = 12$ or $c = -12$

15. $(x - 3)^2 = 25$

    $(x - 3)^2 - 25 = 0$

    $(x - 3 - 5)(x - 3 + 5) = 0$

    $(x - 8)(x + 2) = 0$

    $x - 8 = 0$ or $x + 2 = 0$

    $x = 8$ or $x = -2$

17. $4a^2 + 7a = 2$

    $4a^2 + 7a - 2 = 0$

    $(4a - 1)(a + 2) = 0$

    $4a - 1 = 0$ or $a + 2 = 0$

    $a = \dfrac{1}{4}$ or $a = -2$

19. $(x + 2)(x + 6) = 5$

    $x^2 + 8x + 12 = 5$

    $x^2 + 8x + 7 = 0$

    $(x + 7)(x + 1) = 0$

    $x + 7 = 0$ or $x + 1 = 0$

    $x = -7$ or $x = -1$

21. $x^2 = 49$

    $x = \pm\sqrt{49}$

    $x = \pm 7$

23. $k^2 - 100 = 0$

$$k^2 = 100$$
$$k = \pm\sqrt{100}$$
$$k = \pm 10$$

25. $p^2 = -24$

$$p = \pm\sqrt{-24}$$

There are no real-valued solutions.

27. $3w^2 - 9 = 0$

$$3w^2 = 9$$
$$w^2 = 3$$
$$w = \pm\sqrt{3}$$

29. $(a-5)^2 = 16$

$$a - 5 = \pm\sqrt{16}$$
$$a - 5 = \pm 4$$
$$a = 5 \pm 4$$
$$a = 5 + 4 \quad \text{or} \quad a = 5 - 4$$
$$a = 9 \qquad\qquad a = 1$$

31. $(y-5)^2 = 36$

$$y - 5 = \pm\sqrt{36}$$
$$y - 5 = \pm 6$$
$$y = 5 \pm 6$$
$$y = 5 + 6 \quad \text{or} \quad y = 5 - 6$$
$$y = 11 \qquad\qquad y = -1$$

33. $(x-11)^2 = 5$

$$x - 11 = \pm\sqrt{5}$$
$$x = 11 \pm\sqrt{5}$$

35. $(a+1)^2 = 18$

$$a + 1 = \pm\sqrt{18}$$
$$a + 1 = \pm\sqrt{9 \cdot 2}$$
$$a + 1 = \pm 3\sqrt{2}$$
$$a = -1 \pm 3\sqrt{2}$$

37. $\left(t - \dfrac{1}{4}\right)^2 = \dfrac{7}{16}$

$$t - \frac{1}{4} = \pm\sqrt{\frac{7}{16}}$$
$$t - \frac{1}{4} = \pm\frac{\sqrt{7}}{4}$$
$$t = \frac{1}{4} \pm \frac{\sqrt{7}}{4}$$

39. $\left(x - \dfrac{1}{2}\right)^2 + 5 = 20$

$$\left(x - \frac{1}{2}\right)^2 = 15$$
$$x - \frac{1}{2} = \pm\sqrt{15}$$
$$x = \frac{1}{2} \pm \sqrt{15}$$

41. $(p-3)^2 = -16$

$$p - 3 = \pm\sqrt{-16}$$
$$p = 3 \pm \sqrt{-16}$$

There are no real-valued solutions.

43. $12t^2 = 75$

$$t^2 = \frac{75}{12}$$
$$t^2 = \frac{25}{4}$$
$$t = \pm\sqrt{\frac{25}{4}}$$
$$t = \pm\frac{5}{2}$$

45. $(x+3)^2 = 5$

For $x = -3 + \sqrt{5}$:

$$\left(-3 + \sqrt{5} + 3\right)^2 \overset{?}{=} 5$$
$$\left(\sqrt{5}\right)^2 \overset{?}{=} 5$$
$$5 = 5$$

The solution checks.

47. False; -8 is also a solution.

49. $d = 16t^2$

(a) $d = 16(2)^2$
$d = 16(4)$
$d = 64$ 64 ft

(b) $200 = 16t^2$
$12.5 = t^2$
$\pm 3.5 \approx t$
Since the answer to this problem is a measurement, only the positive value is appropriate.   3.5 sec

(c) $1250 = 16t^2$
$78.125 = t^2$
$\pm 8.8 \approx t$
Since the answer to this problem is a measurement, only the positive value is appropriate.   8.8 sec

51. Use the Pythagorean Theorem.
$x^2 + x^2 = 10^2$
$2x^2 = 100$
$x^2 = 50$
$x \approx \pm 7.1$
Since the answer to this problem is a measurement, only the positive answer is appropriate.   7.1 m

53. Use the area of the circle.
$A = \pi r^2$
$200 = \pi r^2$
$r^2 = \dfrac{200}{\pi}$
$r = \pm \sqrt{\dfrac{200}{\pi}}$
$r \approx \pm 7.9788$
$r \approx \pm 8.0$
Since the answer to this problem is a measurement, only the positive answer is appropriate.   8.0 ft.

Section 9.2 Practice Exercises

1. (a) Completing the square is the process of rewriting any equation $ax^2 + bx + c$ as the square of a binomial equal to a constant.

(b) A **quadratic term** is the term ax^2.

(c) A **linear term** is the term bx.

(d) A **constant term** is the term c.

3. $(x - 5)^2 = 21$
$x - 5 = \pm\sqrt{21}$
$x = 5 \pm \sqrt{21}$

5. Add ½ of 4, squared. $\left[\frac{1}{2}(4)\right]^2 = 4$.
$y^2 + 4y + n$
$y^2 + 4y + 4 = (y + 2)^2$

7. Add ½ of -12, squared. $\left[\frac{1}{2}(-12)\right]^2 = 36$.
$p^2 - 12p + n$
$p^2 - 12p + 36 = (p - 6)^2$

9. Add ½ of -9, squared. $\left[\frac{1}{2}(-9)\right]^2 = \dfrac{81}{4}$.
$x^2 - 9x + n$
$x^2 - 9x + \dfrac{81}{4} = \left(x - \dfrac{9}{2}\right)^2$

11. Add ½ of $\dfrac{5}{3}$, squared. $\left[\dfrac{1}{2}\,\dfrac{5}{3}\right]^2 = \dfrac{25}{36}$.
$d^2 + \dfrac{5}{3}d + n$
$d^2 + \dfrac{5}{3}d + \dfrac{25}{36} = \left(d + \dfrac{5}{6}\right)^2$

13. Add ½ of $-\dfrac{1}{5}$, squared. $\left[\dfrac{1}{2}\ -\dfrac{1}{5}\ \right]^2=\dfrac{1}{100}$.

$m^2-\dfrac{1}{5}m+n$

$m^2-\dfrac{1}{5}m+\dfrac{1}{100}=\left(m-\dfrac{1}{10}\right)^2$

15. Add ½ of 1, squared. $\left[\dfrac{1}{2}\ 1\ \right]^2=\dfrac{1}{4}$.

u^2+u+n

$u^2+u+\dfrac{1}{4}=\left(u+\dfrac{1}{2}\right)^2$

17.
$$x^2+4x=12$$
$$x^2+4x+4=12+4$$
$$(x+2)^2=16$$
$$x+2=\pm\sqrt{16}$$
$$x=2\pm4$$
$$x=2+4=6$$
$$\text{or } x=2-4=-2$$

19.
$$y^2+6y=-5$$
$$y^2+6y+9=-5+9$$
$$(y+3)^2=4$$
$$y+3=\pm\sqrt{4}$$
$$y=-3\pm2$$
$$y=-3+2=-1$$
$$\text{or } y=-3-2=-5$$

21.
$$x^2=2x+1$$
$$x^2-2x=1$$
$$x^2-2x+1=1+1$$
$$(x-1)^2=2$$
$$x-1=\pm\sqrt{2}$$
$$x=1\pm\sqrt{2}$$

23.
$$3x^2-6x-15=0$$
$$\dfrac{3x^2}{3}-\dfrac{6x}{3}-\dfrac{15}{3}=0$$
$$x^2-2x=5$$
$$x^2-2x+1=5+1$$
$$(x-1)^2=6$$
$$x-1=\pm\sqrt{6}$$
$$x=1\pm\sqrt{6}$$

25.
$$4p^2+16p=-4$$
$$\dfrac{4p^2}{4}+\dfrac{16x}{4}=-\dfrac{4}{4}$$
$$p^2+4p=-1$$
$$p^2+4p+4=-1+4$$
$$(p+2)^2=3$$
$$p+2=\pm\sqrt{3}$$
$$p=-2\pm\sqrt{3}$$

27.
$$w^2+w-3=0$$
$$w^2+w=3$$
$$w^2+w+\dfrac{1}{4}=3+\dfrac{1}{4}$$
$$\left(w+\dfrac{1}{2}\right)^2=\dfrac{13}{4}$$
$$w+\dfrac{1}{2}=\pm\sqrt{\dfrac{13}{4}}$$
$$w=-\dfrac{1}{2}\pm\dfrac{\sqrt{13}}{2}$$

29. $x(x+2)=40$
$$x^2+2x=40$$
$$x^2+2x+1=40+1$$
$$x+1\ ^2=41$$
$$x+1=\pm\sqrt{41}$$
$$x=-1\pm\sqrt{41}$$

31. $a^2 - 4a - 1 = 0$

$a^2 - 4a = 1$

$a^2 - 4a + 4 = 1 + 4$

$a - 2\ ^2 = 5$

$a - 2 = \pm\sqrt{5}$

$a = 2 \pm \sqrt{5}$

33. $2r^2 + 12r + 16 = 0$

$r^2 + 6r + 8 = 0$

$r^2 + 6r + 9 = -8 + 9$

$(r + 3)^2 = 1$

$r + 3 = \pm\sqrt{1}$

$r = -3 \pm 1$

$r = -3 + 1 = -2$

or $r = -3 - 1 = -4$

35. $h(h - 11) = -24$

$h^2 - 11h = -24$

$h^2 - 11h + \dfrac{121}{4} = -24 + \dfrac{121}{4}$

$\left(h - \dfrac{11}{2}\right)^2 = \dfrac{25}{4}$

$h - \dfrac{11}{2} = \pm\sqrt{\dfrac{25}{4}}$

$h = \dfrac{11}{2} \pm \dfrac{5}{2}$

$h = \dfrac{11}{2} + \dfrac{5}{2} = 8$

or $h = \dfrac{11}{2} - \dfrac{5}{2} = 3$

37. $y^2 = 121$

$y = \pm\sqrt{121}$

$y = \pm 11$

39. $(p + 2)^2 = 2$

$p + 2 = \pm\sqrt{2}$

$p = -2 \pm \sqrt{2}$

41. $(k + 13)(k - 5) = 0$

$k + 13 = 0$ or $k - 5 = 0$

$k = -13$ $k = 5$

43. $(x - 13)^2 = 0$

$x - 13 = 0$ or $x - 13 = 0$

$x = 13$ $x = 13$

45. $z^2 - 8z - 20 = 0$

$(z - 10)(z + 2) = 0$

$z - 10 = 0$ or $z + 2 = 0$

$z = 10$ $z = -2$

47. $(x - 3)^2 = 16$

$x - 3 = \pm\sqrt{16}$

$x = 3 \pm 4$

$x = 3 + 4 = 7$

or $x = 3 - 4 = -1$

49. $a^2 - 8a + 1 = 0$

$a^2 - 8a = -1$

$a^2 - 8a + 16 = -1 + 16$

$(a - 4)^2 = 15$

$a - 4 = \pm\sqrt{15}$

$a = 4 \pm \sqrt{15}$

51. $2y^2 + 4y = 10$

$y^2 + 2y = 5$

$y^2 + 2y + 1 = 5 + 1$

$(y + 1)^2 = 6$

$y + 1 = \pm\sqrt{6}$

$y = -1 \pm \sqrt{6}$

53. $x^2 - 9x - 22 = 0$

$(x - 11)(x + 2) = 0$

$x - 11 = 0$ or $x + 2 = 0$

$x = 11$ $x = -2$

55. $5h(h - 7) = 0$

$5h = 0$ or $h - 7 = 0$

$h = 0$ $h = 7$

57. $8t^2 + 2t - 3 = 0$

$(4t + 3)(2t - 1) = 0$

$4t + 3 = 0$ or $2t - 1 = 0$

$t = -\dfrac{3}{4}$ $t = \dfrac{1}{2}$

59. $t^2 = 14$

$t = \pm\sqrt{14}$

61. $c^2 + 9 = 0$

$c^2 = -9$

$c = \pm\sqrt{-9}$

There are no real-valued solutions.

63. $4x^2 - 8x = -4$

$x^2 - 2x = -1$

$x^2 - 2x + 1 = 0$

$(x - 1)^2 = 0$

$x - 1 = 0$

$x = 1$

65. Let h represent the height of the suitcase. The width of the suitcase is represented by $h + 4$.

$30h(h + 4) = 4200$

$30h^2 + 120h = 4200$

$h^2 + 4h = 140$

$h^2 + 4h - 140 = 0$

$(h + 14)(h - 10) = 0$

$h + 14 = 0$ or $h - 10 = 0$

$h = -14$ $h = 10$

Since the answer to this problem is a measurement, only the positive answer is appropriate. The suitcase is 10 in. by 14 in. by 30 in.

$10 + 14 + 30 = 54 > 45$

The bag must be checked because the combined linear measurement of length, width, and height is greater than 45 in.

Calculator Exercises

1.
```
( -5+√(17))/4
          -.2192235936
( -5-√(17))/4
          -2.280776406
```

Section 9.3 Practice Exercises

1. $z^2 = 169$

$z = \pm\sqrt{169}$

$z = \pm 13$

3. $(x - 4)^2 = 28$

$x - 4 = \pm\sqrt{28}$

$x = 4 \pm \sqrt{28}$

$x = 4 \pm \sqrt{4 \cdot 7}$

$x = 4 \pm 2\sqrt{7}$

5. $3a^2 - 12a - 12 = 0$

$a^2 - 4a = 4$

$a^2 - 4a + 4 = 4 + 4$

$\left(a - 2\right)^2 = 8$

$a - 2 = \pm\sqrt{8}$

$a = 2 \pm \sqrt{2 \cdot 4}$

$a = 2 \pm 2\sqrt{2}$

7. For $ax^2 + bx + c = 0$

$x = \dfrac{-b \pm \sqrt{b^2 - 4ac}}{2a}$

9. $2x^2 - x = 5$

$2x^2 - x - 5 = 0$

$a = 2, b = -1, c = -5$

11. $-3x(x - 4) = -2x$

$-3x^2 + 12x = -2x$

$-3x^2 + 14x = 0$

$-3x^2 + 14x + 0 = 0$

$a = -3, b = 14, c = 0$

13. $x^2 - 9 = 0$

$x^2 + 0x - 9 = 0$

$a = 1, b = 0, c = -9$

15. $t^2 + 16t + 64 = 0$

$t = \dfrac{-16 \pm \sqrt{16^2 - 4(1)(64)}}{2(1)}$

$= \dfrac{-16 \pm \sqrt{256 - 256}}{2}$

$= \dfrac{-16 \pm \sqrt{0}}{2}$

$= -8$

17. $6k^2 - k - 2 = 0$

$k = \dfrac{-(-1) \pm \sqrt{(-1)^2 - 4(6)(-2)}}{2(6)}$

$= \dfrac{1 \pm \sqrt{1 + 48}}{12}$

$= \dfrac{1 \pm \sqrt{49}}{12}$

$= \dfrac{1 \pm 7}{12}$

$k = \dfrac{1 + 7}{12} = \dfrac{8}{12} = \dfrac{2}{3}$

$k = \dfrac{1 - 7}{12} = -\dfrac{6}{12} = -\dfrac{1}{2}$

19. $5t^2 - t = 3$

$5t^2 - t - 3 = 0$

$t = \dfrac{-(-1) \pm \sqrt{(-1)^2 - 4(5)(-3)}}{2(5)}$

$= \dfrac{1 \pm \sqrt{1 + 60}}{10}$

$= \dfrac{1 \pm \sqrt{61}}{10}$

21. $x(x - 2) = 1$

$x^2 - 2x - 1 = 0$

$x = \dfrac{-(-2) \pm \sqrt{(-2)^2 - 4(1)(-1)}}{2(1)}$

$= \dfrac{2 \pm \sqrt{4 + 4}}{2}$

$= \dfrac{2 \pm \sqrt{8}}{2}$

$= \dfrac{2 \pm \sqrt{4 \cdot 2}}{2}$

$= \dfrac{2 \pm 2\sqrt{2}}{2}$

$= 1 \pm \sqrt{2}$

23. $2p^2 = -10p - 11$

$2p^2 + 10p + 11 = 0$

$p = \dfrac{-10 \pm \sqrt{(10)^2 - 4(2)(11)}}{2(2)}$

$= \dfrac{-10 \pm \sqrt{100 - 88}}{4}$

$= \dfrac{-10 \pm \sqrt{12}}{4}$

$= \dfrac{-10 \pm \sqrt{4 \cdot 3}}{4}$

$= \dfrac{-10 \pm 2\sqrt{3}}{4}$

$= \dfrac{-5 \pm \sqrt{3}}{2}$

25. $-4y^2 - y + 1 = 0$

$y = \dfrac{-(-1) \pm \sqrt{(-1)^2 - 4(-4)(1)}}{2(-4)}$

$y = \dfrac{1 \pm \sqrt{1 + 16}}{-8}$

$y = \dfrac{1 \pm \sqrt{17}}{-8}$ or $\dfrac{-1 \pm \sqrt{17}}{8}$

27.
$$2x(x+1) = 3-x$$
$$2x^2 + 2x = 3-x$$
$$2x^2 + 3x - 3 = 0$$
$$x = \frac{-3 \pm \sqrt{3^2 - 4(2)(-3)}}{2(2)}$$
$$x = \frac{-3 \pm \sqrt{9+24}}{4}$$
$$x = \frac{-3 \pm \sqrt{33}}{4}$$

29.
$$0.2y^2 = -1.5y - 1$$
$$0.2y^2 + 1.5y + 1 = 0$$
$$2y^2 + 15y + 10 = 0$$
$$y = \frac{-15 \pm \sqrt{(15)^2 - 4(2)(10)}}{2(2)}$$
$$y = \frac{-15 \pm \sqrt{225 - 80}}{4}$$
$$y = \frac{-15 \pm \sqrt{145}}{4}$$

31.
$$\frac{2}{3}x^2 + \frac{4}{9}x = \frac{1}{3}$$
$$6x^2 + 4x = 3$$
$$6x^2 + 4x - 3 = 0$$
$$x = \frac{-4 \pm \sqrt{4^2 - 4(6)(-3)}}{2(6)}$$
$$x = \frac{-4 \pm \sqrt{16 + 72}}{12}$$
$$x = \frac{-4 \pm \sqrt{88}}{12}$$
$$x = \frac{-4 \pm 2\sqrt{22}}{12}$$
$$x = \frac{\overset{2}{-2} \pm \sqrt{22}}{12}$$
$$x = \frac{-2 \pm \sqrt{22}}{6}$$

33.
$$16x^2 - 9 = 0$$
$$(4x - 3)(4x + 3) = 0$$
$$4x - 3 = 0 \quad \text{or} \quad 4x + 3 = 0$$
$$4x = 3 \qquad\qquad 4x = -3$$
$$x = \frac{3}{4} \qquad\qquad x = -\frac{3}{4}$$

35.
$$(x-5)^2 = -21$$
$$x - 5 = \pm\sqrt{-21}$$
There are no real-valued solutions..

37.
$$\frac{1}{9}x^2 + \frac{8}{3}x + 11 = 0$$
$$x^2 + 24x + 99 = 0$$
$$x = \frac{-24 \pm \sqrt{24^2 - 4(1)(99)}}{2(1)}$$
$$x = \frac{-24 \pm \sqrt{576 - 396}}{2}$$
$$x = \frac{-24 \pm \sqrt{180}}{2}$$
$$x = \frac{-24 \pm 6\sqrt{5}}{2}$$
$$x = -12 \pm 3\sqrt{5}$$

39.
$$2x^2 - 6x - 3 = 0$$
$$x = \frac{-(-6) \pm \sqrt{(-6)^2 - 4(2)(-3)}}{2(2)}$$
$$x = \frac{6 \pm \sqrt{36 + 24}}{4}$$
$$x = \frac{6 \pm \sqrt{60}}{4}$$
$$x = \frac{6 \pm 2\sqrt{15}}{4}$$
$$x = \frac{\overset{2}{6} \pm \sqrt{15}}{4}$$
$$x = \frac{3 \pm \sqrt{15}}{2}$$

41. $9x^2 = 11x$

$9x^2 - 11x = 0$

$x(9x - 11) = 0$

$x = 0$ or $9x - 11 = 0$

$9x = 11$

$x = \dfrac{11}{9}$

43. $(2y - 3)^2 = 5$

$2y - 3 = \pm\sqrt{5}$

$2y = 3 \pm \sqrt{5}$

$y = \dfrac{3 \pm \sqrt{5}}{2}$

45. $0.4x^2 = 0.2x + 1$

$4x^2 = 2x + 10$

$4x^2 - 2x - 10 = 0$

$x = \dfrac{-(-2) \pm \sqrt{(-2)^2 - 4(4)(-10)}}{2(4)}$

$= \dfrac{2 \pm \sqrt{4 + 160}}{8}$

$= \dfrac{2 \pm \sqrt{164}}{8}$

$= \dfrac{2 \pm \sqrt{4 \cdot 41}}{8}$

$= \dfrac{2 \pm 2\sqrt{41}}{8}$

$= \dfrac{1 \pm \sqrt{41}}{4}$

47. $9z^2 - z = 0$

$z(9z - 1) = 0$

$z = 0$ or $9z - 1 = 0$

$z = \dfrac{1}{9}$

49. $r^2 - 52 = 0$

$r^2 = 52$

$r = \pm\sqrt{52}$

$r = \pm\sqrt{4 \cdot 13}$

$r = \pm 2\sqrt{13}$

51. $-2.5t(t - 4) = 1.5$

$-2.5t^2 + 10t = 1.5$

$-2.5t^2 + 10t - 1.5 = 0$

$-25t^2 + 100t - 15 = 0$

$t = \dfrac{-100 \pm \sqrt{100^2 - 4(-25)(-15)}}{2(-25)}$

$t = \dfrac{-100 \pm \sqrt{10,000 - 1500}}{-50}$

$t = \dfrac{-100 \pm \sqrt{8500}}{-50}$

$t = \dfrac{-100 \pm 10\sqrt{85}}{-50}$

$t = \dfrac{10 \ -10 \pm \sqrt{85}}{-50}$

$t = \dfrac{-10 \pm \sqrt{85}}{-5}$ or $\dfrac{10 \pm \sqrt{85}}{5}$

53. $(m - 3)(m + 2) = 9$

$m^2 - m - 6 = 9$

$m^2 - m - 15 = 0$

$m = \dfrac{-(-1) \pm \sqrt{(-1)^2 - 4(1)(-15)}}{2(1)}$

$m = \dfrac{1 \pm \sqrt{1 + 60}}{2}$

$m = \dfrac{1 \pm \sqrt{61}}{2}$

55. $x^2 + x + 3 = 0$

$$x = \frac{-1 \pm \sqrt{1^2 - 4(1)(3)}}{2(1)}$$

$$= \frac{-1 \pm \sqrt{1 - 12}}{2}$$

$$= \frac{-1 \pm \sqrt{-11}}{2}$$

There are no real-valued solutions.

57. Let x represent the width of the rectangle. The length of the rectangle is represented by $2x - 1$.

$$x(2x - 1) = 100$$

$$2x^2 - x = 100$$

$$2x^2 - x - 100 = 0$$

$$x = \frac{-(-1) \pm \sqrt{(-1)^2 - 4(2)(-100)}}{2(2)}$$

$$x = \frac{1 \pm \sqrt{1 + 800}}{4}$$

$$x = \frac{1 \pm \sqrt{801}}{4}$$

$$x = \frac{1 \pm 3\sqrt{89}}{4}$$

Since the answer to this problem is a measurement, only the positive value is a solution.

$$x = \frac{1 + 3\sqrt{89}}{4} \approx 7.3$$

$$2x - 1 = 2\left(\frac{1 + 3\sqrt{89}}{4}\right) - 1$$

$$= \frac{1 + 3\sqrt{89}}{2} - \frac{2}{2}$$

$$= \frac{-1 + 3\sqrt{89}}{2} \approx 13.7$$

The width of the rectangle is 7.3 m. The length of the rectangle is 13.7 m.

59. Let x represent the width of the rectangular storage area. The length of the rectangular storage area is represented by $x + 2$.

$$6x(x + 2) = 240$$

$$6x^2 + 12x = 240$$

$$6x^2 + 12x - 240 = 0$$

$$x^2 + 2x - 40 = 0$$

$$x = \frac{-2 \pm \sqrt{2^2 - 4(1)(-40)}}{2(1)}$$

$$x = \frac{-2 \pm \sqrt{4 + 160}}{2}$$

$$x = \frac{-2 \pm \sqrt{164}}{2}$$

$$x = \frac{-2 \pm 2\sqrt{41}}{2}$$

$$x = -1 \pm \sqrt{41}$$

Since the answer to this problem is a measurement, only the positive value is a solution.

$$x = -1 + \sqrt{41} \approx 5.4$$

$$x + 2 = -1 + \sqrt{41} + 2 = 1 + \sqrt{41} \approx 7.4$$

The width of the rectangular storage area is 5.4 ft. The length is 7.4 ft. The height is 6 ft.

61. Let x represent the width of the rectangle. The length is represented by $x + 4$.

$$x(x+4) = 72$$

$$x^2 + 4x = 72$$

$$x^2 + 4x - 72 = 0$$

$$x = \frac{-4 \pm \sqrt{4^2 - 4(1)(-72)}}{2(1)}$$

$$x = \frac{-4 \pm \sqrt{16 + 288}}{2}$$

$$x = \frac{-4 \pm \sqrt{304}}{2}$$

$$x = \frac{-4 \pm 4\sqrt{19}}{2}$$

$$x = -2 \pm 2\sqrt{19}$$

Since the answer to this problem is a measurement, only the positive answer is appropriate.

$$x = -2 + 2\sqrt{19} \approx 6.7$$

$$x + 4 = -2 + 2\sqrt{19} + 4$$

$$= 2 + 2\sqrt{19} \approx 10.7$$

The width is 6.7 ft. The length is 10.7 ft.

63. Let x represent the length of the first leg of the right triangle. The length of the second leg of the right triangle is represented by $x + 3$.

$$x^2 + (x+3)^2 = 13^2$$

$$x^2 + x^2 + 6x + 9 = 169$$

$$2x^2 + 6x = 160$$

$$x^2 + 3x = 80$$

$$x^2 + 3x - 80 = 0$$

$$x = \frac{-3 \pm \sqrt{3^2 - 4(1)(-80)}}{2(1)}$$

$$x = \frac{-3 \pm \sqrt{9 + 320}}{2}$$

$$x = \frac{-3 \pm \sqrt{329}}{2}$$

Since the answer to this problem is a measurement, only the positive answer is a solution.

$$x = \frac{-3 + \sqrt{329}}{2} \approx 7.6$$

$$x + 3 = \frac{-3 + \sqrt{329}}{2} + 3 = \frac{3 + \sqrt{329}}{2} \approx 10.6$$

The lengths of the legs are 10.6 m and 7.6 m.

Problem Recognition Exercises

1. $6x^2 + 7x - 3 = 0$

(a) $(2x + 3)(3x - 1) = 0$

$2x + 3 = 0 \quad$ or $\quad 3x - 1 = 0$

$x = -\dfrac{3}{2} \quad$ or $\quad x = \dfrac{1}{3}$

(b) $\dfrac{6x^2}{6} + \dfrac{7x}{6} - \dfrac{3}{6} = 0$

$x^2 + \dfrac{7}{6}x = \dfrac{1}{2}$

$x^2 + \dfrac{7}{6}x + \dfrac{49}{144} = \dfrac{1}{2} + \dfrac{49}{144}$

$\left(x + \dfrac{7}{12}\right)^2 = \dfrac{121}{144}$

$x + \dfrac{7}{12} = \pm\sqrt{\dfrac{121}{144}}$

$x = -\dfrac{7}{12} \pm \dfrac{11}{12}$

$x = -\dfrac{7}{12} + \dfrac{11}{12} \quad$ or $\quad x = -\dfrac{7}{12} - \dfrac{11}{12}$

$= \dfrac{4}{12} \qquad\qquad = -\dfrac{18}{12}$

$= \dfrac{1}{3} \qquad\qquad = -\dfrac{3}{2}$

(c) $x = \dfrac{-7 \pm \sqrt{(7)^2 - 4(6)(-3)}}{2(6)}$

$= \dfrac{-7 \pm \sqrt{49 + 72}}{12}$

$= \dfrac{-7 \pm \sqrt{121}}{12}$

$= \dfrac{-7 \pm 11}{12}$

$= \dfrac{4}{12} \quad$ or $\quad \dfrac{-18}{12}$

$= \dfrac{1}{3} \quad$ or $\quad -\dfrac{3}{2}$

3. Quadratic

$x(x - 8) = 6$

$x^2 - 8x - 6 = 0$

$x = \dfrac{-(-8) \pm \sqrt{(-8)^2 - 4(1)(-6)}}{2(1)}$

$= \dfrac{8 \pm \sqrt{64 + 24}}{2}$

$= \dfrac{8 \pm \sqrt{88}}{2}$

$= \dfrac{8 \pm \sqrt{4 \cdot 22}}{2}$

$= \dfrac{8 \pm 2\sqrt{22}}{2}$

$= 4 \pm \sqrt{22}$

5. Linear

$3\ k - 6 = 2k - 5$

$3k - 18 = 2k - 5$

$k = 15$

7. Quadratic

$8x^2 - 22x + 5 = 0$

$(4x - 1)(2x - 5) = 0$

$4x - 1 = 0 \quad$ or $\quad 2x - 5 = 0$

$x = \dfrac{1}{4} \quad$ or $\quad x = \dfrac{5}{2}$

9. Rational

$\dfrac{2}{x - 1} - \dfrac{5}{4} = -\dfrac{1}{x + 1}$

$4(2)(x + 1) - 5(x - 1)(x + 1) = -(4)(x - 1)$

$8x + 8 - 5x^2 + 5 = -4x + 4$

$-5x^2 + 12x + 9 = 0$

$(-5x - 3)(x - 3) = 0$

$-5x - 3 = 0 \quad$ or $\quad x - 3 = 0$

$x = -\dfrac{3}{5} \qquad x = 3$

11. Radical

$$\sqrt{2y-2} = y-1$$
$$\sqrt{2y-2}^{\,2} = (y-1)^2$$
$$2y-2 = y^2 - 2y + 1$$
$$0 = y^2 - 4y + 3$$
$$0 = (y-1)(y-3)$$
$$y-1 = 0 \quad \text{or} \quad y-3 = 0$$
$$y = 1 \quad \text{or} \quad y = 3$$

13. Quadratic

$$w+1^{\,2} = 100$$
$$\sqrt{w+1^{\,2}} = \pm\sqrt{100}$$
$$w+1 = \pm 10$$

$$w+1 = 10 \quad \text{or} \quad w+1 = -10$$
$$w = 9 \quad \text{or} \quad w = -11$$

15. Rational

$$\frac{2}{x+1} = \frac{5}{4}$$
$$5(x+1) = 8$$
$$5x + 5 = 8$$
$$5x = 3$$
$$x = \frac{3}{5}$$

Section 9.4 Practice Exercises

1. (a) $i = \sqrt{-1}$

  (b) A **complex number** is a number of the form $a+bi$ where a and b are real numbers and $i = -1$

  (c) If $b \neq 0$, then we say that $a+bi$ is an **imaginary number**.

  (d) The **standard form** for a complex number is $a+bi$.

  (e) The **real part** of a complex number is a.

  (f) The **imaginary part** of a complex number is b.

  (g) The complex numbers $(a + bi)$ and $(a - bi)$ are **conjugates**.

3. $\sqrt{-36} = 6i$

5. $\sqrt{-21} = i\sqrt{21}$

7. $\sqrt{-48} = i\sqrt{16\cdot 3} = 4i\sqrt{3}$

9. $\sqrt{-100} \cdot \sqrt{-4} = 10i \cdot 2i = 20i^2 = -20$

11. $\sqrt{-3} \cdot \sqrt{-12} = i\sqrt{3} \cdot i\sqrt{12} = i^2\sqrt{36} = -6$

13. $\dfrac{\sqrt{-81}}{\sqrt{-9}} = \dfrac{\overset{3}{\cancel{9}}\,\overset{1}{\cancel{i}}}{\underset{1}{\cancel{3}}\,\cancel{i}_1} = 3$

15. $\dfrac{\sqrt{-50}}{\sqrt{-2}} = \dfrac{\overset{1}{\cancel{i}}\sqrt{25\cdot 2}}{\underset{1}{\cancel{i}}\sqrt{2}} = \dfrac{5\sqrt{2}}{\sqrt{2}} = 5$

17. $\sqrt{-9} + \sqrt{-121} = 3i + 11i = 14i$

19. $\sqrt{-1} - \sqrt{-144} - \sqrt{-169}$
$$= i - 12i - 13i = -24i$$

21. $10i^2 = 10(-1) = -10$

23. $6 + i^2 = 6 + (-1) = 5$

25. $-i^2 - 4 = -(-1) - 4 = -3$

27. $-5i^2 = -5(-1) = 5$

29. real part: -3, imaginary part: -2

33. real part: 0, imaginary part: $\dfrac{2}{7}$

35. Add or subtract the real parts. Add or subtract the imaginary parts.

37. $(2 + 7i) + (-8 + i) = 2 + 7i - 8 + i = -6 + 8i$

39. $(3 - 4i) + (7 - 6i) = 3 - 4i + 7 - 6i = 10 - 10i$

41. $4i - (9 + i) + 15 = 4i - 9 - i + 15 = 6 + 3i$

43. $(5 - 6i) - (9 - 8i) - (3 - i)$
$= 5 - 6i - 9 + 8i - 3 + i = -7 + 3i$

45. $(2 - i)(7 - 7i)$
$= 2(7) - 2(7i) - i(7) + i(7i)$
$= 14 - 14i - 7i + 7i^2$
$= 14 - 21i + 7(-1)$
$= 7 - 21i$

47. $(13 - 5i) - (2 + 4i) = 13 - 5i - 2 - 4i$
$= 11 - 9i$

49. $(5 + 3i)(3 + 2i)$
$= 5(3) + 5(2i) + 3i(3) + 3i(2i)$
$= 15 + 10i + 9i + 6i^2$
$= 15 + 19i + 6(-1)$
$= 9 + 19i$

51. $\left(\dfrac{1}{2} + \dfrac{1}{5}i\right) - \left(\dfrac{3}{4} + \dfrac{2}{5}i\right)$
$= \dfrac{1}{2} + \dfrac{1}{5}i - \dfrac{3}{4} - \dfrac{2}{5}i$
$= \dfrac{2}{4} + \dfrac{1}{5}i - \dfrac{3}{4} - \dfrac{2}{5}i$
$= -\dfrac{1}{4} - \dfrac{1}{5}i$

53. $8.4i - (3.5 - 9.7i) = 8.4i - 3.5 + 9.7i$
$= -3.5 + 18.1i$

55. $(3 - 2i)(3 + 2i)$
$= 3(3) + 3(2i) - 2i(3) - 2i(2i)$
$= 9 + 6i - 6i - 4i^2$
$= 9 - 4(-1)$
$= 13$

57. $(10 - 2i)(10 + 2i)$
$= 10(10) + 10(2i) - 2i(10) - 2i(2i)$
$= 100 + 20i - 20i - 4i^2$
$= 100 - 4(-1)$
$= 104$

59.

$$\left(\frac{1}{2} - i\right)\left(\frac{1}{2} + i\right)$$

$$= \frac{1}{2}\left(\frac{1}{2}\right) + \frac{1}{2}\,i - i\left(\frac{1}{2}\right) - i\cdot i$$

$$= \frac{1}{4} + \frac{1}{2}i - \frac{1}{2}i - i^2$$

$$= \frac{1}{4} - (-1)$$

$$= \frac{1}{4} - \left(-\frac{4}{4}\right)$$

$$= \frac{5}{4}$$

61. $6 - i^{\,2} = 6 - i\ \ 6 - i$

$$= 6\cdot 6 - 6\cdot i - i\cdot 6 + i\cdot i$$

$$= 36 - 6i - 6i + i^2$$

$$= 36 - 12i + (-1)$$

$$= 35 - 12i$$

63. $5 + 2i^{\,2} = 5 + 2i\ \ 5 + 2i$

$$= 5\cdot 5 + 5\cdot 2i + 2i\cdot 5 + 2i\cdot 2i$$

$$= 25 + 10i + 10i + 4i^2$$

$$= 25 + 20i + 4(-1)$$

$$= 21 + 20i$$

65. $4 - 7i^{\,2} = 4 - 7i\ \ 4 - 7i$

$$= 4\cdot 4 - 4\cdot 7i - 7i\cdot 4 + 7i\cdot 7i$$

$$= 16 - 28i - 28i + 49i^2$$

$$= 16 - 56i + 49(-1)$$

$$= -33 - 56i$$

67. The conjugate of $7 - 4i$ is $7 + 4i$

$$7 - 4i\quad 7 + 4i$$

$$= 7\cdot 7 + 7\cdot 4i - 4i\cdot 7 - 4i\cdot 4i$$

$$= 49 + 28i - 28i - 16i^2$$

$$= 49 - 16(-1)$$

$$= 65$$

69.

The conjugate of $\dfrac{3}{2} + \dfrac{2}{5}i$ is $\dfrac{3}{2} - \dfrac{2}{5}i$

$$\left(\frac{3}{2} + \frac{2}{5}i\right)\left(\frac{3}{2} - \frac{2}{5}i\right)$$

$$= \frac{3}{2}\left(\frac{3}{2}\right) - \left(\frac{3}{2}\right)\left(\frac{2}{5}i\right) + \frac{2}{5}i\left(\frac{3}{2}\right) - \frac{2}{5}i\left(\frac{2}{5}i\right)$$

$$= \frac{9}{4} - \frac{6}{10}i + \frac{6}{10}i - \frac{4}{25}i^2$$

$$= \frac{9}{4} - \frac{4}{25}(-1)$$

$$= \frac{225}{100} - \frac{16}{100}(-1)$$

$$= \frac{241}{100}$$

71. The conjugate of $4i$ is $-4i$

$$4i(-4i)$$

$$= -16i^2$$

$$= -16(-1)$$

$$= 16$$

73. $\dfrac{-3i}{2+i} = \dfrac{-3i}{2+i} \cdot \dfrac{2-i}{2-i}$

$= \dfrac{-3i(2-i)}{4-i^2} = \dfrac{-6i+3i^2}{4+1}$

$= \dfrac{-6i-3}{5} = -\dfrac{6}{5}i - \dfrac{3}{5}$

$= -\dfrac{3}{5} - \dfrac{6}{5}i$

75. $\dfrac{4i}{5-i} = \dfrac{4i}{5-i} \cdot \dfrac{5+i}{5+i}$

$= \dfrac{4i(5+i)}{25-i^2} = \dfrac{20i+4i^2}{25+1}$

$= \dfrac{20i-4}{26} = \dfrac{20}{26}i - \dfrac{4}{26}$

$= -\dfrac{2}{13} + \dfrac{10}{13}i$

77. $\dfrac{4+i}{4-i} = \dfrac{4+i}{4-i} \cdot \dfrac{4+i}{4+i} = \dfrac{16+8i+i^2}{16-i^2}$

$= \dfrac{16+8i-1}{16+1} = \dfrac{15+8i}{17}$

$= \dfrac{15}{17} + \dfrac{8}{17}i$

79. $\dfrac{4+3i}{2+5i} = \dfrac{4+3i}{2+5i} \cdot \dfrac{2-5i}{2-5i} = \dfrac{8-14i-15i^2}{4-25i^2}$

$= \dfrac{8-14i+15}{4+25} = \dfrac{23-14i}{29}$

$= \dfrac{23}{29} - \dfrac{14}{29}i$

81. $\dfrac{2}{7-4i} = \dfrac{2}{7-4i} \cdot \dfrac{7+4i}{7+4i}$

$= \dfrac{14+8i}{49-16i^2} = \dfrac{14+8i}{49+16}$

$= \dfrac{14+8i}{65} = -\dfrac{14}{65} + \dfrac{8}{65}i$

83. $\dfrac{5}{1+i} = \dfrac{5}{1+i} \cdot \dfrac{1-i}{1-i}$

$= \dfrac{5-5i}{1-i^2} = \dfrac{5-5i}{1-(-1)}$

$= \dfrac{5-5i}{2} = -\dfrac{5}{2} - \dfrac{5}{2}i$

85.

$x+4^{\,2} = -25$

$x^2 + 8x + 16 = -25$

$x^2 + 8x + 41 = 0$

$x = \dfrac{-8 \pm \sqrt{(8)^2 - 4(1)(41)}}{2(1)}$

$= \dfrac{-8 \pm \sqrt{64-164}}{2(1)} = \dfrac{-8 \pm \sqrt{-100}}{2}$

$= \dfrac{-8 \pm 10i}{2} = \dfrac{2(-4 \pm 5i)}{2} = -4 \pm 5i$

87.

$$\left(p-3\right)^2 = -8$$

$$p^2 - 6p + 9 = -8$$

$$p^2 - 6p + 17 = 0$$

$$p = \frac{6 \pm \sqrt{(-6)^2 - 4(1)(17)}}{2(1)}$$

$$= \frac{6 \pm \sqrt{36 - 68}}{2(1)} = \frac{6 \pm \sqrt{-32}}{2}$$

$$= \frac{6 \pm 4i\sqrt{2}}{2} = \frac{2(3 \pm 2i\sqrt{2})}{2} = 3 \pm 2i\sqrt{2}$$

89.

$$x^2 - 2x + 4 = 0$$

$$x = \frac{2 \pm \sqrt{(-2)^2 - 4(1)(4)}}{2(1)}$$

$$= \frac{2 \pm \sqrt{4 - 16}}{2(1)} = \frac{2 \pm \sqrt{-12}}{2}$$

$$= \frac{2 \pm 2i\sqrt{3}}{2} = \frac{2(1 \pm i\sqrt{3})}{2} = 1 \pm i\sqrt{3}$$

91.

$$6y^2 + 3y + 2 = 0$$

$$y = \frac{-3 \pm \sqrt{(3)^2 - 4(6)(2)}}{2(6)}$$

$$= \frac{-3 \pm \sqrt{9 - 48}}{2(6)} = \frac{-3 \pm \sqrt{-39}}{12}$$

$$= \frac{-3}{12} \pm \frac{\sqrt{-39}}{12} = -\frac{1}{4} \pm \frac{\sqrt{39}}{12}i$$

93. False. For example $2 + 3i$ is not a real number.

95. True.

97. False. $\sqrt[3]{-64} = -4$

99. False. $(1 + 4i)(1 - 4i) = 17$

101. True.

103. False. $i^4 = 1$

105. True.

Calculator Exercises

1.

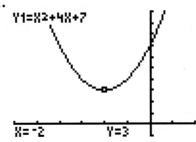

3.

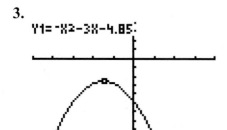

5.

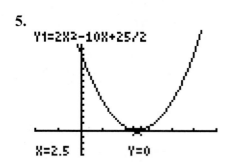

Section 9.5 Practice Exercises

1. (a) A function in the form $y = ax^2 + bx + c$, where a, b, and c are real numbers with $a \neq 0$, is called a **quadratic equation in two variables.**

(b) In general, the shape of the graph of any quadratic function is called a **parabola.**

(c) The **vertex of a parabola** is the lowest or highest point on the graph.

(d) For a quadratic function, the **axis of symmetry** is the vertical line that passes through the vertex.

3.
$$3 + a(a+2) = 18$$
$$3 + a^2 + 2a = 18$$
$$a^2 + 2a - 15 = 0$$
$$(a-3)(a+5) = 0$$
$$a - 3 = 0 \quad \text{or} \quad a + 5 = 0$$
$$a = 3 \qquad\qquad a = -5$$

5.
$$2z^2 + 4z - 10 = 0$$
$$z^2 + 2z - 5 = 0$$
$$z = \frac{-2 \pm \sqrt{2^2 - 4(1)(-5)}}{2(1)}$$
$$= \frac{-2 \pm \sqrt{4 + 20}}{2}$$
$$= \frac{-2 \pm \sqrt{24}}{2}$$
$$= \frac{-2 \pm 2\sqrt{6}}{2}$$
$$= -1 \pm \sqrt{6}$$

7.
$$(x-5)^2 = 12$$
$$x - 5 = \pm\sqrt{12}$$
$$x - 5 = \pm 2\sqrt{3}$$
$$x = 5 \pm 2\sqrt{3}$$

9. Linear

11. Quadratic

13. Neither

15. Linear

17. Quadratic

19. Neither

21. If $a > 0$ the graph opens upward; if $a < 0$ the graph opens downward.

23. $a = 2$; upward

25. $a = -10$; downward

27. $x = \dfrac{-b}{2a} = \dfrac{-4}{2(2)} = \dfrac{-4}{4} = -1$
$y = 2(-1)^2 + 4(-1) - 6 = 2 - 4 - 6 = -8$
Vertex: $(-1, -8)$

29. $x = \dfrac{-b}{2a} = \dfrac{-2}{2(-1)} = \dfrac{-2}{-2} = 1$
$y = -(1)^2 + 2(1) - 5 = -1 + 2 - 5 = -4$
Vertex: $(1, -4)$

31. $x = \dfrac{-b}{2a} = \dfrac{-(-2)}{2(1)} = \dfrac{2}{2} = 1$

$y = (1)^2 - 2(1) + 3 = 1 - 2 + 3 = 2$

Vertex: $(1, 2)$

33. $x = \dfrac{-b}{2a} = \dfrac{-0}{2(1)} = 0$

$y = 0^2 - 4 = -4$

Vertex: $(0, -4)$

35. To find the x-intercept(s), substitute 0 for y and solve for x. To find the y-intercept, substitute 0 for x and solve for y.

$y = x^2 - 7$

x-intercepts: $x^2 - 7 = 0$

$\qquad\qquad x^2 = 7$

$\qquad\qquad x = \pm\sqrt{7}$

$\qquad\qquad \sqrt{7}, 0 \quad -\sqrt{7}, 0$

y-intercept: $\begin{aligned} y &= 0^2 - 7 \\ y &= -7 \qquad (0, -7) \end{aligned}$

This function is graph c.

37. $y = (x + 3)^2 - 4$

x-intercepts: $(x + 3)^2 - 4 = 0$

$\qquad\qquad (x + 3)^2 = 4$

$\qquad\qquad x + 3 = \pm 2$

$\qquad\qquad x = \pm 2 - 3$

$\qquad\qquad x = -1, -5$

$\qquad (-1, 0) \quad (-5, 0)$

y-intercept: $y = (0 + 3)^2 - 4$

$\qquad\qquad y = 3^2 - 4$

$\qquad\qquad y = 9 - 4$

$\qquad\qquad y = 5 \qquad (0, 5)$

This function is graph a.

39. $y = x^2 - 9$

(a) $a = 1$ $\qquad\qquad$ Upward

(b) $x = \dfrac{-b}{2a} = \dfrac{-0}{2(1)} = 0$

$\qquad y = (0)^2 - 9 = -9 \qquad$ vertex: $(0, -9)$

(c) x-intercepts:

$\qquad x^2 - 9 = 0$

$\qquad x^2 = 9$

$\qquad x = \pm 3 \qquad (3, 0) \quad (-3, 0)$

(d) y-intercept: $y = 0^2 - 9$

$\qquad\qquad\qquad y = -9 \qquad (0, -9)$

(e)

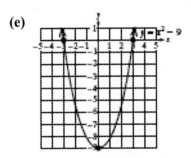

41. $y = x^2 - 2x - 8$

(a) $a = 1$ Upward

(b) $x = \dfrac{-b}{2a} = \dfrac{-(-2)}{2(1)} = \dfrac{2}{2} = 1$

$y = (1)^2 - 2(1) - 8 = 1 - 2 - 8 = -9$

Vertex: $(1, -9)$

(c) x-intercepts: $x^2 - 2x - 8 = 0$

$(x + 2)(x - 4) = 0$

$x + 2 = 0$ or $x - 4 = 0$

$x = -2$ $x = 4$

$(-2, 0)$ $(4, 0)$

(d) y-intercept: $y = 0^2 - 2(0) - 8 = -8$

$(0, -8)$

(e)

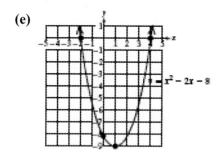

43. $y = -x^2 + 6x - 9$

(a) $a = -1$ Downward

(b) $x = \dfrac{-b}{2a} = \dfrac{-6}{2(-1)} = \dfrac{-6}{-2} = 3$

$y = -(3)^2 + 6(3) - 9 = -9 + 18 - 9 = 0$

Vertex: $(3, 0)$

(c) x-intercept: $-x^2 + 6x - 9 = 0$

$x^2 - 6x + 9 = 0$

$(x - 3)^2 = 0$

$x - 3 = 0$

$x = 3$ $(3, 0)$

(d) y-intercept:

$y = -(0)^2 + 6(0) - 9$

$y = -9$ $(0, -9)$

(e)

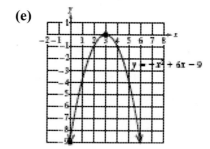

45. $y = -x^2 + 8x - 15$

(a) $a = -1$ Downward

(b) $x = \dfrac{-b}{2a} = \dfrac{-8}{2(-1)} = \dfrac{-8}{-2} = 4$

$y = -(4)^2 + 8(4) - 15$

$= -16 + 32 - 15$

$= 1$

Vertex: $(4, 1)$

(c) x-intercepts: $-x^2 + 8x - 15 = 0$

$x^2 - 8x + 15 = 0$

$(x - 3)(x - 5) = 0$

$x - 3 = 0$ or $x - 5 = 0$

$x = 3$ $x = 5$

$(3, 0)$ $(5, 0)$

(d) y-intercept: $y = -(0)^2 + 8(0) - 15$

$y = -15$ $(0, -15)$

(e)

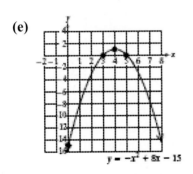

47. $y = x^2 + 6x + 10$

(a) $a = 1$ Upward

(b) $x = \dfrac{-b}{2a} = \dfrac{-6}{2(1)} = \dfrac{-6}{2} = -3$

$y = (-3)^2 + 6(-3) + 10$

$= 9 - 18 + 10$

$= 1$

Vertex: $(-3, 1)$

(c) x-intercepts: $x^2 + 6x + 10 = 0$

$x = \dfrac{-6 \pm \sqrt{6^2 - 4(1)(10)}}{2(1)}$

$x = \dfrac{-6 \pm \sqrt{36 - 40}}{2}$

$x = \dfrac{-6 \pm \sqrt{-4}}{2}$ None

(d) y-intercept: $y = (0)^2 + 6(0) + 10$

$y = 10$ $(0, 10)$

(e)

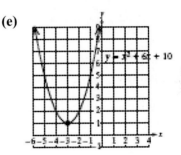

49. $y = -2x^2 - 2$

(a) $a = -2$ Downward

(b) $x = \dfrac{-b}{2a} = \dfrac{-0}{2(-2)} = 0$

$y = -2(0)^2 - 2 = 0 - 2 = -2$

Vertex: $(0, -2)$

(c) x-intercepts: $-2x^2 - 2 = 0$

$-2x^2 = 2$

$x^2 = -1$ None

(d) y-intercept: $y = -2(0)^2 - 2$

$y = -2$ $(0, -2)$

(e)

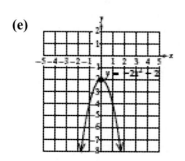

51. Because the graph opens downward, this is a true statement.

53. $a = 1.5$ which indicates the graph opens upward. Therefore, the statement is false.

55. $y = -16t^2 + 40t + 3$

(a) The maximum of the ball is the y value of the vertex. (See part b for the x value of the vertex.)

$y = -16(1.25)^2 + 40(1.25) + 3$

$= -25 + 50 + 3$

$= 28$

The maximum height of the ball is 28 ft.

(b) The length of time needed for the ball to reach its maximum height is the x value of the vertex.

$x = \dfrac{-b}{2a} = \dfrac{-40}{2(-16)}$

$= \dfrac{-40}{-32}$

$= 1.25$

It will take the ball 1.25 seconds to reach its maximum height.

57. $y = -\dfrac{1}{40}x^2 + 10x - 500$

(a) The number of calendars that should be produced to maximize profit is the x value of the vertex.

$x = \dfrac{-b}{2a} = \dfrac{-10}{2\left(-\dfrac{1}{40}\right)}$

$= \dfrac{-10}{-\dfrac{1}{20}}$

$= -10 \div \left(-\dfrac{1}{20}\right)$

$= -10 \cdot (-20)$

$= 200$

200 calendars will need to be produced to maximize profit.

(b) Maximum profit is the y value of the vertex.

$y = -\dfrac{1}{40}(200)^2 + 10(200) - 500$

$= -1000 + 2000 - 500$

$= 500$

Maximum profit is $500.

59. $y = -16t^2 + 32t$

(a) How high will Josh be after 50.5 seconds?

$$y = -16(0.5)^2 + 32(0.5)$$
$$y = -16(0.25) + 16$$
$$y = -4 + 16$$
$$y = 12$$

Josh will be 12 feet high in 0.5 seconds.

(b) What is Josh's hang time? (Hint:compute the time required for him to land. His height will be zero)

$$0 = -16t^2 + 32t$$
$$0 = -16t(t - 2)$$
$$0 = -16t \quad \text{or} \quad 0 = t - 2$$
$$0 = t \quad \text{or} \quad 0 = 2$$

Josh's hang time is 2 seconds.

(c) What is Josh's maximum height? First find the t value of the vertex then calculate the y value.

$$x = \frac{-b}{2a} = \frac{-(32)}{2(-16)}$$
$$= \frac{-32}{-32}$$
$$= 1$$

$$y = -16(1)^2 + 32(1)$$
$$y = -16(1) + 32(1)$$
$$y = 16$$

The maximum height is 16 feet.

Section 9.6 Practice Exercises

1. (a) The set of first components in a set of ordered pairs (x, y) is called the **domain**.

(b) A relation in x and y is a **function** if for every element x in the domain there corresponds exactly one element y in the range.

(c) **Function notation** is an equation used to define a function.

(d) The set of second components in a set of ordered pairs (x, y) is called the **range**.

(e) Any set of ordered pairs (x, y) is called a **relation** in x and y.

(f) The **vertical line test** is used to determine whether a relation defined by a set of points (x, y) defines y as a function of x. If no vertical line intersects the graph of the points in more than one point, the relation is a function.

3. First find the x value of the vertex $\left(x = \dfrac{-b}{2a}\right)$, then determine the y value.

$$y = 4x^2 - 2x + 3$$
$$x = \frac{-(-2)}{2(4)} = \frac{2}{8} = \frac{1}{4}$$

$$\overline{\hspace{3cm}}$$

$$y = 4\left(\frac{1}{4}\right)^2 - 2\left(\frac{1}{4}\right) + 3$$
$$y = 4\left(\frac{1}{16}\right) - \frac{2}{4} + 3$$
$$y = \frac{4}{16} - \frac{8}{16} + \frac{48}{16}$$
$$y = \frac{44}{16}$$
$$y = \frac{11}{4}$$
$$\left(\frac{1}{4}, \frac{11}{4}\right)$$

5. Domain: {4, 3, 0};
   Range: {2, 7, 1, 6}

7. Domain: $\left\{\dfrac{1}{2}, 0, 1\right\}$;
   Range: {3}

9. Domain: {−8, 0, 5, 8};
   Range: {0, 2, 5}

11. Domain: {Atlanta, Macon, Pittsburgh};
    Range: {GA, PA}

13. Domain: {New York, California};
    Range: {Albany, Los Angeles, Buffalo}

15. The relation is a function if each element in the domain has exactly one corresponding element in the range.

17. The relations in Exercises 7, 9 and 11 are functions.

19. Yes; no vertical line intersects the graph more than once.

21. No; at least one vertical line intersects the graph more than once.

23. No; at least one vertical line intersects the graph more than once.

25. Yes; no vertical line intersects the graph more than once.

27. Yes; ; no vertical line intersects the graph more than once.

29. $f(x) = 2x - 5$
    $f(0) = 2(0) - 5 = 0 - 5 = -5$
    $f(2) = 2(2) - 5 = 4 - 5 = -1$
    $f(-3) = 2(-3) - 5 = -6 - 5 = -11$

31. $h(x) = \dfrac{1}{x+4}$
    $h(1) = \dfrac{1}{1+4} = \dfrac{1}{5}$
    $h(0) = \dfrac{1}{0+4} = \dfrac{1}{4}$
    $h(-2) = \dfrac{1}{-2+4} = \dfrac{1}{2}$

33. $m(x) = |5x - 7|$
    $m(0) = |5(0) - 7| = 7$
    $m(1) = |5(1) - 7| = 2$
    $m(2) = |5(2) - 7| = 3$

35. $n(x) = \sqrt{x-2}$
    $n(2) = \sqrt{2-2} = \sqrt{0} = 0$
    $n(3) = \sqrt{3-2} = \sqrt{1} = 1$
    $n(6) = \sqrt{6-2} = \sqrt{4} = 2$

37. The domain is the set of all real numbers for the which the denominator is not zero. Set the denominator equal to zero, and solve the resulting equation. The solution(s) must be excluded from the equation. For this example $x = 2$ must be excluded. The domain is $-\infty, 2 \cup 2, \infty$.

39. Exclude the value for which the denominator is zero. $-\infty, -6 \cup -6, \infty$

41. Exclude the value for which the denominator is zero. $-\infty, 0 \cup 0, \infty$

43. There exists no value for which the denominator is zero. No exclusions.
    $-\infty, \infty$

45. The solution set for the inequality written to indicate that the radicand must be greater than or equal to zero is the domain. $[-7, \infty)$

47. The solution set for the inequality written to indicate that the radicand must be greater than or equal to zero is the domain. $[3, \infty)$

49. The solution set for the inequality written to indicate that the radicand must be greater than or equal to zero is the domain.

$(-\infty, \frac{1}{2}]$

51. No exclusions. $-\infty, \infty$

53. No exclusions. $-\infty, \infty$

55. b

57. c

59. Domain: $(-\infty, \infty)$

Range: $[-2, \infty)$

61. Domain: $[-1, 1]$

Range: $[-4, 4]$

63. The function value at $x = 6$ is 2.

65. The function value at $x = \frac{1}{2}$ is $\frac{1}{4}$.

67. $(2, 7)$

69. $s(t) = 32t$

(a) $s(1) = 32(1) = 32$
The speed of an object 1 sec after being dropped is 32 ft/sec.

(b) $s(2) = 32(2) = 64$
The speed of an object 2 sec after being dropped is 64 ft/sec.

(c) $s(10) = 32(10) = 320$
The speed of an object 10 sec after being dropped is 320 ft/sec.

(d) $s(9.2) = 32(9.2) = 294.4$

The ball was going at a speed of 294.4 ft/sec before it hit the ground.

71. $h(t) = -16t^2 + 64t + 3$

(a) $h(0) = -16(0)^2 + 64(0) + 3$
$= 0 + 0 + 3$
$= 3$
The initial height of the ball is 3 ft.

(b) $h(1) = -16(1)^2 + 64(1) + 3$
$= -16 + 64 + 3$
$= 51$
The height of the ball 1 sec after being kicked is 51 ft.

(c) $h(2) = -16(2)^2 + 64(2) + 3$
$= -16(4) + 128 + 3$
$= -64 + 128 + 3$
$= 67$
The height of the ball 2 sec after being kicked is 67 ft.

(d) $h(4) = -16(4)^2 + 64(4) + 3$
$= -16(16) + 256 + 3$
$= -256 + 256 + 3$
$= 3$
The height of the ball 4 sec after being kicked is 3 ft.

73. (a) $C x = 75 + 50x$

$C(3) = 75 + 50(3)$

$C(3) = 225$

The cost is $225.

(b) $200 = 75 + 50x$

$125 = 50x$

$2.5 = x$

She was charged for 2.5 hours.

(c) If x represents the number of hours the minimum value of x is zero. There is no maximum. $[0, \infty)$

(d) The y-intercept represents the amount of the estimate.

Group Activity

1. The measurements and volume of the gutter are as follows:

Height, x	Base	Length	Volume
0.5 in.	7.5 in.	11 in.	41.25 in.^{3}
1.0 in.	6.5 in.	11 in.	71.5 in.^{3}
1.5 in.	5.5 in.	11 in.	90.75 in.^{3}
2.0 in.	4.5 in.	11 in.	99 in.^{3}
2.5 in.	3.5 in.	11 in.	96.25 in.^{3}
3.0 in.	2.5 in.	11 in.	82.5 in.^{3}
3.5 in.	1.5 in.	11 in.	57.75 in.^{3}

3. (a) Let x represent the height of the gutter. The base is $8.5 - 2x$.

(b) $V = (8.5 - 2x)(x)(11)$
$= 11x(8.5 - 2x)$
$= -22x^2 + 93.5x$

(c) $x = \dfrac{-b}{2a} = \dfrac{-93.5}{2(-22)} = \dfrac{-93.5}{-44} = 2.125$

$V = -22(2.125)^2 + 93.5(2.125)$
$= -99.34375 + 198.6875$
$= 99.34375$

(d) Fold the paper 2.125 in. from the edge. This will produce a maximum volume of 99.34375 in.^{3}

5. Let the optimal distance be x and V the volume.

$x = \dfrac{-b}{2a} = \dfrac{-612}{2(-144)} = \dfrac{-612}{-288} = 2.125$

$V = -144x^2 + 612x$
$= -144(2.125)^2 + 612(2.125)$
$= 650.25$

Fold the aluminum 2.125 in. from the edge. This will produce a maximum volume of 650.25 in.^{3}

Chapter 9 Review Exercises

Section 9.1

1. Linear

3. Quadratic

5. $x^2 = 25$
$x = \pm\sqrt{25}$
$x = \pm 5$

7. $x^2 + 49 = 0$
$x^2 = -49$
$x = \pm\sqrt{-49}$
The equation has no real-valued solutions..

9. $(x+1)^2 = 14$
$x + 1 = \pm\sqrt{14}$
$x = -1 \pm \sqrt{14}$

11. $\left(x - \dfrac{1}{8}\right)^2 = \dfrac{3}{64}$

$x - \dfrac{1}{8} = \pm\sqrt{\dfrac{3}{64}}$

$x - \dfrac{1}{8} = \pm\dfrac{\sqrt{3}}{8}$

$x = \dfrac{1}{8} \pm \dfrac{\sqrt{3}}{8}$

Section 9.2

13. $\left[\dfrac{1}{2}(12)\right]^2 = 6^2 = 36, n = 36$

15. $\left[\dfrac{1}{2}(-5)\right]^2 = \left(-\dfrac{5}{2}\right)^2 = \dfrac{25}{4}, n = \dfrac{25}{4}$

17. $x^2 + 8x + 3 = 0$

$x^2 + 8x = -3$

$x^2 + 8x + 16 = -3 + 16$

$(x+4)^2 = 13$

$x + 4 = \pm\sqrt{13}$

$x = -4 \pm \sqrt{13}$

19. $2x^2 - 6x - 6 = 0$

$x^2 - 3x - 3 = 0$

$x^2 - 3x = 3$

$x^2 - 3x + \dfrac{9}{4} = 3 + \dfrac{9}{4}$

$\left(x - \dfrac{3}{2}\right)^2 = \dfrac{21}{4}$

$x - \dfrac{3}{2} = \pm\sqrt{\dfrac{21}{4}}$

$x - \dfrac{3}{2} = \pm\dfrac{\sqrt{21}}{2}$

$x = \dfrac{3}{2} \pm \dfrac{\sqrt{21}}{2}$

21. Let x represent the length of each of the legs of the triangle.

$x^2 + x^2 = 15^2$

$2x^2 = 225$

$x^2 = 112.5$

$x \approx \pm 10.6$

Since the answer to this problem is a measurement, only the positive value is a solution. The length of the legs is about 10.6 ft.

Section 9.3

23. For $ax^2 + bx + c = 0$, and $a \neq 0$

$x = \dfrac{-b \pm \sqrt{b^2 - 4ac}}{2a}$

25. $x^2 + 4x + 4 = 0$

$x = \dfrac{-4 \pm \sqrt{4^2 - 4(1)(4)}}{2(1)}$

$x = \dfrac{-4 \pm \sqrt{16 - 16}}{2}$

$x = -\dfrac{4}{2}$

$x = -2$

27. $2x^2 - x - 3 = 0$

$x = \dfrac{-(-1) \pm \sqrt{(-1)^2 - 4(2)(-3)}}{2(2)}$

$x = \dfrac{1 \pm \sqrt{1 + 24}}{4}$

$x = \dfrac{1 \pm \sqrt{25}}{4}$

$x = \dfrac{1 \pm 5}{4}$

$x = \dfrac{1 + 5}{4}$ or $x = \dfrac{1 - 5}{4}$

$x = \dfrac{6}{4}$ $\qquad x = \dfrac{-4}{4}$

$x = \dfrac{3}{2}$ $\qquad x = -1$

29. $\dfrac{1}{6}x^2 + x + \dfrac{1}{3} = 0$

$x^2 + 6x + 2 = 0$

$x = \dfrac{-6 \pm \sqrt{6^2 - 4(1)(2)}}{2(1)}$

$x = \dfrac{-6 \pm \sqrt{36 - 8}}{2}$

$x = \dfrac{-6 \pm \sqrt{28}}{2}$

$x = \dfrac{-6 \pm 2\sqrt{7}}{2}$

$x = -3 \pm \sqrt{7}$

31. $0.01x^2 - 0.02x - 0.04 = 0$

$x^2 - 2x - 4 = 0$

$x = \dfrac{-(-2) \pm \sqrt{(-2)^2 - 4(1)(-4)}}{2(1)}$

$x = \dfrac{2 \pm \sqrt{4 + 16}}{2}$

$x = \dfrac{2 \pm \sqrt{20}}{2}$

$x = \dfrac{2 \pm \sqrt{4 \cdot 5}}{2}$

$x = \dfrac{2 \pm 2\sqrt{5}}{2}$

$x = 1 \pm \sqrt{5}$

33. $(x - 1)(x - 7) = -18$

$x^2 - 7x - x + 7 = -18$

$x^2 - 8x + 25 = 0$

$x = \dfrac{-(-8) \pm \sqrt{(-8)^2 - 4(1)(25)}}{2(1)}$

$x = \dfrac{8 \pm \sqrt{64 - 100}}{2}$

$x = \dfrac{8 \pm \sqrt{-36}}{2}$

The equation has no real-valued solutions.

35. Let x represent the height of the parallelogram. The base of the parallelogram is represented by $x + 1$.

$x(x + 1) = 24$

$x^2 + x = 24$

$x^2 + x - 24 = 0$

$x = \dfrac{-1 \pm \sqrt{1^2 - 4(1)(-24)}}{2(1)}$

$x = \dfrac{-1 \pm \sqrt{1 + 96}}{2}$

$x = \dfrac{-1 \pm \sqrt{97}}{2}$

Since the answer to this problem is a measurement, only the positive value is a solution.

$x = \dfrac{-1 + \sqrt{97}}{2} \approx 4.4$

$x + 1 = \dfrac{-1 + \sqrt{97}}{2} + 1 = \dfrac{1 + \sqrt{97}}{2} \approx 5.4$

The height of the parallelogram is 4.4 cm. The base of the parallelogram is 5.4 cm.

Section 9.4

37. $a + bi$ where a and b are real numbers and $i = \sqrt{1}$

39. $\sqrt{-16} = 4i$

41. $\sqrt{-75} \cdot \sqrt{-3} = i\sqrt{75} \cdot i\sqrt{3}$

$= i^2 \sqrt{225} = -1(15) = -15$

43. $-6i^2 = -6(-1) = 6$

45. $12 - i^2 = 12 - (-1) = 13$

47. $(-3 + i) - (2 - 4i) = -3 + i - 2 + 4i$

$= -5 + 5i$

49. $(4 - 3i)(4 + 3i) = 16 + 12i - 12i - 9i^2$

$= 16 - 9(-1) = 25 + 0i$

51. $\dfrac{17-4i}{-4} = -\dfrac{17}{4} + i$

Real part: $-\dfrac{17}{4}$

Imaginary part: 1

53. $\dfrac{2-i}{3+2i} = \dfrac{2-i}{3+2i} \cdot \dfrac{3-2i}{3-2i}$

$= \dfrac{6-4i-3i+2i^2}{9-6i+6i-4i^2} = \dfrac{6-7i+2(-1)}{9-4(-1)}$

$= \dfrac{4-7i}{13} = \dfrac{4}{13} - \dfrac{7}{13}i$

55. $x+12\,^2 = -20$

$\sqrt{x+12\,^2} = \pm\sqrt{-20}$

$x+12 = \pm 2i\sqrt{5}$

$x = -12 \pm 2i\sqrt{5}$

57. $4x^2 - x + 2 = 0$

$a = 4, b = -1, c = 2$

$x = \dfrac{-(-1) \pm \sqrt{(-1)^2 - 4(4)(2)}}{2(4)}$

$= \dfrac{1 \pm \sqrt{-31}}{8}$

$x = \dfrac{1}{8} \pm \dfrac{\sqrt{31}}{8}i$

Section 9.5

59. $a = 1$; upward

61. $a = -2$; downward

63. $y = 3x^2 + 6x + 4$

$x = \dfrac{-b}{2a} = \dfrac{-6}{2(3)} = \dfrac{-6}{6} = -1$

$y = 3(-1)^2 + 6(-1) + 4$

$= 3 - 6 + 4$

$= 1$

Vertex: $(-1, 1)$

65. $y = -2x^2 + 12x - 5$

$x = \dfrac{-b}{2a} = \dfrac{-12}{2(-2)} = \dfrac{-12}{-4} = 3$

$y = -2(3)^2 + 12(3) - 5$

$= -18 + 36 - 5$

$= 13$

Vertex: $(3, 13)$

67. $y = 3x^2 + 12x + 9$

(a) $a = 1$ Upward

(b) $x = \dfrac{-b}{2a} = \dfrac{-2}{2(1)} = -1$

$y = (-1)^2 + 2(-1) - 3$

$= 1 - 2 - 3$

$= -4$

Vertex: $(-1, -4)$

(c) x-intercepts: $x^2 + 2x - 3 = 0$

$(x-1)(x+3) = 0$

$x - 1 = 0 \quad \text{or} \quad x + 3 = 0$

$x = 1 \qquad\qquad x = -3$

$(1, 0) \quad (-3, 0)$

(d) y-intercept: $y = (0)^2 + 2(0) - 3$

$y = -3 \qquad\qquad (0,-3)$

(e)

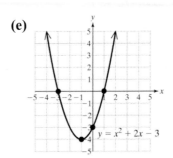

69. $y = -3x^2 + 12x - 9$

(a) $a = -3$ Downward

(b) $x = \dfrac{-b}{2a} = \dfrac{-(12)}{2(-3)} = 2$

$y = -3(2)^2 + 12(2) - 9$
$= -12 + 24 - 9$
$= 3$ (2, 3)

(c) x-intercepts: $-3x^2 + 12x - 9 = 0$
$-3(x^2 - 4x + 3) = 0$
$-3(x - 1)(x - 3) = 0$
$x - 1 = 0$ or $x - 3 = 0$
$x = 1$ $x = 3$
(1, 0)   (3, 0)

(d) y-intercept: $y = -3(0)^2 + 12(0) - 9$
$y = -9$ (0,-9)

(e)

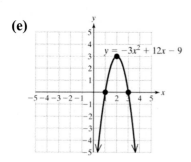

71. $y = -16t^2 + 256t$

(a) The maximum height is the y value of the vertex. (See part b for the t value.)
$y = -16(8)^2 + 256(8)$
$y = -1024 + 2048$
$y = 1024$
The maximum height reached is 1024 ft.

(b) $t = \dfrac{-b}{2a} = \dfrac{-256}{2(-16)} = 8$
The time required for the object to reach its maximum height is 8 sec.

Section 9.6

73. Domain: $\{2\}$
Range: $\{0, 1, -5, 2\}$
The relation is not a function..

75. Domain: $(-\infty, \infty)$
Range: $[-2, \infty)$
The graph is a function. It passes the vertical line test..

77. Domain: $\{3, -4, 0, 2\}$
Range: $\left\{0, \dfrac{1}{2}, 3, -12\right\}$
The relation is a function.

79. $g(x) = \dfrac{x}{5 - x}$

(a) $g(0) = \dfrac{0}{5 - 0} = \dfrac{0}{5} = 0$

(b) $g(4) = \dfrac{4}{5 - 4} = \dfrac{4}{1} = 4$

(c) $g(-1) = \dfrac{-1}{5 - (-1)} = \dfrac{-1}{6} = -\dfrac{1}{6}$

(d) $g(3) = \dfrac{3}{5 - 3} = \dfrac{3}{2}$

(e) $g(-5) = \dfrac{-5}{5 - (-5)} = \dfrac{-5}{10} = -\dfrac{1}{2}$

81. Exclude the value for which the denominator is zero. $-\infty, 11 \cup 11, \infty$

83. The solution set for the inequality written to indicate that the radicand must be greater than or equal to zero is the domain. $[-2, \infty)$

Chapter 9 Test

1. $(x+1)^2 = 14$

$x+1 = \pm\sqrt{14}$

$x = -1 \pm \sqrt{14}$

3. $3x^2 - 5x = -1$

$3x^2 - 5x + 1 = 0$

$x = \dfrac{-(-5) \pm \sqrt{(-5)^2 - 4(3)(1)}}{2(3)}$

$x = \dfrac{5 \pm \sqrt{25 - 12}}{6}$

$x = \dfrac{5 \pm \sqrt{13}}{6}$

5. $(c-12)^2 = 12$

$c - 12 = \pm\sqrt{12}$

$c = 12 \pm \sqrt{12}$

$c = 12 \pm \sqrt{4 \cdot 3}$

$c = 12 \pm 2\sqrt{3}$

7. $3t^2 = 30$

$t^2 = 10$

$t = \pm\sqrt{10}$

9. $6p^2 - 11p = 0$

$p(6p - 11) = 0$

$p = 0$ or $6p - 11 = 0$

$p = \dfrac{11}{6}$

11. $4\pi r^2 = 201$

$r^2 = \dfrac{201}{4\pi}$

$r = \pm\sqrt{\dfrac{201}{4\pi}}$

Since the answer to this problem is a measurement, only the positive value is a solution.

$r = \sqrt{\dfrac{201}{4\pi}} \approx 4.0$ in.

13. $\sqrt{-100} = 10i$

15. $\sqrt{-9} \cdot \sqrt{-49} = i\sqrt{9} \cdot i\sqrt{81}$

$= 3i \cdot 9i = 27i^2 = -27$

17. $5 - 3i^2 = 5 - 3(-1) = 8$

19. $(8 + i)(-2 - 3i) = -16 - 24i - 2i - 3i^2$

$= -16 - 26i - 3(-1) = -13 - 26i$

21. $\dfrac{1}{10 - 11i} = \dfrac{1}{10 - 11i} \cdot \dfrac{10 + 11i}{10 + 11i}$

$= \dfrac{10 + 11i}{100 - 121i^2} = \dfrac{10 + 11i}{221} = \dfrac{10}{221} + \dfrac{11}{221}i$

23. $x^2 + x + 7 = 0$

$a = 1, b = 1, c = 7$

$x = \dfrac{-1 \pm \sqrt{(1)^2 - 4(1)(7)}}{2(1)} = \dfrac{-1 \pm \sqrt{-27}}{2}$

$= \dfrac{-1 \pm i\sqrt{9 \cdot 3}}{2} = \dfrac{-1 \pm 3i\sqrt{3}}{2}$

$x = -\dfrac{1}{2} \pm \dfrac{3\sqrt{3}}{2}i$

25. $y = x^2 - 10x + 25$

$x = \dfrac{-b}{2a} = \dfrac{-(-10)}{2(1)} = 5$

$y = (5)^2 - 10(5) + 25$

$= 25 - 50 + 25$

$= 0$

$(5, 0)$

27. $y = -x^2 - 16$

$x = \dfrac{-b}{2a} = \dfrac{0}{2(-1)} = 0$

$y = -(0)^2 - 16 = -16$

$(0, -16)$.

29. $y = x^2 + 6x + 8$

(a) $a = 1$ Upward

(b) $x = \dfrac{-b}{2a} = \dfrac{-6}{2(1)} = -3$

$y = (-3)^2 + 6(-3) + 8$
$= 9 - 18 + 8$
$= -1$
$(-3, -1)$

(c) $x^2 + 6x + 8 = 0$
$(x + 4)(x + 2) = 0$

$x + 4 = 0$ or $x + 2 = 0$
$x = -4$ or $x = -2$
$(-4, 0)$ and $(-2, 0)$

(d) $y = (0)^2 + 6(0) + 8 = 8$
$(0, 8)$

(e)

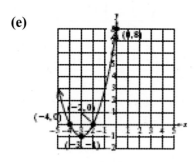

31. $y = -400x^2 + 20,000x$

(a) $x = \dfrac{-b}{2a} = \dfrac{-20,000}{2(-400)} = 25$

The ticket price that will produce maximum revenue is \$25.

(b) $y = -400(25)^2 + 20,000(25)$
$y = -250,000 + 500,000$
$y = 250,000$
The maximum revenue is \$250,000.

33. $f\ x\ = \dfrac{1}{x + 2}$

$f\ 0\ = \dfrac{1}{0\ +2} = \dfrac{1}{2}$

$f\ -2\ = \dfrac{1}{-2\ +2} = \dfrac{1}{0} = \text{undefined}$

$f\ 6\ = \dfrac{1}{6\ +2} = \dfrac{1}{8}$

35. Domain: $[-7, \infty)$

37.

$D\ x\ = \dfrac{1}{2} x\ x - 3$

a $D\ 5\ = \dfrac{1}{2}\ 5\ 5 - 3\ = 5$

A five sided polygon has 5 diagonals.

b $D\ 10\ = \dfrac{1}{2}\ 10\ 10 - 3\ = 35$

A ten sided polygon has 35 diagonals.

c   Substitute 20 for $D\ x$

$20 = \dfrac{1}{2} x\ x - 3$
$40 = x(x - 3)$
$40 = x^2 - 3x$
$0 = x^2 - 3x - 40$
$0 = (x - 8)(x + 5)$
$x - 8 = 0$ or $x + 5 = 0$
$x = 8$ $x = -5$

$x + 5$ is an extraneous solution.

A polygon with 20 diagonals has eight sides.

Cumulative Review Exercises
Chapters 1–9

1.
$$3x - 5 = 2(x - 2)$$
$$3x - 5 = 2x - 4$$
$$3x - 2x - 5 = 2x - 2x - 4$$
$$x - 5 = -4$$
$$x - 5 + 5 = -4 + 5$$
$$x = 1$$

3.
$$\frac{1}{2}y - \frac{5}{6} = \frac{1}{4}y + 2$$
$$6y - 10 = 3y + 24$$
$$6y - 3y - 10 = 3y - 3y + 24$$
$$3y - 10 = 24$$
$$3y - 10 + 10 = 24 + 10$$
$$3y = 34$$
$$y = \frac{34}{3}$$

5. $y = -37.6x + 1353$ where $9 \leq x \leq 13$

(a) Decreases

(b) $m = -37.6$
For each additional increase in education level, the death rate decreases by approximately 38 deaths per 100,000 people.

(c) $y = -37.6(12) + 1353$
$y = -451.2 + 1353$
$y = 901.8$
The expected death rate would be 901.8 per 100,000.

(d) $977 = -37.6x + 1353$
$-376 = -37.6x$
$10 = x$
The approximate median education level for a city with 977 deaths per 100,000 is about 10th grade.

7. $(5.2 \times 10^7)(365) = 1898 \times 10^7$
$$= 1.898 \times 10^{10} \text{ diapers}$$

9.
$$(2x - 3)^2 - 4(x - 1)$$
$$= (2x)^2 - 2(2x)(3) + 3^2 - 4x + 4$$
$$= 4x^2 - 12x + 9 - 4x + 4$$
$$= 4x^2 - 16x + 13$$

11. $2x^2 - 9x - 35 = (2x + 5)(x - 7)$

13. Let x represent the height of a triangle. The length of the base of the triangle is represented by $x + 1$.
$$\frac{1}{2}x(x + 1) = 36$$
$$x(x + 1) = 72$$
$$x^2 + x - 72 = 0$$
$$(x - 8)(x + 9) = 0$$
$$x - 8 = 0 \quad \text{or} \quad x + 9 = 0$$
$$x = 8 \qquad\qquad x = -9$$
Since the answer to this problem is a measurement, only the positive value is a solution.
$x = 8$
$x + 1 = 9$
The base is 9 m and the height is 8 m.

15.
$$\frac{x^2 + 10x + 9}{x^2 - 81} \cdot \frac{18 - 2x}{x^2 + 2x + 1}$$
$$= \frac{(x + 1)(x + 9)}{(x - 9)(x + 9)} \cdot \frac{-2(x - 9)}{(x + 1)^2}$$
$$= -\frac{2}{x + 1}$$

17.
$$\frac{\frac{1}{x+1} - \frac{1}{x-1}}{\frac{x}{x^2 - 1}} = \frac{\frac{1}{x+1} - \frac{1}{x-1}}{\frac{x}{(x-1)(x+1)}}$$
$$= \frac{\frac{1}{x+1} - \frac{1}{x-1}}{\frac{x}{(x-1)(x+1)}} \cdot \frac{(x-1)(x+1)}{(x-1)(x+1)}$$
$$= \frac{(x-1) - (x+1)}{x}$$
$$= \frac{x - 1 - x - 1}{x}$$
$$= -\frac{2}{x}$$

19. $y - 3 = \dfrac{1}{2}(x - (-2))$

$y - 3 = \dfrac{1}{2}(x + 2)$

$y - 3 = \dfrac{1}{2}x + 1$

$y = \dfrac{1}{2}x + 4$

21. $4x + 12 = 0$

(a) x-intercept: $4x + 12 = 0$
$$4x = -12$$
$$x = -3 \qquad (-3, 0)$$

(b) y-intercept: $4(0) + 12 = 0$
$$12 = 0 \quad \text{None}$$

(c) It has been shown in part b that this equation can be written in the form $x = $ a constant. This indicates the line is a vertical line whose slope is undefined.

(d)

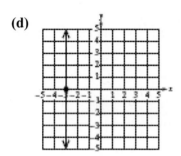

23. $\quad 2x - y = 8$
$\quad 4x - 4y = 3x - 3$

Since the coefficient on y in the first equation is -1, solve this equation for y.
$$2x - y = 8$$
$$-y = -2x + 8$$
$$y = 2x - 8$$

Substitute this value for y into the second equation and solve for x.
$$4x - 4(2x - 8) = 3x - 3$$
$$4x - 8x + 32 = 3x - 3$$
$$-4x + 32 = 3x - 3$$
$$-7x + 32 = -3$$
$$-7x = -35$$
$$x = 5$$
Substitute the value found for x into the first equation and solve for y.
$$2(5) - y = 8$$
$$10 - y = 8$$
$$-y = -2$$
$$y = 2 \qquad (5, 2)$$

25.

	Number	Value	Total value
Dimes	x	0.10	$0.10x$
Quarters	y	0.25	$0.25y$
	27		4.80

$$x + y = 27$$
$$0.10x + 0.25y = 4.80$$

Solve this system of equations by the substitution method. Solve the first equation for x.
$$x + y = 27$$
$$x = 27 - y$$

Multiply the second equation by 100 to eliminate the decimals.
$$0.10x + 0.25y = 4.80$$
$$10x + 25y = 480$$

Substitute the value found for x into the above equation.
$$10(27 - y) + 25y = 480$$
$$270 - 10y + 25y = 480$$
$$270 + 15y = 480$$
$$15y = 210$$
$$y = 14$$

Substitute the value found for y into the first equation and solve for x.
$$x + 14 = 27$$
$$x = 13$$
There are 13 dimes and 14 quarters.

27. $\pi, \sqrt{7}$

29. $\dfrac{\sqrt{16x^4}}{\sqrt{2x}} = \sqrt{\dfrac{16x^4}{2x}}$

$\qquad = \sqrt{8x^3}$

$\qquad = \sqrt{4 \cdot 2 \cdot x^2 \cdot x}$

$\qquad = 2x\sqrt{2x}$

31. $-3\sqrt{2x} + \sqrt{50x} = -3\sqrt{2x} + \sqrt{25 \cdot 2x}$

$\qquad\qquad\qquad = -3\sqrt{2x} + 5\sqrt{2x}$

$\qquad\qquad\qquad = 2\sqrt{2x}$

33. $\sqrt{x+11} = x+5$

$\left(\sqrt{x+11}\right)^2 = (x+5)^2$

$\quad x+11 = x^2 + 10x + 25$

$\quad\quad 0 = x^2 + 9x + 14$

$\quad\quad 0 = (x+2)(x+7)$

$x+2 = 0 \quad$ or $\quad x+7 = 0$

$\quad x = -2 \qquad\qquad x = -7$

When checking these values in the original
equation, $x = -7$ does not check.
Solution: $x = -2$

35. b

37. Domain: $\{2, -1, 9, -6\}$
Range: $\{4, 3, 2, 8\}$

39. $-4x - 5y = 10$

$\quad -5y = 4x + 10$

$\qquad y = -\dfrac{4}{5}x - 2$

$m = -\dfrac{4}{5}$

41. $2x^2 + 12x + 6 = 0$

$\quad x^2 + 6x + 3 = 0$

$\quad x^2 + 6x = -3$

$x^2 + 6x + 9 = -3 + 9$

$\quad (x+3)^2 = 6$

$\quad x + 3 = \pm\sqrt{6}$

$\qquad x = -3 \pm \sqrt{6}$

43.

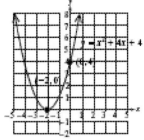

Vertex: $(-2, 0)$
x-intercept: $(-2, 0)$
y-intercept: $(0, 4)$

45. $3i(4i - 1) = 12i^2 - 3i$

$\qquad\qquad = 12(-1) - 3i = -12 - 3i$

Appendix

Calculator Exercises

1. and 2.

```
4/9
        .4444444444
7/11
        .6363636364
```

2. and 4.

```
3/22
        .1363636364
5/13
        .3846153846
```

Section A.1 Practice Exercises

1. Tens

3. Hundreds

5. Tenths

7. Hundredths

9. No; the symbols I, V, X, and so on each represent certain numerical values but the values are not dependent on the position of the symbol within the number.

11.
```
        0.7
   10)7.0
        7 0
```
Solution: 0.7

13.
```
        0.36
   25)9.00
        7 5
        1 50
        1 50
```
Solution: 0.36

15.
```
        1.22
   9)11.00
      9
      2 0
      1 8
        20
        18
         2
```
Solution: $1.\overline{2}$

17.
```
        0.2121
   33)7.0000
      66
       40
       33
        70
        66
         4
```
Solution: $0.\overline{21}$

19. 214.1

21. 39.268

23. 40,000

25. 0.73

27. $0.45 = \dfrac{45}{100} = \dfrac{5 \cdot 9}{5 \cdot 20} = \dfrac{9}{20}$

29. $0.181 = \dfrac{181}{1000}$

31. $2.04 = \dfrac{204}{100} = \dfrac{4 \cdot 51}{4 \cdot 25} = \dfrac{51}{25}$ or $2\dfrac{1}{25}$

33. $13.007 = \dfrac{13,007}{1000}$ or $13\dfrac{7}{1000}$

35. $0.\overline{5} = \dfrac{5}{9}$

37. $1.\overline{1} = 1 + 0.\overline{1} = 1 + \dfrac{1}{9} = 1\dfrac{1}{9}$ or $\dfrac{10}{9}$

39. $30\% = 30 \times 0.01 = 0.30$

$30\% = 30 \times \dfrac{1}{100} = \dfrac{3 \cdot 10}{10 \cdot 10} = \dfrac{3}{10}$

41. $75\% = 75 \times 0.01 = 0.75$

$75\% = 75 \times \dfrac{1}{100} = \dfrac{75}{100} = \dfrac{25 \cdot 3}{25 \cdot 4} = \dfrac{3}{4}$

43. $3\dfrac{3}{4}\% = 3.75\% = 3.75 \times 0.01 = 0.0375$

$3\dfrac{3}{4}\% = 3\dfrac{3}{4} \times \dfrac{1}{100}$

$\quad = \dfrac{15}{4} \times \dfrac{1}{100}$

$\quad = \dfrac{3 \cdot 5}{4} \times \dfrac{1}{5 \cdot 20}$

$\quad = \dfrac{3}{4} \times \dfrac{1}{20}$

$\quad = \dfrac{3}{80}$

45. $15.7\% = 15.7 \times 0.01 = 0.157$

$15.7\% = \dfrac{157}{10} \times \dfrac{1}{100} = \dfrac{157}{1000}$

47. $270\% = 270 \times 0.01 = 2.70$

$270\% = 270 \times \dfrac{1}{100} = \dfrac{270}{100} = \dfrac{27 \times \cancel{10}^{1}}{10 \times \cancel{10}_{1}} = \dfrac{27}{10}$

49. Multiply by 100 and apply the % sign.

51. $0.05 = 0.05 \times 100\% = 5\%$

53. $0.90 = 0.90 \times 100\% = 90\%$

55. $1.2 = 1.2 \times 100\% = 120\%$

57. $7.5 = 7.5 \times 100\% = 750\%$

59. $0.135 = 0.135 \times 100\% = 13.5\%$

61. $0.003 = 0.003 \times 100\% = 0.3\%$

63.
$$\begin{array}{r} 0.06 \\ 50\overline{)3.00} \\ \underline{3\ 00} \end{array}$$

$0.06 = 0.06 \times 100\% = 6\%$

65.
$$\begin{array}{r} 4.5 \\ 2\overline{)9.0} \\ \underline{8} \\ 1\ 0 \\ \underline{1\ 0} \end{array}$$

$4.5 = 4.5 \times 100\% = 450\%$

67.
$$\begin{array}{r} 0.625 \\ 8\overline{)5.000} \\ \underline{4\ 8} \\ 20 \\ \underline{16} \\ 40 \\ \underline{40} \end{array}$$

$0.625 = 0.625 \times 100\% = 62.5\%$

69.
$$\begin{array}{r} 0.3125 \\ 16\overline{)5.0000} \\ \underline{48} \\ 20 \\ \underline{16} \\ 40 \\ \underline{32} \\ 80 \\ \underline{80} \end{array}$$

$0.3125 = 0.3125 \times 100\% = 31.25\%$

71.
$$\begin{array}{r} 0.833 \\ 6\overline{)5.000} \\ \underline{4\ 8} \\ 20 \\ \underline{18} \\ 20 \\ \underline{18} \\ 2 \end{array}$$

$0.83\overline{3} = 0.83\overline{3} \times 100\% = 83.\overline{3}\%$

73.

$$
\begin{array}{r}
0.933 \\
15{\overline{\smash{\big)}\,14.000}} \\
\underline{13\,5} \\
50 \\
\underline{45} \\
50 \\
\underline{45} \\
5
\end{array}
$$

$$0.93\overline{3} = 0.93\overline{3} \times 100\% = 93.\overline{3}\%$$

75. The discount is 30% of the original price of the suit. *of* translates as multiplication.
$30\%(140) = 0.30(140) = \$42$

77. Tom's taxes are 27% of his income. *of* translates as multiplication.
$27\%(12,500) = 0.27(12,500) = \$3375$

79. $\dfrac{5.95}{85} = 0.07 = 0.07 \times 100\% = 7\%$

81. 33% of the monthly income is spent on rent. *of* translates as multiplication.
$33\%(2400) = 0.33 \times 2400 = \$792$

83. 8% of the monthly income is spent on utilities. *of* translates as multiplication.
$8\%(2400) = 0.08 \times 2400 = \$192$

85. 75% of the mortgage has been paid. *of* translates as multiplication.
$75\%(90,000) = 0.75(90,000) = \$67,500$

Section A.2 Practice Exercises

1. (a) The **mean** of a set of numbers is the sum of the values divided by the number of values.

(b) The **median** is the "middle" number in an ordered list of numbers.

(c) The **mode** of a set of data is the value or values that occur most often.

(d) If two data values occur most often in a data set, the data are **bimodal.**

(e) When data values in a list appear multiple times, a **weighted mean** can be found. Each data value is "weighted" by the number of times it appears in the list.

3. Mean $= \dfrac{3+8+5+7+4+2+7+4}{8} = \dfrac{40}{8}$
$= 5$

5. Mean $= \dfrac{7+6+5+10+8+4+8+6+0}{9}$
$= \dfrac{54}{9} = 6$

7. Mean $= \dfrac{(-22)+(-14)+(-12)+(-16)+(-15)}{5}$
$= \dfrac{-79}{5} = -15.8$

9. Mean $= \dfrac{5.5+6.0+5.8+5.8+6.0+5.6}{6}$
$= \dfrac{34.7}{6} \approx 5.8 \text{ hr}$

11. (a)

$$
\begin{array}{r}
360 \\
370 \\
380 \\
400 \\
400 \\
+\ 470 \\
\hline
2380
\end{array}
$$

$\text{Mean} = \dfrac{2380}{6} \approx 397 \text{ Cal}$

(b)

$$
\begin{array}{r}
310 \\
325 \\
350 \\
390 \\
440 \\
+\ 500 \\
\hline
2315
\end{array}
$$

$\text{Mean} = \dfrac{2315}{6} \approx 386 \text{ Cal}$

(c)

$$
\begin{array}{r}
397 \\
-\ 386 \\
\hline
11
\end{array}
$$

There is only an 11-Cal difference in the means.

13. (a) $\text{Mean} = \dfrac{98 + 80 + 78 + 90}{4} = \dfrac{346}{4}$
$= 86.5$
Zach's mean test score was 86.5%.

(b) $\text{Mean} = \dfrac{98 + 80 + 78 + 90 + 59}{5} = \dfrac{405}{5}$
$= 81$
The mean of all five tests was 81%.

(c) The low score of 59% decreased Zach's average by 86.5% − 81% = 5.5%.

15. Arrange the numbers in order from least to greatest.
13   14   16   <u>17</u>   19   20   22
Median = 17

17. Arrange the numbers in order from least to greatest.
100   109   <u>110   111</u>   118   123

$\text{Median} = \dfrac{110 + 111}{2} = \dfrac{221}{2} = 110.5$

19. Arrange the numbers in order from least to greatest.

−58   − 55   <u>-55   -50</u>   − 40   − 40

$\text{Median} = \dfrac{-55 + -50}{2} = \dfrac{-105}{2} = -52.5$

21. Arrange the numbers in order from least to greatest.

3.82   3.87   <u>3.93</u>   4.09   4.10

Median = 3.93

23. Arrange the numbers in order from least to greatest.

−8   −5   -3   <u>-1   1</u>   2   4   8

$\text{Median} = \dfrac{-1 + 1}{2} = \dfrac{0}{2} = 0$

25. Arrange the numbers in order from least to greatest.

42.4   45.4   46.5   48.3   <u>51.7</u>
56.4   71.2   86.8   91.6

Median = 51.7 million passengers

27. The data value 4 appears most often. The mode is 4.

29. The data values -21 and -24 appear most often. The modes are -21 and -24.

31. No data value occurs most often. There is no mode.

33. $600

35. 5.2%, 5.8%

37. Mean $= \dfrac{92 + 98 + 43 + 98 + 97 + 85}{6} = \dfrac{513}{6}$
$= 85.5\%$

Arrange the numbers in order from least to greatest.
43 85 92 97 98 98

Median $= \dfrac{92 + 97}{2} = \dfrac{189}{2} = 94.5\%$

The median gave Jonathan a better overall score.

39. Mean $= \dfrac{\begin{array}{c}312 + 225 + 221 + 256 + 308 \\ + 280 + 147\end{array}}{7}$
$= \dfrac{1749}{7} \approx \$250$

Arrange the numbers in order from least to greatest.
147 221 225 <u>256</u> 280 308 312
Median = \$256

There is no mode.

41. Mean
$\begin{array}{c}850,000 + 835,000 + 839,000 \\ + 829,000 + 850,000 + 850,000 \\ + 850,000 + 847,000 \\ + 1,850,000 + 825,000\end{array}$
$= \dfrac{}{10}$
$= \dfrac{9,425,000}{10} = \$942,500$

Arrange the numbers in order from least to greatest.
8.25 8.29 8.35 8.39 <u>8.47</u> <u>8.5</u> 8.5 8.5 8.5 18.5

$\dfrac{8.47 + 8.5}{2} = 8.485$

Median = \$848,500

Mode = \$850,000

43. $\dfrac{4(3) + 1(2) + 3(4) + 5(1)}{13} = \dfrac{31}{13} \approx 2.38$

45. $\dfrac{3(3.5) + 4(2) + 1(0) + 3(4)}{11} = \dfrac{30.5}{11} \approx 2.77$

47. $\dfrac{3(4) + 1(2) + 2(3.5) + 4(3)}{10} = \dfrac{33}{10} \approx 3.3$
Elmer's GPA improved from 2.5 to 3.3.

49.
$\dfrac{3(1) + 9(2) + 3(10) + 9(4) + 6(5)}{37} = \dfrac{117}{37} \approx 3.2$
The mean number of residents is approximately 3.2.

Section A.3 Practice Exercises

1. b, e, i

3. $P = 2w + 2l$
$= 2(6) + 2(10)$
$= 12 + 20$
$= 32$ m

5. $P = 4s$
$= 4(4.3)$
$= 17.2$ miles

7. $P = 2\dfrac{1}{3} + 5\dfrac{1}{6} + 4$
$= \dfrac{14}{6} + \dfrac{31}{6} + \dfrac{24}{6}$
$= \dfrac{69}{6}$
$= \dfrac{23}{2}$
$= 11\dfrac{1}{2}$ in.

9. $C = 2\pi r = 2(3.14)(5) = 31.4$ ft

11. a, f, g

13. $A = lw = (3)(11) = 33$ cm^2

15. $A = s^2$
$= (4.1)^2$
$= (4.1)(4.1)$
$= 16.81 \text{ m}^2$

17. $A = bh = (14)(6) = 84 \text{ in.}^2$

19. $A = \dfrac{1}{2}bh = 0.5(8.8)(2.3) = 10.12 \text{ km}^2$

21. $A = \pi r^2 = (3.14)(2.1)^2 = 13.8474 \text{ ft}^2$

23. $A = \dfrac{1}{2}(b_1 + b_2)h = \dfrac{1}{2}(14 + 8)6 = 66 \text{ in.}^2$

25. $A = \dfrac{1}{2}bh = \dfrac{1}{2}(9)(7) = 31.5 \text{ ft}^2$

27. c, d, h

29. $V = \pi r^2 h$
$= (3.14)(3.5)^2(8)$
$= 307.72 \text{ cm}^3$

31. $V = lwh = (6.5)(1.5)(4) = 39 \text{ in.}^3$

33. $V = \dfrac{4}{3}\pi r^3$
$= \dfrac{4}{3}(3.14)(3)^3$
$= \dfrac{4}{\cancel{3}}(3.14)(\cancel{27}^9)$
$= 113.04 \text{ cm}^3$

35. $V = \dfrac{1}{3}\pi r^2 h$
$= \dfrac{1}{3}(3.14)(9)^2(20)$
$= \dfrac{1}{\cancel{3}}(3.14)(\cancel{81}^{27})(20)$
$= 1695.6 \text{ cm}^3$

37. To find the amount of helium is to find the volume of the spherical balloon.
$V = \dfrac{4}{3}\pi r^3 = \dfrac{4}{3}(3.14)(9)^3 = 3052.08 \text{ in.}^3$

39. The volume of the snow cone is
$V = \dfrac{1}{3}\pi r^2 h = \dfrac{1}{3}(3.14)(3)^2(12) = 113.04 \text{ cm}^3$

41. The area of the wall is $(20)(8) = 160 \text{ ft}^2$.

(a) To find the price per square foot, divide the cost by the area of the wall.
$\$40 \div 160 \text{ ft}^2 \approx \$0.25/\text{ft}^2$

(b) The areas of the remaining walls are $(20)(8) = 160 \text{ ft}^2$, $(16)(8) = 128 \text{ ft}^2$, and $(16)(8) = 128 \text{ ft}^2$. The total area is $160 + 128 + 128 = 416 \text{ ft}^2$. The total price is $416(0.25) = \$104$.

43. Perimeter

45. To find the fence is to find the perimeter of the triangularly shaped garden.
$P = 12 + 22 + 20 = 54 \text{ ft}$

47. (a) The area of the field is
$360(160) = 57{,}600 \text{ ft}^2$

(b) The area of a piece of sod is $1(3) = 3 \text{ ft}^2$
To find the number of pieces of sod, divide the area of the football field by the area of a piece of sod.
$57{,}600 \div 3 = 19{,}200 \text{ pieces}$

49. (a) The area of the 8-in. diameter circular pizza is $A = \pi r^2 = (3.14)(4) = 50.24 \text{ in.}^2$

(b) The area of the 12-in. diameter circular pizza is
$A = \pi r^2 = (3.14)(6) = 113.04 \text{ in.}^2$

(c) Two 8-inch pizzas have
$2(50.24) = 100.48 \text{ in.}^2$ One 12-inch pizza has 113.04 in.^2 Therefore one 12-inch pizza has more.

51. The volume of a soup can in the shape of a right circular cylinder is
$$V = \pi r^2 h = (3.14)(3.2)^2(9) = 289.3824 \text{ cm}^3$$

53. True

55. True

57. True

59. Not possible; acute angles are less than 90°.

61. Answers vary. One example: 100°, 80°

63. 45°

65. **(a)** $\angle 1$ and $\angle 3$, $\angle 2$ and $\angle 4$

(b) $\angle 1$ and $\angle 2$, $\angle 2$ and $\angle 3$, $\angle 3$ and $\angle 4$, $\angle 1$ and $\angle 4$

(c) Since $\angle 1$ and $\angle 4$ are supplementary, $m(\angle 1) + m(\angle 4) = 180°$.
$m(\angle 1) + 80° = 180°$
$m(\angle 1) = 100°$
It follows that $m(\angle 3) = 100°$ and $m(\angle 2) = 80°$.

67. $90° - 33° = 57°$

69. $90° - 12° = 78°$

71. $180° - 33° = 147°$

73. $180° - 122° = 58°$

75. Vertical angles: $m(\angle 5) = m(\angle 7)$

77. Corresponding angles: $m(\angle 5) = m(\angle 1)$

79. Alternate exterior angles: $m(\angle 7) = m(\angle 1)$

81. Alternate interior angles: $m(\angle 3) = m(\angle 5)$

83. $m(\angle a) = 45°$ (Supplementary angles); $m(\angle b) = 135°$ (Vertical angles are equal); $m(\angle c) = 45°; m(\angle d) = 135°$ (Corresponding angles are equal); $m(\angle e) = 45°$; $m(\angle f) = 135°; m(\angle g) = 45°$

85. Scalene (no equal sides)

87. Isosceles (Two sides equal)

89. True

91. No; a 90° angle plus an angle greater than 90° would make the sum of the angles greater than 180°.

93. 40°; the sum of angles of a triangle is 180°.

95. 37°; the angles of a right triangle are complementary.

97. $m(\angle a) = 80°$ (The sum of angles of a triangle is 180°); $m(\angle b) = 80°$ (Vertical angles are equal); $m(\angle c) = 100°$ Supplementary angles); $m(\angle d) = 100°; m(\angle e) = 65°; m(\angle f) = 115°; m(\angle g) = 115°; m(\angle h) = 35°; m(\angle i) = 145°; m(\angle j) = 145°$

99. $m(\angle a) = 70°; m(\angle b) = 65°; m(\angle c) = 65°; m(\angle d) = 110°; m(\angle e) = 70°; m(\angle f) = 110°; m(\angle g) = 115°; m(\angle h) = 115°; m(\angle i) = 65°; m(\angle j) = 70°; m(\angle k) = 65°$

101. $P = 20 + 2(16) + 2(5) + 20 = 82 \text{ ft}$

103. $\left(\begin{array}{c}\text{Area of} \\ \text{outer square}\end{array}\right) - \left(\begin{array}{c}\text{Area of} \\ \text{inner square}\end{array}\right) = 10^2 - 8^2$
$= 100 - 64$
$= 36 \text{ in.}^2$

105. $\left(\begin{array}{c}\text{Area of outer} \\ \text{rectangle}\end{array}\right) - \left(\begin{array}{c}\text{Area of inner} \\ \text{circle}\end{array}\right)$
$= (6.2)(4.1) - (3.14)(1.8)^2$
$= 25.42 - 10.1736$
$= 15.2464 \text{ cm}^2$

Notes

Notes